Yankee Stories Untold

ALSO BY RICH MARAZZI

Yale Football Through the Years (McFarland, 2020)

ALSO BY RICH MARAZZI AND LEN FIORITO

Baseball Players of the 1950s: A Biographical Dictionary of All 1,560 Major Leaguers (McFarland, 2004; paperback 2010)

Yankee Stories Untold

*An Insider's Memoir
from Ruth to Jeter*

Rich Marazzi

McFarland & Company, Inc., Publishers
Jefferson, North Carolina

Unless otherwise noted, all photos in this book are the author's.

ISBN (print) 978-1-4766-9380-4
ISBN (ebook) 978-1-4766-5128-6

LIBRARY OF CONGRESS AND BRITISH LIBRARY
CATALOGUING DATA ARE AVAILABLE

Library of Congress Control Number 2024002098

© 2024 Rich Marazzi. All rights reserved

No part of this book may be reproduced or transmitted in any form or by any means, electronic or mechanical, including photocopying or recording, or by any information storage and retrieval system, without permission in writing from the publisher.

Front cover: (top) Rich Marazzi on the 50th anniversary of his first game at Yankee Stadium, sitting in the same area (author's collection); (bottom) overview of Yankee Stadium (Matt Hecht)

Printed in the United States of America

*McFarland & Company, Inc., Publishers
Box 611, Jefferson, North Carolina 28640
www.mcfarlandpub.com*

To my wife, Lois,
a longtime Yankees fan who has given me the space
to take this journey into the fog-thick history of Yankee baseball.
Our wedding vows included "for better or worse
and in wins and losses."

Acknowledgments

Author Interviews or Conversations with Players

Mickey Mantle, Roger Maris, Yogi Berra, Whitey Ford, Phil Rizzuto, Joe Torre, Bobby Murcer, Ralph Terry, Bill Skowron, Bobby Richardson, Tony Kubek, Luis Arroyo, Ryne Duren, Rocky Colavito, Don Zimmer, Hank Bauer, Eddie Robinson, Billy Martin, Don Larsen, Art Ditmar, Gil McDougald, Charlie Keller, Tommy Henrich, Frank "Spec" Shea, Phil Linz, Al Downing, Johnny Ellis, Ron Blomberg, Don Mattingly, Bernie Williams, Derek Jeter, Alex Rodriguez, Jorge Posada, Paul O'Neil, Roger Clemens, David Cone, Gary Sheffield, Bobby Hofman, Dom DiMaggio, Ferris Fain, Gus Zernial, Jimmy Piersall, Dick Radatz, Luis Tiant, and Von Joshua.

Author Interviews with Umpires

Nick Bremigan, Mark Hirschbeck, Steve Palermo, Dale Ford, and Jim Evans.

Author Interviews or Conversations with Others

Bob Sheppard, Mel Allen, Suzyn Waldman, Ed Fastook, Ray Kelley, Andy Strasberg, Barry Halper, Bill Jenkinson, Bob Wolff, Richard Ben Cramer, Paul Kleiber, Joe Carrieri, George Grande, Linda Ruth Tosetti, Lew Rothgeb, Kevin Huard, Maury Allen, Jerry Vale, Arthur George Rust, Jr., Merritt Riley, Arthur Richman, Ed Lucas, Sal Durante, Dick Kunath, Ceil Kunath, and Jeff Devine.

Special Thanks to the Following

Marty Appel: New York Yankees historian and author of *Pinstripe Empire, Munson, Casey Stengel* and other books. Marty is a former Yankees public relations director and a TV producer. He provided unique insights into the careers of Joe DiMaggio and Mickey Mantle. He also reviewed this book for historical accuracy. His most recent book is titled *Pinstripes by the Tale: Half a Century In and Around Yankees Baseball*.

Sarah Langs: An ESPN, MLB Network, and MLB.com reporter and researcher for her impeccable review of this book for statistical accuracy. In 2021 Sarah was diagnosed with ALS. On January 28, 2003, she was honored with the Casey Stengel "You Could Look It Up" Award, presented at the annual Baseball Writers Association of America New York Chapter dinner in New York City.

Gary Mitchem: My editor for this project who properly guided me along the way.

John Labombarda: The senior historian for MLB at the Elias Sports Bureau, the official statistician for major league baseball.

Bob Ellis: For his review of all chapters in this book. A Lou Gehrig collector, Bob provided interesting information about Gehrig's private life and an auction of Gehrig items never seen before.

Tom Peters, Ed Lysak, Joe Lenti, Hank Violin, Jeff Lownds, and Howie Shafran: For reviewing selected chapters in this book.

David Conti: A graphic artist at Arrow Printers in Ansonia, Connecticut, for his assistance in gathering the photographs in this book.

John Horne: Coordinator of rights and reproductions at the National Baseball Hall of Fame and Museum for his assistance in photograph research.

Table of Contents

Acknowledgments	vii
Introduction: From the Upper Deck to the Press Box	1
1. Power of the Media Credential	7
2. Bob Sheppard: "The Voice from Center Field"	28
3. The Babe and "Little Ray"	38
4. The Babe's Last Hurrah	48
5. Babe, Helen, and Claire	54
6. Lou Gehrig: A Reluctant Hero	61
7. Gehrig's $312,000 Cap	69
8. Joe DiMaggio: A Lonesome Hero	74
9. The Streak, the Stolen Bat and Final Years, 1941–1951	82
10. Dorothy, Marilyn, and Memorabilia	88
11. "The Mick"	97
12. The Two Mickeys	107
13. Yogi: From Dago Hill to D-Day	115
14. The Real "Mr. October"	123
15. "Scooter"	132
16. The Broadcaster, the Hall of Famer, the Humanitarian	138
17. Roger Maris: Chasing a Ghost	145
18. Don Larsen: The Imperfect Yankee	161
19. Mel Allen: The "Voice of the Yankees"	172
20. The Pine Tar Game	183
21. Joe Torre: "The Godfather"	192

22.	Derek Jeter: The Captain	199
23.	Suzyn Waldman: A Pioneer in Her Field	206

Epilogue: My Field of Dreams   215
Bibliography   219
Index   221

Introduction

*From the Upper Deck
to the Press Box*

My inaugural journey to Yankee Stadium came on Wednesday, July 21, 1954. It was a steamy, asphalt-melting New York City day. I went with the local YMCA in my hometown of Ansonia, Connecticut, a leafy factory town where high school football is the sacred cow. I bristled with excitement boarding the bus with my mother's brown bag lunch in one hand and, in the other, the $2.25 that allowed me to purchase a hot dog, an orange drink, and a *1954 New York Yankees Yearbook*. I still have it, minus the many photos I foolishly (in retrospect) cut up and taped to a wall in a spare room in the house that I dubbed my "Wall of Fame."

The two-hour, 65-mile trip to East 161st Street and River Avenue felt like 10 hours. That week, time could not pass quickly enough in anticipation of the trip. The excitement I felt when the bus pulled up outside the stadium was overwhelming. The sight filled my five senses. Before me stood the iconic copper frieze that circled the upper deck, giving Yankee Stadium its signature look. The magnificent green lawn was breathtaking. It was nothing like the parched sandy lots I played baseball on back home. My heart was pounding in my chest like a jackhammer. It was a visceral experience that hit me like a semitruck and continues to resonate.

The game pitting the Yankees and White Sox was an afterthought. For a 10-year-old baseball junkie, who played Little League and earnestly collected baseball cards, it would be the first time those pasteboards that I put on my bicycle spokes would come alive—Mickey Mantle, Yogi Berra and Whitey Ford on one side, and Nellie Fox, Minnie Miñoso and "Jungle Jim" Rivera on the other. I paid rapt attention to all of them.

The attendance that day was 18,597, but it seemed more like 100,000. We sat in the upper deck in left field near the foul pole among the pigeons. I expected the Bronx Bombers to win easily. This was an era when the Yankees piled up championships like cordwood, having won an unprecedented five straight World Series from 1949 to 1953, a record that no team has since equaled. They were steeped in tradition going back to bigger than life figures like Babe Ruth, Lou Gehrig, and Joe DiMaggio and a cascade of other stars. But before I could finish my hot dog, the White Sox dashed my expectations when they scored five runs in the top of the first inning en route to a 15–3 romp. That season the Yankees would win 103 games but finish a disappointing second to the Cleveland Indians, who won 111 led by their vaunted pitching staff of Early Wynn, Bob Lemon, Mike Garcia, Art Houtteman, and Bob Feller.

It was a simpler era. The game was not awash with stats. Terms like "launch angle," "exit velocity," "spin rate" and WAR were unheard of. I listened to games on WINS radio when broadcaster Mel Allen painted a picture of the action. I watched baseball on a black-and-white 12-inch Admiral TV that my father purchased in 1950. Before WPIX picked up Yankee telecasts in 1951, I recall watching Yankee games with my dad on Channel 5, WABD on the DuMont network, my *Captain Video and the Video Rangers* station. Announcers Curt Gowdy and Dizzy Dean shared the booth with Allen. Little did I know that Allen would be a guest in my father's living room many years later and I would have the privilege of working with him on various projects.

This book is a deep dive into the sea of experiences I've had with Yankee players, past and present, broadcasters, writers, front office personnel, umpires, and celebrities whom I've come across during my travels.

Of course, I never did get the chance to meet Ruth or Gehrig, but I have encountered individuals who had a very close connection to the Yankee greats and who would serve as a conduit of interesting information.

A former high school and college baseball umpire, I was hired to write a rules column for the *Yankees Magazine* in the early '80s. This led to an incredibly privileged assignment of umpiring the Old-Timers' Day games for 16 consecutive years (1989–2004).

I have also been a rules columnist for *Baseball Digest, USA Today Sports Weekly Collegiate Baseball*, and other publications. In 1997 I launched a radio talk show titled

I'm umpiring home plate in the August 14, 1999, Old-Timers' Game at Yankee Stadium. Rick Cerone is the catcher and Willie Randolph is the batter.

Introduction

Inside Yankee Baseball. The show that started on WICC 600 AM in Bridgeport, Connecticut, ran for 17 years and finished on ESPN 1300 in the New Haven, Hartford, and Springfield area. It allowed me to interview many Yankees and others both past and present.

My affiliation with the Yankees was enhanced when I was hired as the team's rules consultant in 2004. I realized that players, coaches, managers, and broadcasters struggled with a poorly written rulebook that was about as exciting to read as watching paint dry. And on occasion the umpires stumbled as well. This led me to launch a rules-education program titled "Ruleball" designed to help teams win games. The operative word is "win" because that puts money in pockets.

My program involves a spring training video presentation to the Yankees coaching staff and weekly reports during the season involving current rule-related situations illustrated with a viewing link.

Over the years I got to know Yankees general manager Brian Cashman very well and would often see him in the press dining room at the stadium. He once told me that he used to read my rules column in *Baseball Digest* when he was a kid. Of course, that did not make me feel any younger, but I did enjoy hearing that and I realized he had a proclivity toward the importance of knowing the rules.

In January 2004, with snow on the ground, I called Cashman and asked if the Yankees would be interested in my Ruleball program as way to educate the players and coaches on all levels of the organization about the baseball rules. I explained that my mission was not to make players and coaches into umpires, but to teach them various rules from a playing perspective to help them win games.

"I think it's a great idea," said Cashman. "I'll have to call [Joe] Torre, who is vacationing in Hawaii."

Torre liked the idea, and the Yankees were the first team to hire me as a baseball rules consultant. Thanks to Cashman and the Yankees organization, since 2004 I have worked with 25 of the 30 major league teams and have expanded my program into the broadcasting arena.

Ironically, I work for both the Yankees and the Red Sox. I am often asked how I could serve the two rivals. My answer simply is that I provide information to the coaching staffs. How they communicate or teach it to the players is an organizational decision. When it comes to rules education, I divorce myself from any fan affiliation.

Thanks to Cashman and Torre, I'm the first and only person in baseball history to be given the honor and privilege of such an assignment and it didn't take long for the Yankees to benefit from the value of my program.

Phone Call to the Yankee Dugout

As part of my agreement with teams, I am available 24/7 to deal with rule situations. The first time this was utilized came on Sunday, July 31, 2005, when the Angels and Yankees played at Yankee Stadium. In the top of the eighth inning the Angels took a 6–2 lead and appeared to be cruising to an easy win. With Vlad Guerrero on second base and Garret Anderson on first and two outs, Torre went to the bullpen. He replaced Alan Embree with Felix Rodriguez to face Bengie Molina. Rodriguez had control problems and posed a risk.

Rodriguez threw two pitches before Guerrero was gunned down by Posada in his attempt to steal third base to end the inning. In the bottom of the inning the Yanks began to rally when I received a phone call from Cashman, who had received the following question from Torre in the dugout. "Because Rodriguez never retired a batter, nor did a batter reach base, does Rodriguez have to return in the ninth inning to pitch to one batter?" asked the Yankees' GM. If the Yankees tied the score or took the lead, Torre would bring in Rivera, the greatest closer in baseball history. But they had to be sure that Rodriguez was not required to return to face one batter.

My answer was "You can remove Rodriguez." As soon as the inning ended Rodriguez was no longer required to return.

Cashman then said, "I'm going to put you through to the Yankees dugout and I want you to tell that to [trainer] Gene Monahan who is sitting next to Torre." This was perfectly legal because I wasn't sign stealing or doing anything that was a rule violation. So, I told Monahan to tell Torre he could burn Rodriguez for the game. It was a surreal experience for me because while watching the game on TV, I could hear the fans near the dugout when I was talking to Monahan.

The Yanks scored four runs to tie the game and won 8–7 in 11 innings. Rivera pitched two innings in relief, allowing one run, and Tom Gordon pitched the 11th inning to earn the win.

July 21, 2004, marked the 50th anniversary of my first game ever at Yankee Stadium. I sat in the same area where I did on July 21, 1954.

Introduction

When the season ended the Yankees and Red Sox were tied for first place with the same record (95–67), but the Yankees won the division because of their better record in the season series against their division rival. In retrospect, if the Yankees were under the impression that they had to allow Felix Rodriguez to pitch to one batter and he walked that batter, it could have changed the outcome of the game and the race for the division title. So, I think I played a very small but important role in helping the Yanks win the AL East in 2005 and perhaps put a few extra bucks in their pocket.

On July 21, 2004, 50 years to the day after I first walked into Yankee Stadium, I was there to do some interviews before the Yankees crushed the Blue Jays, 10–3, behind the pitching of Javier Vázquez. About 90 minutes before the start of the Wednesday night game, I decided to revisit the area where I sat exactly 50 years earlier. I walked up to the third deck in left field of the renovated stadium and took a seat for about 15 minutes while the crowd filed in. This allowed me to reflect on one of the most memorable days of my life.

The 1974–75 renovation that closed the stadium for two years changed the face of the stately stadium that opened in 1923. The classic frieze or awnings no longer draped the upper deck. Instead, a replica one stood atop the center field bleachers I call Yankee Stadium II. I never embraced the replica and thought it was out of place above the bleachers. The support beams that often caused a visual obstruction were thankfully eliminated, and the stadium had escalators that accompanied the walking ramps assisting fans in their trek to the upper deck. But the field where immortals played remained. I visualized Mickey gripping the bat and with his picture-perfect swing swatting a majestic home run, and I saw Yogi jumping into the arms of Don Larsen after he tossed the only perfect game in World Series history. The heroes of my youth rippled with time, but the game always seems to cultivate new stars like Derek Jeter, Mariano Rivera, and Aaron Judge.

While I was going back to the future a young boy and his dad took their seats in front of me. Ironically, it was the boy's first game ever and he was filled with excitement. I knew exactly how he felt. I volunteered to take a photo of the two with the father's camera. I'm sure it's a photo they continue to cherish.

Time had robbed me of my parents, many relatives, and friends. And time is no longer on my side, but it cannot erase the vivid memories I have from my first visit to Yankee Stadium and the many experiences I enjoyed as a fan and a writer that carved a path into the amazing world of Yankee baseball.

It wasn't long before Bob Sheppard, the eternal voice of Yankee Stadium, greeted the fans with his signature opening: "Good evening, ladies and gentlemen, welcome to Yankee Stadium." It's the same voice I heard on July 21, 1954.

1

Power of the Media Credential

I am forever grateful to Harry "Lime" Katzman, the sports editor of the *Evening Sentinel* in my hometown, who requested my initial press credentials from the Yankees. The rest is history. My media credentials gave me access to parts of Yankee Stadium that fans could only dream of. That would include the press box, the field, the dugout, the clubhouses, the managers' offices, the umpires' room, the press dining room and other areas. This put me in a position to meet some interesting people including players, managers, umpires, writers, Hollywood personalities and others which at times turned into an impromptu interview. Needless to say, most of the material in this book was gained from my access to virtually all parts of the stadium. I thank such media relations directors as Irv Kaze, Jeff Idelson, Harvey Greene, Rick Cerrone and others for providing the invaluable media credentials.

The Press Gate

Entering the press gate was always a thrill for me. The most unusual time was two weeks after the horrific 9/11 terrorist attacks in 2001 in NYC. Major league baseball was shut down for several days following the tragedy. The Yanks returned to action on the road on September 18 and beat the White Sox 11–3 in Chicago. They took two out of three in the Windy City before dropping two of three in Baltimore.

The Bronx Bombers returned home on September 25 before 33,777 fans. I didn't know what to expect and to be honest I thought the stadium might be a terrorist target, but I felt the need to be there. I parked my car in the garage along the right field line and was ID'ed four times before I got to the clubhouse. Security was extremely tight. For the first time I had to put my business bag through an X-ray machine. This would become the new norm.

The stadium was a police state that night. There were two cops in front of every entrance throughout the ballpark. And in the press box there were almost as many New York policemen as there were media members. I interviewed one of them and thought I would use it on my radio show. This particular member of the NYPD was involved in the recovery of dead bodies. The stories he told were so graphic and upsetting I could not use the material on the air.

The eerie night ended when the Tampa Bay Devil Rays put the Yankees to sleep winning 4–0 behind the pitching of Tanyon Sturtze. I was happy to get home safely.

Yankee Stadium is a "who's who" that continues to attract denizens from a variety of backgrounds and was a springboard for many interviews that I was able to conduct.

Arthur Richman (left), one of baseball's all-time ambassadors, stands with Pete Gray, the one-armed outfielder with the St. Louis Browns in 1945.

It was also a haven of photographs. On Opening Day in 1983 I was in the press gate line standing behind actor Cary Grant. I couldn't help but take a photo of the screen legend. One night I rode the press elevator with actor Mickey Rooney. I've met several celebrities in Arthur Richman's office. Richman, a former writer for the *New York Daily Mirror* who had been around baseball forever, served as a senior advisor to majority owner George Steinbrenner. He was always very helpful. Arthur was hired by the nascent Mets as director of promotions and served the organization for many years before his role with the Yankees. He knew everybody from presidents to actors to baseball legends. He was unfiltered, and he enjoyed a cocktail or two or three. In my travels I even met Dick and Ceil Kunath, the unknown Yankee Stadium sign-painters who had their fingerprints all over the hallowed ballpark that included the retired numbers and emblems and blue plaques in Monument Park.

The Press Box

I've seen actors Kevin Costner, Billy Crystal, and Christopher Reeve in the press box. I sat near such legendary writers as Roger Kahn, Roger Angell and David Halberstam, while being sure to remain mute. *New York Daily News* writer Bill Madden was a live wire among the knights of the keyboard. When a pitcher had a bad outing and his pitching line was announced in the press box, he would shout, "He was horseshit." I always got a chuckle out of that. I'm not sure others did.

For most games I sat next to Bob Rosen from the Elias Sports Bureau and Bill Shannon, the longtime official scorer for the New York major league venues. Both were consummate professionals in their fields. Rosen, a longtime Brooklyn Dodgers fan, always carried a season ticket in his wallet from the old Ebbets Field. Shannon was a ballpark historian and rules expert and an impeccable scorer. He often arrived just before the first pitch. One night he was not in his normal perch at game time when the Yanks played an interleague game against the D'backs. Cerrone asked me if I would pinch-hit for him and handle his official scoring duties. I did for an inning and was a nervous wreck because my expertise is in the playing rules, not the scoring rules. I did a deep exhale when he showed up about 20 minutes later.

In 2010, Shannon died tragically in a three-alarm house fire in West Caldwell, New Jersey, where he lived with his 92-year-old mother, who was thankfully rescued. I was devastated when I heard the news.

During one game I sat next to former Mets shortstop Bud Harrelson, a very nice guy. And there was the day I sat with former umpire Ron Luciano, whose flamboyant style and on-the-field histrionics were entertaining to some and annoying to others. When I learned that he took his own life in 1995, it was upsetting. I often sat near Ed Randall, who hosted a popular Sunday morning baseball talk show for many years on WFAN radio titled *Ed Randall's Talking Baseball*. He was normally busy cutting up newspaper articles in preparation for his show.

I developed a friendship with Barry Halper, a Yankees minority owner, who had perhaps the largest collection of baseball memorabilia in the country. He would always be in Steinbrenner's suite while I was in the auxiliary press box a few feet away. We enjoyed bouncing baseball trivia questions off each other. He invited me to his home in Livingston, New Jersey, that was a veritable baseball museum. I regret I never took him up on the offer before his passing. His collection was auctioned by Sotheby's in 1999 for $22 million.

Jim Abbott

I was in the press box for Jim Abbott's no-hitter on September 4, 1993. It was certainly a thrill watching Abbott achieve greatness that day considering the physical challenge he had with part of his right arm missing. Abbott's right arm ends about where his wrist should be. He doesn't have a right hand, just a loose flap of skin at the end of his underdeveloped arm. Otherwise, he was a strapping 6-foot-3, 200-pounder in his prime whose physique could have served as a model for the ideal baseball player.

Little did I realize that the following year I would be involved in a personal meeting with the Yankees left-hander through the efforts of Mr. Richman.

My longtime childhood friend and best man in my wedding, Don Kosakowski, and his wife, Gail, adopted two children, Stephanie and Donnie. Donnie was born in 1986 with part of his right arm missing. Don was very interested in building Donnie's esteem ever since he was a young child to make his life as normal as possible. Don even went lengths to have his son meet Pete Gray who lived in Nanticoke, Pennsylvania.

Richman arranged for Donnie to meet Abbott on August 11, 1994, the final day before the record 232-day baseball strike that extended into the 1995 season resulting in a 144-game schedule. It was the fourth work stoppage in 22 years and the first time since 1904 that there was no World Series.

The crowd was sullen at the stadium on that overcast day. The crowd of 37,333 fans did not know what the future would bring. They did get their money's worth, however, when the Blue Jays beat the Yankees 8–7 in a 13-inning marathon contest. The deciding blow came in the top of the 13th when Ed Sprague homered off the Yankees' Joe Ausanio.

But I was primarily focused on the meeting with Abbott. Richman met Don, his son, Donnie, and me just inside the press gate and ushered us down to the area of the Yankee clubhouse before the game. Richman then brought Abbott to meet Donnie, who was thrilled, but I think his father and I might have gotten a bigger kick out of it. Like Gray, Abbott served as a motivator for Donnie,

Young Donnie Kosakowski, Jr., with former Yankees pitcher Jim Abbott on August 11, 1994. Abbott, who was also born with part of his right arm missing, served as a motivator for Donnie.

who went on to have much success playing Little League and Babe Ruth League baseball as a pitcher, a first baseman, and an outfielder. But Donnie's best sport would be track and field. At St. Joseph High School in Trumbull, Connecticut, he was an all-stater winning the Class M state championship in the long jump. He also excelled in the javelin and 400-meter run.

Donnie competed in the Paralympics in the Netherlands, Canada and Brazil. His 4 × 100-meter team set a world record in the Netherlands. Today, Donnie has found success as an IT computer technician for hotels.

No-Hitters

I was also there the night of June 11, 2003, when six Astros pitchers combined to no-hit the Yanks. When three Houston pitchers no-hit the Yankees on June 25, 2022, it brought back negative memories. But the no-hitter that still grabs me is the perfect game David Cone pitched on July 18, 1999, when he put down the Montreal Expos, 6–0. Needless to say, it was one of the more exciting days I spent in the big Bronx ballyard.

Maury Allen

I often sat with *New York Post* writer Maury Allen. When Yankee pitchers Fritz Peterson and Mike Kekich traded wives, children and dogs in 1972, it became a national story and very upsetting to the Yankees' front office. "Peterson and Kekich came to my home for a cookout," Allen revealed. "When my wife and I were about to retire for the evening, we heard the four of them talking in my driveway deep into the night. It was then that they made the agreement for the family swap."

From my research the date was July 15, 1972. When the two couples left Allen's house it was reported that they went to a diner in Fort Lee, New Jersey, and finished business. Kekich and Peterson held separate press conferences on March 4, 1973—Kekich at 10 a.m., Peterson at 4 p.m.—to announce the swap.

Allen was a great storyteller. One of my favorite stories involved an unfortunate experience he had with Earl Torgeson, the moody, bespectacled former first baseman who enjoyed a 15-year career that started with the old Boston Braves and ended with the Yankees in '61. "When I was a kid growing up in Brooklyn, I went to a Dodgers-Braves game on the subway," recalled Allen. "I was going home, and I had my scorecard with me. I looked up and right opposite me was Torgeson. I was a little bit nervous because here I am, a 13-year-old on a subway car with a major league player. I wanted to get his autograph, but I didn't have the nerve to ask him. Finally, I got the confidence and went up to him and said, 'Mr. Torgeson, can I have your autograph?' He looked up and growled, 'Get the fuck outta here.'"

Twenty years later Allen, now a sportswriter, was at a winter banquet in Manhattan that was held by the state of Florida to promote the upcoming spring training. There was a beauty queen at every table representing the different cities in the Sunshine State. Miss Tampa was at Allen's table. "We started talking about different experiences in baseball," said Allen. "She told me that she collected autographs, so I told her about my experience with Earl Torgeson. Well, her face almost dropped. She shook her head three or four times and looked at me and said sheepishly, 'Earl Torgeson is my father. I'm Ina Torgeson.'"

Art Rust, Jr.

Another one of my press box friends was Art Rust, Jr. His sports talk show on ABC radio in the '80s was very popular and along with Bill Mazur laid the groundwork for current New York talk radio. He was a former newspaper columnist and author of several books, many of which focused on the interplay of race and athletics. As a black man, he had a deep sensitivity for the black athlete. His first book, the controversially titled *Get That Nigger Off the Field*, published in 1976, explored the rocky beginnings of blacks in baseball. He was especially proficient on the subject of baseball and boxing. He loved talking about Joe DiMaggio.

He said that he saw Negro League star Josh Gibson hit a ball out of Yankee Stadium. This has never been officially documented but Rust was emphatic that it was true. I was a guest one night on his radio show and he immediately set the record straight when he said loud and clear, "Remember, you're on my fucking show."

Jerry Vale

I attended the Yankees home opener on April 10, 1998, when the Yankees outslugged the Oakland A's, 17–13. The 30 combined runs were the most ever scored in a game at Yankee Stadium. Tino Martinez provided the only home run of the day, a three-run blast in the third inning off the A's right-hander Jimmy Haynes.

Before the game I was in the press dining room when I came across Jerry Vale, the Columbia Records recording star. Vale (born Genaro Louis Vitaliano) was one of my favorite vocalists over the years. No, he never enjoyed the celebrity and fame of Frank Sinatra or Elvis Presley, but his talents grabbed my heart, leading me to many of his performances. I loved such songs as "Have You Looked into Your Heart" and "Pretend You Don't See Her." Vale also appeared in such movies as *Goodfellows* and *Casino*. But it was his tasteful, straightforward rendition of the national anthem, which he sang live at Yankee Stadium several times, that got him to the Baseball Hall of Fame with a little help from Joe DiMaggio, his good friend. "I was given a gold record for my recording of the national anthem from Columbia Records," he explained. "I gave the gold record to Joe, and he took it took Cooperstown."

At one time 14 different teams were using Vale's version of the national anthem. There was a time when the Yankees would rotate his version with Robert Merrill's, whose rendition the Yankees used for many years beginning in 1969 that included opening days covering three decades. He usually wore his Yankees jersey number 1½ while positioned in the area of home plate.

When I went upstairs to the press box, all the seats were taken so I sat in the visitors' TV broadcast booth, which was empty because the A's weren't televising the game. Shortly after I was seated, Vale walked in the booth with a friend and took a seat next to

Columbia Records recording star Jerry Vale sat with me in the press box at the Yankees' 1998 home opener when the Yanks beat the A's, 17–13.

me. I was a bit uncomfortable, not knowing how engaging I should be without being an intrusion. So, I basically remained quiet until some small talk led to some serious baseball conversation between Vale and me. It wasn't long before I realized that he was a knowledgeable baseball junkie.

Once I saw he was on a roll talking about his baseball experiences, I asked if I could interview him for a weekly column that I wrote for *Sports Collectors Digest*. He seemed more than happy. The column led to a friendship, and he even invited me to his Palm Desert, California, home. He died in 2014 and I regret never taking him up on his invitation. I do have a signed photo of him from that day that hangs in my man cave.

The Field

I've had numerous memorable experiences on the field before games. One I will never forget involved Tony Kubek, the shortstop on the great '61 Yankees team.

My wife, Lois, an avid Yankees fan, grew up in Weehawken, New Jersey. She adored Kubek and had a surprising phone conversation with him when he was a Yankees announcer for the MSG network teaming with Dewayne Staats.

Here is what happened.

On Friday, September 7, 1990, I had plans to take my family to the A's-Yankees night game. This was not a proud Yankee era. It was a dismal season with the Yanks finishing in seventh place in the AL East at 67–95. Bucky Dent was fired as the team's manager after the first 49 games in which the Yanks only won 18 times. He was replaced by Stump Merrill, who didn't fare much better at 49–64.

When I came home from my teaching duties at the O'Brien Tech in Ansonia, Connecticut, I saw that our bedroom had been turned upside down. I soon realized that we were robbed. My wife had $8,000 worth of jewelry stolen and I had some baseball and football cards stolen from my man cave valued at only $500. Fortunately, the robber had no clue as to the value of sports cards since most that were stolen were of the more recent variety. My vintage cards from the '40s, '50s, and '60s were untouched.

Tony Kubek, the shortstop on the great '61 Yankees team, made a thrilling phone call to my wife Lois two days after our house was robbed.

My family was obviously upset, and we weren't sure if we would go to the game. After the police dusted everything for fingerprints, we decided to go since staying home wouldn't make things any better.

The crowd that night numbered a little over 27,000 fans. But the game did not lift our spirits as the Yankees were no match for the AL pennant-winning A's of Rickey Henderson, Mark McGwire, and Jose Canseco who cruised to a 7–1 win with a five-run uprising in the sixth inning and would sweep the series. Seeing Willie Randolph in an Oakland uniform seemed a bit odd.

I returned on Sunday, September 9 for business reasons and ran into Kubek on the field near the Yankee dugout before the game. I had established a good relationship with the former Yankee shortstop and explained to him that my wife was a huge fan of his and she was flying low this weekend because of the robbery. I asked him if he would talk to her over the phone to help lift her spirits and he was happy to do it.

When I got Lois on the phone I said, "Someone wants to talk with you." She waited in anticipation before Tony said, "This is your old boyfriend."

Lois was too perplexed to answer.

Kubek then added, "Is it true you liked Mickey better than me?"

Lois then reacted, "Oh my God—Tony Kubek."

My wife was elated, and it certainly softened the sting of a horrible weekend.

The Clubhouse

Having access to the clubhouse was invaluable. It allowed me to conduct numerous interviews that I used on my radio show. When you walked in the Yankee clubhouse, if you made a quick right, you would be at Bernie Williams' large locker stall. And you wouldn't be surprised if you found this classical guitarist playing the guitar with his mind a million miles from baseball.

The speedy center fielder was not the first Bernie Williams in major league baseball. The original one had a mediocre career as a back-up outfielder with the Giants and Padres in the early '70s. I had his 1971 Topps baseball card. One day I entered the clubhouse and gave it to Bernie. He got a big kick out of it, but I'm sure he never heard of the previous Bernie Williams.

The Manager's Office

During one of Billy Martin's stints as Yankees manager, I was in his office when I ran into Bobby Murcer, the former Yankees center fielder turned broadcaster. I reminded him of an experience I had with him several years earlier.

In the early '80s Murcer was the featured speaker at the Connecticut Pinstripe Club dinner at the Ambassador restaurant in Hamden, Connecticut. The Pinstripe Club was a very active Yankee fan base group that held an annual dinner that drew about 500 people. I was the warm-up guy for Murcer. I had recently written a book with Len Fiorito from Seattle, Washington, titled *Aaron to Zuverink: A Nostalgic Look at Baseball Players of the 1950s*. Len and I chronicled every player who appeared in a ML box score from 1950 to 1959 and also included the post–playing careers of the players. I was asked to speak about former Yankees and the lives they led after the cheering stopped. I talked about known players like Gil McDougald and Andy Carey plus obscure bonus babies like Frank Leja and Tommy Carroll.

The speaking program followed the dinner as usual before the club held a raffle. The winning prize was a seat from the original Yankee Stadium that was removed during the 1974–75 renovation. At the time, I would estimate the seat was valued at about $150 to $200.

Lo and behold Murcer was the winner of the raffle. Instead of keeping the seat, he said, "Why don't we auction it and use the proceeds for the Pinstripe Club?" Everyone thought it was a great idea. The bidding climbed to about $550 if I recall—considerably above the market price. The guy who won the bid was elated.

I asked Bobby if he recalled the night he won the raffle and then auctioned the seat.

"Yes," he answered. "But you know, it was fixed that I would win the raffle so the seat could be auctioned."

I was astonished.

The Dugout

"The Boss"

The Yankee dugout is usually a hub of interesting traffic. One night during the 1998 season I found George Steinbrenner, the strong-willed Yankees owner, sitting at the end of the bench during batting practice. He agreed to give me a few minutes for my radio show. I had known he was upset about the amount of money the D'backs gave infielder Jay Bell, a free agent, the year before. The middle infielder signed a five-year contract at $34 million, more than three and a half times the league average. Steinbrenner was very critical that a middle infielder could sign for that kind of money, and he let his feelings be known.

It was during this time that Steinbrenner had threatened to move the Yankees to New Jersey. I asked him where the Yankees would be playing in 10 years. The interview abruptly ended. "Goodnight, Bridgeport. I love Bridgeport, but goodnight," said "the Boss."

End of interview.

Over the years I've spent a lot of time with Eddie Fastook, who heads the security at Yankee Stadium. Fastook has served as Steinbrenner's bodyguard and in general was a good utility man for the Boss. He has seen both sides of a man who is often portrayed in the media as iron-fisted and autocratic, a despot. "One thing you never wanted to do is lie to him," he commented. "I've seen him fire many people over little white lies."

Steinbrenner was known to frequently discharge employees but take them back the next day. "I've been fired about four times," chuckled Fastook. "If he meant it, he would tell you to pack your bags and clean out your office. If he's calling you the next day, you know you're okay."

Publicly Steinbrenner was normally amicable and charming. He could be a master psychologist while in the midst of a hostile crowd. Fastook recalled an incident during the 1998 World Series in San Diego.

"People were heckling him," said Fastook. "George always looked around to see who had the loudest mouth. This one night in San Diego during the 1998 World Series he broke away from his security which was common and walked right up to the heckler and asked him what his problem was. The loudmouth was in such shock he didn't know what to say. George then walked away, and the crowd cheered."

Steinbrenner could be boorish and contemptuous. He demanded perfection and loyalty from the top down as he intensely strived to maintain a winning Yankee tradition. But the man also had a philanthropic, compassionate side, one that is seldom publicized. He could be a very caring, loving person who enjoyed signing autographs.

"He's the most generous man you'd want to meet," stated Fastook. "Once we were at a horse auction in Ocala, Florida. Somebody told George that there was a woman who had to sell her whole farm because she had a brain tumor. George paid for everything including her 24-hour care."

The ultimate nightmare for any security guard is not being able to protect what you are being paid to protect. Fastook once had a close call with Steinbrenner.

"One time I was driving, and we were on Park Avenue and came to a stop when a car pulled up alongside us. Two guys opened their windows and were yelling, 'Hey George, we love you, we love you.'"

"I told George not to put his hand out the window to shake their hand and sure enough he did. They started driving away and wouldn't let go. I had to try and keep the car as close to them as possible until George was able to yank his arm back in."

(From left) George Steinbrenner, Ed Fastook, and Gulf War general Norman Schwarzkopf at the 1993 Penn relays. Steinbrenner was an accomplished hurdler on the Williams College track and field team (courtesy Ed Fastook).

"Donnie Baseball"

I have many fond memories of Don Mattingly's career, but my favorite occurred in the summer of '93. My oldest son, Rich, was about to study sports management at the University of Massachusetts. So I arranged for him to spend time with Mr. Richman. Following their meeting, Richman escorted Rich to the Yankees' dugout where he had a photo taken with Mattingly, who also signed a ball for him. The ball is currently displayed with Mattingly's 1984 Topps rookie card and the 8x10 photo is framed.

It was a core memory for both my son and me.

My initial contact with "the Hit Man" came on April 22, 1983, before the Yankees-Twins night game. I was sitting in the Yankees dugout next to Mattingly, a relatively unknown product who wore number 46. To his right was catcher Butch Wynegar. Mattingly had turned 22 just two days earlier. We were watching the Twins take batting practice and I said to Mattingly, "If you were on the other side of the field, you would probably be starting tonight." He gave me a smile that indicated I was probably right.

Mattingly vs. Winfield Race

In '84, Yankees manager Yogi Berra gave Mattingly the first base job after he had been used as a swing man between first base and the outfield. It was cemented when Steve Balboni was traded to the Royals before the '84 season. It had to be one of the best decisions Yogi ever made.

Mattingly and Dave Winfield battled for the AL batting title in '84. The two went head-to-head down to the last game of the season when the Yanks beat the Tigers 9–2 on September 30. The race wasn't as dramatic as the Mantle-Maris home run derby in '61, but the competition became the best running story for the New York tabloids the final month of the season since the Yanks and the Mets weren't going anywhere.

Going into the season's final weekend, Mattingly led Winfield .342 to .341. They were scheduled to face three Detroit right-handers in a row to close out the season, which favored the left-handed-hitting Mattingly, but he went just 1-for-7 on Friday and Saturday. He entered the last day of the season trailing Winfield .341 to .339.

On this pleasant Sunday afternoon, I sat in the press box with excitement. To be honest, I was rooting for Mattingly to win the crown because he was a homegrown Yankee. But I also liked Winfield and really didn't have a horse in the race. Mattingly didn't disappoint, going 4-for-5 while Winfield went 1-for-4. After Mattingly got his last hit in the bottom of the eighth, Winfield, batting against Willie Hernandez, hit a sharp grounder to Howard Johnson at third. He fired to second, forcing out a sliding Mattingly. As the new batting champ walked toward the dugout, the 30,000-plus fans roared in approval. It was a chilling scene.

Just as Maris emerged from the dugout when he hit number 61, Mattingly made a curtain call. He then walked to first base where he and Winfield, in a memorable stadium moment, shook hands and waved their caps to the crowd. They walked off the field together as the crowd cheered. It was a touching piece of stadium lore, a lasting memory.

Mattingly had won the race, .343 to .340. He was the first Yankee to win a batting title since Mantle in '56. To go along with his batting title, Mattingly topped the American League in hits (207) and doubles (44). He also finished in the top five in RBI, total bases, slugging percentage, and extra-base hits. The Yankee first baseman became the first left-handed Yankee hitter to bat over .340 since Gehrig hit .351 in 1937.

Following the game, I raced down to the Yankee clubhouse that was packed with media members. Mattingly sat on a table in the middle of the clubhouse with his knees to his chest and answered questions. "To be separated by that minute amount of points, I don't think there was a loser today," said Mattingly in his humble way.

Hall of Fame

There have been cries that he belongs in the Hall of Fame as his stats are comparable to Kirby Puckett (.318; 207 home runs; 1,085 RBI; .837 OPS). Perhaps an even better comparison is Mattingly with Tony Oliva, who was elected in 2022 by the Golden Days Era Committee.

Mattingly: .307/222/1099, OPS .830, one batting title, nine Gold Gloves, AL MVP (1985), six-time All-Star

Oliva: .304/220/947, OPS .830, three batting titles, one Gold Glove, two-time WS champion, eight-time All-Star

Don Mattingly sits on a table in the Yankees clubhouse and answers questions after winning the American League batting title on September 30, 1984.

But in Mattingly's 15 years on the baseball writers' ballot, he was never favored by more than 28.2 percent of the voters. One of his staunch supporters for election to the Hall is former Royals third baseman George Brett, a contemporary opponent and rival.

"If I'm going to be in a fox hole, who do I want with me?" said Brett in the 2022 MLB Network documentary *Donnie Baseball*. Playing against Don Mattingly, he was the guy. "In my mind he's a Hall of Famer. He's one of the best ballplayers I ever played against."

Marisa Tomei

Some of my most memorable stadium moments that occurred in the Yankees dugout did not exclusively involve baseball personalities. June 28, 1997, was a sunny, 85-degree day in the Bronx. Before the Yankees-Indians game, there was a celebrity softball exhibition. I was sitting in the Yankees' dugout which was empty, but seated about 30 feet to my right there was an attractive young lady who was garnering significant attention. Curious, I asked someone to identify her. I was told it was actress Marisa Tomei. Two things came to mind.

I recalled the *Seinfeld* episode when George Costanza was engaged to be married, living with Susan. He has a chance for a blind date with Marisa. Susan catches him watching all of Marisa's movies on TV, wonders if he has a crush on her. In the end he does meet her, and they are getting along fine until he casually mentions that he's engaged.

What I best identify Tomei with was her Oscar-winning role in the 1992 movie *My Cousin Vinny*, in which she co-starred with Joe Pesci and Fred Gwynne. I told her how much I enjoyed her work. She thanked me for my praise, and I took a seat next to her. We talked a bit about her casual interest in baseball and her Brooklyn roots.

Within a few minutes, a conga line of Yankee players came by to greet Tomei after word spread through the clubhouse that the popular actress was in the dugout. I had a camera with me and took photos of a number of players with her, including Wade Boggs, David Cone, Derek Jeter, Tino Martinez, Jeff Nelson, and Andy Pettitte. They appeared in awe of the talented actress, but I'm not so sure she was as impressed meeting the players.

The pre-game activities proved to be more satisfying than the game that followed as the Indians outslugged the Yankees 12–8, disposing Yankee starter David Wells after three innings.

I even had someone take a photo of Marisa with me that was placed on the refrigerator in the kitchen of my home.

I have an understanding wife.

A couple of weeks later I returned to the stadium and distributed the photos. I

Former pitcher Andy Pettitte was one of several Yankees who were photographed with actress Marisa Tomei on June 28, 1997, while watching a celebrity softball game at Yankee Stadium.

stopped by each of the players' cubicles in the Yankee clubhouse and presented them with the photo they took with the celebrated actress. You would think I gave them gold. They were excited and appreciative.

The Closers

April 27, 1996, was a beautiful baseball Saturday—the kind of day when Ernie Banks would say, "Let's play two." The Yanks played one that day and lost 8–6 to the Twins in 10 innings. I walked into the Yankees dugout about 10:15 a.m. and found Ryne Duren, the Yankees' premier reliever in the late '50s, sitting there by himself, perhaps reflecting on days gone by when he was throwing a baseball at mach speed. It wasn't long before John Wetteland, the current Yankees closer, entered the dugout. I asked Wetteland if he knew the guy I was talking to.

He said, "No."

I then introduced the two and they shook hands. It was a Kodak moment. I snapped a photo bridging the Yankee bullpen aces past and present.

The Prodigal Yankee

Between 1958 and 1960 Duren was arguably the best relief pitcher or "fireman" in baseball. The baseball term "closer" was not yet in use. Duren's trademark was the Coke

Former Yankee closers Ryne Duren (left) and John Wetteland bridge 38 years of Yankees history.

bottle glasses he wore because of his poor eyesight. His blazing fastball, estimated to be around 100 mph, was the standard for how hard throwers were ranked. Add this to his wildness, and his reputation as a heavy drinker, and you can bet he had many hitters shaking in their shoes. Stengel declared, "I would not admire hitting against Ryne Duren, because if he ever hit you in the head, you might be in the past tense."

Anecdotes about the nearly blind fireballer inspired the character Ricky Vaughn, "Wild Thing," from the movie *Major League*. "On one occasion when he came in to pitch, he knelt down to manicure the mound," wrote Steve Rushin in an April 2021 issue of *Sports Illustrated*. The Orioles' Gus Triandos was batting. After watching Duren for a moment, he turned to Yogi Berra and asked what Duren was doing. Yogi said, "He's looking for the pitching rubber!"

Duren's life was plagued by the evils of alcohol, an insidious drug that usually gets the last out. His addiction affected his career and cost him his marriage to his first wife, Beverly. He threw hard on the field and drank hard off the field. Following games in New York, he and Mantle, a buddy boozer, would often ride together over the George Washington Bridge and have a few pops at some of their favorite New Jersey haunts. He was emphatic that he has pitched with hangovers but never took the mound drunk.

Duren was the prodigal Yankee. When he came into the game, he would fervently fire the ball 20-feet over the catcher's head high off the backstop screen for the purpose of getting into the head of the on-deck batter. On occasion, Duren would intentionally uncork a wild pitch from the bullpen.

Duren found multiple ways to rub management the wrong way. While he was a member of the Angels, the team headed for Washington following a series in New York. But the unpredictable chucker took the wrong plane and wound up in Boston. "I told the airline people about it, and they got me another plane to go down to Washington. I was lucky enough to get there in time for the game."

Because of his alcohol problems Duren was released by the Reds and finished with the Phillies and Washington Senators in '65. At this point in his life, he was on a mapless road with no exit in sight.

There would be attempts to end his life to alleviate the pain of his alcoholism. Once he parked his car on a railroad track in Texas. "The switch engine came rather than the first freight and I ended up in jail," Duren revealed.

Another episode occurred when he attempted to drown himself in the frigid waters of Lake Michigan. "I was desperate because I had just lost my job," uttered the depressed former flamethrower. "I went into the water with a concrete block over my head. The water was cold, being late May. My thought was to drown myself. That's how my father-in-law died. I went into the water over my head and like any true addict I believed the next fix became more important than life itself, and so, at that particular time, I thought it was silly to die so cold. I decided it was better to have a few Brandy Manhattans and warm up before I go."

His post–playing career was a mix of triumphs and tragedies. It was reported that he lost all his money from baseball and worked odd jobs like a gas station attendant and dishwasher. He was living in a flophouse before he was committed to the Texas State Mental Hospital. Later he moved to Wisconsin where he continued drinking, and he finally wound up at the DePaul Hospital in Milwaukee where he underwent 22 months of treatment for alcoholism.

From 1968 until his death on January 6, 2011, at age 81, at his home in Lake Wales,

Florida, he worked as an alcohol counselor and alcohol rehab director. He had conquered a deadly enemy. He started a drug and alcohol rehabilitation clinic in Stoughton, Wisconsin. He was prouder of that than anything he ever did in baseball.

"Zim"

Don Zimmer was a member of the Dodgers during the '55 WS and had a front row seat when Jackie Robinson stole home against the Yankees. One night I was in the Yankee dugout during batting practice when "Zim," who at the time was on Joe Torre's coaching staff, was playing trivia with a friend. They were trading questions when Zim asked him, "Who was the Dodgers' batter when Robinson stole home?"

He had his friend stumped.

I was sitting about 20 feet away with the answer but did not want to be rude and spoil Zimmer's fun. Finally, when I saw the question would go unanswered, I shouted, "Frank Kellert." Zimmer looked at me angrily and barked, "I've asked that question for almost 50 fuckin' years and nobody ever got the answer." I didn't know whether to laugh or show compassion for raining on his trivia parade.

Yankees coach Don Zimmer, known as "Popeye," meets the real Popeye outside the Yankees dugout.

"The Rocket"

On one occasion I found myself alone with Roger Clemens in the dugout before a Sunday afternoon game. He owns seven Cy Young awards, the most all-time. He won 354 games and collected 4,672 strikeouts, third behind Nolan Ryan and Randy Johnson. Twice he fanned 20 batters in a game. Yet, because of his link to performance enhancing drugs, he is not in the Hall of Fame. Like Barry Bonds, he is no longer on the BBWAA ballot but could be considered by the Contemporary Baseball Era Committee.

When we met, he had a baseball in his hand. So I asked him how he gripped the ball differently for his two-seam vs. his four-seam fastball. He proceeded to give me a personal clinic. It was fascinating but 40 years too late. I found the fireballer to be very cordial and friendly. I never had to bat against him, but Mike Piazza did.

There was bad blood between the two after Clemens plunked the Mets catcher in the head during a July 8, 2000, interleague battle just three months before the Series. Piazza suffered a concussion and missed the All-Star game. The three previous times they faced each other, Piazza was the victor, hitting three home runs in three different games. The beaning certainly had the look of retaliation. Piazza has said that he thought Clemens was throwing at his head but did not want to hit him.

Fast forward to the top of the first inning of game two of the Yankees-Mets 2000 subway series. Piazza was facing Clemens with two outs while the crowd of more than 56,000, knowing the toxic history between the two, watched with heightened interest. The count reached 1-and-1 when Piazza hit a foul ball that rolled into the Yankee dugout. The inside fastball shattered Piazza's Mizuno Pro bat, sending the sharpened barrel toward Clemens. The barrel of the broken bat bounded off the ground and Clemens fielded it like a ground ball and shockingly flung it in the direction of Piazza low to the ground as he began to run up the first base line holding the handle of the bat. Plate umpire Charlie Reliford immediately got between the two as did catcher Jorge Posada while Clemens was asking for a new ball to continue the game.

The jagged piece missed Piazza, but it triggered a bench-clearing skirmish that did not involve any punches or ejections.

Umpire Tim Welke stood between Piazza and Clemens to prevent any further engagement. Mets broadcaster Gary Cohen bellowed, "Is Clemens out of his mind? What was he thinking?"

Clemens kept saying, "I thought it was the ball." Did his mind snap? Piazza then grounded out to second to end the inning.

"I had no idea Mike was running on the foul ball. There was no intent there," Clemens told reporters following the game. Clemens ended up throwing eight innings of two-hit ball, allowing no runs in the Yankees 6–5 win.

In the incident's aftermath, Clemens was charged with "inappropriate conduct" by the commissioner's office and reportedly fined $50,000 after a review, which considered Clemens' history with Piazza.

Strange but true, baseball's odd couple were batterymates in the 2004 All-Star game at Minute Maid Park in Houston when Clemens, wearing an Astros uniform, gave up six runs in top of the first inning with Piazza as his catcher. I doubt if the two went out for dinner.

The Broken Bat

The Clemens-Piazza broken bat episode was resurrected in 2014 when the barrel of the bat was sold for an incredible $47,500 in a Heritage Auctions event. The consigner of the notorious piece of wood was Jeff Mangold, the Yankees' strength and conditioning coach from 1984 to 1988 and 1998 to 2006.

Appearing on Connecticut's WCTX *Inside New York Baseball* show in 2021, Mangold explained how the piece fell into his hands. "The barrel of the bat went flying toward Clemens," recalled Mangold. "All hell broke loose. As usual the bat boy ran out and grabbed the pieces of the bat and brought them back into the dugout. They put the discarded broken pieces in the area for collection. I was standing by the bat rack. When I saw the Piazza bat, I said to myself, 'This can't be thrown away.' I grabbed the barrel and took it to my locker."

Mangold, who lived in Oakland, New Jersey, displayed the bat in his home office for 13 years.

Mangold said he decided to sell it to help pay for his children's college tuition. He also said he planned to make a contribution to the CJ Foundation for SIDS (Sudden Infant Death Syndrome), saying that he lost a daughter at just two and a half months old in 1991.

The Downing-Aaron Connection

This visitors' dugout also presented many opportunities.

Former Yankees left-hander Al Downing wore pinstripes from 1961 to 1969, during which time he went 72–57 with a 3.23 ERA. The hard-throwing Trenton, New Jersey, native led the Yankees pitching staff in strikeouts four consecutive seasons (1964–67). In '64 he led the AL in strikeouts when he recorded 217 Ks.

Downing finished his career with the Los Angeles Dodgers. He gave up Hank Aaron's 715th record-breaking home run in 1974. His roommate that year was outfielder Von Joshua. I had a chance to chat with Joshua one night at the stadium in the visitors' dugout when Joshua was a coach with an opposing team. Joshua recalled that he and Downing were ready to leave spring training and open the season at Dodger Stadium against the Padres (April 5–7). Downing expected to pitch in one of those games when he received a call from the Dodgers' front office that they were not going to pitch him in Los Angeles. He was told that he would be pitching on Monday, April 8, in Atlanta.

Downing was upset that he was not going to pitch in Los Angeles. Joshua believed they wanted a black man to pitch against Aaron who was on the brink of breaking Babe Ruth's career 714 mark.

"Before we left the hotel in Atlanta, I asked Al if he [Aaron] was going to get the historic home run tonight," recalled Joshua. "But he never answered me. He just gave me a funny look."

Aaron got number 715 that night.

Downing connects with Aaron in a numerological oddity. Aaron, who wore number 44 for the Braves and Brewers, hit 44 homers in a season four times in his career. His record-breaking 715th home run came off Downing, who also wore number 44. In 1963, Aaron and Willie McCovey both hit a league-leading 44 round trippers. And yes, McCovey also wore number 44. In the year Aaron passed away (2021), the Braves won 44 games before the All-Star break and 44 games after the break.

The Umpires' Room

The late sportswriter Furman Bisher once said of umpires, "They're submerged in the history of baseball like idiot children in a family album." There's some truth to that. But for me, these are my people. They are generally honest, salt of the earth guys.

I have spent a great deal of time in the umpires' room where some of the greatest stories are told.

One year while dressing in the umpires' room following the Old-Timers' game, I had an uncomfortable experience. Former major league umpire Bill Haller worked the plate for the Old-Timers' game and was near me. It wasn't long before the currently active umpires entered the room and began to dress for the regular game. This was a time when there was bad blood among the umpires with two current umps, Derryl Cousins and John Shulock, who worked as replacements during the 1979 umpires' strike.

Haller, a grizzly, strong union guy, wasn't happy to be in the same room with Cousins. At one point he shouted, "I hate fucking scabs." I was braced for a contentious battle. There was three seconds of silence that felt like three hours. But Cousins ignored Haller and thankfully nothing escalated.

Earl Weaver Ejection

Most stories from the umpires' room were humorous and colorful. One of my favorite baseball yarns came from Dale Ford, who was an American League umpire from 1974 to 1999 before he was elected to the Tennessee House of Representatives, serving in that chamber from 2006 to 2012. Like many umpires he had his share of run-ins with the combative Earl Weaver, the long-time Orioles manager who, according to Baseball Reference, was ejected 96 times in his career. I was sitting in the umpires' room one night at the stadium when Ford told this incredible story about the night he ejected Weaver during the national anthem.

"Everything in the big leagues is a four-letter word," Ford said. "Most of those guys have like a 25-word vocabulary and 24 of those are four letters. It doesn't take a brain surgeon to deal with that."

"The problem with Weaver started the previous night. I was working first base and tossed him in the seventh inning after he came out to argue four times," remembered Ford. "The umpires called Weaver 'Rooney' because he was short like actor Mickey Rooney. He came out there the fourth time, and I said, 'Rooney, you've been out here more than I have tonight. Why don't you just stay 'cause I know I can manage better than you.'" Ford continued, "He [Weaver] said, 'I'll be out here every time I don't get one of these calls.' I said, 'No, you won't. Once you get to that door right there behind the dugout, just keep on trucking 'cause you're done for the night.'"

The next night, Weaver was standing next to Ford while a large woman sang the national anthem standing between the pitcher's mound and the plate. Ford said, "Out of the corner of his mouth he [Weaver] said, 'Dale, how many plays are you gonna fuck up tonight?' I said, 'Rooney, it don't matter 'cause when this fat lady's done, you are too and if you try to kick dirt on me 50,000 people are going to think you've gone nuts because nobody knows I dumped you but you and me.' When she finally finished, he looked up and he says, 'Are you serious?' I said, 'As a heart attack, get out of here.'"

"Nobody knew that Weaver had been ejected, so in the second inning the bat boy brought me a note from broadcaster Jon Miller. It read, 'Dale, where's Rooney?' I put one word, 'Guess,' and sent it back. I turned around and they're yelling and giving me a thumbs up and stuff. They loved it."

President Bush and the Secret Service Umpire

There was a night I wasn't in the umpires' room that I wish I was.

One of my closest umpire friends is Mark Hirschbeck who umpired in the major leagues from 1987 to 2003. Mark and his brother John were the first pair of brothers to umpire in the big leagues. They have since been joined by Tim and Bill Welke.

Mark worked the 2001 World Series played between the Diamondbacks and Yankees. Game Three was played at Yankee Stadium on October 30, just 49 days after the terrorist attacks in NYC. Security was very tight throughout the stadium and in the umpires' room as well. When Hirschbeck arrived, he found President George W. Bush sitting at a table in the middle of the room. No president had ever visited Yankee Stadium during a World Series. Hirschbeck also noticed a guy in his locker stall with a gun strapped around his leg who was strangely putting on Hirschbeck's umpire trousers. "The agent's name was Ray," according to Jim Joyce, who also umpired the game that night. "He had smoke grenades, concussion grenades, two guns on his belt and wore a bullet proof vest under his jacket."

Perplexed, Hirschbeck asked the president, "What's going on here, did I get fired or something?"

Bush answered, "Mark, would you to take one for the president of the United States?"

Hirschbeck responded, "For you, I would do anything."

Hirschbeck was then told that the guy in his locker stall was a secret service agent, and he was going to go on the field with the other umpires before the game dressed as an umpire. He would be armed in case there was a terrorist in the crowd.

Hirschbeck, taking full advantage of the situation, said to the president, "Would you take one for the umpires and sign six dozen baseballs for us?"

The president obliged and signed 72 baseballs. The clubhouse man stacked six boxes of baseballs and peeled off the paper of each ball and gave the ball to the president to sign.

"I gave each umpire one dozen," said Hirschbeck. "I still have most of them."

Bush, a former general partner of the Texas Rangers, went to the batting cage area under the stands to take a few warm-ups and get ready to make his first pitch when Yankees captain Derek Jeter ambled in to take some swings. "He was taking it pretty serious, trying to get loose," said Jeter, who urged the leader of the free world to stand on the rubber rather than in front of the mound and joked that the fans would boo him if he bounced it.

When the umpires entered the field before the start of the game, "Ray" inconspicuously joined the regular umpires, Dale Scott, Ed Rapuano, Dana DeMuth, Steve Rippley and Joyce. Nobody noticed the unidentified umpire, not even the writers on press row.

But Hirschbeck's daughter, Nikki, who was sitting in the stands with her mother, noticed that her father was not among the umpires in the home plate pre-game meeting.

"Where's Dad?" she asked her mother. Mrs. Hirschbeck had no answer.

Bush, who was waiting in the Yankees dugout wearing an NYPD flak jacket, was introduced by Yankee Stadium public address announcer Bob Sheppard. In his measured and recognizable voice, Sheppard said, "Ladies and gentlemen, please direct your attention now to the area in front of the pitcher's mound for tonight's ceremonial first pitch and please welcome the president of the United States."

It was a chilling moment when Bush took the mound, electrifying the crowd of 55,820. The noise was deafening. It was a city saying, "We're back, we're OK."

He waved a number of times and gave a thumbs up. I witnessed this from the stadium press box where it appeared there were more NYC police doing security duty than writers performing their jobs.

It was reportedly only the second time a sitting president threw out a first pitch in the WS. President Dwight D. Eisenhower was the first to do so when he performed the task in the 1956 Fall Classic played between the Yankees and Dodgers.

Bush threw a perfect strike to Yankees catcher Todd Green that preceded one of the most extraordinary games in Yankees history. The Yankees won, 2–1.

The crowd then chanted, "USA, USA, USA."

"Standing on the mound at Yankee Stadium was by far the most nervous moment of my presidency," said the 43rd president of the United States years later.

Soon after, the president was rushed home, not on a passenger jet, but on an F-18.

Only the umpires and the president knew that Hirschbeck remained in the Yankee dugout dressed in one of his uniforms.

It is one of the best kept secrets in World Series lore.

2

Bob Sheppard

"The Voice from Center Field"

"Babe Ruth gave Yankee Stadium a face and Bob Sheppard gave it a voice."
—AP writer Ron Blum

The voice was measured, dignified and strong. The former St. John's speech professor preached the importance of being "clear," "concise" and "correct," droplets of sound advice. He refused to acquiesce to the contemporary de facto cheerleader public address style of many current PA announcers. "A public address announcer is not a cheerleader, or a circus barker, or a hometown screecher," Sheppard once said. "He's a reporter. He's not there to stir up the crowd."

Sheppard was a favorite among Yankee players as well as opponents. "You're not in the big leagues until Bob Sheppard announces your name," stated Red Sox Hall of Famer Carl Yastrzemski.

The haunting voice from center field was eternally timeless. It was a constant throughout my life as it was for so many generations of fans. As a youngster, each new season I waited to hear "the Voice," always worried it would no longer be there. A trip to Yankee Stadium without Sheppard's trademark greeting "Good afternoon ladies and gentlemen ... welcome to Yankee Stadium" was akin to going to Niagara Falls without seeing the falls. He was as much of a part of "the House That Ruth Built" as the monuments that pay homage to the Yankee gods beyond the center field wall.

Sheppard was an integral component of the Yankee Stadium experience. Although his face was not recognizable to most fans, his sonorous voice certainly was. It

Bob Sheppard, the legendary Yankee Stadium public address announcer, spent 57 seasons in his broadcast booth.

reverberated through the stadium for more than five decades, creating everlasting memories. He announced more than 4,500 regular season games in a career that lasted 56 years. He was at the mic for two All-Star contests and introduced 70 Hall of Famers. His streak of 121 consecutive postseason games, which included 62 World Series contests, will most likely never be broken. His legacy included 13 of the Bombers' 27 World Series championships. He witnessed 22 pennant-winning seasons, six no-hitters, and three perfect games.

Although he is most identified as the Yankees PA announcer, he was the public address voice of the New York football Giants for half a century and many other venues. Sheppard spent so many games behind the mic at Yankee Stadium that his greeting became rote. This caused a bit of embarrassment when he worked the first New York Giants football opener at Giants Stadium in New Jersey against the Dallas Cowboys. He began, "Ladies and gentlemen, welcome to Yankee Stadium."

Sheppard was born on October 20, 1910, in Richmond Hill, a neighborhood located in the southwestern section of the borough of Queens in New York City. His age remained a mystery for many years. It was a secretive, forbidden topic that he found irrelevant and refused to discuss. When the 2001 season began, he was 90 years old, but he remained vigorous for several more years and never lost his fastball. Bill Madden of the *New York Daily News* wrote, "It was his spirit that kept him forever young. And besides, did anyone ever ask how old God was?"

Former Yankees pitcher Jim Bouton, working for CBS-TV, once arranged an interview with Sheppard in his booth during a game. When Bouton for the second time attempted to get Sheppard to reveal his age, the iconic public address announcer tersely replied, "This interview is over."

Sheppard rated Don Larsen's perfect game in Game Five of the 1956 WS as his top stadium baseball memory. Also near the top was the home run that Mickey Mantle hit off Pedro Ramos on Memorial Day in 1956 that almost left the stadium, Roger Maris' 61st home run, and Reggie Jackson's three-home run game in Game Six of the 1977 Series when the Yankees played the Los Angeles Dodgers.

Sheppard never missed an Opening Day at Yankee Stadium from 1951 until 2006, when he suffered an injury to his artificial hip the night before at his Long Island home. During his first 50 years he reportedly was absent for only five games, all of them for family commitments. "My particular job because it's less wearing and tearing allows me to continue," he once told me. "I know from my work in speech that the vocal cords are about the last to go. The great opera star Giovanni Martinelli was able to sing opera when he was in his 80s."

Sheppard loved the charm of the big ballyard in the Bronx where he worked. "Yankee Stadium is a cathedral, not a ballpark," he articulated. And his stately voice and elegant presentation was a perfect fit for the storied venue, a New York landmark. When there was talk in the 1990s of moving the Yankees to New Jersey or to other parts of New York City, he lamented, "Taking the Yankees out of the Bronx would be like taking the Vatican out of Rome."

The renovation of the stadium took the Yankees out of the Bronx to Queens when they played at Shea Stadium in 1974 and 1975. This prompted Sheppard to adjust his greeting to "The Yankees welcome you to Shea Stadium."

His voice and presentation were often imitated but never duplicated. Is there a greater form of flattery? As a youngster playing in the street, I would announce the lineups in Sheppard style playing with my friend Don Kosakowski, who would also offer his imitation.

Mine was better.

And even in my adult years, I would go down into my man cave with an empty Pringles can and announce lineups in the midnight hour while my wife and sons slept upstairs. The Pringles can was used to simulate the classic echo in Sheppard's voice that resulted from the bounce-back of the speakers in center field. Tooling around town in my car, I would often give a Sheppard lineup and still do on occasion. "Number 12… Gil McDougald … shortstop…. Number 12…."

Is this normal behavior for a man born between Pearl Harbor and D-Day?

Sheppard was well aware of the many impersonators out there such as San Francisco Giants broadcaster Jon Miller, actor Billy Crystal, Reggie Jackson and others. "But they don't sound like me," he told writer Eddie Lucas. "They sound like somebody trying to impersonate me."

Jackson likes to talk about the day Sheppard announced his name at—of all places—Fenway Park. Sheppard was visiting Boston and took in the game. Veteran Fenway PA announcer Sherm Feller asked him if he would do an inning. He obliged and shocked Jackson when he came to bat. He announced, "Number 44 … Reggie Jackson … number 44." Startled, Jackson stopped in his tracks and looked up at the booth and waved to the familiar voice that made it from New York to Boston.

I once asked Bob Sheppard if he considered himself a legend. He responded, "Longevity gives you something. I imagine if you're around long enough you become a legend. I assume nobody here is used to any other voice. Like you, they have grown up with me."

His legend continues to grow. A representative from Leland's Auction House recently said his autograph is valued at $500. To put that in perspective, the value of a Joe DiMaggio single signed baseball is between $400 and $600.

* * *

Dinner with Bob and Eddie

On August 18, 1981, I wrote Mr. Sheppard a letter requesting an interview. At the time I was writing for the *Baseball Bulletin*, a small monthly magazine published in Royal Oak, Michigan. He answered almost immediately. In a letter dated August 22, he wrote, "I'd be happy to grant you an interview." He suggested that I contact Dave Szen, a Yankee official, for press credentials. Several days later I did the interview with him which launched a 29-year relationship with a man I deeply admired. Through time, our friendship grew stronger because of my affiliation with the Yankees.

On most of my visits to the stadium I would have dinner in the press dining room with Sheppard and Eddie Layton, a mogul in the music industry. Rick Cerrone, the media relations director, would often join us. Layton spent 29 years as the stadium organist from 1967 to 1970 and then again from 1978 to 2003. He replaced Toby Wright, the first-ever organist at Yankee Stadium, who entertained the fans in 1965 and 1966. Layton also played for the Knicks, Rangers and Islanders and wrote scores for several soap operas, including *The Secret Storm* and *Love of Life*.

The two were a fixture at the same table before games in the press dining room. They went together like salt and pepper. Every night they would both bet a penny on a variety of mundane stats such as the game's length of time, the total number of hits in the contest, how many innings a starting pitcher would go, etc. There was one dinner I will forever remember. It involved Chico Carrasquel, the first notable of the many outstanding Venezuelan shortstops to play in the major leagues.

On June 1, 1994, Carrasquel was in town covering the White Sox on Spanish-language radio. I looked forward to interviewing him since he was the White Sox shortstop in the first major league game I ever saw. He was also one of my Topps bubble gum baseball card heroes back in the day.

I spent time interviewing him in the White Sox dugout between 4 and 5 p.m. About an hour later, I was having dinner with Sheppard and Layton in the press dining room when I noticed Carrasquel sitting at a distant table. Knowing Sheppard's affinity for announcing the Latino players, I asked him if he had ever met Carrasquel, and he said, "No." I then said, "Would you like to meet him?" and he answered "Yes" with some excitement in his voice. So I walked over to Carrasquel's table and asked him if he would like to meet Bob Sheppard. With similar interest, he obliged.

I escorted Carrasquel to Sheppard's table and said, "Chico Carrasquel, meet Bob Sheppard. And Bob Sheppard, meet Chico Carrasquel." The two shook hands and suddenly Sheppard went back in time and announced, "The shortstop ... number 17 ... Chico Carrasquel ... number 17."

It blew my mind and for one moment it was July 21, 1954, and I was 10 years old again.

The Latino players especially appreciated how Sheppard correctly announced their names. Minnie Miñoso, the former White Sox outfielder, was Minnie "Min-yoso," not "Min-oso." Washington Senators shortstop José Valdivielso was Jose "Val-di-vee-elso."

His favorite names included an eclectic ensemble that included Mickey Mantle, Salomé Barojas, Álvaro Espinoza, Shigetoshi Hasegawa, and Valdivielso.

"Anglo-Saxon names are not very euphonious," he remarked. "What can I do with Steve Sax? What can I do with Mickey Klutts? If I had to pick just one it would probably be the Japanese pitcher for the Angels, She-ge-TOE-shi Ha-se-GA-wah! Just wonderful! How much fun it was to work my tongue around that one!"

If Bob was with us today, I wonder how he would handle Isiah Kiner-Falefa.

Mantle was high on his list because of the alliteration of his name. "It was a perfect name for a ballplayer," noted Sheppard. It had a nice rhythm. "The Mick," who deeply respected Sheppard, made an appearance on the TV show *Good Morning America* several years after he retired. Sheppard was invited to appear on the show with Mantle for the purpose of majestically introducing him the way he did for 18 years at Yankee Stadium.

The Hall of Fame center fielder was surprised to see Sheppard at the studio. "Bob, what are you doing here?" asked Mantle. "Did they think I wouldn't show up?" Sheppard explained that he was there to introduce him. On cue Sheppard announced, "Ladies and gentlemen, the center fielder, number 7 ... Mickey Mantle ... number 7." Mantle turned to the interviewer and said, "I get chills up and down my spine every time I hear Bob say that." Sheppard added, "Well, you know I get a chill when I introduce him."

Sheppard was a multi-talented man who enjoyed talking baseball rules with me at dinner. He got a kick out of the off-beat, esoteric stuff. I explained to him in 1997 that if a batted ball hits a flying bird, the ball remains in play, and if the ball is caught, it's a put-out. This triggered his poetic juices. A published poetry writer, he went upstairs to his broadcast booth following dinner and penned the following poem, which I have saved.

> *Your attention please, Flying Birds.*
> *Listen carefully to my words:*
> *Stilled your lovely bird-like calls*
> *if you're hit by flying balls.*
> *And if you swoop or soar or dive.*
> *You're not impervious to a line drive,*
> *unless you fly with caution and propriety*
> *and join the Audubon Protective Society.*

A Backup to His Backup

One night I went to the press food bar in the middle of a game to get a bite to eat. His broadcast booth was located a few feet away. He spotted me and invited me into the booth where he made me an offer I couldn't refuse.

"Rich, how far do you live from here?" he asked.

I answered, "About 65 miles."

He countered, "Would you like to be a backup to my backup Jim Hall?"

I was stunned and speechless, but of course, I accepted the offer. He then requested that in my next several stadium visits I join him in his booth for the purpose of learning his routine. This set off my imagination. Could this lead me to be the heir apparent to Sheppard? It proved to be the Walter Mitty experience of my life. I found myself announcing lineups in my home, at stop lights, in the shower, you name it. At the stadium I would tape every word and every announcement he made. Then I would go home and replay it. He was my Socrates, and I was his Plato.

I waited for the call to pinch-hit for Mr. Sheppard. A couple of years went by, and on the morning of July 14, 2006, I woke up with a bad case of laryngitis. I sounded like Marlon Brando in the movie *The Godfather*. I had planned to go later in the day to the stadium where the Yanks would be hosting the White Sox, and since having a good voice was not necessary for what my agenda called for that evening, I drove to the Bronx. When I arrived late in the afternoon, Mike Bonner, the senior director of scoreboard and broadcaster operations, asked, "Did Shepp call you?" "No," I answered. He then said, "Well, Bob has a bad case of laryngitis, and you might have to do the public address announcing tonight." He added, "Bob will start the game, but he might need help."

My legs turned to jelly. In my raspy, hoarse voice I told Bonner, "I'm not sure I can do it." He directed me to go down to the press dining room and drink tea and honey. I immediately called my wife, Lois, and told her to watch and listen carefully to the telecast and to alert my sons that I might be the Yankee Stadium public address announcer at some point during the game. This was surreal. Pinch-hitting for Bob Sheppard, in my mind, was like a marginal player pinch-hitting for Babe Ruth. I knew I better be good. I was dealing with royalty.

I ran out to my car to get some throat lozenges before drinking the tea. I was excited but scared. The opportunity was amazing, but would I make a fool of myself and regret this night forever?

My master, who had a lesser case of laryngitis than I had, started the game. I did not know if I could do the job if called on. And I think he was aware that I was struggling.

I practiced speaking in a very low voice to mask the hoarseness. But to be honest, I was hoping he would ask me to take over or perhaps announce a few names because I knew I might never again get this opportunity.

I thought, would this be the 15 minutes of fame in my life that Andy Warhol allegedly guaranteed?

It never happened.

The Yankees held a 6–3 lead entering the top of the ninth. Manager Joe Torre brought in Mariano Rivera to close. Normally when Rivera came into the game to Metallica's "Enter Sandman," opponents would be put to sleep. But not on this night. Mo gave up three hits and two earned runs as the Chisox closed the gap to 6–5. With two outs in the ninth inning, Chicago had the tying run on third base in Jermaine Dye. Rivera was facing A.J. Pierzynski when Sheppard literally had one foot out of the broadcast booth door. He was prepared to jog down the hall to the elevator and get out to the street where Herb Stein, his neighbor and driver, would be waiting.

"Where are you going?" I nervously asked. He answered with calm, "Nothing to fear—the great Rivera is pitching."

Yes, the great Rivera, the only player voted unanimously to the Hall of Fame was on the mound, but he was not classic Rivera on this Friday night. But Sheppard was correct as Pierzynski flied to Bubba Crosby in right field to end the game. This would be another of his 652 saves—the same man who got the final out in four World Series. In 96 postseason games his record stands at 8–1 with 42 saves like the number on his jersey. His postseason ERA was a microscopic 0.70.

I never did get the chance to pinch-hit for Bob Sheppard, but we remained close friends. He asked if I would write a book about his life. I was flattered at such a request, but the time was not right for me and, regrettably, I never did.

Favors

I never wanted to compromise our relationship, but I did ask Sheppard for three favors over the years. He never asked for money, but I would on occasion give him a little money or a good bottle of Scotch.

I asked Sheppard if he would tape the opening for my radio show. At the start of every show, my producer would begin with the Yankees theme song. He would lower the volume and then Sheppard's voice would enter with "Good morning, ladies and gentlemen … welcome to *Inside Yankee Baseball* … and now, here's your host … baseball writer Rich Marazzi."

I would come on and say, "Ah, thank you, Bob Sheppard."

That was a real kicker. Imagine being announced weekly several hundred times by the most famous public address voice in baseball history. Could there be a better intro?

In one show we had a Bob Sheppard imitation contest. The winner won two tickets to a Yankees game and a tour for two of Yankee Stadium, compliments of my long-time friend Tony Morante, who was in charge of the stadium tours. I had three contestants in place from various parts of the state of Connecticut. I asked Bob if he would be the judge of the contest. He declined but chuckled, "I will be a bogus contestant."

That was even better.

For fairness, I mailed the "four" contestants the same announcement for when they went on the air with me. It read, "Your attention, please, ladies and gentlemen ... coming in to pitch for the Yankees ... number 42 ... Mariano Rivera ... number 42."

On the day of the show, only my producer (who had to call Sheppard) and I knew that "Walter" from Rye, New York, would actually be Bob Sheppard. I did not tell my wife or Bill Pucci, my co-host, of the ruse that was about to unfold.

The first three contestants went on the air and did a nice job with the real Bob Sheppard waiting in the wings. I then said, "We have our final contestant, Walter from Rye, New York." I greeted him and asked, "So you want to participate in the Bob Sheppard contest?" He said, "Yes." He then went into the Rivera announcement. The look on Pucci's face was priceless. His jaw dropped. "This guy has got to win," he muttered. I struggled not to laugh.

My wife, who was listening to the show at home, thought that Walter was cheating by using a tape of the stadium public address announcer. Anyway, we all had a good laugh and having Bob as a bogus contestant proved to be more effective than having him as a judge.

It would have been an honor to have Bob attend my oldest son Rich's wedding on September 30, 2006, and announce the wedding party as they entered the reception room at the Aqua Turf Club in Southington, Connecticut. But the travel distance from his home on Long Island would be too long of a drive for a man nearing his 96th birthday. I decided to ask the voice of Yankee Stadium if he would make a tape introducing the wedding party that would be used at the reception. As usual, he agreed.

Fast forward to the wedding reception. He began in his mellifluous tone, "Good evening, ladies and gentlemen ... welcome to the Bartone/Marazzi wedding. Please rise for the introduction of the families...."

None of the 200 or so guests were aware that Sheppard would be doing the intros. When the DJ brought the iconic voice into the room, the wedding guests searched the facility in pursuit of Sheppard's location. Heads turned in all directions. The DJ played the *Star Wars* theme while intermingling the introductions. Sheppard went through the wedding party and ended with "And now, ladies and gentlemen ... please welcome for the first time as husband and wife, Mr. and Mrs. Richard Marazzi."

I will take that tape to my grave.

A Man of Faith

It was widely known that Sheppard was deeply religious. I once asked him who he would like to see walk out of that Iowa cornfield in the movie *Field of Dreams*. He answered without hesitation, "Jesus of Nazareth."

Every Sunday morning there would be a mass in the Yankee Stadium auxiliary dressing room that I often attended. A local priest in the Bronx area would be the celebrant and Sheppard, a devout Roman Catholic and a eucharistic minister, would be the lector and do the readings which he delivered in a mystical tone. His nickname was fittingly "the Voice of God."

The Climb to Yankee Stadium

The youngest of three children (he had two older brothers), Shepperd went to St. John's College, now St. John's University, on an athletic scholarship. He was a left-handed first baseman and played quarterback on the football eleven from 1928 to 1931. He later played semi-pro football with the Valley Stream Red Raiders and the Hempstead Monitors earning $25 per game. He received a master's degree in speech at Columbia University.

Sheppard served his country during World War II in the Navy as a gunnery officer aboard cargo ships, both in convoys and independent missions in the Pacific Theater. Following his military stint, he was teaching speech at Grover Cleveland High School in Ridgewood, New York, when he saw an advertisement about a charity exhibition football game that was going to be played between the New York Yankees and Chicago Rockets, both members of the All-America Conference. He sought out the promoters and volunteered to be the public address announcer for the game. This led to him landing the job with the Brooklyn Dodgers of the All-American Football Conference. Like the baseball Dodgers, they played their games at Ebbets Field. The owner was Branch Rickey, the man who shattered baseball's color line when he brought Jackie Robinson to the major leagues in 1947. When the football team folded after '48, Sheppard moved to the New York Yankees football team in the same league.

Dan Topping, co-owner of the baseball Yankees, was impressed with Bob after he heard Sheppard make a tribute to Babe Ruth who had recently passed. In 1951, Sheppard replaced Red Patterson, who doubled as the Yankee Stadium PA announcer and PR director. He was reportedly paid $15 a game and got $17 for doubleheaders. The Yankees allowed him to use a pinch-hitter when needed and he chose Walter McLoughlin, the former athletic director at St. John's. Prior to Sheppard, the Yankee Stadium public address announcers were Jack Lenz, George Levy, Fred Sharp, and Patterson.

Sheppard worked his first game as the Yankee Stadium public address announcer on April 17, 1951, the same day Mantle made his debut playing right field and wearing number 6. The two also share the same birthday 21 years apart. On this Tuesday afternoon the Yankees beat the Red Sox, 5–0, before 44,860 fans as Vic Raschi pitched a complete-game shutout for the Yanks. Jackie Jensen, who started in left field for the Bombers, hit the game's only home run. In the Yankees lineup were five future Hall of Famers: Joe DiMaggio, Yogi Berra, Phil Rizzuto, Johnny Mize and Mantle. The Red Sox had three of their own in Ted Williams, Bobby Doerr, and Lou Boudreau.

The first player Shepp introduced was Dom DiMaggio. I can still hear him. "Leading off for the Red Sox ... number 7 ... Dom DiMaggio ... center field ... number 7." "The Little Professor" proceeded to collect an infield bunt single. The first Yankee player who came to bat in the bottom of the inning was Jensen who fanned facing Bill Wight.

Sheppard's body of work was virtually flawless, but he did have one hiccup at Yankee Stadium. In a 1982 game, Yankee reliever Shane Rawley entered the contest with the bases loaded and immediately gave up a bases-clearing double. Not realizing the pedal to his microphone had gotten stuck, he sarcastically asked a visitor in his booth, "Now that's relief pitching?" His words had gone out to everyone in the stadium, including Rawley. Sheppard was mortified, and in a display of character, he went down to the clubhouse the next day and personally apologized to the Yankee reliever.

The Ninth Inning

For many years at the conclusion of a game, Sheppard would give his send-off with the words "Now, please drive carefully and arrive home safely." Bob Sheppard arrived at his Baldwin, New York, home safely on September 5, 2007, following the Yankees' win over the Seattle Mariners. He would never return to Yankee Stadium. At the time, the 96-year-old announcer was battling a bronchial infection that would permanently sideline him. Mariano Rivera, who pitched the ninth, was the last Yankee name he ever announced. And the M's Ben Broussard, who hit into a game-ending double play, was the final name that left his tongue over the mic. Excluding his hip injury the year before, the following night was the first time he ever missed a game due to illness.

Jim Hall, his long-time backup, succeeded Sheppard the remainder of the 2007 season and handled the assignment in 2008. But when the Yankees moved into the new Yankee Stadium in 2009, Paul Oldin was handed the keys and has been there since.

During Sheppard's illness, Derek Jeter asked him to tape his introduction, "The shortstop ... number 2 ... Derek Jeter ... number 2." The Yankees captain used that throughout the remaining years of his career at Yankee Stadium. "I grew up a Yankee fan and it was the voice I always heard," Jeter said. "He is as much a part of this organization as any player."

In failing health, Sheppard recorded a greeting to the fans that was played at the old Yankee Stadium's final game on September 21, 2008, when the Yankees hosted the Baltimore Orioles. It was a touching moment. He pre-recorded the Yankee lineup from his home that was shown on the Diamond Vision screen at the stadium for the fans. Each player that was announced ran out to his position. "Playing left field, number 18 ... Johnny Damon ... number 18." That was a night to remember.

He had hoped to be behind his mic when the new Yankee Stadium opened in 2009. It never happened, but the media dining room was appropriately named "Sheppard's Place" in honor of the beloved "Voice."

Shortly after the Yankees defeated the Philadelphia Phillies in the 2009 World Series, Sheppard formally announced his retirement two weeks before his 99th birthday.

Bob Sheppard's voice was stilled when he passed on July 11, 2010, at age 99 at his Baldwin, Long Island, home. Two nights later at the All-Star game in Anaheim, MLB honored Sheppard's legacy by using his voice to introduce Jeter. The Yankees wore a commemorative patch on the left sleeve of their home and road jerseys for the remainder of the 2010 season.

Yankees owner George Steinbrenner passed away on July 13. It was a week of mourning for the Yankee family.

I attended Bob's funeral on July 15 at the Church of Saint Christopher in Baldwin, New York. Yankees GM Brian Cashman, VP of Marketing Debbie Tyman and Cerrone led a contingent of front office personnel and behind the scenes staff including the team's former PR director Marty Appel.

Cashman delivered the eulogy.

Unfortunately, no players attended.

The Yankees returned to a somber stadium on July 16 in their 5–4 win over the Tampa Bay Rays mourning the loss of their owner and Bob Sheppard. In his honor, his PA booth was empty and there were no announcements during the game.

Bob Sheppard Day

After more than 50 years on the job, Bob Sheppard was given his due when New York City mayor Michael Bloomberg declared May 7, 2000, Bob Sheppard Day. I was there with my camera, clicking away. Several members of his family joined him including his wife Mary and his four children from his first marriage to Margaret, who died in 1959. Walter Cronkite read the inscription on his plaque:

> BOB SHEPPARD
> PUBLIC ADDRESS ANNOUNCER
> "THE VOICE OF YANKEE STADIUM"
> FOR HALF A CENTURY, HE HAS WELCOMED GENERATIONS OF
> FANS WITH HIS TRADEMARK GREETING, LADIES AND GENTLEMEN,
> WELCOME TO YANKEE STADIUM. HIS CLEAR, CONCISE AND CORRECT
> VOCAL STYLE HAS ANNOUNCED THE NAMES OF HUNDREDS OF
> PLAYERS BOTH UNFAMILIAR AND LEGENDARY WITH EQUAL DIVINE
> REVERANCE MAKING HIM AS SYNONYMOUS WITH YANKEE
> STADIUM AS ITS COPPER FAÇADE AND MONUMENT PARK.

In a gesture that personified the man, Bob Sheppard donated his public address microphone to the Baseball Hall of Fame in 2000. He earned his rightful place in the coveted Hall along with all the other Yankee greats.

3

The Babe and "Little Ray"

I launched my radio show titled *Inside Yankee Baseball* on September 7, 1997. It was aired on WICC 600 AM in Bridgeport, Connecticut, the largest city in the state located in Fairfield County, a heavy Yankees demographic area. I grappled with the idea as to who would make an interesting guest on the inaugural show. In a perfect world the answer would be Babe Ruth, the iconic Yankee who grabbed the wheel of history and turned baseball in a different direction from small ball to home runs.

Of course, Ruth wasn't an option as a guest, so the next best thing was to have an unknown guy named Ray Kelly, a.k.a. "Little Ray," who served as one of Ruth's mascots, a fancy name for "gofers" who ran errands for baseball's mega star and ferried his bats.

I first met Kelly in the Yankees dugout at the July 12, 1997, Old-Timers' Day game at Yankee Stadium a couple of months before I began my show. I was dressed in my umpire's uniform prepared to ump the Old-Timers' exhibition when he approached me. Kelly, a man short in stature, was wearing a bright green blazer and a shirt and tie. He stared me in the eye and said, "Do you know who I am?"

Somewhat embarrassed, I answered, "No."

He said, "I was Babe Ruth's mascot from 1921 to 1931."

"Mascot?" I quizzically asked.

Intrigued by Mr. Kelly, I traveled on August 4 to his

Ray Kelly, shown here in his Valley Cottage, New York, home on August 4, 1997, has many memories from the years he served as Babe Ruth's mascot.

Valley Cottage, New York, home to get his story for my column in *Sports Collectors Digest* that plays like a fairy tale.

By 1921, the Babe was a burgeoning star in his second season with the Yankees when he saw Little Ray, a three-year-old boy playing catch with his father in an underdeveloped area of Riverside Drive in New York City. "One day Babe, who lived on Riverside Drive, was coming back from a ball game," recalled Kelly, who served three and a half years in the Air Corps as a radio operator in World War II. "He stopped his car when he saw this crowd of people that were assembled. He thought there was an accident. Babe walked over to the crowd and stood there for about 10 minutes watching me play ball with my dad. He then introduced himself to my father, who almost dropped dead. Here was Babe Ruth standing in front of him. Ruth asked my dad if he could take me out to the Polo Grounds where the Yankees played before Yankee Stadium was built."

"'Absolutely,' my dad replied."

Ray and his father went to the Polo Grounds the following day, guests of the peerless slugger. Kelly and his father sat in the Yankees dugout the entire game, an unforgettable experience for both father and son.

"At one point during the game, Babe turned to my father and asked, 'I'd like to have Little Ray as my personal mascot. Would that be alright with you?'"

"My father answered, 'That'll be fine with me.'"

This led to the dream job of being one of Babe Ruth's mascots. It was pretty much a public relations stunt on and off the field. Kelly ran a variety of errands for the Yankees' mega star. "There used to be a buffet in the clubhouse," Kelly remembered. "Babe would send me in there to get hot dogs during the game. I would come back with two dogs in one hand, plus a bottle of pop. Then I'd go back and get him a couple of more hot dogs."

Kelly's father would usually drive his celebrity child to the ballpark. On occasion, Ruth or Eddie Bennett, the official Yankees bat boy, would pick him up at his house on 102nd Street. Little Ray was the envy of the neighborhood. "My classmates called me the 'King of the Block,'" smiled Kelly. His friends and other kids would often ask if he could get Babe's autograph for them. But Little Ray declined, thinking it would be an imposition on the wildly popular Yankee. "I felt if they wanted his autograph they could go to the games," Kelly commented. "He was a liberal signer before and after games."

As is widely known, Babe loved kids. As far-fetched as it seems, he would sometimes play ball with them outside Yankee Stadium after games. "He would take me to Macombs Dam Park, and we would play ball with the kids," remembered Kelly. "Imagine, someone as famous as Babe Ruth doing that!"

On occasion the "Sultan of Swat" would take Little Ray and his father to Beefsteak Charlie's between 97th and 98th Street on Broadway after a game. He used to put his tiny mascot up on a stage and show him off to the patrons of the restaurant. "He would have me give the lineups of the 1923 or 1924 Yankees," said Kelly. "Then he would say to my father, 'Ned [his real name was Edward] pass the hat around and see how much people enjoyed it.'"

The Babe had three uniforms made for Kelly. One read "Babe Ruth," another read "New York," and the other was labeled "Yanks." Throughout his life, Kelly kept the hat he wore, a pair of pants, stockings, and a red sweatshirt he wore under his jerseys. But the full uniforms were lost in time.

As Little Ray got older, he took care of Ruth's bat and glove. "The glove Babe wore just about covered his mitt," revealed Kelly. "He used to cut out the palm of his glove so he could get the feel of the ball."

The Monarch of Baseball

George Herman Ruth was a larger-than-life figure. The bedrock of the Yankee legacy, he was a transcendental star. His accomplishments were amazing. The monarch of baseball batted .342 lifetime with 714 home runs. He is listed as collecting 2,214 RBI, but because the RBI stat did not become official until 1920, he is not officially credited with the 224 he had before 1920. If he received credit for those RBI, he would have 2,438, 141 more than Hank Aaron who is listed as the all-time RBI leader with 2,297. The Babe ranks number one in baseball history for the best lifetime OPS (slugging plus on-base percentage) at 1.164 and is one of four players to reach base via base-on-balls more than 2,000 times along with Barry Bonds, Ricky Henderson, and Ted Williams. He even stole 123 bases and was known to slide head-first on occasion. Of his career home runs, 10 were of the inside-the-park variety.

The Babe's legend refuses to die. In December 2019, the bat used by Ruth to hit his 500th career home run in 1929 sold for more than $1 million through SCP Auctions.

Over the past couple of seasons, the Los Angeles Angels' two-way star Shohei Ohtani has drawn comparisons to the Babe. Although Ruth never was a full-time player and a regular pitcher at the same time as is Ohtani, the Bambino's career totals overall will likely go unmatched. An argument can be made, certainly, that Ruth is the only player to have demonstrated the skills to be elected to the Hall of Fame as a pitcher and a position player. Time will tell whether Ohtani will join him.

Ruth's pitching statistics place him among the elites in the history of the game. He went 94-46 with a glossy 2.28 ERA. A total of 89 wins came with the Red Sox between 1914 and 1919, a period in which he helped them win three world championships. In 1916, he threw 323⅔ innings, went 23–12 and led the American League in both shutouts (nine) and ERA (1.75). A year later, he went 24–13 with a 2.01 ERA in 326⅓ innings and led the AL with a whopping 35 complete games—a figure topped only once since then, by Bob Feller in 1946 when "Rapid Robert" hurled 36 complete games. Ruth was also a Yankee killer. According to the Elias Sports Bureau, he made 23 starts in his career against the Yankees and went 17–5 with a 2.21 ERA.

He sparkled in the postseason when on the mound. In Game Two of the 1916 World Series, Ruth pitched a 14-inning complete game to beat the Dodgers 2–1. It's still the most innings ever thrown by one pitcher in a single postseason game. Ruth posted a 0.87 ERA in three World Series starts for the Red Sox and his record of 29⅔ consecutive scoreless innings in the Fall Classic stood from 1918 until Whitey Ford broke it in 1961. In Game 4 of the 1918 WS between the Cubs and Red Sox, he batted sixth and went 1-for-2 with a two-run triple and a sacrifice in Boston's 3–2 win over the Cubs. Since that time the only other pitcher not to bat ninth in the World Series was the Astros' Zack Greinke who batted eighth in Game Four of the 2021 Fall Classic against the Atlanta Braves at Truist Field. The right-hander went 1-for-2, collecting a single off Kyle Wright in the Braves' 3–2 win.

Ruth is the only player since the turn of the 20th century to lead his league in Triple Crown categories as both a hitter and a pitcher and he did it in a span of three years.

Ruth's feats were superhuman. In 1921 he underwent a battery of tests at Columbia

University. According to Geoff Miller in his book *Intangibles: Big-League Stories and Strategies for Winning the Mental Game—in Baseball and in Life*, "the tests revealed Ruth was 90 percent efficient compared with a human average of 60 percent and his eyes were about 12 percent faster than those of the average human being."

As a member of the Red Sox, he collected his first major league hit off the Yankees' Leonard Cole on October 2, 1914, at Fenway Park in Boston's 11–5 win. His first big league home run came against the Yankees' Jack Warhop at the Polo Grounds on May 6, 1915, when he led off the third inning. In that game he went the distance and took the loss. Pitching 12⅓ innings in the Yankees' 4–3 win. Two umpires worked the game. Hall of Fame ump Billy Evans called balls and strikes while Dominick Mullaney worked the bases. Exactly three years later, in the same ballpark, batting sixth in the Red Sox batting order, Ruth hit a home run in his first start at a position (1B) other than pitcher. In his career he made 23 starts at first base.

The Yankees were unwanted tenants at the Polo Grounds, under Coogan's Bluff, a venue the Yanks shared with the Giants from 1913 to 1922. Giants manager John McGraw, a traditionalist of small-ball baseball, was no fan of Ruth's power game. And the fact that the Yankees outdrew the Giants created a strained relationship between the two clubs. Because of Ruth's attraction, the Yankees became the first professional sports team to draw more than a million spectators when they drew almost 1.3 million to the Polo Grounds in 1920. In '20 and '21, the Yanks drew more than 1.2 million each year while the Giants, much to the chagrin of McGraw, drew just over 929,000 in 1920 and 973,000 in '21. That was considered good at the time, but it did not match the Yankees. From 1920 to 1930, the Bombers drew more than one million fans nine times thanks to the gate attraction of the mighty Babe.

The Yankees, aware they were not welcomed in the Polo Grounds, pursued their own park. And in the process, they had a landing spot of all places—Fenway Park—if they were evicted from the Polo Grounds.

The Sale of Babe Ruth

The genesis of the Yankees–Red Sox rivalry can be traced to January 5, 1920, when New York purchased Ruth for $100,000. (Some sources report that it was $125,000.) The deal included a personal loan of $350,000 from Yankees co-owners Colonel Jacob Ruppert and Tillinghast L'Hommedieu Huston. The loan was secured by a mortgage of Fenway Park. Following the sale of Ruth, the Red Sox did not win another championship until 2004. For Boston fans, the sale led directly to the championship drought, and the team's inability to win it came to be known as "The Curse of the Bambino."

It's a long-standing myth that Red Sox owner Harry Frazee sold Babe Ruth to the Yankees to finance his Broadway play *No, No, Nanette,* which featured the song "Tea for Two." In fact, it wasn't until 1925 that the play hit Broadway, five years after Ruth was sold to the Yankees. From 1918 to 1923, Frazee sold 17 players to the Yankees. Just as the Kansas City A's would in the '50s, the Red Sox took on the look of a Yankees farm team, cultivating talent before shipping it to New York.

Except for his troubled seasons in 1922 and 1925, he led the league in homers every year from 1918 through 1931. He hit multiple home runs in a record 72 games. He was in a league of his own.

Little Ray had a front row seat to the greatest hitting show on Earth. Ruth's raw power epitomized the emerging "live ball era" and fans flocked to see the celebrated Yankee whose prodigious home runs might be described as life imitating art.

Kelly wasn't even of school age when the Bambino enjoyed a spectacular 1921 season. He set a new single-season home run record for the third consecutive year hitting an astounding 59 homers, while out-homering eight of the 16 big league teams. The Sultan of Swat, enjoying one of the greatest seasons in the history of the game, also led the majors in RBI (168), runs scored (177), walks (145), on-base percentage (.512), and slugging percentage (.846). His 1.359 OPS was off the charts. Ruth's 457 total bases and 119 extra base hits remain major league records. Despite hitting .378, he finished in batting behind Harry Heilmann (.394) and Ty Cobb (.389) in the AL. Rogers Hornsby (Cardinals) led the ML in batting at .397.

Ruth moved into first place on the career home run list in '21 with number 139, breaking the record of Hall of Fame first baseman Roger Connor that had stood since 1895. The record-setting home run came off Tigers reliever Bert Cole in Detroit on July 18, at Navin Field (later called Tiger Stadium). It was a titanic blast that, according to Ruth expert Bill Jenkinson, might have traveled 575 feet.

Otto Young Schnering headed the Curtiss Candy Company, located in Chicago, a pop fly from Wrigley Field. The company launched the Baby Ruth candy bar in 1921 when Ruth was a burgeoning star. According to a 2014 article written by Christopher Klein and published at History.com, "By 1926, the candy bar totaled one million dollars a month in sales. The company's candy making facilities had become the largest of their kind in the world."

Although the company maintained that the candy bar was named after former president Grover Cleveland's daughter Ruth—a dubious claim, given that she had passed away in 1904—the Babe believed that Curtiss Candy was capitalizing on his name, so he took action. "In 1926," writes Klein, "Babe Ruth entered the candy business himself and licensed his name to the George H. Ruth Candy Company, which sought to register 'Ruth's Home Run Candy' with the U.S. Patent and Trademark Office."

It was just a matter of time before Ruth and the Curtiss Candy Company faced each other in court. Klein notes that in 1931, the company successfully defended itself against a suit filed by Ruth, as a patent court ruled that the similarity between the slugger's nickname and the candy bar was coincidence.

Ruth was known to thumb his nose at rules. Even Commissioner Kenesaw Mountain Landis wasn't going to get in his way. In October 1921, Ruth and Yankees teammate Bob Meusel joined a postseason barnstorming tour in direct defiance of the commissioner, who had outlawed such tours. Both players were suspended the first six weeks of the 1922 season. Despite missing the first 33 games, the rule-breaking Yankee slugged 35 homers. It was the only year between 1918 and 1924 that he failed to lead the league in four-baggers. In the next nine years, he led the junior circuit in home runs eight times. Ruth and Meusel debuted on May 20 of the '22 season when the Yankees named Ruth captain of the team. The honor lasted only six days because of an incident at the Polo Grounds on May 25 where the Yankees met the Senators. In the second inning he tried to stretch a single into a double and was called out at second base by umpire George Hildebrand. According to the *New York Times*, "Ruth leaped to his feet with the quickness of a cat, and he brought up with him a handful of dirt which he threw in the direction of the umpire." The encounter led to his ejection.

According to Mike Lynch, who wrote an article about the game for the Society for American Baseball Research (SABR), "As Ruth walked off the field, many in the crowd jeered and hooted. Ruth returned the favor and mockingly doffed his cap as he headed to the dugout. At this, a fan yelled, 'You goddamned big bum, why don't you play ball?'"

Ruth climbed into the stands, but the heckler was nowhere to be found. Then, as Lynch notes, "Someone in the crowd yelled, 'Hit the big stiff!' Rather than continue his pursuit, the slugger returned to the dugout roof and challenged anyone and everyone to a brawl. 'Come on down and fight. Anyone who wants to fight,' he shouted, 'come down on the field!' As he exited the Polo Grounds, the catcalls grew louder." Ruth missed one game and was fined $200 by AL president Ban Johnson.

In the middle of June, Ruth was again involved in an ugly incident with an umpire. Playing left field, he charged into second base to argue a call with umpire Bill Dineen. What he said led to a three-day suspension. The following day Ruth challenged Dineen to a fight under the stands which was avoided but Johnson added two more days to the suspension. In late August, Ruth was suspended three more days following an ejection for disputing a called third strike.

His most publicized ejection occurred on June 23, 1917, at Fenway Park as a member of the Red Sox when he argued balls and strikes with home plate umpire Brick Owens. The two got into a scuffle when Owens issued a walk to Washington Senators second baseman Ray Morgan to open the game. Ruth was replaced by right-hander Ernie Shore, who had a modest seven-year career. Morgan was then caught stealing and Shore retired the next 26 batters to lead the Red Sox to a 4–0 win. Ruth, then, is credited for participating in a combined no-hitter. (A perfect game could not be credited because a runner reached base.)

Despite Ruth's misadventures, he remained the most popular player in the game, a rock star in current terminology. Sports writing reached its gaudy pinnacle in the Roaring Twenties and the greatest home run masher in the world gave the scribes material they had never seen before.

The Birth of Yankee Stadium

Ruppert and Huston paid $675,000 in 1921 for a 10-acre plot from the estate of William Waldorf Astor that was the site of a rocky lumberyard. Ruppert, a brewing magnate and former congressman, bought out Huston's share of the Yankees early in 1922. He then contracted with the Osborn Engineering Co. of Cleveland to be the architect of the new ballpark that would be built on the land that was purchased from the Astor estate. Ruppert said, "I want the greatest ballpark in the world."

His wish was granted.

Construction of Yankee Stadium began on May 5, 1922. In only 284 days the White Construction company built the magnificent new Yankee Stadium at a cost of $2.5 million. It would be the first three-tier stadium in America. The only other athletic facility in the country referred to as a stadium was Harvard Stadium, which was constructed in 1903. The grand new edifice just off the Harlem River was visible for miles.

At the new Yankee Stadium, the right field foul pole measured 295-feet from home plate. Over the years the dimensions have been modified but the stadium continues to be a paradise for lefty hitters with its current 314-foot distance to the right field foul pole. It truly was the "House that Ruth Built."

Yankee Stadium opened on April 18, 1923, when the Yankees hosted the Red Sox. The game started at 3:30 p.m. on a raw, breezy day. Seating held about 58,000–60,000 but the attendance reportedly swelled to 74,200. Newspapers reported that thousands were denied entry by the fire department. Little Ray, at age five, was there for the grand opening. "I'll never forget it," he said. "John Philip Sousa and his band played the national anthem. Al Smith, the governor of New York who later ran for president, threw out the first pitch." It was caught by catcher Wally Schang.

In this era, the public address system was not electronic. "A short, stocky guy [Jack Lenz] used to walk all around the park with a megaphone and announce the lineups," recalled Kelly. "He would make a complete circle of the stadium. In those days it was important to identify the players for the crowd because they didn't have numbers. In 1929 the Yankees became the first team to permanently have numbers on their uniform jerseys."

When the Yankees took the field, their shortstop, Everett "Deacon" Scott, the Yankees original "Iron Man," started his 987th consecutive game. His streak that would extend to 1,307 games would be broken by Lou Gehrig and Cal Ripken.

Ruth reportedly said, "I'd give a year of my life if I can hit a home run in the first game in this new park." In the third inning, a tall, broad-shouldered, flat-bellied Babe connected for a three-run homer off Red Sox pitcher Howard Ehmke with Whitey Witt on third and "Jumpin' Joe" Dugan on first. It was fitting that the Babe would hit the first home run ever hit in Yankee Stadium and it led to the Yankees' 4–1 win. The bat he used was sold by SCP Auctions in conjunction with Sotheby's, fetching nearly $1.3 million in 2004.

He would hit 258 more homers there. Ruth also committed the first Yankee error ever in the new stadium when he dropped a fly ball off the bat of Joe Harris in the top of the fifth inning.

Ruth's '23 season was beyond anyone's imagination when he hit an astounding .393 and led the league in home runs (41) and RBI (131). He was four hits shy of batting .400. The Yanks drew an incredible 1,007,066 fans.

The Yankees won their first World Series when they finally beat the Giants after losing to them the previous two years at the Polo Grounds. On New York's first World Series title team of 1923, half the regular players and six of the seven pitchers to throw more than a dozen innings were acquired from Frazee.

Ruth had a great series, batting .368, including three home runs. Little Ray Kelly played his part in the Yankees win.

"Giants manager John McGraw was always kidding me about the fact that the Giants beat the Yankees in 1921 and 1922," said Kelly. "He predicted that they would bury the Yankees in the '23 Series. Some smart photographer asked me to pose, putting a hex on McGraw and the Giants. The Yanks won the Series—maybe it was because of the jinx I put on McGraw," laughed Kelly.

In the '23 WS, the teams rotated parks every other game. In Game One, played at Yankee Stadium, the score was tied 4–4 in the top of ninth, when the Giants' Casey Stengel hit an inside-the-park home run. "It's ironic that Stengel, who would win seven world championships with the Yankees, would hit the first WS home run in Yankee Stadium," Kelly stated.

Ruth hit three home runs in Game Four of the 1926 World Series, a feat he duplicated against the Cardinals two years later, again in Game Four. That record has since been tied

3. The Babe and "Little Ray"

"Little Ray" Kelly and the Babe at Yankee Stadium in 1923, the year the stadium opened. Note that Ruth posed batting right-handed (National Baseball Hall of Fame and Museum).

three times by Reggie Jackson, Albert Pujols, and Pablo Sandoval but never broken, and Ruth is the only man to have hit three home runs in any postseason game twice.

"By the fall of 1927, Ruth had completely reshaped the game of baseball, bending it to his will," author Jane Leavy wrote in *The Big Fella*. Kelly, now nine years old, recalled Babe's epic 60-home run season and the bats he used. "The Bambino used three different bats that year," said Kelly. "They were named 'Black Betsy,' 'Beautiful Bella,' and 'Big Bertha.' 'Black Betsy' was used to hit number 59, and he used 'Beautiful Bella' to hit number 60."

The great '27 Yankees ran away with the AL pennant, going 110–44–1. The lethal tandem of Ruth and Gehrig tore the AL to shreds before sweeping the Pirates in the WS. Ruth batted .356 and hit a single-season record 60 home runs, including 165 RBI. Gehrig, who was the league's MVP, had superb numbers (.373–47–173) as well.

As Little Ray grew older he was allowed to take batting practice, shag fly balls and field ground balls. He even made some road trips and roomed with Bennett, who lost both parents in the 1918 flu epidemic when he was 15. Bennett received a spine injury when he fell out of a baby carriage. The injury left him hunchbacked and restricted his growth. By the time he was an adult he was considered a dwarf. But there was a belief that small people were good luck charms for star players, a superstition that went back to the 19th century. It was common for elite players to have their own mascot. It's possible the Babe saw Kelly and Bennett as talismans to enhance his game.

In 1932, Bennett was hit by a taxi and suffered a broken leg. He never fully recovered and had to relinquish his bat boy duties with the Yankees. The pain from his injury led to heavy drinking. In 1935 he succumbed to alcoholism in a boarding house on West 84th Street. His room was filled with Yankee memorabilia including "balls and bats signed by Lou Gehrig and Babe Ruth," wrote Benoit Morenne in an April 2, 2021, *New York Times* piece. The Yankees paid for his funeral services, but no players attended on a cold January day. Bennett was buried in an unmarked grave at the St. John's Cemetery in Queens, New York.

Charles Papio, a Yankee fan, was able to get a monument company in Long Island owned by Anthony Spadolini to donate a gravestone in 2019. Bennett was given the dignity of a graveside service. His headstone reads, "New York Yankees Mascot/Batboy, 1921–1932."

Babe was a well-known womanizer and lived a very active social life, but according to Kelly, there was another side of the man. "He used to take me to church when we were on the road on occasion," noted Kelly. Ruth's Catholic background was cultivated at the St. Mary's Industrial School for Boys in Baltimore, where he spent most of his childhood and formative years. The school, run by Catholic monks, had a definite impact on his religious thinking and his baseball career. It was there that his baseball abilities were honed under Brother Matthias. He never forgot his humble origins and often visited orphanages during his career.

The "Called Shot"

Little Ray and his father were guests of the slugger at Yankee Stadium where the first two games of the 1932 World Series were played between the Yankees and the Chicago Cubs. Kelly, now in high school, no longer was Babe's mascot.

"After the second game, Babe said to my dad, 'I want to take Little Ray out to Chicago because I think we're going to take four straight from these guys,'" recalled Kelly.

"My dad respectfully answered, 'No, Babe. He's got to start concentrating on his studies.'"

"Babe said sternly, 'Listen, Little Ray is coming out to Chicago with me. End of story.'"

"So I went to Wrigley Field and sat in a box seat right alongside the Yankee dugout."

The eternal question remains—did the Bambino call his home run shot in Game Three, or did he point to pitcher Charlie Root, indicating he had one strike left, or was he waving off hecklers in the Cubs dugout? The controversy continues and is an important chapter in the game's lore.

In the fifth inning the score was tied 4–4 when the Bambino stepped to the plate. He took a big swing and missed the first pitch for strike one. Ruth then raised a finger as if to say, "That's one strike." The next pitch was a ball, and the third pitch was called a strike. With the count 1-2, Ruth put up two fingers, most likely indicating he had two strikes but one more left. At that point, Kelly insisted, "I heard him yell vividly to Charlie Root, 'It only takes one.'"

"The next pitch was a ball to even the count. Before the next pitch, Babe took his arm and elevated it over Root's head. I've read four or five different books that said he was pointing to Root. That's baloney. I was there on ground level. Ruth's arm was elevated over Root's head. The next pitch came in and Babe banged it right where he had pointed to the center field bleachers at Wrigley Field."

Kelly claims he asked Ruth if he specifically pointed to the bleachers with the intention of calling his shot.

"Absolutely," stated the Yankee slugger.

From teammates like Lefty Gomez to Wrigley PA announcer Pat Pieper to Supreme Court Justice and diehard Cubs fan John Paul Stevens, who attended the game as a kid, swore that Ruth called it.

Cubs catcher Gabby Hartnett was in the "no" camp, but if you watch film of this event, Hartnett had his back turned at the time Ruth was pointing.

Halper invited Kelly to his New Jersey estate, a veritable baseball museum, and asked if he would put his account in writing. Before Kelly's testimony, he had documentation from six players who were in uniform that game that said no. They included Billy Herman, Guy Bush, Frank Crosetti, Johnny Moore, Ben Chapman and Red Lucas. Paul Gallico, one of the writers at the game, supported Kelly. Umpire George Magerkurth, who was behind the plate, always said that Ruth called it.

The original footage of Ruth's "called shot" was taken by Kirk Kandle of St. Louis. In 1999 a treasure trove of new footage emerged that was filmed by a man named Harold Warp, a prominent businessman from Chicago, who was at Game Three of the 1932 WS with a 16-millimeter camera. The film was taken from the third base side. Jacobs claims that Ruth's arm was extended toward the Cubs' dugout. He did not think Ruth's arm was elevated, countering Kelly's account.

"I'm sure he made a gesture, to indicate 'I'm going to hit one,'" said Robert Creamer, the author of *Babe: The Legend Comes to Life*. "But he did that a lot. It doesn't matter if he's pointing to a spot. He did something. He challenged them. He gestured. He stuck it to the Cubs, and he loved it."

Lou Gehrig was the on-deck batter. He proceeded to homer off Pat Malone, who had replaced Root. In the 12 years Ruth and Gehrig played together they combined for 859 home runs, Aaron and Eddie Mathews combined for 863..

Five days later, on October 6, Gehrig appeared on a radio show hosted by vocalist and bandleader Rudy Vallee titled *The Fleischmann's Yeast Hour*. Gehrig declared, "I've played a lot of baseball, but I've never seen so much nerve on display before. Babe had two strikes on him. There was the old Bronx cheer."

"So what does he do? He stands there and tells the world that he's going to sock it into the center field stands. A few seconds later the ball was just where he pointed in the center field stands. He called his shot and made it."

It has been questioned if Gehrig was reading from a script or if those were his own words. He never denied that Ruth pointed.

4

The Babe's Last Hurrah

A young ballplayer can hide behind the veneer of invincibility, but not even the Babe had an answer for Father Time. Ruth was a fading star, and on January 15, 1934, he signed his final contract with the Yankees for $35,000, accepting a pay cut of $17,000. He was the highest-paid player in the game for 13 consecutive years from 1922 to 1934, topping out at $80,000 for both the 1930 and 1931 seasons.

The Babe finished his career with the bedraggled Boston Braves in 1935. Judge Emil Fuchs, the team's owner plagued by financial problems, took a chance on the aging slugger to help improve attendance. It was a failed experiment. Appearing in 28 games, the tired 40-year-old Bambino batted a weak .181 with six home runs. His final three homers came in the same game on May 25 at Forbes Field in an 11–7 loss to the Pirates. The Behemoth of Bust did everything big. His first came against Red Lucas and his last two off pitcher Guy Bush with the final one clearing the right field roof—the first time in the ballpark's 26-year history that a ball was hit out of the park. He also singled that game.

After Ruth circled the bases for his third home run, instead of going to the Braves dugout, he headed toward the showers. To do so he had to go through the Pirates dugout. He spotted an open seat on the bench and sat next to pitcher Mace Brown. "I'll never forget it," Brown said in a 1998 interview with the *Greensboro News and Record*. "He sat down on our bench right beside me. 'Boys,' he says, 'that last one felt good.'"

In addition to playing for the Braves, Ruth's contract called on him to serve as a vice president and assistant manager of the organization. He would also take home a percentage of profits on top of his salary. And there was a glimmer of hope that he would one day succeed Bill McKechnie as manager of the team.

Ruth sought permission from Fuchs to attend a reception on the French luxury liner *Normandie* on its maiden voyage when it docked in New York City. It was a day off for the Braves, but they were scheduled to play an exhibition game in Bridgeport, Connecticut. "Fuchs refused, saying Ruth's place was with the team," wrote Bob LeMoine of the Society for American Baseball Research. "I do not have to put up with this sort of treatment," Ruth blasted.

Ruth's final career at-bat occurred at the Baker Bowl in Philadelphia on May 30, 1935. Facing the Phillies' Jim Bivin in the first game of a doubleheader, he grounded out to Dolph Camilli at first base in the bottom of the first inning. He then went out to play left field. This might sound strange because he was primarily a right fielder, the position he always played at Yankee Stadium. But he started more than 1,000 games in left field during his career. There is a reason for this. According to a 2013 *Sports Illustrated* article titled "99 Cool Facts About Babe" by Cliff Corcoran, courtesy of the National Baseball Hall of Fame, "After losing a ball in the sun in the Polo Grounds' left field on July

4. The Babe's Last Hurrah

16, 1922, Ruth refused to ever play the sun field again. His position thereafter was determined by the geographic orientation of the ballpark in which he was playing. For the rest of his career, Ruth played exclusively in right field at the Polo Grounds and Yankee Stadium, as well as in Washington and Cleveland but exclusively in left field at the other AL cities (Boston, Chicago, Detroit, Philadelphia and St. Louis)."

According to *Baseball Almanac*, Ruth started 1,121 games in right field and 1,041 games in left field. He also started games in center field (64) and first base (23).

Ruth now struggled defensively in his final game. First a ball dropped in front of him because of his lack of speed. Then Lou Chiozza hit a ball that rolled past him to the wall. Babe threw to Pinkey Whitney, the cutoff man, who erased Chiozza at the plate in his attempt to hit an inside-the-park home run. Ruth was credited with an assist on the play, but the big guy knew it was over. The inning over, Ruth exited through the center field fence where the clubhouse was located. It was like walking through that corn field in the movie *Field of Dreams*, never to return.

By this time, Ruth's relationship with the Braves front office was toxic. He called a press conference while a game was in progress on June 2. *Time* reported the following lacerating comments by Ruth. "Judge Fuchs is a double-crosser. His word is no good. He doesn't keep his promises. I don't want another damn thing from him—the dirty double-crosser." Ruth added, "I will not return to the Braves so long as Fuchs remains in control of the club." "Fuchs had actually informed Ruth of his release on June 1," wrote LeMoine.

Ruth was one of the five initial inductees to the Baseball Hall of Fame in 1936 along with Ty Cobb, Honus Wagner, Walter Johnson and Christy Mathewson. Out of that group, only Cobb had a higher percentage of the vote than the 95.1 percent Ruth received just six months after his retirement.

Bulkeley Stadium in Hartford, Connecticut, was home to the Hartford Baseball Club, a minor league team nicknamed the Senators, then the Bees and later the Chiefs. Major league stars and the "who's who" of baseball often made exhibition game appearances at the stadium. The *Hartford Courant* reported, "On September 30, 1945, Ruth played in a charity game at Bulkeley Stadium as a member of the Savitt Gems. At 50 years old, Ruth drew a crowd of more than 2,500. He took batting practice before the game and clouted a home run over Bulkeley Stadium's right field fence. During the exhibition, Ruth coached first base. He later entered the game as a pinch-hitter and grounded out to the pitcher." The ballgame was Ruth's final appearance in a baseball uniform.

After a brief stint as a Brooklyn Dodgers coach in 1938, Ruth retired and spent his time golfing, fishing, bowling, and making public appearances. In November 1946, he checked into French Hospital on 29th Street in Manhattan; he had headaches and pain above his left eye. It was cancer, but the newspapers never said that was what it was. The New York *Herald Tribune* reported that Babe Ruth had been sick all winter with "a throat infection."

Following a visit with the Babe, baseball commissioner A.B. "Happy" Chandler, aware of Ruth's rapidly deteriorating condition, declared April 27, 1947, Babe Ruth Day throughout baseball. A Yankee Stadium crowd of 58,339 fans turned out that breezy Sunday afternoon to honor the ailing Bambino. The 10-minute ceremony had several speakers. Cardinal Francis Spellman, then the Archbishop of New York, was among them; he delivered the invocation at Ruth's request. Before Mel Allen introduced Ruth, the Yankees tapped a "freckled 13-year-old" legion ballplayer named Larry Cutler, who said, in part, "From all of us kids, Babe, it's swell to have you back."

A shadow of his former self, greatly affected by 82 days in the hospital, Ruth, in a camel overcoat, waved his cap. His voice, a hoarse, forced whisper, went over the loudspeaker and the WOR radio network to be piped into every ballpark playing organized baseball. "You know how bad my voice sounds," he said, in a frank whisper. "Well, it feels just as bad."

The Yankees retired his number 3 on June 3, 1948, 13 years after his last at-bat. The Indians were in New York that cold, rainy day. Nat Fein's Pulitzer Prize–winning photo from that day shows a frail, fading Ruth leaning on a bat borrowed for the occasion from Indians pitcher Bob Feller. The bat eventually fell into the hands of Eddie Robinson, who was Feller's Indians teammate in '48.

Ruth was in the Indians dugout before the ceremony and Robinson could see that the Babe was in ill health. "I gave him the bat," Robinson told MLB.com writer Michael Clair. "He looked like he needed help physically, and I took a bat out of the bat rack and gave it to him. He carried it up to home plate, and he used it as a kind of a crutch. When he came back, I got the bat and had him sign it."

Robinson kept the bat for more than 30 years, hanging it in the restaurant he owned in Baltimore. Eventually, he decided to sell it—and he called Halper.

"I told my wife, Bette, 'I wonder what that bat's worth.' We had no idea, and I said, 'Well, I'm going to call Halper and ask him for a price that I know he won't give me, but he might come back with a lesser price, give us an idea about what it's worth.' So I called him. I said, 'Barry, I'm thinking about selling that Ruth bat.' He said, 'What do you want for it?' I said, '$10,000.' He said, 'I'll have the money to you tomorrow.' I think it eventually sold for $120,000 to $125,000!"

Robinson died on October 4, 2021, at age 100 on his ranch in Bastrop, Texas. At the time, he was the oldest living former major league player.

Ruth's last public appearance was on July 26, 1948, when he attended the New York premiere of *The Babe Ruth Story*, starring William Bendix as the great slugger. As Cliff Corcoran notes in an article for SI.com, Ruth left before the film ended and made his way back to the hospital. The man who lived a life fit for fiction died three weeks later at age 53, on August 16, 1948. The next two days he lay in state in the rotunda at Yankee Stadium. It's estimated that 105,000 mourners viewed his body. Ruth's funeral was conducted at St. Patrick's Cathedral in Manhattan. His final resting place is the Gate of Heaven Cemetery in Hawthorne, New York, where 6,000 fans said goodbye on the day of his funeral. His second wife, Claire, was buried next to him when she died in 1976.

The *New York Times* began Babe's obituary, "Probably nowhere in all the imaginative field of fiction could one find a career more dramatic and bizarre than that portrayed in real life by George Herman Babe Ruth...."

The Babe Was Robbed

Babe Ruth's lifetime home run record held for 39 years until Hank Aaron eclipsed the mark in 1974. Barry Bonds currently stands atop the homer record board at 762, although tainted by steroid allegations. The Bambino's home run total is a stunning number in any era. But was the most prolific home run hitter of his time short-changed because of the fair-foul rule that existed for most of his career?

Unequivocally, yes!

4. The Babe's Last Hurrah

A relatively unknown rule (Number 48) that affected baseball's most sacred record, the home run mark, existed from 1906 to 1930, minus a couple of months in 1920. It's a slice of baseball history that has generally been ignored by baseball historians. The unfair rule declared that batted balls that left the field fair and curved foul were ruled foul. Umpires had the authority to rule the ball fair or foul where it was last seen. Since Ruth played from 1914 to 1935, a large part of his sterling career fell under this rule that stripped him of many homers.

Since 1931, a batted ball has been judged fair or foul according to where it leaves the playing field. Bill Jenkinson, a prominent baseball historian and author, is confident that the Babe lost a minimum of 62 home runs. His estimate is the result of 40 years of exhaustive research of newspaper accounts.

"I used primary sources to determine if a ball the Babe hit would have been a home run by current rules," said Jenkinson. "I tried to read anywhere from three to ten primary accounts when researching his home runs. I read at least three different newspaper accounts of every game Ruth ever played." Jenkinson's quest took him to libraries in Philadelphia, Pittsburgh and New York and to the Library of Congress.

Several factors made the task a daunting one. "Prior to the 1920s, sportswriters were given virtually unlimited space when reporting a ballgame," explained Jenkinson. "However, with the advent of radio in the 1920s, there was a finite amount of space to cover the games." And, he added, "because what we view as home runs today were often foul balls because of the rule, the long drive was simply a foul ball, and the writers were not going to write about foul balls. Also, doubleheaders reduced the amount of column space as did anything of an unusual nature. All of this invites the conclusion that there were many more home runs that were lost by the old rule."

There is no doubt that Ruth's career home run total was aided by the short right field porches in the Polo Grounds and at Yankee Stadium. A total of 48 percent of his home runs were hit in those parks. He hit 85 in the Polo Grounds where the right field wall measured 256 feet from the plate. In Yankee Stadium he stroked 259 homers, where the distance to right field for most of his career was 296 feet. But during most of Ruth's tenure with the Yankees, center field measured 490 feet from the plate and right center was 429 feet away. Center field in the Polo Grounds was 483 feet from the plate and right center was 449 feet when the Babe played there. Therefore, one has to wonder how many long fly balls that scraped against the sky were caught off the bat of the Bambino. But most likely the greatest home run thief was Rule Number 48 that allowed umpires to call batted balls fair or foul where last seen. The following anecdote provides a good example.

"On August 21, 1920, Babe stroked one far over the right field grandstand roof in the Polo Grounds," Jenkinson. said. "It was obviously fair when it left the park and Ruth proceeded to trot around the bases. When he arrived at home plate, the umpire gave Ruth the bad news. It was a foul ball with the explanation that the ball had landed on foul ground somewhere out in Manhattan Field."

To be fair, it must be taken into consideration that not all of his Polo Grounds shots would have been home runs today. The best example would be balls that were hit into the upper deck there. Since that grandstand was situated closer to home plate than today's fences, some of those drives would have been put-outs or foul balls if hit in a modern ballpark.

Yankee Stadium is often called "the House that Ruth Built." Only Mickey Mantle hit more home runs (266) there in 18 seasons. But because of the quirky fair-foul rule, Yankee Stadium was not as friendly to the Babe as one might think.

While Ruth was a member of the Yankees the upper deck wings in right and left field at the stadium extended only to the foul poles. The wings did not wrap around the pole into fair territory until 1937. This meant there were approximately 60–70 rows of bleachers that went beyond the outfield wall in right field where most of the lefty-batting Ruth's home runs came to rest. Because of the length of the bleachers that went beyond the playing field, batted balls hit over the wall had a good chance of eventually curving foul because there was no upper deck wing in fair territory in right field to intercept the ball as it curved toward foul territory on its downward flight. This was not in Ruth's favor. "The curvature of a batted ball mostly happens at the end of the flight," stated Jenkinson. "Therefore, it's likely that many ended up in foul territory. What would be a home run today was a long foul ball back in the day—and unreported."

Another factor to consider is that when the stadium opened foul poles were only about 20 feet high. So, umpires had to do a lot of guessing on his high flies down the line that were much higher than the pole.

It might surprise you, but Ruth hit more homers on the road (367) than he did at home (347) in his career. Fenway Park, where he played his first full five seasons, was not friendly to lefty hitters.

Babe wasn't the only one affected by the fair-foul rule. Gehrig finished his career with 493 home runs. You can make the argument that under the current fair-foul rule, it's a safe bet that he would have been a member of the 500 home run club. "There's no doubt about that," said Jenkinson. The "Iron Horse" became a regular player starting on June 2, 1925. Therefore, he played almost six years (1925–30) under this rule and one can only speculate how many homers he lost, especially in Yankee Stadium.

And who knows how many tape measure jobs were lost to Rule Number 48? "On Sept. 27, 1928, the 'Sultan of Swat' lost two home runs at Sportsman's Park in St. Louis where the Bronx Bombers met the St. Louis Browns," writes Jenkinson in *The Year Babe Ruth Hit 104 Home Runs*. "The two drives sailed fair and far over the right field pavilion but wound up foul outside the park. One of them was a moon shot that reportedly struck the roof of a building about 500 feet away on the opposite side of Grand Ave."

Babe's single-season record 60th home run (off the Washington Senators' Tom Zachary) on September 30, 1927, at Yankee Stadium was almost voided. "The drive was hit over the right field fence, but by the time it crashed halfway up the right field bleachers, it was just about on a dead-line with the right field foul line," notes Jenkinson. "The Washington Senators argued that it was foul, but on this occasion the umpires ruled in Babe's favor, and baseball history was made."

The fair-foul rule wasn't the only rule that erased home runs in Ruth's era. He also lost a homer to the rule which stipulated that an over-the-fence home run in a game-ending situation (now a walk-off) would only count for as many bases as was necessary to "force" the winning run home. "For example, in a tie game, a ball hit over the wall with a runner on first to end the game would only count as a triple," explains Jenkinson. "It happened at Fenway Park in 1918 when Babe played for the Red Sox."

From 1920 to 1930, a batted ball that bounced over the outfield wall in fair territory was, by rule, a home run. Today it would be a book rule double. Over the years some skeptics have said that Ruth benefited from this rule.

Not true.

Jenkinson says emphatically, "I am one hundred percent certain that Babe Ruth was never credited with a home run in an official major league baseball game that bounced over the fence."

By Jenkinson's research, if Ruth lost at least 62 homers, as stated above, that would give the Babe an incredible total of 776 and he would still the home run king by 14 over Bonds. And according to Retrosheet, he lost two homers because of rain-shortened games.

Whatever, 714 homers are impressive in any era—especially when a home run was not a home run!

5

Babe, Helen, and Claire

"The big fellow wasn't perfect.... But that guy had a heart. He really did. A heart as big as a watermelon and made out of pure gold," said former player Jimmy Austin in *The Glory of Their Times*.

To enhance the understanding of Ruth's family, it's best if I list the cast of characters.

Helen Woodford—Ruth's first wife
Juanita Jennings—a woman with whom Ruth fathered a child named Dorothy
Dorothy—Ruth's only known biological child and daughter of Ms. Jennings
Linda Ruth Tosetti—Dorothy's daughter; Ruth's only known biological granddaughter
Claire Hodgson—Ruth's second wife
Julia—Claire's biological daughter through a previous marriage; Ruth's stepdaughter and Dorothy's stepsister

When Ruth was a Red Sox rookie, he often ate at Lander's Coffee Shop in Boston where he met Helen Woodford, a waitress. The two married on October 17, 1914. The Rev. Thomas S. Dolan conducted the ceremony in St. Paul's Catholic Church in Ellicott City, Maryland, near where the Babe had attended boarding school. He was 19 (or 20) and she was 16. In 1924 he enlisted in the 104th Field Artillery Division of the New York Army National Guard and listed his birth date as February 7, 1894, on his draft card. But mounds of research have documented that he was born on February 6, 1895, in Baltimore, Maryland.

After the Red Sox sold Babe's contract to the Yankees in 1919, he and Helen lived in an eight-room hotel suite in the elaborate Ansonia Hotel located at 2109 Broadway on the Upper West Side of Manhattan during the baseball seasons and wintered at their Sudbury, Massachusetts, farm where for a time Babe tried raising chickens and other barnyard animals. Farm work was not to his liking. Although Ruth had no involvement, the Ansonia Hotel is where plans for the Chicago Black Sox scandal were made to throw the 1919 World Series to the Reds when mobster Arnold Rothstein met with White Sox player Chick Gandil in his apartment at the hotel. The hotel, built by Earl Dodge Stokes, was named in honor of his grandfather, Anson Green Phelps, who in 1845 founded the Ansonia Copper and Brass Co. in Ansonia, Connecticut, where my father worked for many years. I always get a kick out of telling the locals that Ansonia has a connection to Babe Ruth and the Chicago Black Sox for different reasons.

The Babe and Cars

Ruth's love for customized, powerful cars fit his fast-lane, colorful lifestyle. He was a reckless driver known for ignoring stoplights and traffic signals on his drive to Yankee Stadium. He tooled around NYC ignoring stop signs and red lights and he had his share of fender benders or worse.

In July of the 1920 season, he drove his car on a Yankees road trip to Philadelphia and Washington and was in a serious accident. According to Jeff Peek of Hagerty Media, "Ruth was driving late one night just outside rural Wawa, PA, with Helen and three friends from the club [the Yankees]. When he sped dangerously around a curve, the auto skidded out of control. As the machine went off the road, Helen and coach Charley O'Leary were thrown clear as it flipped over. Fortunately, nobody was seriously injured."

Peek's account continued, "The car was another story, and after walking to a nearby farm and spending the night, the group returned to the crash site accompanied by a mechanic. 'Sell it,' Ruth supposedly said of the wreck. 'Take whatever you can get for it. I'm through with it.'"

Two months later Ruth escaped disaster in Wallingford, Connecticut. Following is an article written by Weston Ulbrich for a periodical titled *The Bat and Ball*, first published just after the Civil War in 1866, long before the *The Sporting News* was first published. It sold on the streets of Hartford. Ulbrich wrote,

> After setting a new major league home run record in his first year with the Yankees, Babe Ruth bought a brand-new Packard Roadster for $12,000. On September 30, 1920, Ruth was driving from New York City to Springfield, Massachusetts, to play in an exhibition game. Halfway through his trip, Ruth crashed into a heavy Mack Truck while speeding through a tunnel, the Yalesville Culvert in Wallingford, Connecticut, near the Meriden city line.
>
> Ruth was thrown from the car but luckily walked away from the accident with only a few scratches. His Roadster was totaled, but the Great Bambino refused to miss his appearance and hitchhiked his way to Springfield. The very next day Ruth appeared in another exhibition game for a team called the Hartford Poli's at Muzzy Field in Bristol, Connecticut. He played every position except pitcher and went 4-for-4 at the plate.

The cops would often turn a blind eye to Ruth's careless driving habits because of his celebrity. Take the following story written by Susan Luber and Tony DiRenzo that was published in the *New York Times* on May 28, 1928.

> On May 5, 1928, famed baseball player Babe Ruth made an unscheduled stop in Weehawken (New Jersey) when he was pulled over by police for speeding. A court date was set for May 21st, and as word spread around town that the Bambino was to appear before a municipal judge that morning, "several score of youthful admirers" besieged the courthouse for several hours, waiting for their hero to arrive and be judged. They were disappointed when Weehawken Police Chief Patrick Dolan announced that the charges had been dropped and that the Babe would not be making an appearance. According to a report in the *New York Times*, when the Chief was asked why the ticket was withdrawn, he replied, "The Babe's the greatest ballplayer in the world, isn't he? And he's Irish, isn't he? And we have to stick together, don't we?"

Baby Dorothy

In September 1922, Babe and Helen surprised the Yankees when they brought a 15-month-old girl named Dorothy to the Polo Grounds and introduced her as their daughter. "Not even his closest friends on the team had suspected Ruth was a father," the *Boston Globe* reported. Babe fathered the baby through an affair he had with Jennings.

In 1923, Ruth met Claire Hodgson, whose roots were in Georgia. She came to New York with her daughter Julia after her husband, Frank, died. Claire worked as an illustrator's model and was also a dancer at the Dew Drop Inn in NYC. For a time, she was a Broadway chorus line performer in the *Ziegfeld Follies*. Babe and Claire developed a relationship that led to marriage six years later.

On April 24, 1925, Helen collapsed outside St. Vincent's hospital where Babe was hospitalized with an intestinal abscess. It proved to be her first of two nervous breakdowns. Four months later Helen and Dorothy went to live full-time in Sudbury, Massachusetts. Babe, estranged from Helen, remained in New York the year round.

"In October 1925, a separation agreement called for Helen to receive four annual payments of $20,000, $30,000, $25,000, and $20,000," wrote Jane Leavy in *The Big Fella*. "In addition, she was to receive their property in Pasadena, Florida, and the farm in Sudbury; a Packard; and custody of Dorothy."

In 1927, Helen moved into the Watertown, Massachusetts, house of dentist Edward Kinder. According to the *New York Daily News*, Helen and Edward had known one another since childhood and their families lived in the same South Boston neighborhood. Edward was a World War I veteran who graduated from Tufts dental school in 1924 and established a practice in Boston. Many believed that Kinder and Helen were married, but they never were. They reportedly lived together for 18 months and had a husband-wife relationship. Kinder referred to Helen as his wife.

Babe knew the Kinder family very well. Edward's father was a physician and Ruth was one of his patients.

Ruth reportedly asked for a divorce, which conflicts with earlier reports that because of his Catholic faith, he would not do so. Helen reportedly agreed as long as Babe would give her

Linda Ruth Tossetti, the only known biological granddaughter of Babe Ruth, holds a vase given to Babe as a gift from the 1934 trip to Japan.

$100,000. "That's hogwash," snapped Ruth's only biological granddaughter, Linda Ruth Tosetti, the daughter of Dorothy and granddaughter of Juanita Jennings.

Tosetti, who lives in Durham, Connecticut, bears a strong resemblance to her famous grandfather—she has the same smile and eyes. She came into my life through my radio show and has made several presentations at the Derby (Connecticut) Public Library where I have facilitated weekly meetings since 2006 for a group called Silver Sluggers.

"Claire wanted him to leave Helen, but he refused to get divorced because of his Catholic religion," stated Tosetti. "Babe was very wealthy. He could have easily afforded the $100,000."

Ruth's involvement with the Catholic Church is reinforced by his donation to the St. Angela Merici Church on Morris Avenue in the Bronx. "There are three marble altars there," commented Tosetti. "On one of the altars there is a plaque that lists contributors. On the list is Mr. and Mrs. Babe Ruth and Dorothy. The Mrs. is Helen."

On January 11, 1929, Helen was alone in the Watertown house when she died tragically in a fire. Earlier that evening, Kinder went to the boxing matches at Boston Garden and Dorothy was at a Catholic boarding school in nearby Wellesley, Massachusetts. There was speculation that there was foul play, but it was determined that faulty wiring was the cause of the fire.

About 10 p.m., a passerby saw smoke seeping from the windows. When firefighters arrived, flames had reached the second story. Helen was found dead on the bedroom floor. The *New York Daily News* reported that she had taken sleeping pills but no narcotics were found in her system during the autopsy, nor was foul play indicated. The *Albany Evening News* reported, "Babe Ruth was crushed beneath the weight of tragedy in his wife's death."

After Helen died in the fire, her family wanted custody of Dorothy but that automatically went to Ruth. "My mother [Dorothy] was placed with the Dooley family in the Bronx," said Tosetti. "To protect her identity from the press, she was given the name Marie Harrington. My mother was raised to believe Helen was her biological mother when actually it was Juanita Jennings, the granddaughter of former Mexican president Francisco Madero. My grandmother, Juanita, and my grandfather met in California in 1920 when he was on an exhibition baseball tour."

The truth came tumbling forth in 1980 when Juanita gave Dorothy the news that she was her biological mother. "This was revealed in a 1988 book my mother [Dorothy] wrote with Chris Martens titled *My Dad, the Babe: Growing Up with an American Hero*," Tosetti said. "In her youth, my mother knew Juanita as 'Aunt Nita,' a family friend. They lived together from 1964 to 1980. She also had a good relationship with Helen."

Three months after Helen's death, on April 17, 1929, Babe and Claire were married in St. Gregory's Church in NYC at 5:45 a.m. The idea of the early morning wedding was to escape the media circus and avoid publicity. The next day, the Yankees opened the season at home against the Red Sox, and in his first at-bat, Babe hit a home run down the left field line off Red Ruffing, who would become a four-time 20-game winner with the Yankees.

Twenty-six days later (May 13, 1929) Ruth was in the Yankees lineup at League Park II in Cleveland where the Indians beat the Yanks, 4–3. It was the first time in baseball history that both teams wore numbered jerseys. The Bambino collected a base hit in a losing cause.

Tosetti painted a picture of an unhappy marriage between Babe and Claire. She saw a dysfunctional family torn in different directions. "My grandfather wasn't going to marry Claire," revealed Tosetti. "He was trapped into marrying her but I can't go into the details. Claire lived in a complex social world. She knew some mafia guys who she introduced to my grandfather." Tosetti added, "One day in the Yankee clubhouse there was an ugly incident involving Mark Koenig, the Yankees' shortstop, and my grandfather. As the story goes, Koenig said some unkind words about Claire. Babe was furious and laid Koenig out. But he didn't hold a grudge. When the Cubs would not give Koenig a full World Series share in the 1932 World Series, my grandfather, as were many of the Yankee players, [was] critical of the frugality of the Cubs players."

It was Tosetti's opinion that Babe never changed his carousing ways even after he married Claire. "You don't change a man who was that socially active," said his granddaughter. "When Babe was very sick in the hospital, my mother snuck in a mistress of his to see him. My grandmother, Juanita, was married to Charles Ellias who Babe had known. We called him 'Uncle Charlie.' If I had to bet, I think my grandfather and Juanita had an on-and-off relationship for many years."

Tosetti was very candid about Babe's private life. "Yes, he was with many women," she acknowledged. "But keep in mind that many of them threw themselves at him—especially the socialites. Here was a man with money and fame. He was a national celebrity."

Not long after Babe and Claire were married, they took in eight-year-old Dorothy. This had the look of an adoption, but Dorothy was his biological child. The family setting was comprised of Babe, Dorothy, Claire and her daughter, Julia (12). They lived in an 11-room apartment at 345 West 88th Street in Manhattan. There was tension from the start.

"Claire gave my mother a porcelain doll when they first met and my mother threw it to the ground," stated Tosetti. "This was not a good way for Mom to start a relationship with her stepmother. Over the years they had some rocky times but out of respect to my grandfather, my mother took care of Claire when she became ill in her later years."

Dorothy and Julia never got along. In reference to Babe, Dorothy said, "He's my father, not yours," Tosetti said. She continued, "My mother thought Julia was a spoiled brat. My mother slept in the servant's quarters because she refused to stay in the same room with Julia. When my mother died, Julia wanted to come to her wake, but my mother left instructions that she did not want Julia anywhere near her coffin."

Dorothy felt that Claire gave Julia favored treatment. "I was excess baggage," lamented Dorothy Ruth Pirone in her 1988 memoir. "Raising me was a burdensome job, like a stack of unexpected paperwork dropped in her lap."

In 1934 Philadelphia A's manager Connie Mack led a team of major league All-Stars to Japan for a 22-game tour against the Big Six University League. It was a tour to bridge the cultural gap between the two countries. Mack compiled a sterling contingent with names like Ruth, Gehrig, Jimmie Foxx, Earl Averill, Charlie Gehringer, Lefty Gomez and others, including Moe Berg, a marginal player who was educated at Princeton and Columbia and could speak 12 different languages, "but couldn't hit in one," quipped Casey Stengel.

Berg was on the trip to get intelligence information for the United States government. "My grandfather wanted his family to make the trip, but Claire was against Dorothy going," Tosetti said. "Claire said, 'Julia's going.' She wanted her to go as a scout to hang with my grandfather so he wouldn't meet any women. There was a lot of bickering about this. My mother finally said, 'I'll stay home.' Claire saw my mother as someone who was in her way."

Little did Claire know that Julia would have an experience with Berg, a very handsome man. He "was tall, strong and a womanizer," wrote Jonathan Mark, an associate editor at the *New York Jewish Week*. "Babe Ruth's daughter Julia (18 at the time) remembered dancing with Berg under the Pacific moon, as Berg and the Babe's family sailed to Japan. Said Julia, 'Berg came on to me, which rather surprised me, I must say, but he was an interesting person, well educated, and I enjoyed dancing with him.'"

Tosetti continues to harbor ill feelings toward Claire. She sees Claire as an alcoholic who got in the way of Babe getting a managing job, something he always wanted. "She would call the Yankees and complain they were not being fair to my grandfather," explained Tosetti. "Connie Mack was interested in hiring Babe to manage the A's. When Commissioner Landis heard this, he shot it down. I believe that Mack was aware of Claire's pestering the Yankees and there was concern that Claire would interfere with the operations of the A's organization."

The flip side of the story is that teams did not believe that Babe could manage himself. How would he manage a baseball team?

The Ruth-Gehrig Feud

Ruth and Gehrig were very friendly after Gehrig joined the Yankees. But Gehrig was the anthesis of Ruth, the gregarious party guy. Gehrig was a quiet, sophisticated man. The Babe went to the bar; Gehrig went to the opera. But on the field, they formed a partnership that transfixed the nation.

It was common for Ruth and other Yankee teammates to visit the Gehrig home in New Rochelle, New York where Lou's mother, Christina, would serve the players home cooked meals. The Iron Horse bought the house for his parents in 1928 and he lived there for five years until he married. Ruth, who spoke German fluently, got along very well with the Gehrig family and loved Christina's sauerbraten. Babe and Gehrig often played bridge together. They were a formidable combination on and off the field. As for his gambling habits, Babe enjoyed betting on the dogs and horses.

"My mother [Dorothy] was close to the Gehrigs, and she spent a couple of summers with them at the house in New Rochelle," Tosetti recalled. "My grandfather wanted her to get away from Claire. My mother had a crush on Lou, saying he was very handsome. She remembered him taking each bale of hay and throwing it up into the barn loft. That takes terrific strength."

It was at the Gehrig house in New Rochelle where the seeds for the feud were planted. According to Tosetti, Claire did not give the girls equal treatment. "Claire used to shop at Bergdorf Goodman's in New York City, a high-level fashionable store known for its quality merchandise," Tosetti said. "Claire would buy clothes that would fit Julia, who was a much larger size than my mother. But the clothes did not look good on my mother who got Julia's hand-me downs."

"One day Claire went to pick up Mom [Dorothy] at the Gehrigs' and Lou's mother, Christina, said, 'Why don't you dress Dorothy like you do your own daughter?' Claire was angered by Christina Gehrig's remarks. When she got home, she barked at Babe and instructed him to tell Lou to have his mother not be so tough on Claire because he had to live with her."

"Gehrig was upset being confronted by my grandfather," divulged Tosetti. "Lou was very close to his mother, and nobody was going to talk her down."

Ruth and Gehrig did not talk for several years. What compounded the problem, according to Tosetti, was something that occurred on the baseball trip to Japan. "Lou found his wife, Eleanor, having lunch with my grandfather and Claire and he wasn't happy about that," commented Tosetti. Another theory was Ruth thought little of Gehrig's record-setting consecutive-game streak. And he also was dismayed that Gehrig didn't support his quest to become the Yankee manager.

According to Tosetti, her grandfather made multiple attempts to make amends but Gehrig, a stubborn German, would not reconcile. When Gehrig was in the ninth inning of his life battling ALS, he had a change of heart. "When my grandfather learned that Lou was dying, he was very upset," Tosetti said. "They did make peace and would often play bridge in the final months of Lou's life just like they did earlier in their relationship."

Dorothy left home at age 17 and married a Daniel Sullivan. "My mother wanted to get married and get away from Claire," Tosetti said. "She knew her parents would not allow it. To prevent them from stopping the marriage, my mother purposely got pregnant. She and her husband had three children together before they divorced. My mother had a second husband, Dominick Pirone. They had three children, and I am the youngest."

Tosetti has unsuccessfully tried to get her grandfather's number 3 permanently retired by the major league teams without success. But she did hit a grand slam in 2018 when her lobbying resulted in the Bambino receiving the Presidential Medal of Freedom. The award was accepted by Julia's son, Tom Stevens, at the White House.

Tosetti said her grandfather, with all his "bravado," was a gentle man who loved life and loved children, was a "big man with a big laugh," and was "born with an innate goodness." "Many don't know this but in 1938, Babe gave Julia a blood transfusion because of a serious throat infection she had," noted Tosetti. "I think this shows he cared for both of his daughters."

Julia became the spokeswoman for the Ruth family. In 1999 she threw out the first pitch before Game Five of the ALCS at Fenway Park where the Yankees beat the Red Sox to win the AL pennant. She also threw out the first pitch when the Yankees played their last game at the old stadium on September 21, 2008. On July 10, 2016, three days after her 100th birthday, she threw out the first ball at Fenway Park prior to the Rays-Red Sox game.

Dorothy Pirone passed in 1989 at age 68. Julia Ruth Stevens died in 2019 at age 102.

6

Lou Gehrig

A Reluctant Hero

There's a walking track near my home I go to frequently. The lanes are numbered 1–8. For me, lane four is the "Lou Gehrig lane," the number he wore. There was an uncanny connection with the number 4 in Gehrig's career. Because he batted in the fourth spot in the batting order, he was given number 4. The Yankees retired his number 4 on July 4, 1939. It was the first number retired in baseball history. He was the first American Leaguer to hit four home runs in a game when he went yard four times on June 3, 1932, against the fourth place Philadelphia Athletics.

Gehrig was born on June 19, 1903, and his legend began long before his professional career. He attended Commerce High School in NYC where he graduated on June 27, 1921. He played with Commerce against Lane Technical HS in Chicago on June 26, 1920, as a high school junior. The game, which was sponsored by the city of Chicago, pitted the two schools that were champions of their respective cities. Commerce was winning 8–6 in the top of the ninth inning, when Gehrig hit a grand slam completely out of Cubs Park (renamed Wrigley Field six years later).

This was an unheard-of feat for a 17-year-old high school player. The *New York Daily News* reported that "the bright star of the inter-city game was 'Babe' Gehrig." It may have been the first time that sportswriters compared Lou to the Babe, but it certainly wouldn't be the last.

Gehrig had numerous nicknames, the most famous being "the Iron Horse." Others included "Larrupin Lou," "Biscuit Pants," and "Columbia Lou" because of his two years spent at Columbia University where he played both football and baseball. While at Columbia he would hit mammoth shots that would land on 116th Street. During his collegiate years he played for the Hartford Senators in the Eastern League under the assumed name Lou Lewis to protect his amateur status. When Columbia athletic officials learned that Gehrig had played with a professional team, he was forced to sit out his freshman 1921–22 school year. Despite being disciplined, Gehrig thumbed his nose again at the college rule that forbade athletes to play for money while matriculating in college. In the summer of '22, he played semi-pro baseball for the Morristown, New Jersey, Colonials as a mercenary, risking losing college eligibility and his football scholarship to Columbia for the 1922–23 school year. In 18 games he batted .450 and hit four home runs.

Gehrig's sophomore year at Columbia would be the only year he played collegiately. A member of the Phi Delta Theta fraternity, he played fullback and defensive tackle in the fall of 1922 for the 5–4 Lions coached by Frank "Buck" O'Neil. In the spring of '23 he played first base and pitched. He batted .444 and blasted seven home runs for the university located in Morningside Heights—Columbia.

In a game against Williams College at South Field, he struck out 17 batters in a losing effort on April 18, 1923, the same day Yankee Stadium opened. Eight days later Yankees scout Paul Krichell saw Gehrig play against Rutgers in New Jersey and he hit two home runs in three at-bats. Krichell was so impressed that he telephoned Yankees general manager Ed Barrow and reportedly told him that he had just discovered another Babe Ruth. Krichell signed the Columbia star for $1,500 and he would receive $400 a month. Gehrig's college days would soon end. Putting food on the table for his family was paramount to an engineering degree.

Lou's mother, Christina, was the central figure of his life. Writer Fred Lieb called the unique mother-son relationship the "Gehrig Mutual Admiration Society."

She regularly attended his games throughout his career and closely monitored his dating life. She was virtually impossible to please when it came to her son. Christina did not approve of Eleanor, whom Lou married in 1933 in New Rochelle, New York. Because Christina refused to attend the wedding, Lou and Eleanor had a small, private ceremony.

The Alpha Male

Gehrig was the alpha male—strong, handsome, and athletic. He was a rock of a man. Legendary sportswriter Jim Murray called him "Gibraltar in cleats." His accomplishments are many. Lifetime, he batted .340 with 493 home runs and 1,995 RBI. He had an OPS of 1.0798. Only Ruth and Ted Williams have a higher OPS (slugging and on-base percentage combined). The two-time American League MVP and 1934 Triple Crown winner posted 13 consecutive seasons with 100 runs scored and 100 RBI. He hit a then-record 23 grand slams, since surpassed by Alex Rodriguez (25). His first bases-loaded homer came on July 23, 1925, scoring Aaron Ward, Ruth, and Bob Meusel. Facing the Senators' Firpo Marberry, hit a homer into the left field stands that would have been a book-rule double under current rules. He was also the foremost first baseman of his era.

He was one of the greatest post-season hitters in the history of the game. In seven World Series totaling 34 games and 150 plate appearances, Gehrig hit .361 with 10 home runs and 35 RBI. He played in 2,130 consecutive games, a record that seemed shatterproof until Cal Ripken, Jr., came along and ran a string of 2,632 consecutive games that ended on September 6, 1995. But Gehrig was a reluctant hero sandwiched between Ruth's colossal shadow and DiMaggio's early stardom.

He could beat you in a variety of ways. Gehrig stole 102 bases in his career. He stole home 15 times, all on the front end of double steals. On June 24, 1925, in the Yankees' 5–3 win at Washington, he stole home in the top of the seventh as part of a double steal with Schang, the slow-footed catcher, on the back end. It was the first stolen base of Gehrig's career which raises the question: Was he the only player in baseball history to steal home for the first stolen base of a career?

Major League Debut

After completing his second year at Columbia, Gehrig made his major league debut on June 15, 1923, at Yankee Stadium where the Yankees were punishing the St. Louis

Browns, 10–0. Yankees manager Miller Huggins sent the 19-year-old prospect (he would turn 20 in four days) into the game in the top of the ninth to replace Wally Pipp at first base. Gehrig handled an easy grounder off the bat of Jack Tobin for the final out of the game, giving Pennock his seventh win of the season.

Gehrig's first at-bat came three days later, on June 18, against the Detroit Tigers. Pinch-hitting for second baseman Aaron Ward in the ninth inning of a game the Yankees lost 11–3, he struck out facing Ken Holloway. His first big league hit was on July 7 at Sportsman's Park in St. Louis. With the Yankees trailing 13–3, in the ninth inning Gehrig pinch-hit for pitcher Oscar Roettger and singled to right field against Browns right-hander Elam Vangilder. Several days later he returned to Hartford in the Eastern League for more seasoning and hit 24 home runs in only 59 games. His prodigious clouts at Clarkin Field and throughout the EL earned him the nickname "the Eastern Babe." It wouldn't be long before he was playing alongside the real Babe.

Gehrig returned to the Yankees late in the '23 season and on September 27 he hit his first major league homer. It came off Boston's Bill Piercy and drove in Ruth from third in the first inning in the Yankees' 8–3 win at Fenway Park. And on the same date 15 years later, he hit his 493rd and last home run in the fifth inning off Dutch Leonard of the Senators in a 5–2 Yankees win at Yankee Stadium before a paltry Tuesday afternoon crowd of 2,773.

After spending most of the 1924 season in Hartford where he terrorized Eastern League pitchers, batting .369 with 37 home runs, he leaped to the big leagues permanently.

The Streak Begins

Although it's a popular belief that Gehrig's iron man streak began on June 2, 1925, when he replaced Pipp at first base, it actually started the day before, when he pinch-hit for Pee-Wee Wanninger in the bottom of the eighth inning. Facing Walter Johnson, he flied to Goose Goslin in left field in the Yankees' 5–3 loss at the Stadium. The following day Huggins started Gehrig at first base in place of Pipp, who was hitting an anemic .244 with the Yankees floundering in seventh place. Gehrig, the former Columbia fence-buster, then played almost 14 full seasons without missing a game from June 1, 1925, to May 2, 1939. (An interesting note: According to Ray Gonzalez, writing in the 1975 *Baseball Research Journal,* "Only in 1931 did Lou play every inning, and one game was in the outfield.")

The Iron Horse flourished in the late 1920s. He was a key force in the Yankees Murderers' Row lineup in 1927 when he belted 47 home runs and knocked in 173, the latter number an AL record he would tie in 1930 and break in 1931 when he drove in 185 runs. For many years Gehrig was credited with 184 RBI until the exhaustive research by Herm Krabbenhoft of the Society for American Baseball Research revealed that Gehrig should be credited with 185, which is the accepted total today.

"Luckless Lou"

Amyotrophic Lateral Sclerosis, the disease that led to his death, not only robbed him of his motor skills but it also deprived him of several significant baseball milestones.

Gehrig never played after age 35. He missed the coveted 500 home run club by seven and 2000 RBI by a mere five. Hank Aaron (2297), Albert Pujols (2218) and Alex Rodriguez (2086) are officially the only players in the 2000 RBI club. Historians estimate Gehrig would have had in the area of 2,400 if his career had not ended prematurely. Although Ruth is listed with 2,214 RBI and Cap Anson is credited with 2,075, they both played several years before RBI became an official stat in 1920, as stated earlier.

The baseball rule book as well as his disease were damaging to his career stats. In addition to the fair-foul rule, Number 48, as previously covered, a running faux pas cost the ill-fated Yankee the sole home run title in 1931. Here is what happened. The Yankees played the Washington Senators on April 26, 1931, at Griffith Stadium. In the top of the first inning the Yankees had Lyn Lary on first base and two outs when Gehrig hit a rocket off Marberry so fast and hard that the ball popped out of the center field bleachers and into the hands of center fielder Harry Rice. Yankees third base coach Joe McCarthy, who was also the team's manager, reportedly told Lary to slow down. Apparently Lary thought the ball was caught when he saw it fall into the hands of Rice. He left the basepath and Gehrig kept running. He was called out by umpire Bill McGowan for passing Lary. The Iron Horse was credited with a triple. The Yankees lost two runs on the play in a game they lost 9–7. Thanks to Lary's misadventure, Gehrig ended the season with 46 home runs, tied with Ruth for the AL home run title. Under current rules, Lary would be called out for abandonment. Because there were two outs, Gehrig would lose the home run. With less than two outs, Lary would be called out, but Gehrig would not be called out for passing his teammate and his home run would count.

Gehrig, who won the AL MVP award in 1927, arguably could have won it two other years. The Yankees' slugger had a banner season in '31 when he batted .341 and led the league in home runs (46), RBI (185), hits (211) and total bases (410). His OPS was a gaudy 1.108. But the AL MVP went to A's pitcher Lefty Grove who led the league in wins (34), ERA (2.06), CG (27), and Ks (175).

In '34, Gehrig enjoyed one of the greatest campaigns in the history of the game when he won the Triple Crown (.363–49–166) and also led the league in getting on base the most times (321), total bases (409) and OPS (1.172). But inexplicably, the MVP award went to Tigers catcher Mickey Cochrane who batted .320 with two home runs and 76 RBI. The Iron Horse of course played in all 154 games while Cochrane played in 129. This might have been baseball's all-time ultimate snub.

Three years later Griffith Stadium was again the site where "Luckless Lou" was deprived of an amazing accomplishment. On June 30, 1934, the baseball weather gods erased a feat that few have achieved. Gehrig hit three triples in the first five innings that went down the drain when the game was rained out while the Senators were batting in the bottom of the fifth, trailing 4–1. If the inning could have been completed, Gehrig's triples would have been saved and so would the Yankees' win. He could have retired with 166 three-baggers instead of 163. He also lost a home run in the '35 season because of a rain-shortened game in Washington.

On July 14, 1934, it was reported that the Iron Horse was suffering acutely from a cold in the back that made breathing difficult and batting a torture. To keep Gehrig in the lineup and allow his playing streak to continue, manager Miller Huggins got creative and listed him as a left-handed starting shortstop and batted him in the leadoff spot. Gehrig, facing Vic Sorrell, slapped a single to right to start a four-run rally. Red Rolfe pinch-ran for Gehrig. When the Yankees took the field, Rolfe played shortstop and

6. Lou Gehrig

Gehrig was done for the day. The Tigers won the game 12–11 when they scored four runs in the bottom of the ninth.

Under current rule 9.23 (c), Gehrig's one at-bat would still extend his playing streak. The rule reads, "A consecutive game playing streak shall be extended if a player plays one half-inning on defense or if the player completes a time at bat by reaching base or being put out. A pinch-hitting appearance only shall not extend the streak…."

Gehrig was the Yankees captain from 1935 to 1939. When he retired, Yankees manager Joe McCarthy retired the Yankee captain position. The idea was the Iron Horse would be the last captain the Yankees would ever have. But the tradition was broken when George Steinbrenner bestowed the honor on Thurman Munson in 1976. His tenure ran until his untimely death in 1979.

Gehrig's final full season came in 1938 when he hit .295 with 29 home runs and 114 RBI. Those aren't bad numbers, but they were sub–Gehrig. "There's present research that essentially confirms he played that season with ALS symptoms," said MLB.com researcher Sarah Langs. "This puts his .295 as perhaps his most impressive accomplishment, on a broader scale."

In the first 13 games of the '38 season he hit an anemic .116 and went homerless. Yet he had a Gehrig-like 25-game stretch from August 7 to 26 when he batted .352 with nine homers, eight doubles, three triples and 36 RBI. During this stretch the Yankees gained the double-digit lead in the AL standings that they would not relinquish. Skeptics who deny that Gehrig played with the onset of the dreaded disease might point to those numbers, or in the grand scheme of things ask whether his greatness allowed him to overcome a disease that does not taste defeat.

Lou Gehrig signs a contract, circa 1937. From left are Gehrig, Jacob Ruppert (Yankees owner), Joe McCarthy (manager), and Joe DiMaggio (National Baseball Hall of Fame and Museum).

"I almost think it was the greatest season anybody has had," says Dan Joseph, author of *Last Ride of the Iron Horse: How Lou Gehrig Fought ALS to Play One Final Championship Season*. "He had to start from such a high level of strength and coordination and determination to do this. It's just astounding to me."

MLB.com writer Anthony Castrovince writes, "The '38 season was a disappointing drop from his career norms, but more modern metrics tell us he had a .932 OPS and a 132 OPS + (32% better than league average) and was worth 4.7 Wins Above Replacement."

Neurology researchers have offered differing opinions as to when Gehrig's ALS became symptomatic. According to Castrovince, "Months after his ALS diagnosis in 1939, Gehrig would tell the famed sportswriter Grantland Rice that the spring of 1938 is when he first knew something was wrong inside him. 'I knew there was no reason for this,' he said, 'as I was still young enough and should have been strong enough. I knew I had kept myself in the best possible condition but lacked the old snap.'"

A bat used by Gehrig in '38 sold for $715,120 in early April 2021 to a private collector through SCP Auctions. The bat—a 34-inch, 36-ounce Bill Dickey model Louisville Slugger—is believed to be the bat Gehrig used in a World Series sweep of the Chicago Cubs that year and the next spring, said the company, which indicated that it had received 26 bids for the bat.

Gehrig gave the bat, which was made from ash, to Earle Combs, a former Yankees teammate and coach who, like Gehrig, was elected to the Baseball Hall of Fame, the company said. "It's one of the best Lou Gehrig bats ever discovered and, obviously, the provenance is impeccable," David Kohler, the auction house's owner, president and chief executive, said in an interview.

The Yankees opened the 1939 season at home against the Boston Red Sox. In his first at-bat, Gehrig came to the plate with two men on base and hit a weak liner to right field that was caught by Sox rookie Ted Williams. In retrospect, the at-bat symbolized the end of one era and the beginning of another.

The final game of Lou Gehrig's career came on Sunday, April 30, 1939, when the Senators beat the Yankees, 3–2, at Yankee Stadium. Batting in the number five slot behind Dickey, he went 0-for-4. His last at-bat came in the eighth inning. Facing pitcher Pete Appleton, with Red Rolfe on second and Dickey on first, he flied to George Case in center field.

On May 2 the Yankees captain was hitting an anemic .143 with one RBI when he told McCarthy before a game in Detroit that he thought it was time for him to sit out, at least for a while. Gehrig's consecutive games streak of 2,130 games was over. He was replaced by another Babe in his life—Babe Dahlgren.

Dr. Rock Positano, in his book *Dinner with DiMaggio: Memories of an American Hero*, wrote about a teary encounter DiMaggio had with Gehrig in the clubhouse when the Iron Horse realized he no longer could do the job. DiMaggio recalled, "Lou said to me, 'Joe, I don't think that I can play baseball anymore. I want to take myself out of the lineup before McCarthy takes me out.'"

"The Clipper was shocked by Lou's words," wrote Positano. "He had told no one else on the team what Lou was going through." Decades later, thinking about the conversation made Joe tear up. "Doc, this was the first time I ever showed any emotion inside the locker room," said DiMaggio. "It was just the two of us, alone, and Gehrig started to cry. I cried, too."

For the next month, Gehrig traveled with the Yankees, but he did not play. Instead, he took the lineup card to home plate often with a teammate accompanying him. He went to the Mayo Clinic in Rochester, Minnesota. A team of doctors headed by Charles William Mayo himself reviewed Gehrig's case and it was determined that he was the victim of Amyotrophic Lateral Sclerosis, a degenerative disease that affects nerve cells in the brain and spinal cord. It eventually robs its victims of the ability to initiate or control muscle movement.

On June 21, 1939, two days after his 36th birthday, the Yankees announced Gehrig's retirement and said July 4 would be Lou Gehrig Appreciation Day, a day to celebrate the life and career of their ailing hero. On that sweltering day, the Yankees welcomed back their Murderers' Row team of 1927 between games of a doubleheader against the Washington Senators. It laid the foundation of the annual Old-Timers' Day that has been held every year since 1947 with the exception of 2020 and 2021 because of the pandemic. The day was filled with painful emotions with love pouring out from all corners of Yankee Stadium, filled with 61,808 teary-eyed fans. It was at this event that Gehrig made his "Luckiest Man" speech in which he claimed to be "the luckiest man on the face of this earth." He gave the oration in measured, heartfelt words.

Most likely very few, if any, of the stadium crowd were aware that the great Yankee was terminal. It's generally acknowledged that Gehrig himself did not know the nature of his illness. At the time, most people did not know much at all about ALS.

"It's certainly baseball's most tragic moment, its greatest speech and probably the game's most humane moment, too, when baseball became a lesson in life," claimed Jonathan Eig, who wrote the 2005 book *Luckiest Man: The Life and Death of Lou Gehrig*. For many, it has become known as "Baseball's Gettysburg Address." It remains the most momentous speech in American sports history.

It's been well documented that Gehrig grappled with the idea of giving the speech. It was not known until the last minute that he would step to the mike not far from the batter's box where he helped lead the Yankees to six championships.

I'm not quite sure I ever understood what Gehrig meant when he said, "Fans, for the past two weeks you have been reading about the bad break I got. Yet today I consider myself the luckiest man on the face of this earth."

Here was a once indestructible man now reduced to a tragic figure, his body ravaged by a horrific illness. It remains a mystery if he knew he was dying. Gehrig often wrote letters to his wife Eleanor, and in one note written shortly after his diagnosis, he said, "The bad news is lateral sclerosis, in our language chronic infantile paralysis. There isn't any cure … there are very few of these cases. It is probably caused by some germ…. Never heard of transmitting it to mates…. There is a 50–50 chance of keeping me as I am. I may need a cane in 10 or 15 years. Playing is out of the question."

If this letter has been properly recorded in history, it's apparent that Gehrig was aware that his playing days were over but not that his illness was terminal. In the movie *Pride of the Yankees*, Gary Cooper, who played the part of Gehrig, said, "Give it to me straight, doc. Is it strike three?" Most likely that was Hollywood, and the dying Yankee never asked such a question.

In reference to Gehrig's words "I might have been given a bad break," Yankees historian and author Marty Appel stated, "That didn't translate to fatal." He added, "The general belief is that he knew he had a form of infantile paralysis, and if the doctors thought it was fatal and they told Eleanor, she didn't tell him. But remember, the speech was only about eight weeks after his last game and the Mayo Clinic tests were still ongoing. It's safe to assume Lou didn't know it was fatal but it's still a bit of mystery to it, because Lou might have chosen not to tell Eleanor, and so they both may have held the secret."

Gehrig ended his speech with these words: "So I close in saying that I might have been given a bad break, but I have an awful lot to live for! Thank you."

It certainly appears that he believed he had a future when he said, "I have an awful lot to live for."

In October 1939, Gehrig accepted Mayor Fiorello La Guardia's appointment to a 10-year term as a New York City parole commissioner and was sworn into office on January 2, 1940. He had rejected other job offers that paid far more than the $5,700 a year commissionership. Gehrig's job was to make judgments about the time of release for prisoners. One of them was a 19-year-old inmate named Thomas Rocco Barbella. Gehrig refused to release him and the two battled verbally. Barbella went on to a successful boxing career as Rocky Graziano, world middleweight champion. About a month before his death, no longer able to do the job, Gehrig quietly resigned.

During a winter meeting of the Baseball Writers' Association of America on December 7, 1939, Gehrig was elected to the National Baseball Hall of Fame and Museum in a special election related to his illness. At age 36, he was the youngest player to be so honored to date (until Sandy Koufax in 1972). He never had a formal induction ceremony. On July 28, 2013, Gehrig and 11 other deceased ballplayers, including Rogers Hornsby, received a special tribute during the induction ceremony held during Hall of Fame induction weekend, July 26–29, in Cooperstown, New York.

On June 2, 1941, at 10:10 p.m., 16 years to the day after he replaced Wally Pipp at first base, Henry Louis Gehrig died at his home on 5204 Delafield Avenue in the Fieldstone section of the Bronx in New York. He was 37 years old. According to James Lincoln Ray of the Society for American Baseball Research, "Upon hearing the news of the 'Iron Horse's' passing, Babe Ruth and his wife, Claire, went to the Gehrig house to console Eleanor. Mayor La Guardia ordered flags in New York to be flown at half-staff, and major league ballparks around the nation did likewise."

President Franklin D. Roosevelt sent his condolences. The following month, a monument was erected for Gehrig in Yankee Stadium, next to that of Miller Huggins.

Lou Gehrig's body was cremated. His ashes reside at Kensico Cemetery in Valhalla, New York.

There may not be a greater baseball story.

7

Gehrig's $312,000 Cap

My connection to Lou Gehrig is a New York Yankees baseball cap he wore circa 1929–32. In 2019 the cap was in the possession of a friend, Bob Ellis. The Bethany, Connecticut, resident, who had a 30-year career with IBM Corporation in systems engineering, event planning and marketing, had a massive collection of vintage Gehrig memorabilia that he inherited through marriage.

Ellis had informed me that his adult children, Kim and Scott, were Red Sox fans and not interested in most of the collection. He asked for my advice over lunch at a local diner. Since Father Time, who is undefeated, was ticking away, I recommended that he put his Gehrig collection in an auction which the Ellis family wisely agreed to. Bob and his wife, Jill, earmarked most of the proceeds for their two children and the future college educations of their grandchildren.

On February 23, 2019, the Yankees cap worn by the Iron Horse auctioned, among other items, for a staggering $312,000. When the auction was over, Ellis had hit it out of the park.

The Trail of the Gehrig Memorabilia

How Ellis came into possession of the Gehrig memorabilia and the final hours of the auction with its frenetic bidding make a fascinating story.

"My wife Jill's parents, George and Laurel Steigler, were married in Mamaroneck, New York, and for many years they were very close friends with Lou's parents, Christina and Heinrich," said Ellis. "As has been well publicized, Lou's mother was the center of his life. She was very protective of him and always saw his potential girlfriends as a threat to her losing him. There were two significant Ruths in Lou's life. One was Babe Ruth, and the other was Ruth Martin. Christina discouraged Lou from dating Miss Martin and that was the end of that."

On June 23, 1934, Ruth Martin married Herbert Quick. They would become lifelong friends of Lou's parents and named in her will when she passed.

On September 29, 1933, Lou married Eleanor Grace Twitchell from Chicago in New Rochelle, New York. They were married nine years and had no children. When Lou died he bequeathed his estate to his wife Eleanor, his parents, and the National Baseball Hall of Fame.

In 1946, Lou's father passed, and in the early 1950s, his mother moved from Mount Vernon, New York, to Milford, Connecticut, and lived with Ellis' in-laws, the Steiglers, for some time before they purchased a home for Mrs. Gehrig in Milford.

Lou's mother died on March 12, 1954, in Milford Hospital. In her will, she bequeathed $500 to the Milford Little League and one of their fields was named the Milford National Lou Gehrig Little League Field.

"Mom Gehrig willed the assets in her estate to Ruth Martin and Herbert Quick, my wife Jill's parents, and the National Baseball Hall of Fame, including many of his trophies and awards," explained Ellis. "It seems strange that Christina would will assets to the Quicks since she did not support the relationship between Ruth Martin and her son Lou."

In the mid–1990s, Ellis' mother-in-law asked if he would like any items in the collection as Father's Day gifts. Ellis thanked her and accepted the Lou Gehrig cap and a baseball signed by Ty Cobb, Tris Speaker, Babe Ruth and Eddie Collins.

In the late '90s Jill Ellis asked her mother to divide the memorabilia between her brother and herself. This proved to be a windfall for Bob Ellis. He recalled, "When we moved my mother-in-law into a condominium, we found an old box in the attic containing documents and over 150 photographs. My mother-in-law gave this box to us. So the trail of the Gehrig memorabilia went from Lou, to his parents, to the Hall of Fame, to my in-laws and finally to us."

Thus, the provenance of the Lou Gehrig collection was firmly confirmed.

On August 30, 2018, I invited Ellis to share some of Lou's memorabilia and photographs with the Silver Sluggers, a baseball group I facilitate during the baseball season at the Derby, Connecticut, Public Library. Several of the Sluggers, including yours truly, took photos wearing the Gehrig cap. We were unaware that the cap would be valued at more than $300,000.

When Bob mentioned that he was considering selling the collection, I recommended Heritage Auctions, headquartered in Dallas, Texas. Several days later Bob called the auction house and was directed to Rob Rosen, vice president of private sales and consignments in the sports department. He was very interested in reviewing the memorabilia. Ellis emailed him pictures of some of the most important and unique items. Highly impressed, Rosen traveled from Dallas to New York City. Two weeks later Ellis and his son, Scott, met with Rosen at the Heritage Auctions office on Park Avenue.

Auction Preparation

In the first two weeks of September 2018, Ellis and his son inventoried the materials in a spreadsheet with accompanying background information. On Thursday, September 14, Ellis packed everything in a medium-sized piece of luggage and took a train from Milford to Grand Central Station in New York City. Arriving around 11:00 a.m., he walked up to St. Patrick's Cathedral to attend daily Mass at noon. "Whenever I'm in New York City, I try to attend Mass at St. Patrick's," noted Ellis. "I took a seat alone near the altar in the fourth row of pews. As communion approached, I began to get anxious about leaving the luggage in the pew. Thinking the worst, I'm telling myself, 'My goodness, what if someone steals it?' I quickly exited the pew, walked up to receive communion and scurried back to the fourth row. How grateful I was that no one had stolen my luggage that was heavily packed with valuable Lou Gehrig memorabilia."

From the cathedral, Ellis walked uptown and met Scott. The two headed over to the Heritage Auctions office for a one o'clock meeting with Rosen. For about four hours

Rosen reviewed the extraordinary collection with excitement. "Throughout the afternoon, he often made remarks like 'Wow. This is the first time we've ever seen anything like this,'" remarked Ellis. "He estimated that the value of the Gehrig cap would be $200,000."

Among the memorabilia were a number of items owned by Gehrig that he received during the 1931 tour of Japan featuring a team of National and American baseball stars, including Hall of Famers Lefty Grove, Mickey Cochrane, Al Simmons and Rabbit Maranville. They traveled to Japan to play exhibition games with professional players representing Japan.

On September 24, everything was shipped to Dallas, where the Heritage staff began to authenticate each item and signature, take professional pictures for the auction catalogue and website, write descriptions and determine background information about where and when an item might have been used or seen. This was an ongoing process right up to the start of the two-day online and telephone auction scheduled for Saturday and Sunday, February 23 and 24, 2019.

All of the lots were reviewed by a group called Professional Sports Authenticator (and designated as PSA) to determine if they were authentic. The 1929–32 Yankees cap worn by Lou Gehrig was authenticated by Memorabilia Evaluation and Research Services (MEARS). They represent the first website of its kind within the sports memorabilia industry and are an Internet-based organization serving both individual collectors and select auction houses. "Mr. Gehrig" was sewn on the headband in the interior of the cap. This was a first for Heritage Auctions and most likely added value to the cap.

The media publicity parade quickly gained traction. In early February 2019 Heritage called Ellis regarding interest by the Associated Press and the *New York Times* to write articles. There was one stipulation: the Ellis family had to agree to use their full names and share where they lived.

They obliged.

The story gained energy. On Tuesday, February 12, Corey Kilgannon of the *New York Times* drove from New York City to the Ellis home and spent more than two hours learning more about the collection. He also took many photos to help him provide background for his story. Five days before the auction, the AP published its article with the headline "Is cap worn by New York

This baseball cap worn by Lou Gehrig circa 1929–1932 auctioned for $312,000 in 2019 (courtesy Bob Ellis).

Yankees Lou Gehrig worth $200,000?" In just a few hours the story was posted on more than 35 websites, including in China and Canada.

On February 19, Monica Jorge, a photographer for the *New York Times*, traveled to Ellis' home and took more than 400 pictures. Three days later the *New York Times* article was headlined "Trove of Lou Gehrig Items Goes Up for Auction." That same day Ellis did two live interviews in his home with WCBS-TV in New York and WFSB-TV in Hartford. He also did an interview with WINS radio in New York. Ed Randall had Ellis on his Sunday morning WFAN radio baseball talk show in NYC on February 24 and the following Sunday as well to discuss the final results.

The Auction

Bids were taken up until 10 o'clock EST on the night of each of the sessions.

On a lot-by-lot basis, starting at 10, any person who had bid on the lot previously was allowed to bid on that lot until there were no more bids for 30 minutes.

A Day to Remember

"Saturday, February 23, 2019, was a day I will never forget," Ellis said. "It was the first day of the auction, and at 12:27 p.m., my son Scott's wife, Jennifer, gave birth to their first child and our third grandchild, a beautiful baby girl. Her name is Ayla, and there still is some hope that we can convince her to become a Yankee fan."

The bidding for the cap opened at $60,000, then quickly jumped to $72,000. On Saturday night the bidding virtually exploded. At 11:00 p.m., the bid climbed from $132,000 to $144,000 and then almost instantly to $156,000. At 11:02 p.m., the bid increased to $180,000. At 11:03 p.m., the bid reached $192,000, then $204,000. At 11:04 p.m., the bid escalated to $216,000 and then four minutes later the bid jumped to $228,000. At 11:09 p.m., a bid came in at $240,000. The bidding was now extended to 11:39 p.m. because of the 30-minute extended bidding rule. At 11:32 p.m. bidding reached $264,000. Ellis' heart was on overload.

At 12:01 a.m., a bid arrived at $312,000. "I was hyperventilating," stated Ellis. This proved to be the final bid and the cap would sell for a record-breaking $312,000.

* * *

Other interesting lots including the selling price:

- A notarized copy of Lou Gehrig's birth certificate ($720).
- The earliest known photograph of Lou Gehrig ($9,600). This picture was taken in a studio in Manhattan and is dated 1903. On February 20, David Siedeman penned a second story, "Lou Gehrig's Newly Surfaced Baby Photo, His True Rookie Card."
- The original 1926 Lou Gehrig signed automobile registration ($26,400). "It was graded Mint 9 for Lou's top-of-the-line Peerless Coupe Roadster," explained Ellis. He added, "Clearly this lot was one of a kind." This was one of five lots which were signed "Henry Louis Gehrig," a signature Heritage had only encountered in legal documents. This signature is considered quite rare, as most of his autographs were signed "Lou Gehrig."
- A 1929 Lou Gehrig–signed check graded Mint 9 condition ($33,600). This check was dated December 18, 1929. All ink is in the bold, black fountain pen ink of

the Iron Horse and most notably his rare and desirable "Henry Louis Gehrig" autograph. Two other near-perfect checks sold for $21,600 and $20,400.

- A 1928 baseball signed by Ty Cobb, Tris Speaker, Babe Ruth and Eddie Collins ($10,800)
- A 1931 Christmas card from Babe Ruth to Lou ($3,600)
- A Silk kimono from the 1934 Tour of Japan trip ($16,800)
- A 1934 American Kennel Club championship certificate won by Gehrig's German Shepherd "Afra of Cosalta" ($1,800)
- A circa 1930 silver cigarette case ($2,520)
- Three typed legal pages discussing the legendary first baseman's financial holdings ($7,200)

Ellis had a baseball signed by the 1936 Yankees World Series championship team. It was the only item that was pulled from the auction. It includes signatures of six Hall of Famers: Bill Dickey, Joe DiMaggio, Lefty Gomez, Tony Lazzeri, Charles "Red" Ruffing and Gehrig. The pre-auction value was $24,000. In late January, there was an opening bid for $6,000, but within days, the Heritage group re-confirmed that the autographs of DiMaggio and Gomez had been deemed "secretarial," meaning they weren't signed by the players but someone else who worked in the Yankee clubhouse. Heritage called the initial bidder, and he accepted their offer to withdraw his bid. Collectors must be aware of team-signed baseballs because it was common for bat boys and other team personnel to forge the signatures of star players. (One former Yankee personnel employee told me that he would sign balls for Dave Winfield.)

By Monday afternoon, February 25, the Ellis family went through an emotional letdown as the activities moved toward a conclusion. A few weeks later, on March 12, Heritage Auctions surprised them with a memento of the event—a framed copy of the *New York Times* story.

For one day in his life, Bob Ellis was the luckiest man on the face of the earth.

This is the earliest known photograph of Lou Gehrig. He was born on June 19, 1903, in New York City. In 2019, the photograph auctioned for $9,600 (courtesy Bob Ellis).

8

Joe DiMaggio

A Lonesome Hero

> "If you said to God, 'Create someone who was what a baseball player should be,' God would have created Joe DiMaggio ... and he did."
> —Tom Lasorda

As stated earlier, Eddie Fastook is the Yankees executive director for team security. He has served the organization for many years in a number of capacities. Before his role with the Yanks he was a member of the NYPD where he worked in uniform and undercover in various assignments. While he was preparing to become a detective a knife-wielding rapist brought his career to an abrupt halt. "I had my right thumb severed and that was the end of my police career," lamented Fastook.

The robust-looking Fastook learned that George Steinbrenner was looking for a bodyguard. He interviewed with the Boss and was hired almost immediately. The former Bronx cop entered a fantasy world going to baseball games at Yankee Stadium and other venues, guarding the rich and famous, including the majority owner of the Yankees, in all areas of life. He often was dispatched to chauffeur Yankee dignitaries to and from airports plus other places. One of his frequent passengers was Joseph Paul DiMaggio, with whom he developed a great relationship.

Fastook took his father to Hofstra University in Hempstead, Long Island, where DiMaggio was doing a signing at a baseball card show. To get him to sign a baseball, a photo or some other item, the fee was $150 per ticket. Once you got to DiMaggio's table, he would sign the requested item after the ticket was handed to Morris Engelberg, "Joltin' Joe's" attorney and confidante. Engelberg was one of the few who were allowed into DiMaggio's private life during his later years. It's estimated the "Yankee Clipper" made $350,000 that weekend after signing 2,000 pieces, including baseballs, photos, and other items.

Unbeknownst to DiMaggio, Fastook, who was in line with his father for three hours, purchased two tickets, one for his father and one for himself. Fastook was carrying two baseballs to be signed. He could have had DiMaggio sign the balls free of charge, but he didn't want to compromise his relationship with the Yankee great. When they got to where the Yankee Clipper was signing, Fastook got his attention, saying, "Hey, Mr. DiMaggio."

DiMaggio was not happy that Fastook would pay $300 to get the two baseballs signed. "Joe got up and had this look of rage on his face," remembered Fastook. "He grabbed the two baseballs I brought and signed both. He said, 'Don't you ever do that again. Anytime you want my autograph, you just ask me for it.' I said, 'Thank you very much, Mr. DiMaggio.'"

A few weeks later Fastook picked up "DiMag" at the airport and took him to Yankee Stadium where he would throw out the first pitch on Opening Day. The security guy found the Yankee Hall of Famer in a sour mood because of the incident at the card show, and the two did not talk on the drive to the stadium. Fastook recalled, "When we got into the elevator at the stadium, DiMaggio angrily said, 'I got a bone to pick with you, young man. Why did you stand in line and pay $300 for my autograph? I told you any time you want my autograph, just ask me for it. Don't you ever pay for one of my autographs again.'"

Later that day, before DiMaggio threw out the first pitch, the two were in Steinbrenner's office. DiMaggio directed Fastook to do him a favor that took Fastook by surprise. "DiMaggio said, 'When you go downstairs, ask Nick Priore [the Yankees clubhouse attendant] for an extra dozen baseballs,'" recalled Fastook.

Priore filled Fastook's request. When Fastook got back upstairs, DiMaggio said to him, "Do you have the key for George's bathroom?" He did and he opened the door for DiMaggio and locked him inside. "DiMaggio went into the bathroom because he didn't want anybody to see him signing autographs," said Fastook. "There were others in the room who would have wanted his autograph and he was not about to fill any requests."

The Yankee Clipper signed a dozen baseballs for Fastook and left his engraved gold Mont Blanc pen in the box. "Ironically, this was a guy who hated people making money off his name," stated Fastook. "He handed me the 12 baseballs and the pen. He said, 'Now, when I'm gone, you make sure you don't get less than $500 a ball for these.'"

This story is a revelation of Joe DiMaggio's character and personality. Late in his life, he could be cranky, moody, and pessimistic, but he had a heart as big as the venerated stadium he played in—if he liked and trusted you.

My First Hero

World War II had ended, the boys were back home, and life was good. Summer Sundays meant church, family, good food and Yankee baseball. Italian songs blared from radios on this day of rest in the three-story apartment house I lived in. The aroma of different sauces from different apartments permeated the hallways. My mother wore an apron from morning until night. My father and uncles talked, read the Sunday papers, ate dinner, smoked cigars, watched the Yankee game and then ate again. When the Yankees and Red Sox played there was noticeable excitement in the air. It was Joe DiMaggio vs. Ted Williams.

DiMaggio was the first sports hero in my life. His grace and class transcended the playing field in American culture. His résumé was impeccable. A three-time MVP (1939, 1941, 1947), the Yankee Clipper batted .325 lifetime during his 13-year career from 1936 to 1951. He hit 361 home runs and incredibly struck out only 369 times. Only once in his career did he strike out three times in a game. It happened on June 19, 1942, in Cleveland Stadium, where Indians pitcher Mel Harder accomplished the almost impossible.

DiMaggio collected 2,214 hits and knocked in 1,537 runs despite missing three years in military service during World War II in his prime years, age 28–30. His OPS (on-base percentage and slugging average) was a glittering .977. His record 56-consecutive game hitting streak in 1941 will most likely never be broken.

Former writer Dan Daniel described DiMag, who appeared in 11 All-Star games, as "a picture athlete if ever there had been one in the major leagues, the very apotheosis of poetry in motion." He embodied the Italian term *sprezzatura* for making difficult things look easy when he ran down a fly ball with loping grace. The Yankees star center fielder was your proverbial five-star player. He could run, throw, field and hit for average and power. But his legacy of style and finesse can't be defined by numbers. "Baseball isn't statistics; it's Joe DiMaggio rounding second," wrote Jimmy Breslin. DiMaggio running the bases was baseball art. Former teammate Frank Crosetti claims he was never thrown out running from first to third. It reportedly was in 1939 when DiMaggio was nicknamed the Yankee Clipper by Yankee's play-by-play announcer Arch McDonald, when he likened DiMaggio's speed and range in the outfield to the then-new Pan American airline.

In 1952, the year following his retirement, DiMaggio hosted a Sunday morning TV show titled *The Buitoni Show*. I watched the show faithfully. Three different teenagers from the NYC area were invited on the show each week. They were asked a series of trivia questions. The winner would receive a Bulova watch. The runner-up would receive a year's supply of Buitoni macaroni. Joltin' Joe would often have Yankee players as guests. On one show, Phil Rizzuto, the mahatma of bunting, taught the kids and the audience the art of bunting.

My interest in Yankee baseball and DiMaggio was fostered by my father, a "Joe D." fan. My Sicilian uncles who were born in Italy were fans too. When I was six years old, my parents bought me a baseball jersey and I insisted that my mother sew the number 5 on the back of it. My first image of DiMaggio was gained from baseball cards in the late '40s.

I would watch DiMaggio bat on TV in the twilight of his career and then go out to the backyard and emulate his batting stance. Like Joe, I held the bat high and steady with my arms away from my body. Like Joe, I stood stock still with feet wide apart. I was now ready to cause some damage. After the count went to 2–2, I would smash a home run and circle the bases around the perimeter of the house that was located on a hill. And like Joe, I was sure to tip my cap, a lost gesture, to the appreciative crowd.

America's First Italian Hero

At age 16 Joe dropped out of Galileo High School to dedicate his life to baseball. To many, DiMaggio came across as distant and removed. He was socially uncomfortable in his early baseball years because of his lack of formal education and often had a third party accompany him to dinner to stimulate conversation. The seeds for his mystique and remarkable baseball journey were planted and cultivated by a friendly New York press. He was treated like royalty early on by the New York media and was very aware of his popularity and the idolatry generated by his legion of fans throughout his life.

DiMaggio, who was born to Italian immigrant parents, was the first Italian hero in this country. He helped erase the Italian mobster stigma of gangsters like Al Capone and Lucky Luciano. His cultural impact on his Italian following was immense as he represented the hopes and dreams of all Italian Americans. His teammates called him "the

Dago" or "Dag" in reference to his Italian heritage. Political correctness was unheard of in this era. His brothers Dom and Vince also enjoyed big league careers.

Wearing the number 9, DiMaggio made his ML debut in the middle of the Great Depression on May 3, 1936, at Yankee Stadium where the Yankees thrashed the inept St. Louis Browns 14–5 before a Sunday crowd of 25,430. He played left field; center field was still reserved for Ben Chapman. This was the first year the Yankees' famous interlocking NY logo became a permanent part of the Yankees' jerseys.

DiMaggio's first at-bat came in the first inning against Browns right-hander Jack Knott which resulted in a crazy play. With Crosetti on third and Red Rolfe on first, the Yankee Clipper grounded to Knott and appeared to be an easy out at first base. But Lady Luck whispered in Crosetti's ear to lend the 21-year-old rookie a hand. "Cro" started for home, drawing Knott's attention. Seeing he couldn't make it, Crosetti ducked back to third and Knott threw the ball away. Crosetti scored, Rolfe went to third and DiMaggio ended up on second. He proceeded to score after Gehrig walked and Chapman doubled.

DiMaggio collected his first hit off Earl Caldwell in the bottom of the second, a looping single to center field. For the day he went 3-for-6, including a triple off Chief Hogsett in the sixth. He batted .323 with 29 home runs and 125 RBI his rookie season. This was the harbinger of a brilliant career.

DiMaggio finished second in the MVP vote in 1937, despite leading the American League in home runs, slugging percentage, runs, and total bases. He won the first of his three MVP awards in 1939, when he led the major leagues with a career-best .381 average; he also hit 30 home runs and 126 RBI. DiMaggio's stats his first four years were off the charts—maybe the best in baseball history. He remains the only player in major league history to be on a world championship team his first four years in the big leagues.

You can measure a man's height and you can measure a man's weight, but you can't measure his heart. DiMaggio had heart. He played the game with ferocity, sliding into bases with thunder. When he got into the batter's box, he was all business. Joltin' Joe always had the unabashed admiration of his peers. I had the chance to talk to a couple of them at the 1991 Old-Timers' Day game.

"He was the greatest baserunner I ever saw, the greatest competitor I ever saw, just the best ballplayer of our time," said Charlie "King Kong" Keller, who shared the same outfield with DiMaggio and Tommy Henrich for several years. "When he was going up against Bob Feller you could see the determination, the veins in his neck. He was working to do well." Henrich added, "He was the only right-handed power hitter that stayed in there against Feller. Jimmie Foxx and Hank Greenberg gave way to Feller because of his wildness. DiMaggio had too much pride to give in to him. Even Ted Williams gave in from the left side."

DiMaggio was Feller's kryptonite. Cleveland writer Tony Lariccia of the *Plain Dealer* wrote, "In 58 games, he [DiMaggio] faced Feller more than any other pitcher in his career with 217 plate appearances and 193 at-bats. His .342 career average against the Hall of Fame right-hander ranked third against pitchers he faced at least 100 times." According to Sarah Langs, "his .342 average was the second highest by any batter who faced Feller at least 100 times … just behind Ted Williams' .344."

DiMaggio was baseball royalty, and he was treated as such by his teammates. Former first baseman Hank Workman had a cup of coffee late in the '50 season, collecting one hit in five at-bats. One of his jobs was to get a cigarette ready for DiMag when he came in from center field between innings. In *Joe DiMaggio: The Hero's Life*, Richard

Ben Cramer wrote, "As each inning ended, he [Workman] had to light a Chesterfield, take one puff and have it burning for the 'Dag.'"

As much as his teammates admired him on the field, most were not close to him off the field. Very few were allowed in his private world. He controlled and protected his life's narrative. "I played 11 years with Joe, and we never had dinner together," said Henrich. "We liked each other but we were just two different kinds of people."

I had Cramer on my *Inside Yankee Baseball* radio show in 2000 to discuss his book. He did not endear himself to many of the DiMaggio fans. He praised the Clipper's baseball talents but portrayed him as a money-hungry, miserable human being. DiMaggio was attending the Giants-A's World Series game at Candlestick Park in San Francisco when the Loma Prieta earthquake occurred. Cramer explained that DiMaggio returned to his old homestead which was now his sister's house. He went upstairs and came back down with a garbage bag filled with $600,000 in cash. And according to Cramer, as a young player, DiMaggio's friends from the underworld set him up with a gigantic "trust fund" at the Bowery bank. Deposits would be made regularly when the high-profile Joe graced certain restaurants with his presence.

Cramer labeled DiMaggio "a miser, never showing any interest in sharing his wealth." This might have been true later in his life but not when he was a ballplayer. I was friendly with former Yankee pitcher Frank "Spec" Shea from Naugatuck, Connecticut. The "Naugatuck Nugget," who won two games in the 1947 World Series, paints a different picture of DiMaggio.

"In 1947, Hank Bauer, Yogi Berra, Joe and myself lived in the Hotel Edison on 228 West 47th Street," said Shea. "There wasn't a morning went by he didn't pay for breakfast. I tried a couple of times to slip money to the waitress to pay the bill. He found out about it and told her, 'If you take that money, I'm going to see that you lose your job. I'm paying for this breakfast.' He did it every morning for the '47 season."

DiMaggio was comfortable around common folk. A former colleague of mine, Hank Violin, tells this story.

"My mother lived in Ft. Lauderdale, Florida, in the early '60s. She had married a Yankee fan named John after my dad died. John would go to the Yankees spring camp in Fort Lauderdale to get a glimpse of 'DiMag' who I believe was a guest hitting coach at the time." John finally connected with Joe and invited him to lunch at the house. Joe accepted and asked, "Does your wife make spaghetti?" John replied, "Yes."

"Joe D. did show up and was a perfect guest. He gave my mother a little gift—can't remember what it was, maybe a plant."

On September 17, 1992, the doors were opened at Joe DiMaggio Children's Hospital at Memorial Regional Hospital in Hollywood, Florida, for which he raised more than $4 million.

There were different sides to the man.

Old-Timers' Day

There was something about Joe DiMaggio that could make a grown man feel like a child. In June of '85, I rode the elevator with him at Yankee Stadium. I was on the first floor waiting for the door to close when he walked in. My tongue was paralyzed for several seconds before I said hello.

My next experience with the Yankee legend was not so unsettling. As previously stated, I had the honor and privilege of umpiring the Old-Timers' Day game at Yankee Stadium for 16 consecutive years. If DiMaggio saw me in my umpire's uniform, he was very cordial, happy to shake hands. He apparently saw me as an integral member of his baseball fraternity. Conversely, if he saw me in regular clothes with my press credential tag hanging from my neck, I was invisible in his eyes, maybe a threat to his protected world.

The 1991 Old-Timers' Day event was special. The Yankees celebrated the 50th anniversary of DiMaggio's historic 56-consecutive game hitting streak. I was standing next to him in the Yankees dugout waiting to ump the Old-Timers' game when a video montage of his career was shown on the Diamond Vision board. The montage was accompanied by the song "Unforgettable," originally sung by Nat King Cole in 1951. In '91 the song was edited and reworked to create a duet with his daughter, Natalie. It was a beautiful rendition and fitting for DiMaggio and his stellar baseball career. He loved it. His eyes reflected a blend of pride, joy and sadness. It has been written that Cole's version in '51 was the favorite song of DiMaggio and his wife Marilyn Monroe.

During the middle of the introductions, the umpires were introduced, and we stood in the area of home plate. Following the pre-game ceremonies and the playing of the national anthem, before I took my position at second base, I walked over to DiMaggio as everyone was exiting the field. I shook his hand and said, "Joe, thanks for the memories."

He politely answered, "Thank you."

My wife, Lois, who was seated several rows behind home plate, was able to capture the Yankee legend and me shaking hands with her camera. It's a photo I will always cherish.

Marty Appel began his tenure with the Yankees in 1968 at age 19 as a fan mail clerk for Mickey Mantle before becoming the Yankees' assistant public relations director under Bob Fishel. In 1973 he became the team's public relations director, a position he held for four years. Appel had several dealings with DiMaggio centered on the annual Old-Timers' Day games.

"Joe DiMaggio was always the best dressed man at the stadium," said Appel. "He was royalty. Everyone was in awe of Joe, even his teammates. Lefty Gomez, his roommate, could needle him but nobody else was able to get away with it."

DiMaggio kept Appel busy during Old-Timers' Day week. "Joe would come into town on Tuesday looking for tickets for a variety of people like the taxi driver, the hotel door man, etc.," recalled Appel. "Whatever he wanted we got him. It was important for us to have him there. Taking nothing for granted, on the day of the event I would greet him with my name, but he'd just walked by, his needs satisfied."

One year the Yankees gave the returning old timers a Longines wristwatch engraved with their name on the back. Those in the PR department also received watches. When Joe died, his watch was auctioned for $25,000. "Looking back, I should have ordered two Joe DiMaggio watches, one for Joe and one for me," laughed Appel.

DiMaggio's ego could get in the way on occasion. The Yankees played at Shea Stadium in 1974 and 1975 while Yankee Stadium was being renovated. One year there was a reception in the Diamond Club following the Old-Timers' game.

"Joe went to the bar to get a drink," Appel remembered. "The bartender said, 'I'm sorry. We're still setting up.'"

"Joe was so upset he left the ballpark and never returned."

It was generally believed that DiMaggio always insisted that he be introduced as "the Greatest Living Player." "DiMaggio never insisted on that when he was announced at the Old-Timers' Day games," clarified Appel. "But he certainly didn't discourage it, and probably, when asked at other gatherings how he'd like to be introduced, he would offer that up. But people have made it seem like a condition for pleasing him, and it was never quite that extreme. He liked it. I would have too."

The Yankee Clipper was always announced last, just after Mickey Mantle, but in 1969 Mantle enjoyed the honor. Mantle became the main attraction of the Old-Timers' Day celebration. His fan base was younger and louder. It was also the year the Yankees honored Mantle and retired his number 7.

"We felt that it would be proper to introduce Mickey last that year because of the honors he had received," explained Appel. "DiMaggio was introduced next to last. When Mickey was introduced, he received a much longer ovation than DiMaggio received which proved to be embarrassing to Joe, who was standing on the field with all the other players."

"Looking back, that was a mistake," admitted Appel. "Joe didn't register a formal complaint, but he let it be known to others, and it made its way back to Fishel. From 1970 on DiMaggio was always announced last."

When DiMag showed up for Old-Timers' Day everything stopped. One year I heard former Yankee Ben Chapman yell in the dugout, "Hey, the Dago is here!" His former teammates and current players were in awe of him, but his changeable moods were challenging. Michael Kay, the Yankees anchor announcer over the YES network, tells the following story:

> One year Joe DiMaggio came in [to the clubhouse] and he was in an absolutely great mood. They put him in a locker about two lockers to the left of Paul O'Neil on the back wall of the old stadium. Players from the present team and old timers as well lined up the length of the clubhouse with baseballs to get them autographed by DiMaggio. You don't realize how big a deal that was because Joe didn't do that very often.
>
> The next year Joe was sitting in the dugout elegantly dressed in his suit, and Wade Boggs, a guy who was going to be in the Hall of Fame, was walking over with a ball [to be signed] and DiMaggio, without looking at him, just put his hand out and said, "No way."

Was DiMaggio baseball's greatest living player in 1969?

His critics argued that his defensive skills fell short based on contemporary defensive metrics. DiMaggio made 105 errors in 13 seasons, but he was protected, playing in the radio era with no TV replay. In a doubleheader against the Red Sox during his hitting streak, he made four errors. In contrast, Mantle, his successor, made 82 miscues from the outfield. Overall, he was charged with 102 errors if you include his infield play.

Some of his contemporaries said his brother Dom was a better flychaser. Up at Fenway, the knights of the keyboard literally sang praise to the Little Professor to the tune of "O Tannenbaum": "You're better than your brother Joe, Dominick DiMaggio."

I once asked Dom how he would compare himself defensively to his brother Joe.

He said, "I'll let the fans decide that." He didn't say Joe was better. Dom was not only an outstanding defensive player, but he was also a great offensive player; during his first 10 seasons (1940–42 and 1946–52), he had more hits (1,679) than anyone in baseball and only Ted Williams scored more runs. From this corner he deserves to be in the Hall of Fame.

8. Joe DiMaggio

Brothers Joe (left) and Dom DiMaggio share memories at the 36th annual Old-Timers' Day on August 7, 1982, at Yankee Stadium.

During Joe's career, mental errors were ignored by the media. In one game, the Detroit Tigers had a runner on third with one out. The batter hit a fly ball to DiMaggio in center field. Thinking it was the third out of the inning, he put his head down and began to run toward the Yankees' dugout. By the time he realized his gaffe, the runner on third had tagged-up and scored. Following the game, he was not asked about it. The flap was never reported in the papers as it would be today.

9

The Streak, the Stolen Bat and Final Years, 1941–1951

Hitting streaks were part of DiMaggio's DNA. As an 18-year-old he hit in 61 straight games in 1933 playing for the San Francisco Seals in the Pacific Coast League. After winning a second consecutive batting title in 1940 (.352), DiMaggio reached a new level of fame in '41 when he set one of the most enduring records in sports by hitting in 56 consecutive games. It would be his crowning achievement. DiMag went from a baseball rock star to a national phenomenon. He was even sanctified in song, "Joltin' Joe DiMaggio," sung by Betty Bonney with the Les Brown orchestra and written by Alan Courtney and Ben Horner.

> He started baseball's famous streak
> that's got us all aglow.
> He's just a man and not a freak,
> Joltin' Joe DiMaggio.

On May 15, 1941, the day the streak began, the Yankees were in fourth place, a mediocre 14–14, and DiMaggio had batted a lowly .194 over the previous 20 games. But things would change. On June 17, the Clipper broke the Yankee hitting-streak record of 29 games, set by Roger Peckinpaugh in 1919 and equaled by Earle Combs in 1931. By mid-June DiMaggio's hitting streak began capturing the hearts of fans from the Bronx to his family's home on 2150 Beach Street in San Francisco.

It was a newsy summer. Whirlaway was chasing horse racing's Triple Crown and Ted Williams was in the midst of batting over .400 for the season. But the winds of war could be felt in the States. In Europe, Germany invaded Russia, escalating the war, while the United States awaited its entry.

As DiMaggio's streak continued to grow it gradually became a national obsession. His legion of Italian fans waved the Italian flag at the stadium. Unfortunately, the Yankee games were not carried on the radio in '41 but radio programs were interrupted for DiMaggio bulletins. Fans waited for Don Dunphy's nightly radio reports.

On June 26 DiMaggio reached his 38th game with a little help from teammate Tommy Henrich. With the Yanks ahead of the Browns 3–1 in the bottom of the eighth, "the Jolter" had gone hitless for the day and was due up fourth in the inning. Johnny Sturm popped out to start the inning. Red Rolfe then walked which gave way to Henrich. If "Old Reliable" bounced into a double play, DiMaggio would not get a chance to bat again that day if the Browns failed to tie the score or take the lead in the ninth. Henrich asked manager Joe McCarthy if he could bunt to avoid the double play. McCarthy gave him the green light. It was a perfect bunt, moving Rolfe to second. DiMaggio showed his appreciation by doubling into the left field corner.

9. The Streak, the Stolen Bat and Final Years, 1941–1951

DiMaggio got number 40 at Philadelphia on June 28 in a game that created considerable interest. The A's pitcher that day was a hard-throwing right-hander named Johnny Babich. A native of Albion, California, Babich had announced how he was going to stop the streak. He said he would get DiMaggio out his first time up and then walk him in each of his following at-bats. This did not sit well with the Yankees and DiMaggio.

In the top of the first inning, the Yankee Clipper hit a fly ball in his first at-bat to shortstop Al Brancato. Babich had his out. Joltin' Joe batted again in the top of the third and worked the count to 3–0. It appeared that Babich was done pitching to DiMaggio. But on the next pitch DiMaggio whizzed a liner past Babich's ear and the Yankee slugger ended up with a double.

"It was probably my most satisfying hit of The Streak," DiMaggio later told the *San Francisco Chronicle*.

On June 29 the Yankees visited Griffith Stadium in Washington for a doubleheader. In between games, his bat, "Betsy Ann," was stolen. In the seventh inning of the second game, DiMaggio, using Henrich's bat, hit a single to pass George Sisler's 41-game streak set in 1922, commonly referred to as the "modern record" to distinguish it from Wee Willie Keeler's 44-game streak, the "all-time record" set in 1897.

But who stole the bat?

DiMaggio enlisted friends Jerry Spotola, a funeral director, and Jimmy "Peanuts" Ceres from Newark, New Jersey, to help him find the valuable lumber. Ceres had the reputation as a small-time rackets guy.

In the early '90s I had a chance to interview Paul Kleiber for *Sports Collectors Digest*. Kleiber was an advanced DiMaggio collector, and his home was a veritable DiMaggio museum. He had inside information on the pilfered bat.

"Ceres heard that a man who lived in Lyndhurst, New Jersey, had the bat," said Kleiber. "Ceres went to the man and recovered the bat on the grounds it was stolen property. Ceres promised the guy future passes to Yankee games as a show of gratitude on DiMaggio's part. The Lyndhurst man said the bat had gone through several hands before reaching him."

It's possible Ceres made the Lyndhurst guy an offer he couldn't refuse. "The streets of Newark had ears, and most of those ears funneled back to 'Peanuts,'" wrote Mike Vaccaro in his book *1941: The Greatest Year in Sports*.

The story had a happy ending. Betsy Ann was back in the hands of the Yankee Clipper and nobody got hurt.

On July 2, DiMaggio broke Keeler's 44-game single-season all-time record with a fifth-inning home run off Red Sox pitcher Dick Newsome. (Keeler actually hit in 45 straight games if you include the hit he collected in the final game of the 1886 season.) It's assumed that DiMaggio used Henrich's bat for games 42, 43, 44, 45 and 46. If true, Keeler's record was broken with Henrich's bat. "Henrich subsequently broke the bat and gave it to DiMaggio on his request," said Kleiber

On July 17, the streak ended in Cleveland's Municipal Stadium in front of 67,468 fans, at that time the largest crowd ever to see a night game, when Indians third baseman Ken Keltner robbed DiMaggio of hits with two spectacular plays. I asked Keltner at the 1984 Yankees Old-Timers' Day what he recalled about that night.

"DiMaggio had a large Italian following in Cleveland," noted Keltner. "After the game, my wife and I received a police escort to the parking lot."

Over the course of the streak the Yankees went 41–13 and moved from fourth place, five and a half games back, to first, seven games ahead of Cleveland. DiMaggio went on to hit safely in his next 16 games, and the Yankees went on to win the pennant and then beat the Brooklyn Dodgers in the World Series.

During the streak he batted .408 with 91 hits, including 15 home runs and 55 RBI. In his 223 times at bat, DiMaggio struck out only five times. In fact, he fanned only 13 times the entire season. Strange but true, in his 56-game streak, he scored 56 runs and had 56 singles. The streak overshadowed Williams' marvelous achievement of batting .406 that season.

DiMaggio rewarded the efforts of Spotola and Ceres. He showed his gratitude by giving the cleats he wore in 1941 to Spotola and Peanuts became his part-time driver. Spotola gave the cleats to his daughter, Bina. In 1991, she consigned the DiMaggio cleats from the '41 season to a Sotheby's auction in NYC. It was at that auction that Kleiber purchased them. It was the only piece of equipment known to still exist that DiMaggio wore during the streak. As for the provenance of the cleats, Kleiber has a letter from Bina as proof she consigned them to Sotheby's.

"Also, there was newspaper stuffed in the shoes dated November 12, 1941," stated Kleiber. "I also have a 1941 newspaper article that states Joe gave the cleats he wore during the streak to Jerry Spotola."

Another piece of evidence that would authenticate the DiMaggio cleats is the wear and tear. "A little-known fact is that DiMaggio had a habit of kicking his right foot into the ground when he entered the batter's box in key situations," Kleiber explained. "The cleats I have are worn at the tip of the top section of the shoe worn on the right foot."

As for the bat that DiMaggio used for 51 games of the streak, the whereabouts remains a mystery. But Kleiber offers a possible answer. "DiMaggio had promised to give the bat to USO officials in San Francisco for an auction to raise funds for soldiers," said Kleiber. "I believe that the late comedian and DiMaggio friend Lou Costello [of Abbott and Costello fame] got the bat at the auction. It has been speculated that the bat that Abbott and Costello used in the popular 'Who's on First' routine was the bat DiMaggio swung during the streak."

Barry Halper, one of the nation's foremost baseball collectors, invited Kleiber to have dinner with him and DiMaggio at Yankee Stadium in early April 1991. "Barry presented Joe with a baseball that was thrown out on Opening Day by General Colin Powell," recalled Kleiber. "This was just after the Desert Storm action that Powell had commanded." The general later retrieved the ball and wrote a short note on it to Joe, basically stating, "Joe, I'm a great fan of yours." He signed his name and asked Barry to give it to Joe.

Joe then asked Barry for a baseball, and I sat there watching Joe write a message on it to General Powell. Joe wrote, "General, yours was an MVP performance." Joe also had a ball signed by former president Ronald Reagan and Mikhail Gorbachev, the former general secretary of the Communist Party of the Soviet Union and head of state. Gorbachev took part in summits with Reagan to limit nuclear weapons and end the Cold War.

Joe DiMaggio was not happy with the Yankees contract offer and held out in '42. Because the country was at war and fighting the Rome-Berlin-Tokyo Axis which Italy was a part of, the hold-out was not popular with many in the baseball world. His Italian heritage exacerbated the problem. During times of war, all natives, denizens, and subjects of countries with which the United States is at war are deemed by the federal government as alien enemies (also known as enemy aliens). This was a time when Italians who were not American citizens were registered as "enemy aliens." Most were located on the West Coast. Ten thousand Italian immigrants were forced from their homes in the Bay Area, Santa Cruz, Monterey, Los Angeles and the coastal areas in between as a result of this wartime policy. DiMaggio's parents weren't U.S. citizens, but the government didn't intern them as enemy aliens. Doing so would probably have created a public outcry. About 2,000 Italians were arrested and sent to internment camps. Eight months later, on Columbus Day 1942, President Roosevelt lifted the restrictions on Italian enemy aliens, citing their loyalty to America. In 2010, the California legislature passed a resolution apologizing for U.S. mistreatment of Italian residents during the war.

DiMaggio Struggled during his holdout '42 season, hitting .305 with 21 homers and 114 RBI. He received hate mail from patriotic citizens who saw him as a self-centered man during this time of conflict.

On February 17, 1943, he enlisted in the U.S. Army Air Forces. According to an article by Branden C. Potter, "While Joe DiMaggio worked as a physical instructor, he was assigned to military baseball teams such as the Seventh Army Air Force team. The New York Post wrote, 'He felt "exploited" and displayed an "aversion" to the use of his special skill.'"

After a so-so season in '46 (.290–25–95) he bounced back and won his third MVP in '47, after beginning the season a little late coming off bone spur surgery on his heel. John Drebinger of the *New York Times* wrote that DiMaggio "seems to be giving more prominence to the human heel than it has received since the days of Achilles."

Critics of DiMaggio's third MVP argued that the award should have gone to Williams. DiMaggio's numbers (.315–20–97) paled in comparison to Williams' Triple Crown stats (.343–32–114). I'm sure defensively DiMaggio was more valuable, but most likely Williams' frigid relationship with the media affected the voting.

It was around this time that the Yankees and Red Sox talked about swapping the two stars. "I was at Toots Shor's restaurant one night when I was privy to a conversation between Red Sox owner Tom Yawkey and Yankees co-owner Dan Topping," recalled Mel Allen, the longtime "Voice of the Yankees." "They were talking about trading DiMaggio for Williams. But Yawkey finally said, 'If I do that, they'll kill me in Boston.'"

Topping, an heir to a tin mining fortune, was a socialite who was married six times. One of his wives was Sonja Henie, the Norwegian Olympic gold medal figure skater.

In the '47 Fall Classic against the Dodgers, DiMaggio hit only .231, but he did hit two home runs, one of which gave the Yanks a 2–1 win in Game Five. In this series, however, he is best remembered for his reaction to Al Gionfriddo's spectacular catch in Game Six at Yankee Stadium. In the sixth inning, the Yankees, trailing 8–5, put two men on with two out, bringing DiMaggio to the plate as the tying run. Gionfriddo, a seldom-used outfielder, had entered the game that inning as a defensive replacement. The Yankee slugger, facing Joe Hatten, launched a long drive toward the visitors' bullpen in deep left, but Gionfriddo was able to track it down and make a lunging catch just short of the bullpen before crashing into the waist-high gate near the 415-foot sign.

David had beaten Goliath and the Dodgers went on to an 8–6 victory. No less memorable than the catch was DiMaggio's reaction. In a rare display of emotion, the famously stoic star kicked at the dirt near second base when he saw that Gionfriddo had caught the ball.

I had a chance to talk with Gionfriddo about the catch many years later. "Shotton [the Dodgers' manager] put me in because of my defense and I could run pretty good," he said. "They moved me over close to the line in left field. I was playing a little out of position. Joe hit the ball deep into left center field near the bullpen. I just put my head down and ran toward the bullpen. I looked over my shoulder and knew the ball was going in that direction."

"I caught the ball over my shoulder," he continued. "I'm jumping as the ball was going into the bullpen. I jumped with my back toward home plate and made the catch over my shoulder. When I came down, I hit the fence. If I didn't catch it, it would have gone over for a three-run homer scoring Snuffy Stirnweiss and Yogi Berra."

Strange but true, Gionfriddo never played another big-league game. His fame gained from the WS was more valuable to the Dodgers' franchise minor league teams as a drawing card than it was in Brooklyn.

Yankee Stadium and its vast left field and left-center Death Valley, 457 feet from home plate, was not friendly to right-handed batters and DiMaggio was no exception. Of his 361 home runs, only 148 were hit in the house that Ruth built; 213, or 59 percent, were hit on the road. The Yankee Clipper hit eight World Series home runs, all on the road.

Nineteen forty-eight proved to be DiMaggio's last great season, at least in terms of statistics. Playing in 153 games, in spite of a bone spur on his right heel, he led the league in home runs (39), RBI (155) and total bases (355) and finished second to Lou Boudreau in the MVP vote. The 1949 season was one of frustration with a happy ending. After missing most the first half of the season because of his heel spur, he returned from the injury in mid–June for a weekend series at Fenway Park and helped cement his reputation as an inspirational team leader when he hit four home runs and collected nine RBI in three games. In the 76 games that remained after his return, he hit a robust .346 while averaging almost a run batted in per game. At age 35, he showed his tank was not empty.

DiMaggio and manager Casey Stengel had a frosty relationship at best. Stengel tried an experiment on July 3, 1950, at Griffith Stadium in Washington that didn't go over well with number 5. He moved DiMaggio to first base to rest his legs. Unfortunately, Stengel reportedly instructed Topping to tell DiMaggio he would be playing first base because of injuries to Henrich, Johnny Mize and Joe Collins. DiMaggio, who had never played that position in his career, worked out at first base the day before. The idea was a disaster.

Although DiMaggio handled 13 put-outs without an error, he looked extremely awkward on one play. This was terribly embarrassing to a man known for his amazing grace in the outfield. It happened on a swinging bunt down the first-base line. DiMaggio raced in, but pitcher Tom Ferrick got to the ball first and yelled, "I got it." Trying to scramble back to the bag, DiMaggio fell and nearly was stepped on by the runner. Cameras clicked, and papers the next day carried a picture of the great DiMag crawling around on his hands and knees. "He was furious to look so clumsy," Ferrick said many years later. "He was enraged."

He never played first base again.

Perhaps the most humiliating moment for DiMaggio occurred on July 7, 1951, at Fenway Park where the Yanks got spanked by the Red Sox, 10–4. In the second inning, with the Yankees trailing 6–1, Stengel asked reserve first baseman-outfielder Johnny Hopp to go to DiMaggio in center field and tell him he was being substituted by rookie

Jackie Jensen. It was reported that the Yankee slugger was humiliated and seething but Stengel told the press the move was made because DiMaggio was injured. When DiMaggio cooled off, he admitted that he had pulled a leg muscle. He told reporters, "I didn't want to take a chance on hurting it anymore, so I got out." He did miss the next two weeks, but Stengel sending a messenger (Hopp) out to tell Joltin' Joe that he was coming out of the game did not sit well.

DiMaggio's final career at-bat came in Game Six of the '51 World Series against Larry Jansen and the New York Giants. In the bottom of the eighth, he led off the inning and doubled to right field. Gil McDougald then tried to sacrifice DiMaggio to third, but Jansen fielded the ball cleanly and got the 36-year-old Yankee sliding into the base. The Yankees won the game, 4–3, and the Series. Of the 10 World Series DiMaggio played with the Yankees, the Bombers won nine. The only loss was to the Cardinals in 1942. In the jubilant Yankee clubhouse following the game, DiMaggio told his teammates, "I've played my last game."

Jon Pessah in his book *Yogi: A Life Behind a Mask* wrote, "Soon every Yankee walks over to Joe, each carrying a glove, a ball, a bat, a uniform, all things they ask DiMaggio to sign."

10

Dorothy, Marilyn, and Memorabilia

On July 10, 1939, the day before the All-Star game that was played at Yankee Stadium, Joe DiMaggio and Dorothy Arnold, the daughter of a railroad conductor from Duluth, Minnesota, announced their engagement. He promised his fiancée he would hit a home run for her which he delivered in storybook fashion in the fifth inning off Bill Lee. DiMaggio met Arnold, a singer, dancer, and actress, while filming a cameo in the movie Manhattan *Merry-Go-Round*.

On November 18, 1939, the two were married at San Francisco's St. Peter and Paul Cathedral and as many as 20,000 well-wishers (most of them described as "laughing Italians") reportedly lined the streets near the church to get a glimpse of the couple. *Life* magazine described the event as having "a carnival spirit that jammed streets and broke police lines" and noted that "even the wedding party had to battle the crowd for 15 minutes to get inside the church" and that "one woman fainted in the crush of the doorway." The magazine also informed readers that although Arnold was raised a Protestant, she had been accepted into the Catholic Church just a week before.

They lived in a $300 per month penthouse in midtown Manhattan. On October 23, 1941, Dorothy gave birth to Joseph Paul DiMaggio III. The couple split up in 1942 but later reconciled. But they separated for good in October of '43 and were divorced on May 12, 1944. Arnold reportedly accused Joe of being cruel and indifferent. She received $500 a month in alimony, custody of Joe Jr. and $150 in monthly child support. They resumed an on-again, off-again relationship that turned off in 1946 when Arnold married George C. Schubert in Baltimore, Maryland, her second of three husbands.

Ferris Fain, who won AL batting titles in 1951 and 1952 as a member of the Philadelphia A's, was in the Army with DiMaggio. In an interview I did with Fain he noted, "DiMaggio was quiet, not very social. We were both staff sergeants. One time the commanding officer gave Joe and I a pass to get off the field. All I did was spend the night outside the telephone booth while he was on the phone talking to his wife, Dorothy, trying to reconcile with her."

Marilyn

"The Yankee Clipper had a penchant for blondes," said one former Yankee bat boy. DiMaggio met actress Marilyn Monroe, the most famous blonde in Hollywood in the '50s, through Gus Zernial, known as "Ozark Ike," a power-hitting outfielder for the

Chicago White Sox and Philadelphia/Kansas City A's in the '50s, who led the AL in home runs in '51 with 33. In 1951, the blonde bombshell showed up at the White Sox spring training camp in Palm Springs, California, and posed for a photo with Zernial. A rising Hollywood star, she was shooting *Monkey Business* at the time, a movie she starred in with Cary Grant, Ginger Rogers, and Charles Colburn. She had received a lot of publicity from different calendar photos. In 1949, desperate for money, she posed nude for a "Golden Dreams" calendar that hung in gas stations and garages.

"She was wearing a halter top, short shorts and very high heels," Zernial said. "She posed in a batter's stance. I was told to stand behind her, wrap my arms around her and show her how to hold a bat." DiMaggio saw Zernial at a charity game of retired old timers. "Joe saw the photo and asked about Marilyn," said Zernial. "I gave him the name of her business manager David March."

The two began to date seriously. DiMaggio hosted a Yankee pregame show in '52. "When Marilyn came to town, she would sit in the stands at Yankee Stadium or in the studio under the stands and watch him interview ballplayers," wrote Maury Allen in his book *Where You Have You Gone Joe DiMaggio? The Story of America's Last Hero*.

"A lot of guys would hang around that studio just to see her," recalled Rizzuto. "She was really gorgeous. She'd sit in the stands before the games and talk to some of the players. They were kids and just liked the idea of going home and telling their friends they knew a movie star. They really liked and admired her."

After two years of dating, America's most famous couple were married at 3:00 p.m. on January 14, 1954, at San Francisco City Hall. It was a marriage that captivated the nation. He was 37 and she was 25. Some theorize that it was a publicity stunt on the part of Monroe allowing her to leverage DiMaggio's stardom to add to her own. But credible accounts support the idea they were deeply in love.

The ceremony took place in the chamber of Municipal Court Judge Charles S. Perry. DiMaggio's friend Reno Barsocchini handled the arrangements. The game plan was to have a quiet, media-free ceremony. But word leaked out, and before it was over numerous photographers, reporters and curious fans were in the corridors outside the judge's chambers. Some believe that it was Marilyn who tipped off certain media members to the wedding plans.

It was reported that Mr. and Mrs. DiMaggio spent the first night of marriage at the Clifton Motel in the tiny beach town of Paso Robles before honeymooning in Mexico. The following month they went to Japan to extend their honeymoon and help kick off the baseball season there. Seeking refuge from intense media scrutiny, they accepted a three-week baseball junket invitation, their schedule put together by the *Yomiuri Shimbun* newspaper in coordination with the Japanese professional baseball league. Lefty O'Doul and his wife, Jean, accompanied the DiMaggios. O'Doul, a two-time NL batting champion, was a highly successful manager in the Pacific Coast League and managed DiMaggio during the nascent part of his professional baseball career when he played with the San Francisco Seals. O'Doul was known as the "father of modern Japanese baseball" due to his efforts to teach and popularize the sport in the "Land of the Rising Sun."

While enroute, Marilyn was offered a chance to entertain the troops in Korea. According to Liesl Bradner,

> Pan American Airways' new Boeing 377 Stratocruiser was just beginning its descent into Tokyo on February 1, 1954, when a high-ranking U.S. Army officer approached the plane's most celebrated passengers: Joe DiMaggio, the New York Yankees legend, and Marilyn

Monroe, the famous Hollywood star and sex symbol, whom DiMaggio had married just weeks earlier. Speaking with a slight Texas twang, Major General Charles W. Christenberry, the assistant chief of staff at the army's Far East Command, leaned over their seats to ask a question. "How would you like to visit Korea for a few days and entertain the American troops currently stationed in Seoul as part of the UN occupation force?" he asked.

"I'd like to," DiMaggio replied, "but I don't think I'll have time this trip."

"I wasn't asking you, Mr. DiMaggio," the general said. "My inquiry was directed at your wife."

Marilyn jumped at the offer.

Other accounts say she was asked to go to Korea after she was in Japan for several days.

Thousands of admirers were at the airport to get a glimpse of Marilyn, a 1953 *Playboy* centerfold and the star of the movie *Niagara*. She attracted more attention than her famous husband. She was the clean-up hitter on this trip.

The Korean War had ended but there were still 330,000 American troops there for the purpose of containing the Soviet sphere of influence. Mrs. DiMaggio left for Korea on February 16. The cultural icon made 10 stops and entertained an estimated 100,000 troops over a four-day run. The quickly thrown together show was titled "Anything Goes." The face of Hollywood dazzled the servicemen with her tight dresses that hugged her curvaceous body while she sang in a sexy voice "Diamonds Are a Girls's Best Friend," a song she sang in the 1953 movie *Gentlemen Prefer Blondes*.

My late father-in-law, Bill Kelly, was a cinematographer who often filmed NYC street scenes. He was on the crew that filmed *Pride of the Yankees* (the Lou Gehrig story), and on September 14, 1954, he was one of the movie photographers who recorded *The Seven Year Itch*. He was on location for the classic skirt-blowing scene in front of Manhattan's Trans-Lux 52nd Street Theater on Lexington Avenue. Bill Kobrin, 20th Century–Fox's East Coast correspondent, told the *Palm Springs Desert Sun* that it was director Billy Wilder's idea to turn the late-night shoot into a media circus. "It was two hours of craziness," said Marilyn's friend Amy Greene in the 2022 CNN series *Reframed: Marilyn Monroe*. "We thought it would be over in a minute and half. Wilder shot the scene 80 times to get one shot."

There was a large crowd of gawkers and onlookers, one of which was an unhappy Joe DiMaggio. "I was standing next to Joe," recalled Greene. "After about the tenth time the skirt went up, Joe began to tremble. I put my hand on his arm and said, 'It's just a movie, it's not real.'" He said, "I realize that but it's my wife showing off her panties." Joe turned around and left.

"DiMaggio was so embarrassed he walked away with Walter Winchell, the syndicated newspaper gossip columnist and radio news commentator, with whom he came with that day," said Mr. Kelly. "I had warned Winchell to take Joe off the set. I knew DiMaggio would be very upset what he was going to see." It was reported that later that evening, the DiMaggios quarreled in their St. Regis hotel room. It was also speculated that DiMaggio had struck her but that has never been proven.

The ill-fated union lasted only nine months, with the divorce coming in October of 1954, just 274 days after they were married. According to author Richard Ben Cramer, DiMaggio was abusive. The Yankee Clipper was looking for a housewife, a woman he could raise children with, but Marilyn's career came first. In her filing, Monroe accused her husband of "mental cruelty."

DiMaggio wanted the relationship to work and held on to it the rest of his life. The two became close friends. They attended the Yankees' 1961 spring training and were at the stadium together during the '61 season, including on Opening Day when Twins pitcher Pedro Ramos shut out Whitey Ford and the Yankees, 6–0. There were creditable reports that said the two were planning to remarry the day after she was found dead on August 5, 1962, at age 36 in Brentwood, an upper-crust neighborhood on the west side of Los Angeles. An investigation concluded that her death was a probable suicide from an overdose of a sleeping pill and the barbiturate Nembutal. But skeptics say it was a cover up and that she was actually murdered. Over the years her love life became as shrouded in mystery as the circumstances of her death. Those close to her dismiss the idea that she was murdered.

Memorabilia Boom

Following his playing career, DiMaggio spent several years in relative obscurity before appearing, incongruously, in the green and white uniform of the Oakland A's, serving as a coach and vice president for Charlie Finley's newly transplanted franchise in 1968–69. Then, in the 1970s, he reemerged as a national celebrity when he became a television spokesman for New York's Bowery Savings Bank and the Mr. Coffee coffeemaker. There is a generation of fans out there who only knew DiMaggio as "Mr. Coffee." But it was the memorabilia business that changed DiMaggio's financial fortunes. His pen proved mightier than his bat.

In a 2019 article written by Brian Warner for *Entertainment Magazine*, Warner wrote that DiMaggio's net worth in 1983 was $200,000. At the time of his death in 1999, his estate was estimated to be $50 million. During his playing career he reportedly earned $632,250. He earned $100,000 each year in 1949 and 1950, his highest-paying years in baseball, with bonus incentives. He took a $10,000 cut in 1951, his final season.

Joltin' Joe earned enormous sums of money doing autograph signings at various baseball card and memorabilia shows. The Yankee icon also did private signings, putting his John Hancock on bats, paintings, etc. In 1986 he signed 1,941 bats for Pro Sports to commemorate the 45th anniversary of his historic streak. DiMaggio kept numbers 56 and 1,941 for obvious reasons and Jerry Romolt from Pro Sports kept number 5, DiMaggio's uniform number. When he did a signing at a show, if the number of items exceeded a certain number, his fee went up. Industry sources will tell you that he normally received $150,000 per show.

Limited Edition Print

In the summer of '96, I received a call from a guy named Lars Tegenborg, whose New York company was involved with DiMaggio in promoting a limited edition print titled "My 56th Consecutive Game Hit." DiMaggio loved the lithograph that was the work of British realist artist Stephen Gardner, a graduate of Cornwall Art College in England. Gardner researched photos and rented videos to study DiMaggio's form. Not the easiest man to please, DiMaggio was impressed with how Gardner captured his physicality, swing and stance.

DiMaggio and Gardner signed 1,000 of them. The print sold for $495.95 plus $7.05 for shipping and handling. If you wanted the piece to be museum-mounted and framed, another $142.95 plus $18.95 for shipping and handling was added.

I was asked to write some promotional articles about DiMaggio's career in conjunction with the art piece. My desire was to interview him at his Florida home or some other designated location. I felt if I could spend enough time with him, I could gain his confidence and maybe come up with some fresh material instead of reheated popcorn.

I was aware that he never authorized a biography and getting the opportunity to go one-on-one with the Yankee legend would be no easy task. His aloofness was his armor. But his ambivalent relationship with fame always provided a glimmer of hope for writers. He enjoyed the attention the public bestowed upon him while desperately seeking to contain its borders. As David Halberstam wrote, "He was the keeper of his own flame."

After several weeks I was told by Tegenborg that it might be best if I submitted some questions to Morris Engelberg, DiMaggio's attorney. Through Engelberg, DiMaggio would provide answers which would give me some quotes that would embellish my articles.

The day before Game One of the 1996 World Series between the Yankees and the Atlanta Braves, I went to Yankee Stadium to obtain my postseason press credentials. After conducting interviews, I went upstairs to the Yankee offices to do more business. As I was standing in the waiting area, DiMaggio entered the room with a companion, a young fellow in his 30s. The Clipper looked tired, and his almost-82-year-old body was showing its age. He was uncharacteristically dressed in a brown checkered sports jacket. He wore an open collar minus a tie. This was unlike his usual natty dark suit and tie.

I was not quite as awestruck as I was that day in the elevator 11 years earlier. I calmly approached him and explained that I was commissioned to write some articles about his playing career to help promote the Gardner limited edition piece. I explained that I would love to interview him personally but was told it might be best if I submitted my questions to his attorney.

He looked at me a bit surprised and said, "You can interview me, but you know there are certain things you can't ask me."

I knew he was referring to Marilyn. It was well known that the mere mention of the Hollywood goddess would cause the Clipper to disappear. Joltin' Joe would become "Boltin' Joe."

I assured him that this would be strictly a baseball interview.

The next day I called Tegenborg with the exciting news that I met DiMaggio at Yankee Stadium and that he agreed to a direct interview. Tegenborg was equally excited. But to my dismay the interview never came to fruition. I simply took my place in an endless line of frustrated writers when dealing with the Yankee great. I understand that he also nixed a chance to appear on *Good Morning America* to promote the piece. Why DiMaggio would not want to help promote an art piece he loved and was generously paid for remained a mystery.

DiMaggio's Autograph

DiMaggio's signature was as elegant and meticulous as the suits he wore. But forgery of his autograph has been problematic. It was well known that forgeries from

10. Dorothy, Marilyn, and Memorabilia

clubhouse attendants, his sister, and other sources created challenges as to the authenticity of his signature. To be sure of its authenticity, getting a DiMaggio autograph in person was the safest.

Joe Carrieri was one of the first Yankee names in my life, as Mel Allen would often identify the Yankee bat boy on the air. Carrieri lived out the fantasy of every young boy. I always wondered what it was like in the Yankee clubhouse, the team's inner sanctum, which is where Carrieri grew into manhood. Thanks to his brother Ralph, who was a Yankee bat boy from 1946 to 1949, Carrieri was initially hired in '49 as a bat boy in the visiting team's clubhouse. The following year he was a Yankee ball boy before becoming a Yankee bat boy from 1951 to 1955. That was the order of progression.

Carrieri wrote a book titled *Joe DiMaggio: The Promise*. His bat boy activities at Yankee Stadium required him to leave school early when the Yankees played day games in the spring and fall. He was granted permission by Brother Colombo, the principal of St. Jerome's Grammar School in the Bronx, on the condition that he maintain a B+ average in all his subjects and discover why some players succeed where others fail. It proved to be the most meaningful long-term homework assignment that Carrieri ever received and helped in preparation for his Fordham education. Ted Williams said, "I visualize the entire game before I play it." But for a long time, DiMaggio never had time to talk to the kid, which was discouraging to the young bat boy. But he did promise he would have an answer for him.

I interviewed Carrieri on April 1, 1995, at the Queens College gym in Flushing, New York, where there was a Double D Promotions collectors show. The purpose of the show was to commemorate the 40th anniversary of the 1955 World Series. Many former Yankees and Dodgers who played on those teams signed at the show.

When Carrieri arrived on the scene in '49, one of his first objectives was to get DiMaggio's autograph. His first encounter with DiMaggio came during his first day on the job. When he saw the Clipper in the clubhouse he turned to his brother Ralph and asked for a pen and something to write on. Ralph, composed and in control, said, "Gimme a break, Joe. That's bush league."

His brother Ralph talked about DiMaggio's signing habits and his personality. "He is very shy, very reserved," said Ralph. "It will be next to impossible to get him to share his thoughts. He rarely talks and he even rarely talks about himself. In fact, DiMaggio is a loner, has very few friends and is not cooperative when asked to sign a baseball. He rarely gives his autograph out and even refuses to sign a baseball when he knows it's for a fellow player. That's the way he is. Other players leave him alone and don't even bother to ask for his autograph. They go straight to Pete Sheehy [a clubhouse man] who signs a real good 'Joe DiMaggio.'"

Carrieri was shocked by his brother Ralph's bluntness and how uncooperative DiMaggio seemed to be. "I found this awfully strange as I could not separate DiMaggio the ballplayer from DiMaggio the man," lamented Joe.

In Carrieri's book he told how waiters were able to get his autograph. It was rumored that the waiters competed with one another for the honor of serving DiMaggio his dinner and that after he signed the check the waiter never turned in the tabs. "They knew these mementos bearing Joe's signature would be collector's items someday," wrote Carrieri.

Although DiMaggio came across as aloof, Carrieri, who became a lawyer in Mineola, New York, specializing in child adoption cases, found a different side of him with the passing of time. The two developed a cordial relationship. When the bat boy traveled with the team, DiMaggio would have him bring newspapers and cigarettes up to his hotel room and the two on occasion would watch boxing matches together on TV.

Following his retirement in '51, DiMaggio visited the Yankee clubhouse and requested to see Carrieri and offer his formula for success. "Sheehy called me," recalled Carrieri. "I ran 27 blocks to Yankee Stadium. I had waited three years for this moment. DiMaggio said in part, 'Always be a student. And as long as you live, you always have more to learn.'" Following his words of wisdom, the Yankee legend then reached into his locker and handed Carrieri one of his game bats. "It was his 1951 All-Star game bat," said Carrieri. "It was inscribed, 'All Star Game—Joe DiMaggio—Detroit 1951.'"

Joe DiMaggio had kept his promise.

I spoke to Carrieri in December 2021 while he was battling Covid. "I sold the bat for $40,000 about 20 years ago," he said.

The Cracker Jack Classic

I was aware that DiMaggio was highly protective of his privacy and could be moody.

Between 1982 and 1990, an annual old timer's game known as the Cracker Jack Classic was played first at RFK Stadium in Washington, D.C., and then in Buffalo its last three years. It was the brainchild of former Atlanta Braves vice president Dick Cecil. The players each received $1,000 plus travel expenses. No one got more—and the only player who appeared at all nine games was DiMaggio. The 1990 game was believed to be the last time he wore a uniform, although he no longer took a turn at-bat. At the 1985 game it was strange to see him in the red (of all colors) American League uniform.

I attended the Classic the first three years with my wife, Lois, and sons Richie and Brian. I thought this would be a unique way to teach my sons U.S. history, touring the great sites in Washington, D.C., and learning some baseball history. Where else would they be able to see baseball dignitaries the likes of Feller, Warren Spahn, Stan Musial, Hank Aaron, Willie Mays, Sandy Koufax, Roger Maris, Whitey Ford, DiMaggio and others on the same field?

A forever Yankee, Joe DiMaggio shed his pinstripes for his red American League uniform at the July 1, 1985, Cracker Jack Old-Timers' Game in Washington, D.C.

10. Dorothy, Marilyn, and Memorabilia

At the time I was a research assistant for ESPN broadcaster George Grande on a weekly Sunday night show titled *Inside Baseball.* To help Grande with his interviews, my job at the Cracker Jack Classic was to prepare biographical information for the players in attendance.

On July 18, 1982, the night before the first Cracker Jack Classic Old-Timers' game, I attended a party for the players and their wives at the Hyatt Regency while Lois stayed at our hotel with the boys. The large banquet room was filled with former great players and their wives, many of whom played in DiMaggio's era. There were luminaries like Luke Appling, Hal Newhouser, Phil Cavaretta, Mize and others. They ate, drank and exchanged stories from the halcyon days of baseball. Music added to the merriment of the evening. To the amazement of everyone, Appling, at age 75, would hit a home run the following night.

In 1982, I co-authored a book with Seattle native Len Fiorito titled *Aaron to Zuverink: A Nostalgic Look at the Baseball Players of the 1950s.* Every player who appeared in a big league box score between 1950 and 1959 is profiled in the book along with their post playing careers. It totaled more than 1,500 players. As a hobby I decided to get as many players as I could to sign their profiles. At this writing I have about 330 signatures.

The gathering proved to be an autograph bonanza. I circled the room, took photos, and politely asked many players to sign their profile in the book. They all obliged with kindness and interest. During the evening, I inadvertently encountered the reclusive DiMaggio sitting in a conference room in the rear of the main room isolated from the crowd of 200 or more. I couldn't believe my eyes. I nervously paced for a while wondering if I should break the barrier that was protecting DiMaggio from the large crowd. I knew DiMaggio, who belonged on baseball's Mount Rushmore, could be difficult. But I adhered to one of life's great lessons: "if you don't ask, the answer is always no."

I finally mustered up enough courage and identified myself before asking if he would sign his profile in my book. I thought with his Sicilian blood he might see me as a Paisano, a compatriot Italian friend. But that did not impress him one bit. He gave me a sustained strained look before he acknowledged my request. It was the longest unnerving five seconds of my life.

In retrospect I had invaded, if only briefly, a tiny enclave of his guarded private life. He most likely saw me as a media guy infringing on his privacy or some yahoo that wanted to sell his autograph. But I lucked out.

The last time I saw the Yankee Clipper was Joe DiMaggio Day, celebrated on September 27, 1996, at Yankee Stadium, a picturesque fall afternoon. Rizzuto presented him with a set of replica World Series rings since his were stolen many years before. DiMaggio was driven around the stadium in a '56 Thunderbird to commemorate his enduring hitting streak. He waved to the crowd in his papal way. It proved to be his goodbye.

Joe DiMaggio died on March 8, 1999, at age 84 in Hollywood, Florida, of lung cancer. His troubled son, Joe DiMaggio, Jr., who battled drug and alcohol problems, passed five months later on August 6 at age 57 of what was reported as natural causes. He spent one year at Yale where he played on the freshman football team in 1960 before joining the Marines. The father and son were estranged for many years. But Joe was very close to his son's adopted two daughters.

To generations of fans, Joe DiMaggio was always a hero despite his shortcomings. Simon and Garfunkel's 1968 hit song "Mrs. Robinson" expressed nostalgia for a simpler, more innocent time by asking, "Where have you gone Joe DiMaggio? A nation turns its lonely eyes to you." The song was a reaction to the turmoil of the time—the Vietnam War, the assassinations of Dr. Martin Luther King, Bobby Kennedy, and other events. The country was hungry for a hero. In Simon's eyes the Yankee Clipper remained an American hero at a time when genuine heroes were in short supply.

Joe DiMaggio was an American hero. But at his funeral a niece said, "My uncle was a lonesome hero."

11

"The Mick"

The name Lew Rothgeb probably doesn't ring a bell. I became acquainted with Rothgeb through my radio show in the late '90s. According to Rothgeb, he was Mickey Mantle's closest friend after Billy Martin died in a motor vehicle mishap on Christmas Day in 1989. Rothgeb provided me with numerous Mickey Mantle calendars that he published in the late '90s that I used for trivia prizes on my show.

Based in San Francisco, he was an executive film producer who developed a style of documentary in which there is no narrator and the interviewer is not seen but his questions are heard. It captures the essence of the subject's personality through his own stories, selected and told by the individual himself in his own way. Mantle agreed to sit with Rothgeb and in 1988 *Mickey Mantle: The American Dream Comes to Life* hit the market with a clout as loud as one of Mantle's 536 blasts.

Rothgeb's relationship with the Mick goes back to his childhood. When Rothgeb was seven years old, he had a fantasy-like experience when he met Mantle at Griffith Stadium in Washington, D.C. Rothgeb had a special gift for the Yankee slugger. "I made a plaque of Mickey and titled it 'Mickey Mantle, the World's Greatest Player,'" said Rothgeb. "I went down near the dugout and asked the usher if I could see Mickey. I showed my project to the usher, and he told me to wait."

To the pleasant surprise of the young boy, Mantle emerged from the dugout and the usher allowed young Lew to present the plaque to Mantle. "He was very gracious," recalled Rothgeb. "He took me down to the field. Every time the Yankees were in town I went down by the field and chatted with him."

The Rothgeb/Mantle relationship grew over the years. During the '80s and '90s, Mantle was a rock star at baseball card shows, and like DiMaggio, he made loads of money. "Mickey called me one night at midnight," Rothgeb remembered. "He said, 'Hey, bud. It's Mickey.'"

Rothgeb said, "Where are you?"

"I'm in a limousine," Mantle answered. "I'm on the way to the Fairmount Hotel [in San Francisco]."

"I got to the hotel at 1:00 a.m. and went up to his room," Rothgeb said. "We talked and decided to go down to the cocktail lounge for a couple of drinks when he asked if the room was safe. He wanted to know if it would be okay if he stashed money under the bed mattress. He said, 'I've got $100,000 in cash.' I immediately told him to put the money in a hotel safe."

In 1987 Rothgeb visited Mantle at Christmas. At the time, the film producer had not planned to do anything with him, but while the two talked, bells went off. "In the middle of explaining to him my concept of videography, I realized it would work with him," stated Rothgeb. "Mickey obliged so my attorney put together an agreement with his attorney."

Rothgeb was well aware of Mantle's drinking problems and friends told him to stay away from the Hall of Fame center fielder concerning the video project because he was a drunk. "When I went to Mickey's house in Dallas, Texas, to begin the production, he was smashed and in no condition to do it," lamented Rothgeb. "I told him that I had a lot of money invested in the project. I went back to San Francisco and returned to Dallas a short time later. This time Mickey was ready, and we did it."

In April of '88 Rothgeb and his crew began shooting for several days at Yankee Stadium. In June, the taping was completed in Mantle's home. "I monitored Mickey's drinking carefully," recalled Rothgeb. "Fortunately, things worked out well."

The premiere of *Mickey Mantle: The American Dream Comes to Life* took place at the Hilton in Oakland in September 1988, with Mantle in attendance. The video was shown to all of the Yankees and A's players since the Yankees were in town. Don Mattingly was there along with Dave Righetti, Jose Canseco, Dave Parker and others. The party was embellished with a cast of 200 gorgeous models. With invitees and select others, the audience numbered about 500.

That's quite a splash for a baseball video.

The expectation of the crowd was not very high as they anticipated another corny baseball film. However, it was a great excuse for a party and Mantle was elated. It was no secret that women and booze were a strong part of his DNA. And to the surprise of many, the video proved to be a grand slam. "The people went nuts," noted Rothgeb. "At the end I introduced Mickey. I said, 'Ladies and gentlemen, Mickey Mantle.'"

"Mickey was overwhelmed by the Roger Maris material in the video—he was crying," Rothgeb added. "Mickey put his arm around me with tears running down his face and said, 'Lew, you done good, you done real good, you really done good.' I almost started crying. It was one of the great experiences of my life," Rothgeb said proudly.

In the sports, fitness and recreation ratings, it ranked number three in '89 and number one in '90. Rothgeb received kudos from celebrities like Paul Simon, Billy Crystal and George Will. He even received a letter from Donald Trump. "It was written on a gold type stationery that had to be valued at $10 a sheet," cackled Rothgeb.

Over the years Rothgeb made several visits to Mantle's Dallas home. On one occasion he was looking through his memorabilia and came across a team signed photo of the '53 Yankees. "This was one of his favorite teams," said Rothgeb, "because that club won an unprecedented five straight world championships. I told Mickey to frame it because it was a really valuable piece."

While admiring Mantle's apparently disorganized collection, he amazingly came across the gift that he had given Mantle at Griffith Stadium when he was a child. "I couldn't believe it when I came across the plaque I had given him many years ago," said the astonished film producer. "The plaque was not well done, and I couldn't believe he kept it."

Rothgeb appeared to be on the brink of a new chapter in his career when his life came to an abrupt halt after he was in a serious car accident at JFK airport in New York City. He suffered a fractured neck and back and was in rehab for six years.

The Rothgeb/Mantle story is comparable to Mickey Mantle's life. It's the story of a beloved baseball hero who was haunted by alcoholism and lived life loosely yet saved a gift given to him by a child that for many would have no value.

It tells you something about Mickey Charles Mantle.

A Fictitious Character

Mantle might not have been the greatest player of his era, but he was arguably the most charismatic. As kids, we imitated his unique baseball mannerisms. We rolled up our shirt sleeves above our developing biceps, we creased our baseball caps, we trotted with his limping gait, head tilted forward, and we tried to switch-hit like he did. We did everything except run and hit a baseball like he did.

A cauldron of noise accompanied each Mantle at-bat. It started with his emergence from the dugout. After he skipped up the stairs, he knelt in the on-deck circle on one knee with his forearms resting on the handle of his bat. His relaxed hands dangled from his powerful wrists and forearms. When it was time for him to stroll to the plate, the roar of the stadium crowd reached a crescendo drowning out Bob Sheppard announcing, "Number 7 … Mickey Mantle … center field … number 7."

When Mantle stepped into the batter's box, time stopped. Ushers as well as fans became totally focused on the Mick. In homes throughout the tri-state area, people arranged their personal schedules around a Mantle at-bat.

If the game of baseball ever had a nearly fictitious character, it was Mantle. He was blond, handsome and well-muscled. Women loved him and men admired him. He was the model male, an Adonis in knickers. He had the speed of a runaway mustang and the power of an Aaron Judge. "With his combination of speed and power, he should win the Triple Crown every year," said former Yankees manager Casey Stengel. Combine his Oklahoma country boy innocence and his ability to hit a baseball to the moon from either side of the plate, and one can say the man bordered fiction. Red Smith wrote, "He didn't just hit the ball, he pounded it into oblivion."

Ruth hit home runs from the left side, DiMaggio hit home runs from the right side. Mantle hit them from both sides. He could beat you playing long ball or getting on base via a drag bunt. "He was the best two-strike bunter I ever saw," said Rizzuto. He was clocked at 3.1 seconds from home to first batting on the left side. Watching the Mick stretch a single into a double, finishing with his patented stand-up slide, and listening to the crescendo of crowd explode with jubilation was baseball beauty.

And he could go get 'em in the outfield. "He always belittled his fielding," said former outfielder Rocky Colavito, who played with Mantle in '68. "But he was an outstanding outfielder. One time he was playing me to pull in left center and I hit the ball to right center. I was coming around first, and he was eating up ground. He made a one-handed catch I couldn't believe."

Mantle rose far above the game. He was the first superstar in the era of televised baseball. Appel respected Mantle's place in the pantheon of Yankee greats. One year in spring training he had every Yankee hopeful in the organization take their picture with Mantle. "I knew they would cherish the photo the rest of their lives," said the former Yankees public relations director.

When Mantle arrived at spring training in '51, clubhouse manager Pete Sheehy gave him uniform number 6, the implication being that Mantle was expected to be the next great Yankee and therefore should succeed Ruth (3), Gehrig (4), and DiMaggio (5). He later would change to number 7. Sheehy proved prophetic.

While Mantle wore pinstripes from 1951 through 1968, the Yankees won 12 American League pennants and seven World Series. He dominated the American League for more than a decade, charting his path to Cooperstown. In 1956, he not only won the

Former Yankees public relations director Marty Appel chats with Mickey Mantle during 1970 spring training in Fort Lauderdale, Florida (courtesy Marty Appel).

Triple Crown in the AL, but he also led both leagues in batting average, home runs and runs batted in when he hit .353 with 52 homers and 130 RBI. This was the last time any player led both leagues in the Triple Crown categories. His 1956 salary of $32,000 jumped to $60,000 in '57, a year he batted .365 with 34 homers and 94 RBI. By the standards of any era, it was an outstanding season. But George Weiss, the frugal Yankees general manager, wanted to cut Mantle's salary $10,000. "That year I didn't lead the league in everything," Mantle quipped. Mantle held out before the start of the '58 season, and Weiss threatened to trade him. "Mr. Weiss said if I didn't sign in a day or two he was going to trade me to Cleveland for Rocky Colavito and Herb Score," recalled Mantle. "I showed up the next day."

In this bygone era of player salaries, the Mick settled for a $5,000 raise for the '58 season and earned $65,000 that year. But Weiss eventually got his $10,000 cut. In '59 Mantle was making $70,000 when he hit "only" .285 with 31 HRs and 75 RBI. For the '60 season he signed for $60,000. After his '61 season, when he hit .317 with 54 homers and a league-leading 126 RBI, he received a $20,000 raise. Apparently, the Yankees realized the injustice and for the final six years of his career he was paid $100,000 each season.

In his career, he batted .300 or better 10 times. He hit 536 home runs and collected

1,509 RBI. He was voted the American League MVP in '56, '57, and '62. The Mick paced the league in OPS six times, finishing with a sterling .977 OPS. For comparison, his counterpart Willie Mays, who many consider the greatest player ever, had a .940 OPS in his 23-year career. Mantle was on 20 All-Star rosters and appeared in 16 games. In '64, facing the Angels' Fred Newman, he recorded his 2,000th hit in the sixth inning, joining Ruth, Gehrig, DiMaggio, and Berra as the only Yankees with 2,000 hits at the time. He became the idol of an entire generation of kids who continued to worship him as adults decades later.

Mantle was a clutch hitter. An underrated aspect of his career is how he performed in late and close games. According to Baseball-Reference.com, he hit .323 in those situations—that is, the seventh inning or later when his team is tied or ahead by one or the tying run is at least on deck.

If there was one pitcher who had Mantle's number, it was Red Sox relief ace Dick "the Monster" Radatz. Mantle had 16 official at-bats versus Radatz and fanned 12 times. As the story goes, on one occasion, Mantle was so frustrated with his inability to hit Radatz that after a strikeout he yelled, "That fuckin' monster." The scribes in the press box picked it up and the "Monster" moniker stuck to Radatz.

The Mick flourished on the grandest stage, batting .257 with a ML record 18 home runs and 40 RBI over 65 WS games. His OPS was a glittering .908. He especially loved the Yankees-Dodgers Subway Series played in '52, '53, '55, and '56. "I loved it—city against city right here in town," recalled Mantle. "I used to love the bus rides from downtown. The Yankee bus would pick up Billy Martin and me and go over to Brooklyn. If we beat them, the Brooklyn fans would throw tomatoes at us while we were in the bus leaving the park."

In an interview he did with Warner Wolff following his career, Mantle talked about the time he was the star of the game in Brooklyn and a guest on Happy Felton's *Knothole Gang* game show. "You had to go through a bar in uniform to get to a back room where the show was televised from," laughed Mantle.

For the most part, Mantle's WS appearances resulted in astounding memories. But the 1960 Fall Classic proved to be a downer that gnawed at Mantle for years. The Yankees outscored the Pittsburgh Pirates 55 to 27. The Bombers batted .338 to Pittsburgh's .256. But the Bucs won the close games and the Series on Bill Mazeroski's walk-off home run in Game Seven at Forbes Field facing Ralph Terry. Game Seven of the '60 series is the only game in postseason history in which not one strikeout was recorded by either team. "With the exception of my dad dying, it was the biggest disappointment of my life," said Mantle somberly.

After years of brilliance, Mantle's career began to decline by 1967, and he was forced to move to first base. The next season would be his last. He retired with a .298 batting average. If he had walked away after the '67 season, his career average would stand at .302. He always regretted riding into the sunset under the .300 mark. He is the cautionary tale for a player who hung on one year too long.

Whether you saw one of his 1,710 strikeouts or 1,733 walks or were able to gasp at his Herculean home runs, the man was electric. One can only speculate how many homers he lost playing in his home park. "When I played, Yankee Stadium was 461 feet to dead center, 457 feet to left center, and 407 feet to right center," noted Mantle. "If I played in Ebbets Field or Detroit, I would have hit over 700 home runs." A natural right-handed hitter who was not a pull hitter, Mantle believed he lost at least 10 homers a year at spacious Yankee Stadium. If so, you can add 180 dingers to his total 536. Of course, the cozy right field porch was an ally for the Yankee slugger as it was for Ruth and Gehrig.

Mantle also had a great knuckleball. "Mickey was a jokester, and most people don't know he had the best knuckleball in baseball," said former second baseman Bobby Richardson. "Anytime a rookie came up, we'd tell him we'd give him $100 if they could catch three of Mickey's knuckleballs in a row. So [catcher] Jake Gibbs came up, he was a football player, a Heisman Trophy candidate out of the University of Mississippi. He caught Mickey's first knuckleball, but the second danced right around his glove and hit him right in the nose and broke it. They had to send him back [to the minors], and we had to stop offering $100 bets to rookies."

"The Mick" and Me

In 1986 Mantle did color commentary for Yankee games for SportsChannel New York, the first regional sports network in this country. This was not his first venture in the broadcast booth. He served as a part-time color commentator on NBC's baseball coverage in 1969, teaming with Curt Gowdy and Tony Kubek to call some *Game of the Week* telecasts as well as that year's All-Star game. In 1972 he was a part-time TV commentator for the Montreal Expos.

One afternoon during the summer of '86 I got to the stadium around four o'clock, three hours before the scheduled night game. I would often go to the press area and research old Yankees scrapbooks to dig out some plays that I could use for my rules column in *Yankees Magazine*. Around 4:45 the Yankees were taking batting practice and I noticed Mantle standing behind the batting cage. I couldn't take my eye off him while I looked at old newspaper clippings. The Mick was always the magnet in the room. His presence was hypnotic. I decided to head downstairs to see if I could meet him and do an impromptu interview for *Sports Collectors Digest*.

I sprinted to the elevator about 100 feet or so from the press area. I got down to the field level and ran toward the tunnel adjacent to the Yankees clubhouse that would get me to the field. My timing was perfect. Just as I emerged from the Yankees dugout, Mantle was headed in my direction. I identified myself and politely asked if he had a few minutes for an interview. He looked at his watch and said, "Sure, let's go to the press dining room."

This was a thrilling experience. It was hard to believe that I was about to go one-on-one with one of baseball's all-time icons. I had my tape recorder ready to go. Fortunately, because of Mantle's popularity and history, I knew enough about his background that I was able to conduct the interview without notes. I reflected a false bravado while my stomach was churning like a cement mixer. But I wasn't about to choke and blow the whole thing.

Born in 1931 in Spavinaw, Oklahoma, Mantle was raised during the Great Depression in the Dust Bowl mining city of Commerce, Oklahoma. His family struggled to survive. His father, Mutt, was a farmer and later a lead miner. Mutt admired Hall of Fame catcher Mickey Cochrane and named his son after him. He also was ahead of the curve and realized the advantages a switch-hitter would have.

"I was lucky I had a father that knew a lot about baseball," stated Mantle. "My dad was a great student of the game. He knew that someday there would be platooning in baseball. If I could hit both ways, I would have a lot better chance of playing." He added, "I had about ten friends. We would choose up sides every day and play ball all day long. I really believe that might be the best thing to do for young kids. Sometimes I would hit 100 times a day. Experience is a great teacher."

Marty Appel tells this story relating to Mantle's roots.

"One spring training, Mick and I and I think two others walked a few hundred feet to a movie theater near our hotel in Fort Lauderdale," remembered Appel. "*The Last Picture Show* was playing. When we walked out, I noticed Mickey wiping a tear off his cheek."

Was Mickey Mantle crying?

"'Hell, that was just like the town I grew up in,' he said. 'We even had a village idiot, just like them.'"

Mantle attended Commerce High School, which did not have a baseball team. But that was not a big deal because football was the sport closest to his heart. Although his fame and fortune came in the game of baseball, he probably would have traded his sliding pads for shoulder pads, if given the choice. His lightning speed was an obstacle for opposing tacklers. He modestly boasted, "I wasn't a head-butter, but if I got around end I could out-run everybody."

Unfortunately, football dogged him throughout his baseball career because of an injury he suffered his freshman year in high school in 1946 when he was kicked in the shin. Within hours his ankle had swollen to three times its normal size, and he developed a 104-degree fever. His parents took him to the local hospital, where doctors diagnosed him with osteomyelitis, a potentially fatal bone disease that had been aggravated by the injury. Doctors reportedly told the Mantles that they had to amputate the leg to save their child's life.

"Mickey's parents sought a second opinion at the Crippled Children's Hospital in Oklahoma City," wrote James Lincoln Ray for the Society for American Baseball Research. "Doctors there agreed that he had osteomyelitis, but they had a much less drastic treatment plan: eight shots a day of a new wonder drug called penicillin. Within a week the swelling in Mickey's ankle dissipated, and he was soon back in sports. His football career was over, but his baseball life was just beginning."

By the time he was 15, Mantle was playing semipro ball with the Baxter Springs Whiz Kids, a local team mostly made up of miners and former high-school stars. One day late in the '48 season, New York Yankees scout Tom Greenwade came to Baxter Springs to evaluate one of Mantle's teammates, a third baseman named Billy Johnson. This was not the Billy Johnson who played third base for the Bombers between 1943 and 1951.

Shortly after high school in '49 Mantle was signed to a Yankee contract by Greenwade as a shortstop for $400 for the remainder of the summer and a $1,150 bonus. After stops at Independence in the Class D Kansas, Oklahoma, and Missouri League and Class C Joplin (1950) where he batted .383 with 26 homers, the Yankees brought him up at the end of the season as a non-roster player, but he did not see any action. He joined the team at Sportsman's Park in St. Louis. The Yanks also brought up Bill Skowron and the two lived together at the Grand Concourse Hotel in the Bronx. "Mickey was very shy," recalled Skowron, the former Yankee first baseman. "He was shy all of his life unless he knew you."

1951

During his rookie season he shared an apartment above the Stage Deli in New York City with Hank Bauer and Johnny Hopp. Bauer saw that Mantle was dressed like a hayseed and took him shopping at some of the finer men's stores to upgrade his wardrobe.

"The day before his first spring training Mickey got off the train wearing a pair of rolled-up pants that looked like Dockers of today," recalled Bauer. "He was wearing white sweat socks and Hush Puppies shoes. I forgot what kind of shirt he had but his tie had a great big peacock on it, and he was wearing a tweed sport coat. When we got to New York I said, 'Mickey, you can't dress like that in New York. Tomorrow morning I'll take you out and buy you two suits.' I took Mickey to Isenberg and Isenberg and bought him two sharkskin suits for $35 each. He never forgot it."

Mantle made his ML debut on April 17, 1951, playing right field in the Yankees opener against the Red Sox at Yankee Stadium that drew 44,860 fans. He batted third in the middle of a cascade of stars that included Jackie Jensen (LF), Phil Rizzuto (SS), Joe DiMaggio (CF), Yogi Berra (C), Johnny Mize (1B), Billy Johnson (3B), Jerry Coleman (2B), and Vic Raschi (P).

Before the game Berra walked up to Mantle and said, "Hey, kid, are you nervous?"

Mantle said, "No."

Yogi joked, "Well, how come you're wearing your jockstrap on the outside of your uniform?"

In his first at-bat in the bottom of the first, facing lefty Bill Wight, he grounded out to Hall of Fame second baseman Bobby Doerr. He collected his first of 2,415 big league hits in the bottom of the sixth off Wight, a line drive to left field that was fielded by Hall of Famer Ted Williams. Berra knocked in Mantle that inning which led to the Yankees' 5–0 win.

Mantle managed to scratch out a few hits but was 0-for-April in the home run department. The glitter and tinsel of the majors was no longer fun. The fans jeered and taunted him. His mastery of kicking water coolers and smashing bats grabbed more headlines than his play on the field.

"It was a bad fault I had," admitted Mantle when we spoke. "I never really did get over it. I still can't stand to lose. If I'm playing golf and make a bad shot, I'll throw a golf club. One time I hit a caddy in the back with a sand wedge. It's a bad habit but I'd rather see a guy who gets mad when he doesn't do good than one who doesn't care."

Mantle's first home run came at Comiskey Park in Chicago on May 1 when he went yard in the sixth inning off White Sox right-hander Randy Gumpert. It was a 450-foot blast that landed in the Yankees bullpen in center field. "He hit a screwball that didn't screw as much as it should have," said Gumpert, who signed a ball for me with the inscription "I gave up Mickey Mantle's first home run—May 1, 1951."

The ball Mantle hit was caught by back-up catcher Charlie Silvera who gave the ball to Mantle. Silvera later told Gumpert, "If I had known what I was doing, I would have kept that ball and gotten $45,000 for it." Of course, Silvera was talking long before the memorabilia boom of the 1980s. A representative of Leland's Auction House said, "With the proper provenance it could go for over one million dollars in today's market—maybe more."

In the late '50s and early '60s, the ball was displayed in Mantle's restaurant in Joplin, Missouri, which opened in 1957. It was called Mickey Mantle's Holiday Inn and

Mantle was part owner with Harold Youngman. Besides lending his name to the restaurant and receiving a share of the profits, Mantle contributed some of his memorabilia for show and came up with the slogan for the fried chicken served there: "To get a better piece of chicken, you'd have to be a rooster." The motel was sold in 1965 for a substantial profit.

On May 18, 1951, he was hitting .316 with four home runs and a team high 26 RBI before crashing the next 21 games when he hit .197 and struck out 21 times. On July 13 the temperamental Yankee rookie was sent to Kansas City, the Yankees Triple-A affiliate. He was crushed and his confidence cracked like a broken bat. He was ready to quit. But his father challenged his manhood and influenced him to stay. In the next few weeks, he went on a tear, hitting .361 with 11 home runs and 50 RBI.

In 1951 he received a draft-examine notice and was about to be drafted by the U.S. Army but failed the physical exam and was rejected as unqualified and given a 4-F deferment for any military service because of his chronic osteomyelitis. He was reexamined and remained classified as 4-F. This led to hate mail and letters from parents of soldiers who called him a draft dodger during the Korean War, which lasted from 1950 to 1953.

It was back to New York in late August. The Yankees had a blue-chip stock in Mantle. Their future was guaranteed. Mantle finished his rookie campaign hitting .267 with 13 home runs and 65 RBI. Despite the fact that he was a marquee rookie and the heir apparent to DiMaggio, teammate Gil McDougald, a master utility infielder, was voted the AL Rookie of the Year in '51 when he hit .306. McDougald would be selected to the All-Star game at second base, shortstop, and third base. He was the glue that held the Yankees infield together in the '50s.

World Series Injury

Mantle's freshman season was a rollercoaster of events. In the World Series against the Giants, bad fortune met the Yankee rookie in the sixth inning of Game Two at Yankee Stadium. Willie Mays hit a pop fly in right center between Mantle and DiMaggio. Mantle heard DiMag yell "I got it" and held up, catching the spikes of his right shoe on the rubber cover of a drain hole buried in the grass. Mantle was removed from the game and sent to Lenox Hill Hospital where he had surgery for torn ligaments. His father, Mutt, rode with him to the hospital. When Mickey leaned on his father on a curb near the hospital entrance, Mutt collapsed. Both ended up in the hospital and watched the '51 World Series together on TV.

Mutt was diagnosed with Hodgkin's disease, a cancer that strikes the body's lymph nodes. He would lose his battle with the disease at age 39. Those who worked for many years in the mines were at risk for lung disease, heart ailments, and cancer. In fact, cancer had been the Grim Reaper of the Mantle family, claiming, among others, Mantle's uncle, his grandfather, and a couple of other relatives, all in their 40s or younger. Because he always thought he would die young, Mantle lived his life full throttle.

During the mid-sixties, the Yankee dynasty collapsed with a dramatic thud. "Everybody got old at the same time," reasoned the Yankee slugger. "It was like a balloon busting. Also, when other teams were paying big bonuses, Dan Topping and Del Webb

[Yankee owners] didn't come out with the $50,000 bonuses so our minor league system deteriorated."

The argument still rages as to who was the greatest center fielder in New York during the '50s? Was it Willie, Mickey or the Duke?

"I never felt a personal rivalry," Mantle said. "Mays has some great statistics. He played many years without getting hurt. The bottom line is what you have to look at and he had it. As for me, Willie was the greatest." But, he added, "there were four or five years through there when I was better than he was."

The Mick stroked the final home run of his career on September 20, 1968, against Red Sox right-hander Jim Lonborg at Yankee Stadium in a meaningless Friday night game before a slim crowd of 15,137. The third-inning clout gave the Yanks a 1–0 lead in a game they would lose, 4–3.

Mantle played his last home game five days later in a 3–0 loss to the Cleveland Indians. He got the only Yankee hit in the game off Luis Tiant. It was a two-out single to center in the first inning. Tiant pitched hitless ball the remaining 8⅓ innings. The Wednesday afternoon tilt drew an announced crowd of 5,723. The Yankees, who finished fifth (83–79–2) in '68, no longer played critical games in front of thousands. This game ended a glorious Mantle era at Yankee Stadium.

Mantle played the final game of his career three days later at Fenway Park. Facing Lonborg in the top of the first inning, he hit a polite pop-up to shortstop Rico Petrocelli. In the bottom of the inning, he went out to his position at first base and threw the customary warm-up ground balls to infielders Horace Clarke (2b), Tom Tresh (ss) and Bobby Cox (3b). Mel Stottlemyre was on the mound taking his warm-ups when Fenway PA announcer Sherm Feller announced Mike Andrews as the first Red Sox batter. At that point, Yankees' manager Ralph Houk sent Andy Kosco to first base to replace Mantle. The Fenway fans gave the broken-down Yankee a standing ovation. Mantle never played another game.

On March 1, 1969, Mantle announced his retirement from baseball. On June 8, Mickey Mantle Day was held at Yankee Stadium. His number 7 was retired before 61,157 screaming fans. Mel Allen, the celebrated Yankees announcer, introduced Mantle. In his eloquent way, he announced, "This is one of the proudest moments I ever had on this hallowed baseball ground. And I'm terribly privileged to have the honor to once again call from the dugout, one of the all-time Yankee greats, the magnificent Yankee, the great number 7, Mickey Mantle." The fans gave him a nine-minute ovation that could be heard on Broadway.

In his speech he said, "I've often wondered how a man who knew he was going to die could stand here and say he was the luckiest man on the face of the earth, but now I guess I know how he felt."

12

The Two Mickeys

"For a baseball biographer, documenting the landscape is an essential part of holding myth accountable to history," wrote Jane Leavy. When chronicling many of Mantle's prodigious home runs, this can be a challenge.

In 1951 the Yankees and Giants switched spring training camps with the Yankees going to Phoenix, Arizona, and the Giants going to St. Petersburg, Florida. Mantle hit .387 with a team high nine home runs and 28 RBI.

The Yankees played the USC Trojans on March 26, 1951, in an exhibition game at Bovard Field on the campus of the University of Southern California. That day Mantle went 4-for-4 including two home runs, one of which was estimated to travel an estimated 550 or 600 feet.

Was that myth, hyperbole, or fact?

The "Commerce Comet" hit 266 of his 536 home runs at Yankee Stadium—two almost left the stately basilica. The first one came on May 30, 1956, in the first game of a Memorial Day doubleheader against the Washington Senators. Batting against Senators right-hander Pedro Ramos, Mantle hit a moon shot that struck the picturesque frieze above the upper deck in right field, fewer than 18 inches from the top, scoring Bauer and McDougald. Courtesy of Mantle, that ball was showcased in teammate Eddie Robinson's restaurant in Baltimore for a time. Robinson played first base for the Yankees that game. He explained how he got the ball.

"The Senators right fielder [Jim Lemon] got it and gave it to the ball boy, who gave it to Mickey. In the clubhouse after the game Mickey yelled over to me and said, 'Hey, Eddie, how would you like the baseball for your restaurant?' He threw it over to me. I displayed the ball behind the bar. I put the ball up for auction at Leland's many years later."

The ball had a reserve of $15,000, meaning if no bid reached that amount, the ball would remain in Robinson's hands. The reserve price was not met. He put up the ball for auction with a Dallas, Texas, memorabilia company. "Mantle signed a letter of authenticity and the ball brought in $46,000," said Robinson.

I once asked Ramos what kind of pitch he threw Mantle. He said, "A bad one."

Ramos was a colorful character who married Miss Cuba in 1960. He called himself the "Cuban Cowboy." He wore boots and a ten-gallon hat. On September 5, 1964, he was traded from Cleveland to the Yankees and helped the Bombers to the pennant by allowing only three runs in 21⅔ innings pitching in relief. Ramos had good foot speed and frequently challenged and beat some of the top speedsters in the game. He perpetually challenged Mantle to a race, but the Mick would never accept since he had nothing to gain and would risk injury.

Ramos would serve time in prison. In 1979 a kilogram of cocaine and two loaded guns were found in his car. He was in the company of a relative of a man who was said by police to be a major figure in the flourishing Miami drug world. Two more kilos of cocaine were found in Ramos's home. But a judge ruled that the search of his house was illegal, and he dodged a bullet.

Then, in 1980, the cigar-smoking Cuban was arrested on a charge of threatening the owner of a bar with a revolver. He pleaded guilty to that charge. And on May 24, 1981, while on probation, he was arrested on charges of driving while intoxicated and possessing a weapon. The probation violation led to a three-year prison sentence.

While in prison, he served as a recreation supervisor and pitched underhand in softball games. He liked to wear his old Yankee cap, but since prisoners are not allowed any signs of individuality, he was forced to take the "NY" insignia off his cap. A model prisoner, Ramos was eventually put on work release and was released from the Miami North Correctional Center after serving about half his sentence.

The Mick was nuclear. On May 22, 1963, Mantle hit a walk-off 11th-inning rocket off Kansas City A's pitcher Bill Fischer that was interrupted in its flight only by the hanging frieze in right field 118 feet high and 370 feet deep. When the ball made contact it was still rising. "That was the only home run I ever hit that the bat actually bent in my hands," said Mantle.

"He hit it so hard it was actually funny," recalled Fischer in an interview I did with him. "The next day we went out to take batting practice and Gino Cimoli, our right fielder, found a ladder underneath the stands at Yankee Stadium. He took it out to right field with him in case he had to climb the ladder to catch a ball."

Ron Blomberg became the first designated hitter in baseball history. On April 6, 1973, the muscular Yankee stepped to the plate at Fenway Park in Boston as a DH. He once told me that he also hit the façade in right field at Yankee Stadium, but that happened during batting practice.

Former Washington Senators pitcher Chuck Stobbs was another of Mantle's pitching victims. On April 17, 1953, Stobbs, facing Mantle in the bottom of the fifth with Yogi Berra on base, served up a pitch that reportedly traveled 565 feet out of Griffith Stadium in Washington. "It was a high fastball," Stobbs said. "When he hit it, it just went. I'm glad he didn't hit the ball straight back at me." After Mantle circled the bases Yankees PR director Arthur Patterson measured the blast. Thus was the birth of tape measure homers.

On August 12, 1964, he hit the longest home run ever inside the cavernous stadium. Batting left-handed against White Sox pitcher Ray Herbert, he launched a 502-foot missile that landed deep in the center field bleachers.

Although it was not a tape measure shot, one of Mantle's most memorable homers was his walk-off in Game Three of the 1964 Series against Cardinals pitcher Barney Schultz. "I thought I threw Mickey a good knuckleball," said Schultz. "But he weighed into it."

One home run that was not a titanic wallop but gained much publicity was number 535 off Detroit pitcher Denny McLain on September 19, 1968, the year McLain won 31 games. It was a lazy Thursday afternoon game that drew only 9,063 fans to Tiger Stadium. The Tigers had already clinched the pennant and had a 6–1 lead in the eighth inning when McLain decided to have a little fun out of respect to Mantle, whom he had idolized as a youngster. The controversial right-hander summoned catcher Jim Price to the mound and told him he was going to groove a pitch for Mantle.

The first pitch came over the plate at about 50 miles an hour, batting practice speed. Plate umpire Russ Goetz called it a strike. "Mantle looked down at Price and said, 'What the fuck was that?'" wrote Leavy in *The Last Boy.*

Mantle wanted to know if McLain was going to throw the same pitch. Price didn't know. As Price started for the mound, McLain yelled, "Just tell him to be ready."

Mantle fouled off the next pitch and the count was now 0–2. McLain yelled to Mantle, "Where do you want it?"

Mantle pointed to the spot.

McLain's next pitch landed in the right field seats.

"I heard what McLain said to Price," recalled Mantle. "But McLain sometimes was a little wacky. You couldn't believe him. He's liable to go back out and nail me behind the head. As I rounded third base, I looked at McLain and he gave me a wink."

The home run allowed him to pass Jimmie Foxx for third place on all-time list. At the time, only Willie Mays and Babe Ruth had hit more homers.

Baseball commissioner William Eckert wrote McLain a letter in essence saying he was attacking the integrity of the game. But nothing came of it. Red Smith cleverly wrote in *Women's Wear Daily,* "When a guy has bought 534 drinks in the same saloon, he's entitled to one on the house." Mantle autographed the ball for McLain. But in 1978 the autographed ball and Eckert's letter were lost in a house fire.

The "Good Boy" and the "Bad Boy"

Despite Mantle's celebrity he had a country boy sincerity that was undeniable. He extended his friendship to unknown rookie players, never trying to big league them. When he signed an autograph for fans his signature was pristine, easy to read. And when he hit a home run, he circled the bases with his head down, never wanting to show up the pitcher. He could be friendly and humorous.

One night I was sitting in the press dining room at Yankee Stadium when Mantle was seated a couple of tables away holding court with friends. He shouted over to my table and said, "Hey, I've got a joke to tell you." He told the forgotten joke, which I didn't think was so funny, but I gave an obligatory respectful laugh. This was not the surly guy painted by the media during his career.

In *The Last Boy: Mickey Mantle,* Leavy brings out the human side of the Yankee hero and exposes his flaws as well. She relates a story shared by former Yankee shortstop Tony Kubek.

"Once on a spring training bus ride from Tampa to St. Pete, he saw a man lying on the railroad tracks. *Hey, bussie, stop!* The driver pulled over. 'Mantle got off and gave him a hundred dollars.'"

"Years later, Kubek was greeted by a homeless man as he left his New York hotel," wrote Leavy. "'Hey, Tony, Mickey just walked by an hour ago and gave me a hundred dollars.' 'He always did it in the dark, so no one knew,' Kubek said. '"I gave him twenty dollars."'

Joe Pepitone once saw Mantle leave a $50 tip on a 50-cent cup of coffee. After Pepitone got divorced, Mantle took him in at his St. Moritz Hotel suite for a year.

When Mantle learned that teammate Roger Maris had been diagnosed with cancer, he called him weekly for two years.

Kevin Huard is a former sports card show promoter and sports art coordinator from Spencer, Massachusetts. In the early '90s he was doing a show at the Cow Palace in San Francisco and Mantle was there to do a signing. "I met Mickey at a hotel room and had him sign some items for me," related Huard. "He was upset for some reason. I asked, 'What's the problem?' He said, 'A guy at the radio station doesn't believe I'm Mickey Mantle. The guy was asking donations for some charity so I called and told him that I would sign a couple of baseballs for him. The guy started laughing and hung up the phone. He didn't believe it was me.'"

"If I got a call like that, I probably wouldn't believe it was you either," responded Huard. "So we both kind of laughed about it."

Bad Boy Mickey

On and off the field, Mantle did everything big. In addition to hitting colossal home runs, his appetite for women and booze was lavish. His dark side was the result of his alcoholism and his treatment of women in general. His off-the-field escapades could easily fill enough chapters for a book. Mantle always said that he was not a good father based on the life he led.

Mantle was no ordinary rookie. A hustler named Allan Savitt reportedly contacted him on April 15, 1951, two days before he made his ML debut. He promised the 19-year-old golden nugget they would both make millions of dollars through endorsements, the sale of his life story, and so on. He promised Mantle an annual salary of $50,000. The naïve kid from Oklahoma hired Savitt as his agent without hiring his own attorney to handle the contract, which proved to be trouble. Savitt developed financial problems and filed for bankruptcy.

Savitt allowed a New York show girl named Holly Brooke to get 25 percent of the action. He reportedly asked Brooke for a $1,500 loan in exchange for 25 percent of his interest in Mantle.

Neither Mantle nor Brooke ever saw any money from Savitt because there was no $50,000 annual guarantee in the contract. Eventually Weiss and Topping's lawyer got Mantle out of the deal, apparently because Mantle was under 21.

But out of the Savitt connection Mantle and Brooke developed a long romantic relationship despite the show girl being seven years older and the mother of a toddler.

In his 2016 book *DiMag & Mick: Sibling Rivals, Yankee Blood Brothers*, author Tony Castro reveals that the Yankees' switch-hitting icon proposed to Brooke during his 1951 rookie season and that they carried on a steamy love affair for years even after he married his high school sweetheart, Merlyn Johnson, on December 23, 1951, just to please his dying father.

In 1957 Brooke gave the story of her relationship with Mantle to *Confidential Magazine*, the *National Enquirer* of the early '50s. The Yankee brass was furious over the magazine story and there were rumblings Weiss was ready to move Mantle to another team. That would indeed have been a fatal error.

According to Castro, Brooke had lived with Mantle much of his rookie year, even when he was sent down to the minors to play in Kansas City. Castro also claims she was the reason Mantle asked to have his uniform number changed from 6 to 7 when he returned to the majors; her birthdate was June 7.

12. The Two Mickeys

Mantle's extracurricular activities began before Brooke entered his life. "Mickey was seduced by one of his high school teachers," revealed Merlyn Mantle in Leavy's book. "She just laid over him. He took her to Independence, Missouri, to meet his roommates, his first year in the minors. She was a hot date."

He spent the final 10 years of his life with Greer Johnson, a former Georgia schoolteacher. Johnson handled Mantle's business affairs, booking him for sports card shows, autograph signings, and other events. The word on the street was that she got 20 percent of the take. She was often seen with Mantle at Yankee Stadium when he did color commentary for SportsChannel New York.

Johnson said, "When Merlyn found out about us, she called me and said, 'I will never divorce Mickey. I like being Mrs. Mickey Mantle.'"

Mantle's documented lack of respect for women was a black mark on his life. He demonstrated it in the ladies he chose for one-night stands and the crude way he talked and acted in front of women when he drank. Diane Shah was a boots-on-the-ground sports reporter in the 1970s. She became the first female sports columnist for a daily paper in the United States at the *Los Angeles Herald-Examiner*. Shah's book, *A Farewell to Arms, Legs, and Jockstraps: A Sportswriter's Memoir*, was published in 2020. In the book she details a strange encounter she had with Mantle while interviewing him back in 1970. Shah's memoir reveals that the Yankee star once hit on her with a lewd message in a greeting card. After asking Mantle how long he had been married, he replied, "Too long." Shah recalls Mantle reaching inside his jacket and pulling out a greeting card. "He handed it to me," Shah writes. "The front showed a picture of flowers, and I assumed this was a card he intended to give his wife. I opened it. Inside, it said, 'Wanna (bleep)…?' He grinned."

Perhaps the seeds for Mantle's drinking and womanizing were planted in his childhood. Leavy wrote that he was molested by an older half sibling named Anna Bea and an older boy in the neighborhood who fondled him.

There were demons in Mantle's life and alcohol seemed to be at the center.

"At the stadium, Mickey would have me go to Louie, the bartender in the press dining room," recalled Appel. "Mickey would say, 'Get me the breakfast of champions.'"

Mickey and Merlyn had four sons: Mickey Jr. (1953–2000), David (born 1955), Billy (1957–1994), whom Mickey named for Billy Martin, and Danny (born 1960). Like Mickey, Merlyn and three of their sons became alcoholics, and Billy developed Hodgkin's disease as several men in Mantle's family had previously.

Author Jon Pessah in his book *Yogi: A Life Behind the Mask* tells this story about a night when Yogi and Carmen Berra invited Mantle and his wife Merlyn to dinner. Yogi had his limit of four vodkas on the rocks and stopped while Carmen had her last glass of wine. But the Mantles continued to drink until they were drunk. The Berras recommended that they should not drive and were welcome to stay.

"'Don't worry, our house isn't that far away,' said Mickey. 'We'll be fine.' But they hadn't got very far when Mantle hit a telephone pole at 70 miles an hour sending Merlyn through the windshield. It took 70 stitches to close all her wounds. A police report was filed, and Mantle paid $400 for the pole. No mention of alcohol appeared in the report, and the story never made the press."

In 1983 the Hall of Fame center fielder worked at the Claridge Resort and Casino in Atlantic City, New Jersey, as a greeter and community representative. Most of his activities were representing the hotel in golf tournaments and at other charity events. Most likely the Yankee icon was in the middle of some heavy socializing, especially at the 19th hole. Merlyn believed that her husband's drinking escalated during his tenure at the casino.

Mantle was suspended from baseball by Commissioner Bowie Kuhn on the grounds that any affiliation with gambling was grounds for being placed on the "permanently ineligible" list. Mays, who had also taken a similar position, had already had action taken against him. Mantle accepted the position though he felt the rule was "stupid." He was placed on the list but reinstated on March 18, 1985, by Kuhn's successor, Peter Ueberroth.

Mantle was involved in various business ventures. Despite the failure of Mickey Mantle's Country Cookin' restaurants in the early 1970s, Mickey Mantle's Restaurant & Sports Bar opened at 42 Central Park South (59th Street) in 1988 and became one of New York's most popular eateries. Mantle was in partnership with Bill Liederman, a 49-year-old workaholic who idolized Mantle as a kid. Halper kept the restaurant stocked with vintage Yankee items such as jerseys worn by Ruth, Gehrig, Mantle and other Hall of Famers.

Mantle let others run the business operations but made frequent appearances. "We had a contract agreement with Mickey that he would make 12 appearances a year," said Liederman. "Mantle's lawyer at the time, Roy True, said, 'Bill, if Mickey likes you, he'll show up 112 times a year. If he doesn't like you, I don't care what the contract says, he's not coming in.' Well, it ended up where Mickey came to the restaurant more like 112 times a year. His favorite booth was number 32. He would sit there all day and sign autographs."

Bob Ahearn, a good friend of mine and a Red Sox fan, went to Mantle's restaurant with several of his friends. They were fortunate that they went on a night Mantle was there and they all got his autograph. When Ahearn approached the Mick, he said, "My friends are all Yankees fans, but I'm a Red Sox fan."

Mantle signed the ball, "Fuck you, Mickey Mantle."

The establishment closed in 2012.

He had another restaurant in West Nyack, New York, Mickey Mantle's, which opened several years after the restaurant in NYC opened. The most prominent item on display was the number 6 Yankee uniform he wore when he made his debut in '51. In 2000 Mickey Mantle's Steakhouse opened in Oklahoma City and as of this writing is still in business.

The King of the Memorabilia Market

It is estimated that Mantle earned $1.1 million during his 18-year career with the Yankees. It is fair to say he was vastly underpaid. Multiple sources report that when he died his net worth was $10 million. Mantle, like DiMaggio, made millions signing his name on baseballs, bats, photographs, and other items. Mantle knew his star power. When he was invited to do a signing at a card show, he often stipulated that his former teammates Bauer, Skowron and Johnny Blanchard would join him so they could make some extra cash in their later years.

Mantle's star continues to shine. It has been 56 years since his last at-bat and his deeds remain a beacon to those who saw him play. He is the poster boy of baseball memorabilia and his 1952 Topps card has been the centerpiece of the baseball card collecting hobby. A PSA (Professional Sports Authenticator) mint 9.5 graded condition card sold for $12.6 million on August 28, 2022, in a Heritage Auctions event, the heftiest price ever paid for a baseball card. The owner of the card was Anthony Giordano, a 75-year-old waste management entrepreneur in New Jersey. Giordano purchased the card for $50,000 at a New York City show in 1991.

Mantle's 1951 Bowman card is actually his rookie card but the '52 Topps card's popularity is based on supply and demand. In '52, Topps printed four different series of cards numbered 1–407. Mantle's number 311 card was part of the final or high-numbered series which came out in late summer. By that time kids were ready to go back to school and storekeepers were ordering football cards.

The surplus stock of cards that didn't sell were dumped into the Atlantic Ocean years later. Experts believe more than 300 cases took the fateful plunge to the bottom of the sea. The demand for the few remaining Mantles skyrocketed.

Several Mantle memorabilia items sold for high prices at various Heritage Auctions. In 2013, his original signed bonus check for $1,150 dated July 11, 1949, and endorsed by the 18-year-old sold for $286,800. In 2015, a game-worn 1954 Mantle jersey sold for $406,300. In 2018, a 1964 Mantle World Series home run record-setting game-worn New York Yankees jersey, MEARS A9 went for $1,320,000. In 2022 the last Yankees jersey Mantle wore in 1968 that was personally signed netted a staggering $2.2 million.

In 1999, actor Billy Crystal purchased a game-used Mantle glove for $239,000 at a Sotheby's auction. The glove was reportedly used by Mantle in the 1961 season.

The bat believed to be the first one he used as a Yankee rookie in 1951 sold for $242,209 in 2015 at a SCP auction.

Although Mantle signed many autographs during his life, the value of his signature remains strong at between $500 and $600. If a fan got Mantle's autograph at a show or anywhere in person, it is certainly 100 percent authentic. However, a Yankees team signed ball signed by the Mick or others that was signed in the clubhouse might prove to be problematic which, as stated earlier, was very common.

Pete Previte, the Yankees assistant clubhouse man for many years, showed up in Jim Bouton's 1970 tell-all book, *Ball Four*. Bouton revealed it was Previte, not Mantle, who signed thousands of baseballs that were sold as autographed by the three-time MVP. Bouton said Mantle was the only Yankee who refused to do his own signing.

Mick's Most Important At-Bat

Mantle's hard-drinking lifestyle eventually struck him out. In 1993, at the urging of football player and close friend Pat Summerall, Mantle checked into the Betty Ford Center in Los Angeles to seek treatment. After he emerged sober from the center, Mantle made a number of public-service announcements regarding the dangers of alcoholism. He traveled the country spreading his message, often saying that if it weren't for alcohol, he would have been a better player and a better man.

The "feel-good" story didn't last very long, however. On January 7, 1994, Mantle was diagnosed with hepatitis, cirrhosis of the liver, and liver cancer. He always thought cancer would defeat him, but it was his drinking that led to his demise.

On May 28, 1995, Mantle was admitted to Baylor University Medical Center with severe stomach pains. His liver was ruined, and he needed a transplant, which he received on June 8. The transplant surgery was a success, but the Yankee slugger was nevertheless given a death sentence.

The transplant resulted in loud criticism by many who felt he did not deserve to be a liver recipient and that he only received the transplant because of his celebrity. "Should we look at Mickey Mantle's transplant as a good research effort? Or was it really an exercise in futile care? Would someone else have done better with Mantle's new organ?" wrote Abigail Trafford in the *Washington Post*.

Perhaps his biggest at-bat came in his final press conference at Baylor when he implored others "not to be like him" and asked people to think of signing organ-donor cards.

Former teammate Bobby Richardson, who became a born-again Christian, has spread the word of the Lord most of his life. Several of his Yankee teammates requested that he preside at their funerals, most notably Mantle.

Four days before Mantle's death, Richardson was summoned from South Carolina to Dallas. He visited Mantle and gave his former teammate spiritual comfort. Mantle told Richardson that he had become a Christian. During Mantle's final week he was also visited by Ford, Bauer, Skowron and Blanchard. For a time, Mantle and Ford's friendship had reportedly cooled due to a dispute over Whitey skimming money out of their fantasy camp. Ford's defense was "We were both supposed to be doing that," said a former Yankees official.

On August 13, 1995, the final curtain came down on baseball's tragic hero at the age of 63. He was undone by his demons which led to his early grave.

His old Yankee teammates reunited at Lovers Lane United Methodist Church in Dallas for the funeral. Ford, Bauer, Berra and Murcer served as honorary pallbearers. Speaking to an audience of 1,500 (plus television viewers) and 3,000 outside at Mantle's interment, Richardson said, "There were two types of people in this world, those who said yes to Christ and those who said no. Mickey said yes."

Bob Costas, who carried Mantle's 1958 Topps card with him for many years, eulogized Mantle. He said, "I just hope God has a place for him where he can run again, where he can play practical jokes on his teammates and smile—God knows no one is perfect. God knows there's something special about heroes. So long, Mick!"

Mantle was laid to rest at the Sparkman-Hillcrest Memorial Park Cemetery in Dallas.

When Mickey Mantle was younger and healthy, I always dreaded the day he would die because I knew a chunk of my childhood would die with him. There are few performers in sports history whose presence immediately evoked a time, a place and an everlasting memory. Mantle was one of them. The day Mantle passed I was sitting in the parking lot of a local Stop & Shop while my wife was getting groceries and a friend, Bob Barth, informed me of his death.

When my friend left, I cried.

13

Yogi

From Dago Hill to D-Day

"Why buy expensive luggage? You only use it when you travel."
—Lawrence Peter Berra

On July 28, 1998, Yogi Berra was a guest on my *Inside Yankee Baseball* radio show. At the time, the Hall of Fame Yankees catcher had boycotted Yankee Stadium for 13 years. Yogi was still irked by how he was fired by the Yankees after only 16 games into the 1985 season. I pleaded with Yogi to go back to Yankee Stadium for the sake of the fans. He was non-committal, but I think he was beginning to soften. He didn't say no.

During the '85 campaign, the Yankees were swept by the White Sox in Chicago in late April and stood 6–10. Following the 4–3 loss in the April 28 Sunday game, Berra was dismissed and replaced by Billy Martin. The appointment of Martin marked the

Yogi Berra was an interesting guest on my *Inside Yankee Baseball* radio show in 1998. Co-host Tom Rogers (left) and I enjoyed talking to Yogi.

12th managerial change since majority owner George Steinbrenner led a group that purchased the Yankees from CBS in 1973.

The unpleasant task of informing Berra of the firing was given to Yankees general manager Clyde King. Sending King to the visiting clubhouse in Chicago to do the dirty work was indefensible. It was a slap in the face to Berra who thought Steinbrenner should have done it himself, especially since he stated pre-season that Yogi would be the manager for the '85 season. Steinbrenner reportedly telephoned Berra an hour later in the visiting clubhouse at Comiskey Park.

Reports circulated that according to King, Steinbrenner had decided to ax Berra even before the Sunday game. He apparently was of the opinion that the team, with players like Rickey Henderson, Willie Randolph, Don Mattingly, Dave Winfield, and Don Baylor, was underachieving. The fact there were 146 games left in the season had meant nothing to the Boss.

The firing was premature and handled in a clumsy manner, but Steinbrenner had no patience for losing, even in April. The Boss had a military mindset. In the tunnel leading to the Yankee clubhouse, for a time he had a sign posted with a statement from General Douglas McArthur that read, "There is no substitute for winning."

Steinbrenner told the media, "I didn't fire Yogi, the players fired him."

In defense of Berra, the Yankees were hobbled with injuries, including Henderson, the Yankees' leadoff-hitting/base-stealing lightning rod who missed the first several games of the season.

Yogi's pride was wounded. He swore he would never return to Yankee Stadium as long as Steinbrenner owned the team. Even when the Yankees unveiled plaques of Bill Dickey and Berra in Monument Park in 1988, Yogi and his family were no-shows.

Houston Astros owner John McMullen reportedly offered Berra the Astros' manager position just three days after he was fired but he turned it down. He did, however, accept a coaching position with the Astros from 1986 to 1989.

Berra had been dismissed twice before, once by the Mets, the team he managed from 1972 to the middle of 1975, taking them to the World Series in '73, and by the Yankees, the team he managed to a pennant in 1964 but which lost the World Series. Both of his Series losses came in a winner-take-all Game Seven. Overall, his ML managerial record is 484–444.

Martin led the Yanks to a 91–54 mark the remainder of the '85 season. The team finished in second place, two games behind the Blue Jays.

The firing wasn't Berra's first brush with Steinbrenner. The impetuous Yankees owner canned Martin after the 1983 season and hired Berra as his manager for 1984. But the AL pennant race was decided early in '84 when the Detroit Tigers came out of the gate going a torrid 35–5, effectively ending the Yanks' chances at the playoffs. Steinbrenner criticized Berra, his players and his coaches. Finally, in July, during a meeting with the owner and the coaching staff just before the All-Star break, Yogi decided he'd heard enough.

He threw a pack of cigarettes at Steinbrenner and launched into a tirade memorialized by Bill Madden and Moss Klein in their book *Damned Yankees*. "This isn't my fucking team, it's *your* fucking team!" Berra shouted. "You make all the fucking decisions. You make all the fucking moves. You get all the fucking players that nobody else wants. You put this fucking team together and then you can sit back and wait for us to lose so you can blame everybody else because you're a fucking chicken shit liar."

On January 5, 1999, a little more than five months after he was on my show, WFAN broadcaster Suzyn Waldman brokered a peace meeting between the Hall of Fame Yankees catcher and Steinbrenner at the Yogi Berra Museum and Learning Center in Montclair, New Jersey. The Yankees were back on top, having won two of the previous three World Series and zeroing in on two more.

When Steinbrenner arrived, the first thing Berra said was "You're late." That broke the ice. The two went into a room by themselves and closed the doors. Their friendship was rekindled.

"It's over," a relieved Berra said.

Steinbrenner had underrated the importance of Berra to both the organization and its fans. Firing a Yankee icon was fundamentally a bad idea. He made a public mea culpa when he stated, "I would have driven across the George Washington Bridge in a rickshaw to get Yogi back. I didn't realize how much I'd screwed up. It was a monumental mistake on my part. Sometimes, it takes a long time to get things right. Yogi is a highly principled man. I messed up. It was the worst mistake I made in baseball."

"George, I forgive you," answered Yogi, in his down to Earth, humble way. "Don't worry about it…. I've made a lot of mistakes in my baseball career too."

Berra then took Steinbrenner on a 45-minute tour of the museum that housed the mitt Yogi wore when he caught Don Larsen's perfect game in the 1956 World Series and other memorabilia.

The feud had come to an emotional end. Yogi returned on Opening Day of the 1999 season, a day also designated as Joe DiMaggio Day. And on July 18 the Yankees celebrated Yogi Berra Day at Yankee Stadium, as the Yankees officially welcomed their

On Yogi Berra Day, July 18, 1999, Andy Parton, Vice President of Chase Manhattan Bank, presents Yogi with a framed No. 8 jersey to be displayed at the Yogi Berra Museum. Michael Kay made the introduction (courtesy Lou Requena).

lovable catcher back where he belonged. I was in the press box that day which proved to be one of the most memorable baseball days of my life.

As part of the day's festivities to honor the Yankee legend, Larsen was also invited to throw the ceremonial first pitch—to Berra! For the gray-haired fans, it was going back in time. This time Yogi did not jump into Larsen's arms!

David Cone took the mound for the Yankees and proceeded to throw the 16th perfect game in baseball history, with Berra and Larsen in attendance!

This was Yankee Stadium theater at its best.

"Lawdie"

Lawrence Peter Berra, born Lorenzo Pietro Berra, came into this world on May 12, 1925, in St. Louis, Missouri. His parents, Pietro and Paulina, were Italian immigrants. In 1909 his father left Robecchetto, a town 25 miles south of Milan, where he was a tenant farmer. He migrated to the United States alone to find a better life. Paulina joined him a few years later.

In Berra's baseball life he was known as Yogi. But growing up he was called "Lawdie" by his family and friends thanks to his mother who had trouble pronouncing "Lawrence." He had three older brothers (Tony, Mike, and John) and a younger sister (Josie). Tony and Mike, who were born in Italy, were also outstanding ballplayers but Pietro put pressure on his sons to work and help with the family finances.

Berra received his nickname Yogi from Bobby Hofman, a childhood friend. Hofman was a slick fielding second baseman who played for the New York Giants before they moved to San Francisco. During his post–playing career he worked in the Yankees organization in a variety of capacities including scouting director, director of minor league operations, and director of player development. I ran into him one day in the '80s in the Yankees dugout prior to a game. He explained how he gave Berra the nickname Yogi.

"It was based on a travelogue movie about India that included a Hindu fakir, or yogi, who was meditating," said Hofman. "I was with Yogi and friends. Because Berra used to sit with his arms folded and legs crossed, I said he looked like the yogi in the movie," explained Hofman.

Yogi admits Hofman gave him the nickname, but his version of the story is a bit different. "I played American Legion ball with Bobby," said Berra. "When we played, we didn't have dugouts. I used to sit on the ground with my arms folded and my legs crossed. Hofman said, 'Lawdie, you look like a yogi.'"

The most recognized moniker in baseball history has endured over multiple generations.

Berra has been stereotyped as a dim-witted, simple-speaking guy who feasted on comic books while his roommate Bobby Brown, who was studying to be a doctor, was reading medical journals. One day Yogi asked him, "How did your story end up?"

The skinny on Yogi was that players did not want to room with him because he watched TV late into the night. "I used to like to watch TV and read my comic books," countered Yogi. "The funny part of it was when I finished reading my comics, they [my teammates] all used to pick them up and read them."

Yogi looked more like a grocery store owner than a baseball player. His teammates and opponents poked fun at his looks. He was short and dumpy with an oversized head. He is the shortest catcher (5'7") to have ever played at least 1200 games in the major leagues which makes his story all the more improbable. Teammates and opponents tormented him with hurtful descriptors like "ugly," "Neanderthal," "caveman," "gorilla," "ape," "nature boy," and so one. Some would swing from the dugout in Yogi's sight imitating an ape or a gorilla. Despite the verbal abuse early in his career, Berra got the last laugh with his bat. Stengel put an end to the ape talk. "No more of this stuff about him keeping house in a tree or swinging from limb to limb like those apes," he said. "And stop feeding him peanuts."

Yogi's reputation for being a character was enhanced by his singular ability to garble the English language. His Yogi-isms and malapropisms are classic. Some are true while others are fabricated. Whatever is true, it's been written that he's the most quoted American since Abraham Lincoln.

He once stated, "I never said most of the things I said." But it's a fact that he did say, "It's not over 'til it's over." It has been said incorrectly this referred to never giving up during a ballgame. Yogi made the statement when he managed the Mets in 1973. Through August 7 the Mets were 50–60, nine and a half games out of first place. It was around this time he spoke those words to the press. "In the last month of September, we had to play the teams we had to beat in our own division," said Berra. "The writers came in and asked me what I thought. I said, 'It's not over 'til it's over.'" The Mets finished 82–79 to win the division.

An avid movie watcher, he even had a bit part in *That Touch of Mink* with Mantle and Maris. The movie co-starred Cary Grant and Doris Day. In 1963 he had a cameo role in the daytime TV soap *General Hospital*, playing the part, believe it or not, of a brain surgeon—Dr. Lawrence P. Berra. Recounting the experience in his book *When You Come to the Fork in the Road, Take It!*, Berra was typically self-effacing: "And I once was a brain surgeon—no kidding—in a *General Hospital* episode, in the early '60s. Those were the days before the soaps got sexy."

But if truth be told, the man was all business. "They say he's funny," said Stengel. "Well, he has a lovely wife and family, a beautiful home, money in the bank and he plays golf with millionaires. What's funny about that?"

When Yogi died his net worth was estimated to be $5 million. If there was a knock on the legendary Yankee, it was that he was a bit frugal. It's been said that he and his amigo Phil Rizzuto had the first penny they ever made. Whitey Ford once said, "The only bad thing I can say about Yogi is that he never bought me a beer."

His New Jersey bowling alley in which he partnered with Rizzuto proved to be a grand slam. He also became a pitchman for several products.

In the '50s he was the face of the Yoo-hoo chocolate drink, becoming a vice president. Rather than receive compensation, he held stock in the company which proved to be quite lucrative down the road. He pitched Visa, Miller Lite, Puss 'n Boots cat food and Aflac insurance to mention a few. The cat's voice in the Puss 'n Boots commercial was that of Ford. At the time of the taping, Berra was unaware that Whitey played a part in the commercial. The Aflac duck and Yogi teamed in the classic barber shop scene. While Yogi was getting a haircut he garbled, "If you get hurt to miss work, it won't hurt to miss work."

Yogi was not afraid to go to court to protect his image. In 1958, a cartoon character (Yogi Bear) was named after the celebrated Yankees' catcher. Berra was not amused by this and sued Hanna-Barbera Productions for defamation, but their management claimed that the similarity of the names was just a coincidence. Berra subsequently withdrew his suit.

In 2005, Yogi filed a $10 million lawsuit against the Turner Broadcasting System for running an ad for its popular show *Sex and the City* asking viewers if a "Yogasm" could be defined as sex with Berra. According to the lawsuit filed with the New York supreme court, Berra claimed TBS violated his right to privacy by using his name without his consent and used his name for commercial gain without compensation. In the end, Berra proved successful. The station and Berra came to an undisclosed settlement through mediation, with his lawyer Louis Smoley calling the payout "substantial."

An All-Around Athlete

Yogi was a natural athlete in his formative years. He loved playing ball on Dago Hill in the Italian southwest section of St. Louis and hated going to school, dropping out before high school. When asked as a child how he liked school he replied, "Closed."

He was an excellent soccer player and even did some boxing in his early teens. In 1940 Berra took a job with the Works Progress Administration, a New Deal agency under President Franklin Delano Roosevelt that worked on public works projects. Berra enjoyed the job because he was able to be around parks and fields, his natural habitat.

The Berras lived at 5447 Elizabeth Avenue across the street from Giovanni Garagiola and his family. Pietro and Giovanni were close friends and worked together as bricklayers. Giovanni had a son named Joe, who was eight months younger than Yogi. Joe and Yogi maintained a lifetime friendship. The two starred for the Stockham American Legion Post team that reached the finals of the legion tournament in 1939 and 1940. Hofman was the second baseman on that team.

Stockham coach Leo Browne arranged for Yogi and Joe to have a tryout with the Cardinals in 1940. The possibility of playing for the Cardinals was more than Yogi could ask for. He grew up a Cardinals fan and followed the exploits of the Gas House Gang during the Great Depression years of the 1930s. Hall of Fame left fielder Joe "Ducky" Medwick was his favorite player. Ducky was the last NL player to win a Triple Crown when he did so in 1934, a year he batted .374 with 31 HRs and 154 RBI. When Yogi was a youngster, he sold newspapers on the street and became the envy of his friends when he became friendly with Medwick.

The Cardinals tryout camp proved to be a success for Garagiola but not for Berra. Garagiola was offered a contract with a $500 bonus with the order to keep quiet about it until he turned 16. Yogi didn't fare well during the tryout but was offered a contract though no bonus. Berra was not about to go home without showing his father the same cash Garagiola had received.

Cardinals general manager Branch Rickey said to Berra, "You will never be a big-league ballplayer—maybe a Triple-A player." Rickey offered Berra a $250 bonus which he declined. Yogi later had a tryout with the St. Louis Browns and once again was offered a contract without a bonus and once again he turned it down.

Browne contacted his old friend George Weiss, who ran the Yankees farm system. "Browne had umpired for Weiss in the old Eastern League where Weiss had a team," said Berra. Krichell, the veteran Yankees scout who signed Gehrig, was high on Berra. He especially liked his lefty bat in Yankee Stadium. Yankees scout John Shulte signed Berra in October 1942 for the $500 bonus he so adamantly desired, plus a monthly salary of $90. He was off to Norfolk, Virginia, to begin his professional baseball career.

The story doesn't end there. In '43 Rickey was now the general manager of the Dodgers. Because of World War II travel restrictions, the Dodgers trained at Bear Mountain near West Point, New York. "Rickey sent me a telegram that said I want you to report to Bear Mountain," recalled Berra. "I told him I already signed with the Yankees." It appears that Rickey knew his time with the Cardinals was ending. His relationship with Cards owner Sam Breadon was strained, partly over Rickey's bonus payments.

Did Rickey downplay Yogi with the Cardinals so he could cover him up?

"That's right," said Yogi.

Seaman Second Class Berra

After a modest '43 season, Berra enlisted in the Navy during World War II. In February 1944, he sailed for the British Isles on the USS *Bayfield* and was a gunner's mate on board a six-man rocket boat in the June 6, 1944, D-Day invasion at Omaha Beach in France. The attack transport vessel got within 300 yards offshore where they fired rockets into suspected German machine gun nests to protect the landing troops at Omaha Beach.

"We had three 30 calibers and a twin 50," Berra stated when describing the support missile boat. "We had 12 rockets on each side."

When the battle commenced at 6:30 a.m., the LCS (landing craft support boat) sprayed bullets and rockets across the heavily fortified beach fronts before the troops landed. "Berra, then 19, manned a machine gun mounted on a ball turret in his LCS and stood tall with a boy's wonder—too busy marveling at the tremendous explosions of lights and sound to consider the danger that would end the lives of 2,500 of his fellow Americans," wrote Tom Verducci for *Sports Illustrated*. "In an LCS, only the steel walls of the boat and the grace of God stood between a sailor and death."

Berra remembered standing with his head out over the armor of the rocket boat which was only 36 feet long. "The officer said, 'You better get your head back if you want it on.' I was looking up and it looked like the Fourth of July," Berra said on my show.

As Berra and his crew continued to run interference for the soldiers who were climbing the cliffs, they had orders to shoot anything that came below the clouds. "One of our own planes came down over the clouds and we shot it down," said Berra in an interview with Keith Olbermann, explaining the friendly fire. Yogi's crew picked up the pilot, who was angry. "You should have heard the words he was saying," said Yogi. He added, "A lot of our guys wanted to get off to go on the beach. I said, 'No, I'm staying on the boat.' And so I didn't go on the beach. We lost one guy. He went on the beach and lost his life."

According to Berra he spent 17 days on the water in Normandy before going to southern France for a day and then returned. Berra, who served in North Africa and Italy as well, won two battle stars, a European Theater of Operations ribbon, a Distinguished Unit Citation, and a Good Conduct medal.

Before he was discharged, Berra was shipped to the submarine base in Groton, Connecticut, but he did not want anything to do with submarines. In 1945, he played for the naval submarine base at New London managed by Lieutenant Commander Jim Gleeson, a former big-league outfielder with the Reds. Gleeson, not impressed by Yogi's appearance, thought Berra was a boxer. Berra's relationship with Gleeson didn't end there. When Berra managed the Yankees in 1964, he brought in Gleeson as the first base coach.

"The naval sub base team was so good that when it lost an exhibition game to the Phillies, it was headlined as an upset," said New Haven area sports historian and writer Joel Alderman. "They had wins over the Giants, Yankees, Dodgers, Senators, Browns and Braves that year. When they beat the Senators, the losing pitcher was Bert Shepard, who only had one leg, the result of a war injury. Appearing in one game for the Senators in '45 against the Red Sox on August 4, he came out of the bullpen and allowed only three hits and one run over 5⅓ innings."

He never pitched in another major league game.

In a game against the New York Giants, Berra went 3-for-4 and impressed Giants manager Mel Ott so much he lobbied Giants owner Horace Stoneham to buy Berra's contract from the Yankees. Stoneham reportedly offered Yankees president Larry MacPhail $50,000, but after conferring with Krichell, he nixed the Giants' offer.

Yogi tore the cover off the ball playing for the sub base team, winning batting championships in two different leagues (.429 and .445).

Berra had odd jobs while on the base that included sweeping out the movie theater at the end of movies and serving as manager for the football team in the fall of '45. He oversaw cleaning the uniforms and performed other jobs. On October 20 they defeated Harvard 18–7 in Boston and on Thanksgiving Day the team traveled to Yankee Stadium to play the Tuskegee Army Air Corps Warhawks.

In 2009, Yogi received the Lone Sailor Award, and in 2010, he received the Audie Murphy Award for his Navy service.

It wasn't long before Berra would have permanent residence in the Bronx.

14

The Real "Mr. October"

Following his discharge from the service in 1946, Yogi prepped one season with the Newark Bears, the Yankees top minor league club, where he hit .314 while banging out 15 homers and knocking in 59 runs.

Wearing number 38, Yogi made his major league debut on September 22, 1946, in the first game of a doubleheader against Connie Mack's Philadelphia Athletics. Batting in the bottom of the fourth, his second at-bat, he homered off A's right-hander Jesse Flores and followed with a single in the sixth inning. For the game, he went 2-for-4 in the Yankees 4–3 win. In his 22 official at-bats covering seven games, he batted .364 with two four-baggers. The following season he wore jersey number 35. In 1948 he was given number 8, the number he wore for the remainder of his career.

Before the '47 season, Yogi met Carmen Short, who worked as a waitress at Biggie's, a popular St. Louis restaurant co-owned by Stan Musial. Their first date was a hockey game in St. Louis and the rest is history. The two married on January 26, 1949, and Garagiola served as his best man. Carmen passed in March of 2014 at age 85, less than two months after their 65th wedding anniversary. Eighteen months later, on September 22, 2015, Yogi died at age 90. Ironically it was the 69th anniversary of the day he broke into the majors. The two had three sons, Larry, Tim, and Dale. Berra is the only baseball Hall of Famer to father a son (Dale) who played major league baseball and a son (Tim) who played in the NFL. Tim held the UMass school record for most career receiving yards with 1,486. He was drafted by the Baltimore Colts in the 17th round (421st overall) of the 1974 NFL Draft. He played in 14 games for the Colts in '74, primarily on special teams, which was the extent of his NFL career.

Dale, a shortstop and third baseman, had an 11-year (1977–87) ML career spent mostly with the Pirates. A lifetime .236 hitter, he struggled with cocaine use and was an important figure in the Pittsburgh cocaine trial in 1985, baseball's biggest scandal since the 1919 Black Sox. A disappointment to his father, Dale has been clean for many years.

Durable and Consistent

Yogi's breakout season was 1950 when he hit .322 with 28 home runs and 124 RBI. Incredibly, he struck out only 12 times. During his 19-year career he whiffed only 414 times in 8,364 plate appearances. My all-time favorite baseball card was his 1950 Bowman pasteboard where he is pictured wearing his catcher's gear in spring training. I think that card inspired me to play the position in high school and college.

The 18-time All-Star topped 30 strikeouts in a season only three times in his career and never fanned more than 38 times in a season. Unlike some hitters who suffer paralysis by analysis, he would say, "If you see it, hit it." He explained, "I could leave a high ball go the first pitch but the next pitch I may swing at it because I saw the ball good." He added, "I get mad when you got men on base and some of these kids today take a good pitch. I always looked for a fastball up to two strikes."

In '50 Berra caught 148 games. According to Pessah in his book *Yogi: A Life Behind the Mask*, "The Yankees played 22 double headers and Berra caught both games 19 times. During his career he caught both ends of a doubleheader a staggering 117 times." Eight straight years (1950–1957) he led American League catchers in games caught. On June 24, 1962, the Yankees beat the Tigers in a 22-inning marathon at Detroit. At age 37, Yogi caught all 22 innings and collected three hits in 10 at-bats. Jack Reed, known as "Mickey Mantle's caddy," hit a two-run homer in the top of the 22nd inning with Maris on base to win it for the Yanks. It was Reed's only home run of his career.

Regardless of Yogi's lumpy looks, his malapropisms and his slips of syntax, the man was a great baseball player. His persona transcended the game of baseball. Of all the elite catchers in the game's history, Bill James wrote in *The New York Yankees: 100 Years—The Yankee Retrospective*, "Berra was the only one who played every day, batted cleanup, did the job defensively, and never had a bad season…. Roy Campanella was as good as Berra was in his best seasons, maybe better, and so was Johnny Bench and maybe Mickey Cochrane, too. Put all three together, and they had about as many great seasons combined as Yogi did by himself."

Did Berra ever feel he was in competition with Campanella, both playing in the same city and World Series arch-rivals?

"No," said Yogi. "He was in the National League, and I was in the American League. We played the Dodgers a lot in spring training. A lot of the guys thought we were enemies. We were all close friends because we saw each other a lot. We used to have a barnstorming trip with Pee Wee Reese. He was a great. We had a lot of fun in those days. You might be friends off the field but once the game started, we were enemies."

New York *Daily News* writer Dick Young wrote, "Yogi was the most consistent gem in the bejeweled George Weiss era." A three-time MVP (1951, 1954, 1955), he batted .285 with 358 homers and 1,430 RBI lifetime. He was named an All-Star 18 times and started behind the plate for the American League 11 times. Berra was "Mr. Consistency." He hit 20 or more home runs a season from 1949 to 1958 and in 1961. He was perhaps the best bad-ball hitter in the game, feasting on the kind of pitches other hitters disdained. His plate coverage was unusual. His batting splits were balanced and he was as consistent as high tide. Batting against right-handed pitchers, he hit .285, and against lefties he hit .279. He hit .286 at home and .283 on the road. When Berra retired, he had recorded more put-outs (8,738) than any catcher in the history of the game.

Mr. Clutch

Stats can be a misleading view of a player's career. It's not always the number of hits a player gets that's important; it's when he gets his hits that counts as well as run production. What the stats don't always show is Yogi's clutch hitting. "Berra is the toughest man in baseball when the game is up for grabs," opposing manager Paul Richards once said. "He is by far the toughest man in the league the last three innings."

Richards' assessment is supported by contemporary metrics. According to *Baseball Reference*, "In situations considered high leverage, he batted .309, with an OPS of .895 during his career. He was poison to opponents in late innings of close games. He surpasses Hall of Fame catchers like Roy Campanella .278, Carlton Fisk .277, and Johnny Bench .271."

Berra led the Yankees each year in RBI from 1949 to 1955. "I liked to hit with men on base," he said. "When there's men on base, you're not in trouble, the pitcher is. If the bases are loaded, he doesn't have any place to put you. He's got to be around the plate somewhere. A sacrifice fly gives you a run batted in. I see kids take a fastball and then take a curveball. What the hell are they looking for?"

Yankees Hall of Fame catcher Bill Dickey was Berra's mentor. "He used to get on me all the time," recalled Berra. "He used to say, 'When nobody's on base, you don't try. You just go up there and swing away.' When somebody was on base, I bore down more."

Thanks to the careless running of Mantle, Berra should have ended his career with 1,431 RBI instead of 1,430 and 2,151 hits instead of 2,150. Here is what happened.

On May 3, 1952, the Yankees and Tigers met at Yankee Stadium. The Bronx Bombers were batting in the bottom of the fifth with Joe Collins on third and Mantle on first when Berra hit a two-out single, apparently scoring Collins and sending Mantle to third. But the Tigers appealed that Mantle missed second base and he was called out by umpire Bill McKinley. Because Mantle was forced to go to second on the play and never legally reached the base because of his failure to touch it, the inning ended in a force when the play was appealed, and Collins' run was nullified since a run cannot score when the inning ends in a force out. The play was scored a fielder's choice.

Also, according to FanGraphs, Berra threw out nearly half of all attempted base-stealers. Berra's WAR (Wins Above Replacement) is high. Wins Above Replacement is a non-standardized sabermetric baseball statistic developed to sum up "a player's total contributions to his team." A player's WAR value is claimed to be the number of additional wins his team has achieved above the number of expected team wins if that player were substituted with a replacement-level player, a player who may be added to the team for minimal cost and effort. Berra's WAR ranks sixth in Yankees history, behind Ruth, Gehrig, Mantle, DiMaggio, and Jeter.

10 Rings

When Yogi passed Derek Jeter in the Yankees clubhouse, he would often raise his 10 fingers to tease the Yankees' captain about his 10 WS rings compared to Jeter's five.

Berra is the real "Mr. October." He holds several World Series records, including the number of World Series played (14), WS won (10), games played (75), plate appearances (295), official at-bats (259), hits (71) and singles (49). He and Frankie Frisch both collected 10 doubles. Berra had home runs in nine different Series, a record he holds with Mantle.

The Hall of Fame catcher batted .274 in Series play, but if you focus on his peak years from 1953 to 1957 when he was age 28 to 32, his performance was nothing short of amazing. In the four WS he played in during that time frame he hit .379 with a slugging percentage of .612

The Yankees faced Brooklyn in the '47 World Series, the first Fall Classic to be televised. The Gillette Safety Razor Company and the Ford Motor Company paid $65,000 between them for the rights to telecast the Series that was won by the Yankees in seven games.

In Game One, Berra teamed with pitcher Frank "Spec" Shea to form an all-rookie battery. The next time an all-rookie battery started a WS game was in Game Four of the 2010 WS when the Giants had Madison Bumgarner on the hill and Buster Posey behind the plate. Shea has the distinction of throwing the first televised pitch in Series history. The first batter to step to the plate was Eddie Stanky. The Yanks won the first two games with Berra behind the plate. Jackie Robinson, who stole a league-leading 29 bases during his rookie season, and shortstop Pee Wee Reese were stolen base threats. In the first game they both stole a base. In Game Two, Reese pilfered two bases but was also caught stealing by a Berra throw.

Because of Berra's Spartan catching skills, Yankees manager Bucky Harris started Sherm Lollar in the catcher's position in Game Three. In the seventh inning he pinch-hit Berra for Lollar, and Yogi, facing Ralph Branca, delivered the first pinch-hit home run in World Series history in the Dodgers' 9–8 win. In Game Four, with Berra catching, Bill Bevens pitched 8⅔ innings of no-hit baseball but issued 10 walks. He lost the game 3–2 when Cookie Lavagetto drove in two runs in the bottom of the ninth. In Game Five, Shea tossed a four-hit masterpiece leading the Yankees to a 2–1 victory with Aaron Robinson behind the plate. Robinson caught the sixth and seventh games with Berra in right field.

It wasn't until 1949 that Berra became the regular backstop thanks to Dickey, who first-year manager Casey Stengel hired to tutor Yogi. Dickey refined Berra's skills and he became a standout receiver. From July 28, 1957, to May 10, 1959, he caught 148 straight games and accepted 950 errorless chances, both records at the time. He had cat-like movements and a strong arm. On July 28 he made an error in the first game of a doubleheader against the Tigers in New York when he made an errant throw to second base in an attempt to pick off Paul Foytack who advanced to third on the play while Harvey Kuenn advanced to second on the throw. The next time Yogi made another error was on May 12, 1959, in a game against the Indians at Yankees Stadium. Again, it came on an errant throw to second base in an attempt to retire a runner. This time it was Minnie Miñoso who was stealing second. Miñoso advanced to third on the throw.

"Dickey worked my butt off, but it was great," Berra said. "I enjoyed it and he learned me a lot. He used to keep me after workouts and work on how to throw a ball to second base. It's very easy."

In 1951 Allie Reynolds pitched two no-hitters. Reynolds, who was part Creek, was known as the "Super Chief." On July 12 he no-hit the Indians and beat Bob Feller, 1–0, in a night game in Cleveland. Gene Woodling homered for the only run in the game. On September 28 he no-hit the Red Sox. Entering the final weekend of the season, the Yankees led the Indians by two and a half games. The Bronx Bombers closed the season hosting the Red Sox for five games that included doubleheaders on Friday and Saturday. Reynolds faced 18-game-winner Mel Parnell in the Friday opener and had an 8–0 lead. In the top of the ninth, Charlie Maxwell grounded out to start the inning. Reynolds then walked Dom DiMaggio before Johnny Pesky struck out looking. Next up was Williams, arguably the greatest hitter in the game. Reynolds was one out from becoming the first American League pitcher to toss two no-hitters in the same season.

Williams hit a high pop-up behind the plate for what appeared to be the last out.

The normally sure-handed Berra misjudged the ball as it moved in the wind. The ball "squirmed out of his glove," wrote *New York Times* sportswriter John Drebinger, "and the catcher tumbled, sprawling on his face." Reynolds, after colliding with Berra and concerned that he might have stepped on his All-Star backstop's hand, went back to the mound. Berra called for the same pitch and Williams hit a foul fly. Yogi caught it and the no-hitter was secured.

Reflecting on that game Yogi explained, "The wind does a lot of funny things in Yankee Stadium. When I dropped the first one, Reynolds stepped on my hand. I was falling back trying to make the catch. He said, 'Are you alright?' I said, 'No. You stepped on my hand.' I called the same pitch and he hit the same ball in the same place, and I caught it. I was lucky. God was on my side."

1955

Berra entered the 1955 season as the highest-paid Yankee ($48,000) by winning his second consecutive MVP award and third overall when he hit .272 with 27 homers and 108 RBI. His OPS was .819. (His highest salary came in 1957 when he earned $65,000.) He was involved in two never-to-be-forgotten plays in the '55 Series.

In top of the eighth inning of Game One, the Dodgers trailed the Yankees 6–4 when Jackie Robinson stole home with Whitey Ford on the mound. Berra, jumping up and down, argued the call vociferously with umpire Bill Summers that Robinson was out. Throughout his life, Yogi never stopped insisting Robinson was out and he even signed photos of the play with "He was out." When Yogi walked by the photo of the play in his museum and learning center, he would bellow, "He was out!"

But I don't think so.

When Berra saw Robinson thundering down the line, he popped out of the catcher's area beyond the front of the plate. In my opinion, Yogi should have been charged with interference. The wording of the rule in 1955 was exactly the same as it is now under rule 6.01 (g). It reads, "If with a runner on third base and trying to score by means of a squeeze play or a steal, the catcher or any other fielder steps on, or in front of home base without possession of the ball, or touches the batter or his bat, the pitcher shall be charged with a balk, the batter will be awarded first base on the interference and the ball is dead." Because the pitcher is charged with a balk, all runners are allowed to advance one base and the run scores. The call became a moot point as the Yanks won the game, 6–5. Critics of the play argued that it was not wise for Robinson to attempt to steal home with his team behind by two runs.

In Game Seven of the '55 Series, the Yankees were down 2–0 in the bottom of the sixth and struggling against Dodgers lefty Johnny Podres. With runners first and second and one out, the Yanks finally had a rally going. Yogi came up in a clutch situation, the kind he craved. He put the ball in play with a long, slicing fly ball to the left field corner. It looked like a for-sure game-tying double. But Sandy Amoros, the Dodgers' left-fielder, made a spectacular one-handed running catch. The nimble Cuban then wheeled and fired the ball to Reese, the cutoff man, who tossed to Hodges at first base to double up McDougald. The rally was over, and the Dodgers went on to win the game 2–0 and their first-ever World Series championship.

"The Dodgers had just changed the outfield," Berra said. "They took Don Zimmer out of the game at second base because he was pinch-hit for by George 'Shotgun' Shuba and put Jim Gilliam there who was playing left field. Amoros was put in left field in place of Gilliam. If Gilliam was out there the ball would have fallen [for a hit] but Sandy being a left hander was able to catch the ball [with the glove on his right hand that was extended]." When I spoke with Yogi he had just seen the play again and realized that Amoros was closer to the line than he thought. "He ran a long way to get that ball," he acknowledged.

When Amoros was asked about the catch he answered, "I dunno. I just run like hell." The shy flychaser reportedly lived like a gypsy while in Brooklyn, never renting an apartment. It was reported that most of the time he lived on Campanella's yacht.

1956 World Series

Yogi had more than baseball on his mind during the '56 World Series when the Yankees again matched up with the Dodgers. His mother, Paulina, who battled diabetes, was scheduled to have a leg amputated the day the Series started. Diabetes, which had already robbed Yogi's 63-year-old mother of most of her sight, was "blocking the circulation of blood into her right leg," wrote Pessar.

On October 2, the night before the start of the Series, the worried Yankee called his father and offered to come home. But his father influenced him to stay in New York.

Despite his worries about mama Paulina, Mr. October batted .360, swatted three homers, had 10 RBI, and caught Don Larsen's historic perfect game in Game Five. Larsen did not shake off Berra once during his masterpiece. Larsen was chosen the *Sport Magazine* MVP of the Series, but Berra clearly was the best player in the Series.

Yogi's wife, Carmen, was seven months pregnant and was at the perfect game with her sister Mary. Carmen was a bundle of nerves when Dale Mitchell, pinch-hitting for pitcher Sal Maglie, came to bat with two outs in the top of the ninth. She told her sister Mary that if Larsen retired Mitchell, she would name her unborn baby Dale. Mitchell struck out.

Dale Berra was born December 13, 1956.

I once asked Yogi about the validity of that story and he deadpanned, "I dunno, Carmen named all the kids."

Berra made a living of making catching teammates back-up receivers. Silvera was a good example. Like the Maytag repairman, he got little work. He spent most of his nine Yankee years in the bullpen. He appeared in one WS game in 1949 and had two at-bats but cashed in on Series money seven times totaling $46,597.05 — chump change today. He kept the mitt he wore to warm up Larsen before the game. When the game ended, Silvera asked Yogi if he had a souvenir from the historic game he could have.

Yogi gave him his jockstrap.

Following Larsen's perfect game Yogi called St. John's Hospital in St. Louis and had an uplifting conversation with his mother. He couldn't wait to see her after the Series was over. Passer wrote Yogi asked, "Momma, is there anything I can do for you?"

"Can you hit a home run for me tomorrow?" she asked.

"Sure, Mom, sure," Yogi said.

The Yankees were held scoreless in Game Six when Clem Labine outdueled Bob Turley in the Dodgers' pulsating 10-inning, 1–0 win. Berra was upset that he failed to keep his promise to his mother. However, he made up for it in Game Seven when he poked two home runs off Don Newcombe in the Yankees' 9–0 win. Right-hander Johnny Kucks blanked the Dodgers on three hits and Bill Skowron's grand slam in the seventh sealed the victory. Trailing 2–0 in the Series, the Yankees won four of the next five games using five different starters (Ford, Sturdivant, Larsen, Turley, and Kucks) to regain the world championship. Credit Berra who guided each pitcher to throwing complete games.

As in the '56 Series, his deeds were forgotten in the '60 Fall Classic against the Pirates. He hit a critical three-run homer in the sixth inning of Game Seven that led to a 5–4 Yankees lead but it has been lost to time because it served as a backdrop to Bill Mazeroski's epic walk-off homer, the first time in the history of the WS that the Series ended in such fashion. Playing left field, Berra helplessly watched the ball sail over the left field wall at Forbes Field.

Berra caught his share of accomplished pitchers during his career. I asked him who he would he want on the mound in Game Seven of a World Series. He answered without hesitation, "Vic Raschi." The "Springfield Rifle," who had a career record of 132–66, was 5–3 in Series play with a 2.24 ERA. As a Yankee he went 120–50 and was a part of the great trifecta that included Reynolds and Lopat who helped lead the Yankees to an unprecedented five straight championships from 1949 to 1953.

Yogi played three more seasons before retiring after the 1963 World Series. He batted just once in the Series, a sweep at the hands of the Los Angeles Dodgers. Even with that loss, he finished with a 10–4 record in Series play as a player.

On October 24, 1963, Berra was named the Yankees' manager to replace Ralph Houk who became the general manager. Berra was paid $35,000, a pay cut from his $52,000 player's contract. The 1964 Yankees were not an easy bunch to manage, especially veteran icons like Mantle and Ford who were famous for wisecracks on and off the field. They were an aging team and players like Pepitone and Bouton were brash. The perception that the clubhouse was out of control did not serve Berra well. Some criticized Mantle and Ford for not being as supportive of Berra as they should have been.

The nadir came in mid–August with a four-game sweep by the Chicago White Sox culminating on August 20 and putting the Bombers in third place, four and a half games behind the first-place White Sox. Following the game, the Yankees were on the team bus headed to the airport where they would board a flight to Boston. It was then that infielder Phil Linz played "Mary Had a Little Lamb" on his harmonica. This upset Berra which led to Yogi knocking the harmonica out of Linz's hands.

Linz, who once co-hosted my radio show, was fined $250 for his actions and apologized to Yogi. But for his part, Linz received a $10,000 endorsement deal from the Hohner harmonica company and was featured in a back-page ad in the 1965 Yankees yearbook that read "Play it again, Phil." He repeated his harmonica playing in 2013 at the Baseball Assistance Team's annual dinner, during which Berra was honored.

"I've always been very conscious of the fact that it was disrespectful, even though I didn't realize what I was doing," Linz told the New York *Daily News* at that event. "I shouldn't have been playing a harmonica after a loss. I did apologize to Yogi."

The incident became national news. "If people remember me at all," Linz told *USA Today* in 2013, "they remember me as a harmonica player, because I sure wasn't too good of a baseball player."

Linz passed on December 9, 2020, at age 81.

With Berra's job already in danger, this appeared to make his firing a *fait accompli*. The Yanks arrived in Boston for the start of a four-game series. They dropped the first two but finished 30–11 the rest of the way to finish one game ahead of the White Sox and two in front of the Orioles for the AL pennant. The Linz harmonica incident was viewed by some as the turning point, both for the players and for Berra, who had been a long-time teammate of many of them. But it didn't save his job—he was fired after the season.

The 1964 WS was a back-and-forth Series that came down to a Game Seven matchup between Cardinals ace Bob Gibson and 22-year-old Mel Stottlemyre, who was called up in mid–August and responded brilliantly, going 9–3 down the stretch run. St. Louis broke through for three runs in the fourth inning with the aid of some sloppy Yankees defense and Gibson held on to clinch the Series.

Across town, the New York Mets had finished their third season of play and two former Yankees were running the show, Weiss (general manager) and Stengel (manager). Berra took Weiss's offer and joined Stengel's staff as a player-coach. He caught only two games and batted .222, playing his final game on May 9, three days before his 40th birthday, when the Atlanta Braves beat the Mets 8–2 in the first game of a Sunday doubleheader. Playing in the first game, Yogi went 0-for-4. His final at-bat came in the bottom of the ninth. The Mets had Ed Kranepool on second base and Joe Christopher on first with one out when Berra, facing Tony Cloninger, hit a ground ball to second baseman Frank Bolling, who tossed to shortstop Denis Menke for a fielder's choice force out.

For Lawrence Peter Berra, his playing days were over!

He then served as the Mets' first base coach through the 1971 season and proved to be a valuable asset to the team, especially with young talent like catcher Jerry Grote coming up.

Berra stayed on to coach under Gil Hodges and won his 11th World Series ring in 1969 when the Miracle Mets upset the Baltimore Orioles. Berra's opportunity to finally manage the Mets came under tragic circumstances when he replaced Hodges after the Mets manager died of a heart attack at age 47 on Easter Sunday, April 2, 1972. Hodges played golf at the Palm Beach Lakes golf course in Florida with coaches Joe Pignatano, Rube Walker, and Eddie Yost. As they walked off the final hole of their 27-hole day toward their rooms at the Ramada Inn, Hodges collapsed and was pronounced dead at 5:45 p.m. in West Palm Beach.

Berra led the 1973 Mets to the NL pennant before losing to the A's in the WS. In 1975 the Mets were 56–53 after being shut out in a doubleheader against the Expos when Berra was fired and replaced by Roy McMillan, a coach on his staff. The team went 26–27 under McMillan.

After a 12-year absence, Yogi returned to the Yankees as a coach under former teammate Billy Martin in 1976. With Berra on board at the renovated Yankee Stadium, the Yanks won their first pennant since 1964. Though they were swept in that Series by the Reds, Berra added two more World Series rings with back-to-back titles in 1977 and 1978. Berra was a constant on the Yankees' coaching staff through the 1983 season despite several managerial changes. He got one more chance to manage when he was named Yankees manager for the 1984 season.

Honors

On May 12, 2000, Yogi's 75th birthday, a new ferry on the Hudson River was christened in his name. Berra was awarded the Presidential Medal of Freedom posthumously on November 24, 2015, by President Barack Obama in a ceremony at the White House attended by members of Berra's family, who accepted the award on his behalf. It is our nation's highest civilian award. At the ceremony, the president said: "Today we celebrate some extraordinary people, innovators, artists and leaders who contribute to America's strength as a nation." Celebrating Berra's military service and remarkable baseball career, Obama used one of Berra's famous Yogi-isms: "One thing we know for sure: If you can't imitate him, don't copy him."

The USPS issued a Yogi Berra stamp in 2021. Charles Chaisson did the artwork. Berra is the 31st baseball player to be featured on a stamp. "His face brought joy to thousands of people," said son Larry Berra. "As players get older and pass away, their legacy wanes and goes down, but hopefully the stamp will keep it going—that means the most to me, to keep him in the public eye, so they don't just forget."

In tribute to the beloved Hall of Fame catcher, Don Mattingly wore the number 8 in his honor when he managed the Miami Marlins.

There has been speculation that Yogi deserves a monument in Monument Park at Yankee Stadium. His baseball career speaks for itself, but he was a monumental national figure as well. He was more than a baseball player. Former broadcaster George Grande served as the master of ceremonies for the Baseball Hall of Fame induction ceremonies for 31 years. "One year I was sitting with Yogi, his wife Carmen, Stan Musial, and his wife Lil," recalled Grande. "They were close friends. Someone asked about George Steinbrenner getting a monument in Monument Park at Yankee Stadium. Stan, who had seven different monuments erected for him from the USA to Poland, said, 'If anyone deserves a monument at Yankee Stadium, it's Yogi—he was the best ever.'"

At an Old-Timers' Day game at Yankee Stadium, Berra was standing with Whitey Ford on the field after being introduced. During the ceremony the Yankees honored those in the Yankee family who had gone on to baseball heaven in the past year. While the names were being read, Yogi said to Whitey, "I hope we never see our name up there."

Classic Yogi!

15

"Scooter"

> "He can't hit like Honus Wagner, but Wagner never made the plays that Phil does. To me Rizzuto is 'Mr. Shortstop.'"
> —Casey Stengel

Phil Rizzuto, the Hall of Fame Yankee shortstop, was best known for his fielding and bunting, but he once pinch-hit for DiMaggio. It proved to be the best at-bat of his life.

Following Rizzuto's rookie 1941 season, DiMaggio was scheduled to speak at a firemen's banquet in Newark, New Jersey. The Yankee Clipper was a national celebrity coming off his 56-game consecutive hitting streak. But DiMag had to cancel his appearance because his wife, Dorothy Arnold, gave birth to his son, Joe, and he needed to be there.

DiMaggio asked Rizzuto to substitute for him. "Scooter" reluctantly obliged, knowing the audience was expecting to see the great DiMaggio. Emil Esselborn, the man in charge of the affair, invited the rookie Yankee shortstop to his home. Esselborn had several daughters, one of which was Cora, an attractive girl of Dutch-Irish descent whom Rizzuto would fall in love with on first sight and later marry.

Born Fiero Rizzuto, he preferred the Americanized name Phil. There has been confusion about his year of birth stemming from Rizzuto's shaving a year off the date at the beginning of his pro career on the advice of teammates. Throughout his career, his birth year was listed as 1918 but it was subsequently reported by the New York City Department of Health that his official birth certificate is, in fact, dated 1917.

Rizzuto's career ended in 1956, but he was the regular Yankees shortstop from 1941 to 1954 minus his years in the military. He was challenged with many fears. He hated to fly and was afraid of anything that crawled. He feared lightning because a minor league teammate was once struck by lightning. He had a weird superstition that involved putting a wad of gum over the metal pin on top of his baseball cap.

Despite his size, Scooter was fearless on the field. The 5'6", 150-pound shortstop was small in stature, but he left a large imprint in Yankee lore. Rizzuto held his ground at second base as runners tried to take him out in the combat zone on the 4–6–3 double play. Believe it or not, the diminutive Italian was even a single wing quarterback on his Richmond Hill High School football team in Queens, New York. "If you think he's a pushover, don't ever bump into him hard," wrote John Drebinger of the *New York Times*. "For you will find him a bundle of steel, heavy-boned and as sturdily built as a brick oven. And his exceptionally large and strong hands and fingers help account for the sureness with which he fields the toughest grounders."

Rizzuto spent his entire career on a dynasty team that captured 10 AL titles and seven World Championships in his 13 seasons. He holds numerous World Series records for shortstops. He was the AL runner-up for MVP behind Ted Williams in 1949 when he fielded .971 and hit .275 leading the Yankees in games played, hits, runs, doubles, and total bases. His best statistical season was 1950, when he batted .324 with 200 hits and was named the American League's Most Valuable Player. He also captured the first Hickock Belt Award that year as the top professional athlete in the United States. In the final 43 games of the season, he hit .326 and scored 42 runs in leading the Yanks to a 31–12 run before sweeping the Phillies "Whiz Kids" in the 1950 Fall Classic. He was hailed by the *New York Times* as "the indispensable man of the world champion Bombers." After DiMaggio retired in '51, Rizzuto was the highest paid Yankee at $50,000 a year.

Big-Game Player

How a player performs in pressure situations is a yardstick for greatness. Rizzuto often stared pressure in the eye and conquered it. The Yankees and Red Sox battled down to the final two games of the 1949 season that were played at Yankee Stadium. The Sox held a one-game lead. In Saturday's game, with the Yankees trailing 4–2 in the fifth inning, Rizzuto singled, then eventually scored on Berra's base hit. Johnny Lindell's homer in the eighth won it for the Yanks, 5–4.

The season came down to Sunday's dramatic winner-take-all grand finale. Raschi opposed Boston's Ellis Kinder, who was described by author David Halberstam in his 1989 best seller *Summer of '49* as an "old fashioned, unreconstructed carouser, cavalier in the extreme about training rules and curfews."

Former Yankees senior advisor Arthur Richman knew Kinder from his days with the St. Louis Browns. "It was well known that the more Ellis drank the night before a game, the better he pitched," Richman stated. "The Boston players asked me to take him out on Saturday night and get him drunk, which I did. When we returned to the hotel, I had a girl with me, and she wasn't a hooker. I left Ellis and the girl in the room and took off."

Richman did his job. Before 68,055 tense fans, Kinder pitched seven innings allowing only one run on four hits. In the bottom of the first, Rizzuto wasted no time getting the Yankees on the board against Kinder when he tripled down the left field line and later scored on Henrich's infield grounder to Doer., The Yanks scored four runs in the bottom of the eighth led by Henrich's home run off Parnell and Coleman's three-run double off Tex Hughson giving the Yankees a 5–0 lead. In the top of the ninth the Sox nicked Raschi for three runs, but the Yanks held on to win the thrilling contest, 5–3. For the weekend series, Rizzuto went 3-for-6.

A defeated Ted Williams lamented, "If we had that little guy [Rizzuto], we would have won [the pennant] by 10 games." Johnny Pesky, Rizzuto's Red Sox counterpart, proclaimed the Yankee shortstop "the best I have ever seen."

Rizzuto was regarded as one of the best bunters in baseball history. He led the majors in sacrifice bunts for four straight years (1949–1952). "Bunting has become a lost art, but Rizzuto is keeping it alive," said Ty Cobb. The Yankee shortstop arguably laid down the greatest bunt in the history of the Yankees' franchise during a pressure-packed game.

On September 17, 1951, the Yankees and Cleveland Indians were tied for first place with just 12 games left in the season when the two rivals clashed on a Monday afternoon in the Bronx in front of 42,072 fans. Rizzuto was facing Bob Lemon in the bottom of the ninth inning with the bases loaded and the score tied 1–1 with one out. It was the perfect situation for a suicide squeeze. Rizzuto took Lemon's first pitch, a called strike, and argued the call with plate umpire Cal Hubbard. That gave him time to grab his bat from both ends, the sign to DiMaggio, who was on third, that a squeeze play was on for the next pitch. But DiMaggio broke early, surprising Rizzuto. Lemon, seeing what was happening, threw high to avoid a bunt, aiming behind Rizzuto. But with Joltin' Joe bearing down on him, Rizzuto got his bat up in time to lay down the bunt. "If I didn't bunt, the pitch would've hit me right in the head," Rizzuto said. "I bunted it with both feet off the ground, but I got it off toward first base." DiMaggio scored the winning run. Stengel called it "the greatest play I ever saw."

In 1982, Yankees owner George Steinbrenner asked Scooter to go down to spring training to teach the Yankees the art of bunting. On the second day, Rizzuto broke his hand which had to be put in a cast. Steinbrenner unwittingly played a part in the injury. Steinbrenner was standing at the cage watching Rizzuto's instruction. "I was getting a little closer to the net behind the plate and talking to the hitters," recalled Rizzuto. "[Jerry] Mumphrey was in there and I said something to him about his stance. He turned to me and let the pitch go. The ball hit the net and then my hand."

The Hall of Fame Yankee shortstop batted .320 in the '51 World Series against the Giants for which the New York chapter of the BBWAA later voted him winner of the Babe Ruth Award as the Series' top player. But Rizzuto was forever upset about an incident in Game Three of the Series when the Giants' Eddie "The Brat" Stanky (real name Stankiewicz) sparked a rally by kicking the ball out of Rizzuto's glove on a tag play. Here is what happened.

The teams had split the first two games. The Giants were leading the Yankees 1–0 in the bottom of the fifth inning. After pitcher Jim Hearn struck out, Stanky walked. With an 0–1 count on Alvin Dark, Berra called for a pitchout. He grabbed Raschi's delivery and fired to Rizzuto, who was covering second.

Rizzuto waited with the ball to tag Stanky, but the Brat moved his right foot into Scooter's glove and kicked the ball toward center field. Stanky then advanced to third. Rizzuto was charged with an error he never forgot. The error led to five unearned runs culminated by Whitey Lockman's three-run homer. Final score, Giants 6, Yankees 2.

Rizzuto and Stengel both argued with second base umpire Bill Summers that interference should have been called on Stanky. Following the game, Scooter told reporters, "Summers was in no position to see the play. I told him, 'Even if you don't call him out for kicking the ball out of my hand—and that's interference—you must call him out for not touching second base.'"

The play haunted Rizzuto for the rest of his life.

Another situation that irked Rizzuto occurred during the '52 season when Pesky was a member of the Detroit Tigers. In the August 25 game at the stadium, Rizzuto led off the bottom of the third and hit a slow roller to Pesky. The shortstop charged the ball but had trouble getting it out of his glove and John Drebinger, the official scorer, scored the play an error. Dan Daniel of the *New York World Telegram* challenged Drebinger's decision, claiming you couldn't call a ball that got stuck in a fielder's glove an error. The error was then changed to a hit.

The call became more controversial as the game went on because by the sixth inning, Detroit right-hander Virgil "Fireball" Trucks had given up no other hits. Finally, Drebinger called down to the Tigers' dugout and talked with Pesky who said he should have been charged with the error because he allowed the ball to squirt out of his hand. The hit was then changed to an error and Trucks went on to no-hit the Yankees in front of a paltry Monday afternoon crowd of more than 13,000.

Rizzuto retired with 1,588 hits instead of 1,589. But losing three years in the military was more of a detriment to his career hits total than Drebinger's reversed decision. Assuming he averaged 160 hits each season, he would have collected more than 2,000 hits.

Rizzuto was the proverbial "small ball" player, noted for his strong defense in the infield. From September 17, 1949, to June 8, 1950, he had a 58-game errorless streak at shortstop. The record was broken by Ed Brinkman (Tigers) who played 72 error free games in '72. Former Orioles shortstop Mike Bordick is the current record holder at 110 consecutive errorless games.

Raschi said, "My best pitch is anything the batter grounds, lines, or pops in the direction of Rizzuto."

Scooter's quick release was his signature. Joe Gordon, one of several second basemen who teamed with Rizzuto, once said he had never seen a shortstop who could get a ball away with so little lost motion. He worked the double play brilliantly with a cadre of second basemen including Gordon, Snuffy Stirnweiss, Jerry Coleman, Billy Martin and Gil McDougald. In 1950 he recorded 123 double plays, three more than Crosetti did in 1938. The little guy was also a master of the hidden ball trick.

During the '89 season I interviewed Rizzuto at Yankee Stadium in the middle of a game. He had agreed that we would meet when he was off the air for a couple of innings. I learned that he did not bleed pinstripes in his youth.

"I was a Dodgers fan, having been born in Brooklyn," he revealed. "But my biggest idol was Babe Ruth. I had an uncle Mike, who was a great sports fan, and he would take me to the Yankees, Giants and Dodgers games. One of the first games I ever saw was the 1934 All-Star game at the Polo Grounds when Carl Hubbell of the Giants struck out Ruth, Gehrig, Foxx, Simmons, and Cronin in succession."

Rizzuto's high school coach, Al Kunitz, played an important role in Rizzuto's life. He told Phil that he should never get ejected from a game because you can't help your team in the clubhouse. During Rizzuto's entire professional career, he never was banished by an umpire. Kunitz wrote to the local New York teams asking them to take a look at his 4'11" scholastic whiz. Dodgers manager Casey Stengel told him to "go get a shoe-shine box. You'll never make it in the big leagues." Giants manager Bill Terry wouldn't even let this little toy soldier put on a uniform. But the Yankees tryout was a week-long camp under the direction of Krichell with games every day. This gave Rizzuto a good chance to show off his assortment of baseball skills.

In 1937 he signed with the Yankees for $75 a month and started off in Bassett, Virginia, a Class D Yankee farm team. "My dad pinned a $20 bill to my undershirt," said Rizzuto. "He read there were thieves on the train." The diminutive Yankee hopeful climbed the ladder quickly. After stops in Norfolk, Virginia, and Kansas City, where he was named the Minor League Player of the Year in 1940 when he batted a glittering .347, it was on to the Big Show.

In 1941, the wide-eyed rookie, the size of an eighth grader, headed for the locker room in spring training in St. Petersburg, Florida, when he was stopped by Fred Logan, the clubhouse man. "Beat it—no kids allowed in here," growled Logan.

The pressure of replacing the veteran Crosetti at shortstop was felt by the fledgling young Yankee. "'Cro' was a big favorite who was the regular shortstop on those four straight world championship teams from 1936 to 1939," explained Rizzuto. "It took all of spring training and possibly a month and a half before the team accepted me." But Rizzuto had nothing but high praise for Crosetti, who told him where to play every hitter and much more, knowing that Rizzuto was trying to take his job.

Phillip Francis Rizzuto made his major league debut on April 14, 1941, at Griffith Stadium in Washington, D.C. McCarthy had him bat leadoff. In his first at-bat, facing Dutch Leonard, he grounded out to shortstop Cecil Travis. Two days later at Yankee Stadium the Yanks lost to the Philadelphia A's 10–7 but "Scooter" went 3-for-4 collecting his first ML hit in the third inning off Nels Potter, a single to left field.

Rizzuto's rookie campaign was a successful one when he batted .307. He roomed with second baseman Jerry Priddy, who was projected to be a star. Rizzuto ended up in the Hall of Fame and Priddy ended up in prison for four and a half months when a California jury found him guilty of a bomb extortion charge involving a cruise ship in 1973. Scooter also had a front row seat his freshman year for DiMaggio's great 56-game run. And he had a 16-game hitting streak of his own, going 28-for-57, which translated into a .491 batting mark. In the World Series against the Dodgers, he handled 30 of 31 chances.

Some called him the "eternal sophomore," but he certainly didn't suffer the proverbial sophomore jinx and helped the Yanks to their second straight AL pennant before falling to the St. Louis Cardinals in the World Series. The loss was no fault of the Yankee shortstop who hit .381 in the Series.

The day after the '42 WS ended, he entered the Navy and served through 1945. Rizzuto was placed at the Norfolk Naval Training Station in 1943 where he played baseball on a regular basis. On June 23 he married Cora. In 1944 he was sent to New Guinea and assigned to lead a 20 mm gun crew on a ship in the Pacific but contracted malaria. "Rizzuto was sent to Australia to recover and coached the US Navy baseball team while there," wrote Gary Bedingfield in his May 2007 *Baseball in Wartime* newsletter. During his time in the Navy, he was plagued by chronic sea sickness.

He returned from the war frail and thin and hit an anemic .257 for the third-place Yankees in '46. It was also the final season for McCarthy, who Rizzuto calls "the greatest manager I ever played for."

The Mexican League

In '46, Scooter considered jumping to the Mexican League. Jorge Pasquel, a wealthy customs broker in Mexico, and his brother Bernardo had a financial interest in a couple of Mexican League teams and were threatening to pirate away many of Major League Baseball's existing stars and key players from the Negro Leagues. Players like Sal Maglie, Mickey Owen, Max Lanier, Nap Reyes, Adrian Zabala and Danny Gardella made the jump. Gardella, an outfielder with the Giants and Cardinals, could walk up a flight of stairs on his hands, quote Plato and sing arias. Overall, 22 major league players defected. When Babe Ruth took his family on an extended Mexican vacation as guest of the Pasquel brothers, it triggered rumors that Ruth was being wooed for a Mexican club manager's job. Having a name like Ruth connected to the Mexican League would give it credibility and a load of publicity but the Bambino never got involved.

Jorge Pasquel met with Rizzuto in a parked car under a viaduct near Yankee Stadium. Pasquel made a reported offer that was difficult to refuse—$100,000, of which $40,000 would be put in escrow in a U.S. bank and $40,000 in a Mexican bank. Rizzuto would get a salary of $20,000, a Cadillac, an air-conditioned apartment in Mexico City and three servants. That was most likely apocryphal. Other reports stated he was offered $12,000 a year for five years plus a $15,000 signing bonus, which is more realistic.

Aware that Rizzuto might defect to Mexico, Weiss, who was then chief of the Yankees farm system, paid the Rizzutos a visit to influence him to stay. That night the Pasquel family invited Scooter and his wife, Cora, to a party at their New York headquarters in the Waldorf Astoria.

"The Pasquel brothers were there along with lawyers and some glamour girls, both Mexican and American," remembered Rizzuto, who was apparently ready to go south of the border. But Pasquel began knocking the Yankees. Cora didn't like the cloak-and-dagger act and persuaded her husband to stay in New York. Realizing where his heart was, Rizzuto stayed and received a $1,000 bonus from the Yankees.

The Pasquel brothers, who also had interests in the large Parque Delta stadium, departed the league in 1952. Jorge was killed in a plane crash three years later.

MLB tried to blacklist the players who defected. In June of '46 Commissioner A.B. "Happy" Chandler had barred any player who jumped to the Mexican League from returning to the major leagues for five years. He cited the reserve clause in the standard player contract, which bound a player to a team for life unless the team traded or released him. In 1948, Gardella brought a claim against the National League and American League as well as their presidents, Ford Frick and Will Harridge. Gardella argued that he was only bound by the reserve clause and not by a contract. An eventual out of court settlement left him with about $30,000 after lawyer fees. MLB then settled with all Mexican League jumpers.

Gardella's successful appeal is recognized as the first major early step toward baseball free agency.

In 1947 Rizzuto led the league in getting hit by pitches (eight time). It's no wonder he became the first player in American League history to wear a reinforced liner inside his cap for protection. It was a hard hat version of the baseball cap. Thanks to the protection, he escaped serious injury when he was beaned by Red Sox pitcher George Susce on September 17, 1955. Rizzuto was carried off on a stretcher but would have suffered worse harm had it not been for his protective cap.

16

The Broadcaster, the Hall of Famer, the Humanitarian

Rizzuto hit for the cycle in life. He excelled as a family man, a ballplayer, a broadcaster, and a humanitarian.

"Winning the MVP in 1950 was my biggest thrill," stated Rizzuto. "The biggest disappointment was when I was released by the Yankees." The bad news came on August 25, 1956. It was on Old-Timers' Day which was not the best public relations move by the Yankees' front office. The Yankees needed a roster spot for Enos Slaughter and Rizzuto was the odd man out.

"I thought that was the end of the world," Rizzuto lamented. "If it wasn't for [my former teammate] George Stirnweiss, I might have done something desperate. Snuffy said, 'Leave your car here and I'll take you home. Take Cora and the kids and go away. Don't talk to the press.' I followed his advice, and it was the smartest thing I ever did."

When he retired, his 1,217 career double plays ranked second in major league history, trailing only Luke Appling's total of 1,424, and his .968 career fielding average trailed only Lou Boudreau's mark of .973 among AL shortstops.

No. 10 Retired

The Yankees retired Rizzuto's number 10 in a ceremony at Yankee Stadium on August 4, 1985. During this ceremony, he was also given a plaque to be placed in the stadium's Monument Park. Humorously, Rizzuto, holding a golf club he had been given, was accidentally bumped to the ground during his own ceremony by a live cow, appropriately named "Huckleberry," a gift from the New York *Daily News*. Rizzuto often used the word Huckleberry in his broadcasts to describe a less-than-gifted player. The cow wore a halo (a "holy cow") in reference to Scooter's often used words to describe a big play or a dramatic home run. Both the honoree and Huckleberry were unhurt.

Rizzuto later described the encounter: "That big thing stepped right on my shoe and pushed me backwards, like a karate move." In that day's game, his future broadcast partner Tom Seaver recorded his 300th career victory pitching for the White Sox.

Most baseball observers, including Rizzuto himself, came to believe that Derek Jeter had surpassed him as the greatest shortstop in Yankees history. Scooter paid tribute to his heir apparent during the 2001 postseason at Yankee Stadium. Jogging back to the Yankee dugout after throwing out a first pitch, he flipped the ceremonial baseball backhanded, imitating Jeter's celebrated game-saving throw to home plate that had just occurred during the Yankees' 2001 American League Division Series triumph against the A's. The photo of Jeter and Rizzuto taken that evening walking back to the dugout is one of Jeter's most prized possessions.

Broadcaster

In 1957 Rizzuto moved into the broadcast booth, and to make room for him, Jim Woods was let go. Some have theorized that this was a way for the Yankees' front office to make amends for the PR faux pas of releasing this popular Yankee on Old-Timers' Day in front of several of his former teammates. But Rizzuto appeared to have his eyes on the job even as a player. During the '56 season when Stengel would take him out of a game, he would on occasion shower and go up to the broadcast booth to observe Mel Allen and Red Barber at their craft.

"I just fell into it," said Rizzuto. "I didn't go to school to prepare for it. Mel Allen helped me the most." Although he credits Allen as a mentor, it has been reported that he faced an unpleasant baptism by Allen and Red Barber, two play-by-play icons.

Rizzuto was once quoted as saying "I was one of the early ones to invade their domain." According to Richard Sandomir, writing in the *New York Times*, Howard Cosell didn't encourage him either. "You'll never last," he told Rizzuto. "You look like George Burns and sound like Groucho Marx."

Rizzuto admitted that he was not a professional announcer. He was not an info guy who would deliver boring, innocuous statistics. As years went on, the broadcast booth became his playpen for having fun. His idiosyncratic style and unpredictable digressions charmed listeners and viewers. Mike Lupica wrote, "He was a character without trying to be one."

His scorekeeping was erratic. If he wasn't paying attention, he would mark the box "WW" for "wasn't watching."

He was self-deprecating, and the viewers loved it. His folksy, homespun practices of reading birthday notices and sending greetings to the ill were generally unheard of during a baseball broadcast. His jabber about leaving early to beat the traffic over the George Washington Bridge and his love for cannolis were often part of his broadcast. Different local pastry shops often sent cannolis to the broadcast booth. But if truth be told, Rizzuto never ate most of them because he feared he might be poisoned. "There was only one lady's cannolis he would eat," said George Grande. "All the rest got sent out to the writers and the press box workers. She was from Brooklyn. She would send one giant cannoli and a box with regular size ones."

Scooter was the head Yankee cheerleader. His recognizable shrieking soprano voice entertained fans for five decades. It made him a broadcasting legend and a pop culture icon that inspired references on an episode of *Seinfeld* and Meat Loaf's "Paradise by the Dashboard Light," a song in which he provided the baseball play-by-play element. But he was not told of the sexual nature of the song before he recorded his portion.

"Holy cow" was the trademark of legendary announcer Harry Carey who reportedly asked Allen to tell Rizzuto to stop using it on Yankees broadcasts. Scooter never got the memo.

For many years he worked with Frank Messer and former player and NL president Bill White. They served as Rizzuto's straight men. The broadcasts were classic. They brought the best or the worst out of Rizzuto. White was his most famous foil. If Rizzuto's comments were going in the wrong direction, White would grab him by the wrist. Of course, the viewers could not see this.

I'll never forget the night Rizzuto came on the air with White and said, "Hi, everyone, welcome to New York Yankee baseball. I'm Bill Wh…." White almost fell out of the booth in laughter. Rizzuto often referenced Cuban cameraman Dulio Costabile, who loved the banter in the booth, in his monologues.

The Telephone Bill Prank

Rizzuto, who was naïve and exuberant with a bubbling personality, was often the target of practical jokes by his teammates who put dead mice, spiders and rubber snakes in his glove. Former pitcher Frank "Spec" Shea once locked the bat rack box with Little Phil in it.

The former shortstop never could escape being the butt of pranks, even in his years behind the mic. Grande, the first face ever on ESPN, worked with Rizzuto and Tom Seaver in 1989 and 1990.

"I loved my time with Scooter," said Grande. "It was like working with your favorite uncle."

Grande and Seaver knew of Rizzuto's frugal reputation. "Before there were cell phones, we had telephones in the broadcast booth," explained Grande. "Phil usually arrived late but one or two times during a homestand he would come up to the booth early and use the stadium phones to call his friends all over the country. He would call Jerry Coleman, Ken Keltner, his doctor in Florida and others. If he made these calls at home, he would be billed but not at the ballpark."

Grande decided to have some fun. He got three pieces of Yankees stationery and made out bogus telephone bills. He designed them to look like an internal order from the Yankees' organization. Grande made out phone bills for Seaver, Rizzuto and himself.

"The bill made out to Seaver was for $120, mine was for $135, and Rizzuto's was an astonishing $4,238," laughed Grande.

The public relations department would place mail from the fans and other sources on the broadcasters' seats in the booth. This one evening the three of them were together about 5:30. "I asked Tom if he got his phone bill," recalled Grande. "Tom said, 'Yes, I did.' I then said, 'I got mine.' I then asked Scooter if he got a telephone bill and he answered, 'No.'"

"Tom and I then left the booth and watched Scooter open his mail from an adjacent booth," Grande continued. "We were standing behind the glass to where Rizzuto was and watched him open his billing letter. When he saw it was over $4,000, he panicked and put the letter to the side of his face. If there was ever a time for him to say, 'Holy Cow,' it was now."

"So I got the guy in charge of finances to go to Phil and ask him about the calls. Rizzuto denied knowing anything about them. He then looked up found Tom and I laughing and knew he was duped," Grande related.

Rizzuto worked the Yankees-Red Sox game in Boston on August 15, 1995, the evening of Mickey Mantle's funeral. It was reported that WPIX refused to let him go to the funeral because "someone needed to do the color commentary." Emotionally drained, Rizzuto abruptly left the booth in the middle of the telecast saying he could not continue.

A source close to the situation disputed the above report. "Rizzuto did blame WPIX. But the truth was, he was looking for an excuse not to go to Dallas because he hated to travel at that time in his life. Of course, WPIX would have let him go. PIX allowed him to tell the story he told, but it wasn't accurate at all."

Late in the '95 season he announced his retirement from broadcasting. Some thought it was because of the falsely reported unfair treatment from WPIX. It was also rumored that he had guilty feelings about not going to Mantle's funeral. But he did return in '96, which would be his final year in the broadcast booth, to witness the rookie seasons of Jeter and Mariano Rivera.

When his broadcasting career ended, he had served the Yankees for 57 seasons, 17 as a player (13 in the majors, four in the minors) and 40 in the broadcast booth.

The Business Man

Although Rizzuto had a long career in the game, if things had turned out differently, he might have been a clothing store magnate. In 1949, he was hired by American Shops, a clothing store on U.S. Route 22 in Newark, New Jersey. He worked there with Berra and Dodgers outfielder Gene Hermanski. Scooter became part owner of the store.

In April 1959, the two amigos (Rizzuto and Berra) opened a 40-lane bowling alley in Clifton, New Jersey, called Rizzuto-Berra Lanes. Business was hot. More than 5,000 people showed up for the official opening aided by the presence of Mantle and Stengel.

Jon Pessah in his book *Yogi: A Life Behind a Mask* wrote, "Business is so good that two armed men showed up just before closing at 3:00 a.m., on April 27. One of the men put a gun to the 21-year-old night clerk's head and ordered him to lead them to the manager's office. As two unaware bowlers finished out their games, the night clerk opened the door to the manager's office, where the assistant manager was counting the weekend's take. The two men took the money—$6,000 in all, cut the phone lines, and ordered the two workers to lie on the floor as they walked out. Police never found the robbers."

Five years later the bowling alley was sold for a substantial profit.

And for 20 years Rizzuto was the celebrity spokesman for the Money Store.

On February 2, 1950, Rizzuto was a mystery guest on the very first Goodson-Todman Productions game show *What's My Line?* hosted by John Charles Daly. Rizzuto also made various TV appearances on programs such as CBS's *Toast of the Town* hosted by Ed Sullivan, *To Tell the Truth* and *The Phil Silvers Show*. In the mid–1950s, Phil and Cora were interviewed by Edward R. Morrow from their home on Windsor Way in Hillside, New Jersey. The police were called to stop several curious bystanders from trampling the Rizzuto lawn.

Some called Scooter "the Little Squire of Windsor Way." He was the first Yankee star to move to northern New Jersey. Berra, Lopat, McDougald, Collins and Woodling would follow.

Hall of Fame

The dream destination for every baseball player is the Hall of Fame located in the bucolic, idyllic village of Cooperstown in central New York. In 1956 *Dell* magazine published a baseball issue titled *Baseball Stars*. I have had it since I was a kid. An article appeared titled "Ten Who Can't Miss the Hall of Fame." Those included were Ted Williams, Casey Stengel, Bob Feller, Stan Musial, Robin Roberts, Jackie Robinson, Roy Campanella, Phil Rizzuto, Yogi Berra, and Pee Wee Reese. Prior to 1994 the only player on the list that was not elected to the coveted Hall was Rizzuto.

Despite his qualifications, Rizzuto was passed over for the Hall of Fame 15 times by the writers and 11 times by the Old Timers committee. The Yankees organization launched a campaign which involved putting together a pamphlet extolling the qualifications of their former shortstop turned broadcaster. Steinbrenner lobbied hard for Rizzuto and threatened to never let the Yankees play in the annual Hall of Fame exhibition game until the former Yankees shortstop was enshrined in Cooperstown. This probably did not serve Rizzuto well. Steinbrenner had a change of heart in 1987, allowing the Yankees to play the game. Neither of these tactics did anything to abet Rizzuto's cause. Finally, a persuasive speech by Williams helped push Rizzuto into the Hall in 1994. Williams, a member of the committee, argued that Rizzuto was the man who made the difference between the Yankees and his Red Sox. He was fond of saying, "If we'd had Rizzuto in Boston, we'd have won all those pennants instead of New York."

When I interviewed Rizzuto, Herb Goren, a longtime writer for the *New York Sun*, sat and observed. Goren, who wrote Rizzuto's long-running daily commentary on the CBS Radio network, covered the Dodgers and saw Reese play every day. I asked him to compare Reese with Rizzuto.

"Pee Wee was a great shortstop and I'm a great fan of his because he was a wonderful guy and a great team leader," said Goren. "But when I saw Rizzuto play not only during the season but in the World Series against Pee Wee and other great shortstops, in my mind Rizzuto was the greatest that ever lived. And that's only a small opinion compared to people like Joe DiMaggio, Ted Williams, and Hank Greenberg who called him the greatest shortstop they ever saw."

Cobb, who often was scornful of the modern player, said Rizzuto could have played in his era.

Lois and I attended Rizzuto's Hall of Fame induction. His speech brought the house down with laughter. It wasn't long before the good-humored shortstop chucked his notes and just ad-libbed as only he could.

Phil Rizzuto proudly sits in the Yankees dugout on Phil Rizzuto Hall of Fame night, August 9, 1994. "Scooter" served the Yankees as a player and broadcaster for 57 seasons.

Throughout his speech he would get sidetracked and tell everyone that they could leave anytime they wanted. So, he said it again while rambling, and as if on cue, Bench and Berra took him up on it and left the stage. While everyone was howling with laughter, they returned. Adding to the humor was a fly that was pestering him while he was speaking, and he tried to swat it away.

The Yankees declared August 9, 1994, as Phil Rizzuto Hall of Fame night. The celebrated shortstop was showered with gifts.

The Humanitarian

Eddie Lucas lost his sight when he was struck by a baseball between the eyes on the same day as Bobby Thomson's "Shot Heard 'Round the World" on Oct. 3, 1951. An ardent 12-year-old Giants fan at the time, Lucas was bubbling with excitement. Following the game, he went out to play baseball with friends in a nearby Jersey City sandlot. Lucas, a lefty pitcher, was struck by a line drive that led to total blindness four years later. The epic Thomson home run would be the last at-bat he ever saw. After he went blind, his mother wrote letters to many of his baseball idols. Giants manager Leo Durocher offered Lucas the opportunity to be a guest at the Polo Grounds for the 1952 season.

Lucas' mother took him to the clothing store where Rizzuto worked. The Yankee shortstop immediately took the blind kid under his wing. Lucas, who graduated from Seton Hall, was a freelance writer for six decades. He wrote for several baseball magazines, was a radio talk show host, and wrote a popular book titled *Seeing Home: The Ed Lucas Story*.

Lucas was also in the insurance business for many years. I often had dinner with Lucas at the stadium and whoever was his walking guide for that game. He no doubt was one of the most remarkable human beings I ever met. He loved to play baseball trivia and tell jokes.

Lucas went through a difficult divorce and Rizzuto testified in court on behalf of his friend. "I was the first blind man in the United States to receive custody of his children," Lucas said proudly. He spoke of his sons, Eddie and Chris. "It was the very first time in U.S. history that a disabled

Ed Lucas interviews Bernie Williams on Opening Day, April 7, 1992.

person was awarded custody over a non-disabled spouse." He was forever grateful to Rizzuto for supporting him in court. Movie producer Penny Marshall had plans to produce a movie about Lucas' extraordinary life, but it never came to fruition.

Rizzuto took an interest in Lucas' St. Joseph's School for the Blind charity in Jersey City. Until his death, Rizzuto raised millions for St. Joseph's by donating profits from his commercials and books and also by hosting the annual Phil Rizzuto Celebrity Golf Classic and Scooter Awards. In 2006 Rizzuto auctioned his 1950 MVP plaque ($175,000), three of his World Series rings ($84,825), and the previously mentioned cap with a wad of gum on it for $8,190. Most of the proceeds went to St. Joseph School for the Blind.

Rizzuto and Lucas remained friendly throughout life. The Hall of Fame shortstop introduced Lucas to his florist, Allison Pfeifle, who was legally blind. After a long courtship, the two were married on March 10, 2006, at home plate in Yankee Stadium. It was the first wedding ceremony ever conducted on the hallowed turf of the original stadium. Steinbrenner handled all the expenses for the affair.

Lucas was one of Rizzuto's last visitors before Rizzuto passed.

Eddie Lucas joined Phil in baseball heaven on November 10, 2021.

Many years ago, Rizzuto was involved in a snow blower accident during the off-season. He stuck his hand in the blower and got his fingers crushed. On the way to the hospital he worried about his golfing career. As he was wheeled into the hospital he made a vow to Sister Ellen, the head of the Elizabeth General Medical Center, that if they saved his hand, he would annually put on a spaghetti dinner to help raise funds for the hospital. He did it every year until Sister Ellen retired.

Phil Rizzuto died August 13, 2007, at age 89 in an assisted-living facility in West Orange, New Jersey. When reviewing Rizzuto's life, DiMaggio said, "People loved watching me play baseball. Scooter they just loved.'"

17

Roger Maris

Chasing a Ghost

"If Roger was going into second base to break up a double play, he would knock the infielder on his ass into left field."
—Rocky Colavito

When I began my radio show in 1997, I set out to find Sal Durante, the 19-year-old Brooklyn truck driver who snared Roger Maris' record-breaking 61st home run on October 1, 1961. The historic blast came off Red Sox pitcher Tracy Stallard. Durante's ticket was in the lower right field stands, box seat 163 D in section 33 about 360 feet from home plate.

Nearly 38 years later, Sal Durante re-enacts his famous catch of Roger Maris' 61st home run, near where he sat on October 1, 1961.

I eventually located Durante, who was living in Staten Island with his wife, Rosemarie. This would lead to a friendship that resulted in a couple of guest appearances on my show and a feature column I wrote in *Sports Collectors Digest*. And on June 19, 1999, Sal and Rosemarie joined Lois and me at Yankee Stadium where we saw the Yankees beat the Angels, 6–2, on a Saturday night. Maris was not there to hit a home run, but Bernie Williams went yard. I purchased tickets in right field, not far from where Durante made the catch of his life—no offense to Rosemarie. I wanted to relive that October 1 day with Durante.

The story of the catch and the events surrounding it would best be told by Durante.

I went to the game with my fiancée Rosemarie [Calabrese], my cousin John [Tortorella] and his girlfriend. Actually, Ro bought my ticket since I didn't have any money. At the time I was making 60 bucks a week delivering auto parts on Coney Island.

I did not go to the game that day with the intention of sitting in the right field grandstand in anticipation of possibly catching a record-breaking home run. I just went there to pass the day and to catch a baseball in batting practice. Would you believe that John dropped a ball during batting practice that Maris hit!

The four of us sat in a six-seat box with three seats in front and three seats in back. I was sitting in the front three seats with John and his girlfriend the first three innings while Rosemarie sat behind us with strangers. Before the start of the fourth inning when Roger hit the home run, I decided that it would be best if Rosemarie sat with John and his girlfriend, so we traded seats. If I never changed seats, I would never have caught the ball.

As for the home run, as soon as the ball left Roger's bat, I knew it was over my head. So, I jumped on the seat and reached as high as I could reach. The ball hit the palm of my hand and knocked me in the row behind me and that was it. There was no competition for the ball. I caught the ball on the fly, and it was just a matter of regaining my feet and getting up. I never lost control of the ball.

As soon as I jumped up two burly Stadium security guards were there to protect me. They escorted me through the Yankee bullpen to the tunnel along the right field line where I met Roger. I told the guards that I wanted to give the ball to Roger. I had no intention of keeping it.

It was publicized prior to Maris hitting the home run that Sam Gordon, a restaurant owner in Sacramento, California, would offer a $5,000 reward for the ball and apparently Maris knew about it. When I met Roger, he said, "Keep the ball and make yourself some money, kid." That's the kind of guy Roger was—a very thoughtful, generous man. I met him a couple of times after that, and he was the same way.

I wanted to take the ball home with me, but Yankee executives refused to let me go home with it because they feared for my security. They asked me how I felt about keeping the ball in a safe in Yankee Stadium. I said, "Wait a minute. How will I know the authenticity of the ball when I pick it up?" So, to guarantee the ball was the one I caught, I initialed it "S.D."

Gordon had someone contact me to come out to Sacramento where I would exchange the ball for $5,000. I actually went out there on my honeymoon. I got the ball back from the Yankees on October 28. I got married on the 29th and we flew to Sacramento on the 30th. Sam gave me a free honeymoon. He even offered to pay for the wedding if we got married in Sacramento.

We got there on a Monday and Roger arrived on Wednesday with his brother [Rudy]. When we arrived at the airport, Sam met us in an armored car. The media took photos of him like he was putting the ball in a vault.

The exchange of the ball and the money took place at Sam's Original Ranch Wagon restaurant. It was one of several restaurants that Sam owned. It was supposed to be done quietly but when we got there, we found many photographers and newspaper reporters. There were well over fifty people in the restaurant. Sam was voted Man of the Year out there. It was all a big publicity stunt for him. For many years he gave out his business card that had a picture of him giving the ball to Maris.

After I gave the ball to Sam, he gave it to Roger on the spot. Roger subsequently gave the ball to the Hall of Fame. I have been to Cooperstown and have viewed the ball. My initials are still on it.

Sam's publicity strategy almost turned into a nightmare. At the restaurant that night, a light fell from a high pole and hit Roger on the head. Roger was cut but he didn't say a word. However, I was embarrassed.

Sam offered me a job and said that I could stay in his home in Palm Springs. He said, "In New York you're either rich or you're poor. Get out while you can." We decided to go back to New York.

When we were in Sam's restaurant, Roger gave me his Yankee cigarette lighter. I have a signed baseball from him and a sterling silver gravy bowl he sent to us for our wedding. He was a great man.

The Yankees gave me two season passes for the 1962 season. In 1976, on the 15th anniversary of Roger's record-breaking home run, I threw the ball from my seat in right field to Graig Nettles, who also wore number 9. The Yankees invited me back for Roger's 25th anniversary in 1986 and I threw out the first ball. My wife and I were invited to sit in George Steinbrenner's suite. It was an Old Timer's Day and Mickey Mantle was there. We took a picture together. To be honest during the Mantle-Maris home run race I was rooting for Mickey, who was my idol. I didn't know Roger at the time.

By the way, I was at Yankee Stadium on September 26, 1961, when Roger hit number 60. We sat in the mezzanine in right field.

I feel like I'm part of history. I'm a part of Maris. I still have Maris in me.

The ball Maris hit for home run number 61 remains at the Baseball Hall of Fame.

In addition to honeymooning in Palm Springs, Sal and Rosemarie were on stage with the Mills Brothers in Reno and backstage with Louis Armstrong—and everywhere Sam Gordon took them there were media people. At the 1962 Seattle World's Fair, Durante missed catching a ball tossed by Stallard from the top of a Ferris wheel 100 feet away. It was originally to be thrown from the top of the 605-foot Space Needle but that was considered too dangerous. There were TV commercials and a question on the TV show *Jeopardy!* involving Durante and his famous catch.

For a moment of his life, he was a rock star. "One day I'm signing autographs and they're calling me an icon," Durante said. "The next day I'm just another working stiff. I've led two lives, and I have enjoyed it, but it hasn't changed me at all."

Durante allowed me to represent him in a Sotheby's auction in the late '90s. The items included his ticket from the historic game that was signed by Maris and a cigarette lighter from the Yankee slugger. The ticket sold for around $9,000 and the lighter went for $1,000. In today's market, the signed ticket would bring in a bundle.

Sal Durante died on December 1, 2022, at age 81 on Staten Island.

The Quiet Hero

Roger Eugene Maris was born on September 10, 1934, in Hibbing, Minnesota, to Croatian Americans Rudy and Corrine Maras. While playing minor league ball in 1954 at Keokuk, he changed his name to Maris.

"My father was tired of the way people incorrectly pronounced the name," said Randy Maris, one of Roger's six children (four boys and two girls). "Even though it was spelled 'Maras,' it should have been pronounced like it was spelled, 'Maris.' So, the pronunciation of the name never changed except there was a more consistent pronunciation of it." Other accounts say Maris was tired of opposing fans making unflattering rhymes with the word "ass."

Maris was your typical low-key guy from the Midwest. The bright lights of Broadway were not a part of his DNA. He wasn't like Babe Ruth, the man whose single-season record he broke. Maris was "introverted, troubled, and shy," wrote *Sports Illustrated* writer Leigh Montville. "He struggles to wear the heavy overcoat of fame."

I met his son, Randy, at a sports card show in White Plains, New York. At the time, he was attempting to market his father's brand nationally, promoting Roger Maris logoed T-shirts, sweatshirts, golf shirts, and sweaters.

A great athlete at Shanley High School in Fargo, North Dakota, Maris once returned four kickoffs for TDs in a 32–27 victory against Devils Lake in 1950. Some consider it a national high school record, but because Maris' feat was never submitted to the National Federation of State High School Associations, he is not officially credited with the record. "He was recruited by the legendary Oklahoma football coach Bud Wilkinson but turned down the athletic scholarship," said Randy. "Dad didn't like school very much."

Maris signed with the Cleveland Indians in 1953. From 1954 to 1956 he crushed 69 homers down on the farm and led the Indianapolis Indians to the '56 Junior World Series title. He made his major league debut playing left field on April 16, 1957, in a game that was an 11-inning classic pitching duel between White Sox southpaw Billy Pierce and the Indians' Herb Score. Maris collected three hits off Pierce, but the Indians were edged, 3–2. Two days later in Detroit, Maris' 11th-inning grand slam in his second big league game iced a five-run victory.

On June 15, 1958, Maris was traded to Kansas City along with Dick Tomanek and Preston Ward for Woodie Held and Vic Power. "From my understanding, the A's were interested in Maris and me," said Colavito, who roomed with Maris in spring training in '57. "But they decided on taking Roger."

The probability of anyone owning a Maris A's uniform is slim to none. But Hall of Fame closer Rollie Fingers has one. "When I got to spring training with the A's in '65 they gave me a uniform out of a bin and I kept it," explained Fingers in an interview I did with him several years ago. "It's an old, gray Kansas City Athletics flannel road uniform. On the back is the number 3 and in the collar is written 'Maris.' It's Roger's 1958 road uniform."

In '59 Maris earned a spot on the American League All-Star team. He batted .273 with 16 homers playing in only 122 games because of appendicitis. On December 11, 1959, he was traded to the Yankees along with Kent Hadley and Joe DeMaestri for Don Larsen, Hank Bauer, Norm Siebern and Marv Throneberry. When Yankee catcher/outfielder Johnny Blanchard heard the news that Maris was coming to the Yankees, he said to his wife, "I'm going to buy a new car tomorrow." Mrs. Blanchard asked, "How do you plan to pay for it?" Blanchard answered, "With my World Series check." Blanchard was prophetic as the Yankees would appear in the World Series in each of the next five seasons, winning in '61 and '62.

Maris hit the ground running. The Yanks opened the 1960 season at Fenway Park on April 19 when Maris went 4-for-5, including two home runs and a double. Batting in the leadoff spot, Maris doubled in his first at-bat. He then homered in the fifth inning off Sox right-hander Tom Brewer and took Ted Bowsfield deep in the eighth leading the Yankees to an 8–4 win. He captured the AL MVP award hitting .283 with 39 home runs, one short of Mantle and led the league in RBI (112). In the World Series loss to the Pirates, Maris played a minor role hitting .267 with two home runs.

The 1960 season was the only year he won a Gold Glove. Then again, he was competing with Detroit's Al Kaline. It should be noted that the first four seasons of the award (1957 to 1960), individual awards were presented by position. From 1961 through 2010 the phrase "at each position" was no longer strictly accurate, since the prize was presented to three outfielders irrespective of their specific position. Since 2011, the award has again been presented by position.

1961

Needless to say, 1961 was one of the most memorable years of my life. It was the year of my high school graduation, and I was coming off a pretty good season as a catcher on the Ansonia High School baseball team. Patsy Cline had a big hit with "I Fall to Pieces," and we danced to the "Bristol Stomp" by the Dovells. It was a newsy year. Yuri Gagarin, the Soviet cosmonaut, became the first man to travel to space; Alan Shepard became the first U.S. astronaut to travel to space; and Cuban exiles and the CIA mounted an unsuccessful attempt to overthrow Cuban dictator Fidel Castro in the Bay of Pigs operation.

But my attention was centered on the great AL pennant race between the Yankees and Tigers and the riveting home run derby staged by Mantle and Maris that by July was a national story. It was also an expansion year in the American League with two new teams—the Washington Senators and the Los Angeles Angels. The original Senators had been transplanted to Minnesota and become the Twins.

Rookie Yankee manager Ralph Houk inserted Maris in the number three spot in the batting order in front of Mantle. With the Mick batting behind him, Maris never had an intentional walk the entire season despite his robust home run output.

Maris did not homer in his first 10 games. At May's end he had a dozen. By the end of June, he had pounded 27. From May 17 through June 22, he stroked 24 homers in 38 games. The ball was jumping off his bat like a firecracker. The only other player to come close to that type of home run streak was Ruth, who hit 24 in 41 games in 1927.

Maris and Mantle both hit home runs off O's pitcher Hal "Skinny" Brown on July 17 that were lost to rain. That day Commissioner Ford Frick gave the edict that if Maris, or anyone, were to break the existing home run record of 60, held by Ruth, he would have to do it in 154 games or less—even though the season had been expanded that year to 162 games. The reason was that Ruth had hit his 60 home runs in 1927 in a 154-game schedule. If anyone hit 60 or more homers in more games than 154, it would qualify only as a specialized 162-game record. New York *Daily News* writer Dick Young suggested that an asterisk be attached to the record if the record was broken in more than 154 games.

What should have been the most rewarding and exciting year of Maris' career turned into one of agony and torment. Maris was attempting to break the Bambino's single season home run record. For some, that was akin to tampering with the sacred cow. In essence, he was chasing the ghost of Ruth, an honor Yankee fans believed would be reserved for Mantle. Instead, he was attempting to beat out Mantle, the homegrown Yankee legend. Yankee fans, Yankee players and several acerbic Yankee beat writers openly rooted for Mantle in the home run sweepstakes. Many viewed Maris as an interloper who rolled into town to take the shine off the Mick.

Maris did not communicate well with the newspaper writers who openly endeared themselves to Mantle. Maris made himself available to the media, but he was not good copy. The veteran writers like Jimmy Cannon, Dan Daniel, John Drebinger, Arthur Daley and Jim Ogle were much more supportive of Maris than the younger set of scribes that became known as "the Chipmunks." One of the Chipmunks was Maury Allen, who admitted years later that he was unfair to Maris. In *Roger Maris: Baseball's Reluctant Hero*, by Tom Clavin and Danny Peary, Allen said, "I wrote negatively about Maris for one reason—he didn't help my career." Allen added, "I look back and say, 'I'm embarrassed. I was not fair to him. I hurt him. I think a lot of us did.'"

George Vecsey was another Chipmunk along with Phil Pepe, Leonard Shecter, and Steve Jacobson, all young story-telling writers who rode the wave of new journalism. In defense of the criticism laid on the Chipmunks, Vecsey stated in the Clavin and Peary book, "We Chipmunks did our research, whereas the older guys were too fucking lazy to go down and talk to somebody. If they had one quote or just a glimmer of an idea, they'd make up a story."

But the Chipmunks were on the attack. They did what they could to take the varnish off Maris' spectacular season, asking questions like "Is the ball a lot livelier this year? How much does it help batting in front of Mantle? Is the pitching a lot worse because of expansion?"

Andy Strasberg grew up in the shadows of Yankee Stadium. His admiration for Maris began as a young boy when he was befriended by Maris. It turned into a lifelong friendship that extended to Maris' family. Over the years, he has made many appearances promoting Roger Maris the man and Roger Maris the player. He became a marketing executive with the San Diego Padres and served as a technical consultant for the movie *61** directed by Billy Crystal and written by Hank Steinberg, a made-for TV flick that first aired on HBO in 2001 depicting the '61 home run race.

Strasberg provides an example of how Maris was treated unfairly by the New York media.

"Once a writer asked Maris if he ever went on dates or played around," said Strasberg. Roger explained, "I'm a married man." The reporter then replied, "I'm married too, but I play around." Rog ended the conversation by saying, "That's your business."

Baseball was Maris' mistress.

"One time my father missed an appointment with a writer because he went to see a kid in the hospital with Mickey," said Randy. "He explained to the writer what happened, but the writer still criticized him in print and there was no retraction."

The writers improperly called him "Redneck Roger" or the "Last Angry Man," borrowing the title from the popular 1959 movie. Redneck is a derogatory term chiefly but not exclusively applied to white Americans perceived to be crass and unsophisticated, usually rural whites in the South. Its meaning originates from the 19th century and the sunburn found on farmers' necks.

"Unfortunately, that inappropriate term 'Redneck' has now been perpetuated by lazy writers who don't know Rog," stated Strasberg. "The term 'Redneck' was used because writers and the newspapers they worked for wouldn't use the baseball term 'red *ass*,' a term baseball people use for a player who is intense and filled with competitive spirit. Because it included the word 'ass' the writers wouldn't use it." As for the "angry

Andy Strasberg had virtually a lifetime relationship with Roger Maris. This 1966 photograph was taken in right field at Yankee Stadium (courtesy Andy Strasberg).

man" label, Maris said, "If I'm mad, I act mad. Nothing wrong with that. If you're mad, aren't you mad? If you weren't, you'd be a phony."

Fred Bengis was a Yankee bat boy from 1959 to 1962. He bled pinstripes growing up on Morris Avenue about 10 blocks from Yankee Stadium. I became friendly with Bengis who I met at an Old-Timers' Day. Bengis would talk how he enjoyed drinking Yoo-hoos and eating Hostess cupcakes with Maris in the clubhouse. It upset Bengis that the media depicted Maris as a surly, unsatisfactory hero. "Roger felt the press was overbearing," said Bengis. "To me, Roger was sincere, a good family man, a great guy and a great ballplayer. A lot of what the press said was wrong."

Because Mantle was the Yankees' golden boy, many fans had a fickle attitude toward Maris and had little tolerance for failure. "He didn't like the idea that when he would strike out, he would go back to the dugout and hear people say, 'You stink' and then when he hit a home run, these same people would cheer him," stated Bengis.

Journalists manufactured a non-existent feud between Mantle and Maris. They claimed that bickering and animosity existed between Mantle, who earned $75,000 that season, and Maris, who was paid $37,000, a hearty but well-deserved raise from his $18,000 salary in 1960. The truth is they were friends who recognized a kindred spirit in each other's devotion to the game they played. They even lived together during the season for a couple of months in Queens, sharing an apartment with Bob Cerv.

The Home Run Race

Maris hit his 50th home run on August 22, becoming the first player to ever hit his 50th homer in August. The Tigers came into Yankee Stadium on September 1 trailing the Yankees by one and a half games to start a huge Labor Day weekend three-game series. Maris was leading Mantle 51 to 48. Whitey Ford was matched up with Don Mossi for the Friday night game. Ford left the game after pitching 4⅔ scoreless innings. He was replaced by Bud Daley who then pitched shutout baseball through the eighth inning. Luis Arroyo blanked the Tigers in the ninth. Mossi pitched eight scoreless innings. In the bottom of the ninth, Maris led off the inning and flied to Kaline in right. Mantle struck out looking before Howard singled to center and Berra singled to right sending Elston Howard to third. Skowron, who swung a monster-sized 36-ounce, 36-inch bat, then singled to left field to drive in the winning run. The M&M boys had a quiet night going a combined 0-for-8. "Third base coach Frank Crosetti was able to steal the sign for the pitch that was called by Tigers catcher Mike Roarke," revealed Skowron.

I attended the game with two friends. We were among the 65,566 sweaty fans on this sultry New York night. If I recall, the gates opened at 5:30. The three of us were 17 years old at the time and it was much easier to buy a beer in New York where the legal drinking age was 18 as compared to Connecticut where it was 21. We wasted no time getting started.

We began knocking 'em down long before the 8:00 p.m. start. It was a macho thing to show my friends that I could handle my booze. When the game ended at 10:44 I was smashed. The field was turning like a Ferris wheel when Bill "Moose" Skowron knocked in the winning run. I staggered to the subway train beyond the bleachers as we headed to Grand Central Station after stopping at an Italian restaurant in the city where I made a fool of myself.

The following day Maris hit home runs 52 and 53 to lead the Bombers to a 7–2 win and the Yanks finished the sweep on Sunday with a come-from-behind 8–5 victory. Mantle went yard twice for numbers 49 and 50. He led off the bottom of the ninth to tie the game 5–5 when he homered off Gerry Staley. Elston Howard then hit a two-out, three-run homer to give the Yankees an 8–5 win and a four-and-a-half-game lead in the standings. The Yankees' climb to the pennant was buttressed by a 13-game winning streak that began on September 1 while the Tigers crashed. After beating the Indians 9–1 on September 8 in New York, the Yanks held a commanding 10-game lead. The pennant race was over, but the home run battle created considerable interest. If you're keeping score, it was Maris 55 and Mantle 52.

The Mick managed just two more homers. Mantle, hobbled with a hip abscess, was no longer a factor in the home run race, and with the Yankees having wrapped up the pennant, all the pressure was totally on Maris. And with each passing day the joy Maris had for the game was being stolen. As he drew closer to the record, things got worse. "I

Tony Kubek interviews '61 Yankees teammates Roger Maris (left) and Mickey Mantle at the August 7, 1982, Old-Timers' Day at Yankee Stadium.

absolutely remember him coming out of the shower and cursing while combing his hair because his hair was falling out," Bengis said.

The Climb to 61

The home run journey continued for Maris. At Baltimore on September 20 in the 154th game of the season, he hit number 59 off Milt Pappas. The O's right-hander was fond of Maris and was upset with Frick's 154-game ruling. Pappas tried to take matters into his own hands. In a 2003 article written by Bruce Amspacher for *Baseball by the Letters*, Pappas confessed,

> The night before the 154th game I saw Maris and Mickey Mantle walking under the stadium. We stopped to talk, and I told Maris that I wanted to see him break the record. I told him that I was going to give him nothing but fastballs tomorrow. Maris said, "Really?!" I told him, "Absolutely."
> Mantle was listening to all of this with wide eyes. Finally, he said, "What about me?"
> "You're on your own, big boy," I said.
> So, the next night the game was nationally televised, which was a big deal in 1961. Maris was sitting on 58 homers for the year, so he needed two to tie and three to break the record. The first time up he tagged it, but it stayed in the park. The second time up he hit it out and now had 59 for the year. I didn't get to finish the game, or he might have tied or broken the record that night.

Home run number 60 came at Yankee Stadium in the 159th game of the season on September 26 off Orioles right-hander "Fat Jack" Fisher, a solo shot in the bottom of the third that helped the Yankees to a 3–2 win. The ball hit a concrete step in the upper deck in right field and bounced back onto the field where O's right fielder Earl Robinson retrieved it and tossed it to the infield. The ball would eventually end up with Maris.

Following is Mel Allen's call, "There it is, there it is, if it stays fair, it's number 60 … and it's number 60. How about that! … A standing ovation for Roger Maris who got number 60. And they're calling him out of the dugout. This is most unusual.…"

The term "curtain call" was not in vogue in '61. And frankly, I don't recall ever seeing a player emerge from the dugout to take a bow for the fans. But it wouldn't be long before Maris made another one.

The Yankees finished the season hosting the Red Sox in a three-game weekend series. Maris came up empty on September 29 and 30.

Sunday, October 1, was a mostly cloudy but dry day in NYC. The 2:03 p.m. game time temp was 70 degrees. One weather outlet reported a wind speed of nine miles per hour—maybe a good sign for number 9. Across the bridge at the Polo Grounds, the New York Titans defeated the Boston Patriots 37–30 in an American Football League matchup before a little more than 15,000 fans.

An exhausted Maris, playing center field, had one more game to reach number 61. In the bottom of the first, Maris flied deep to left into the glove of Carl Yastrzemski. Kubek led off the bottom of the fourth and struck out. Maris then stepped to the plate, facing Stallard, the 24-year-old right-hander. The count reached 2–0 and the drama escalated with each pitch. In the Yankee bullpen in right field, pitchers and catchers anxiously watched. Players in both dugouts observed with excitement as did the four umpires—Bill Kinnaman (plate), Red Flaherty (1b), Jim Honochick (2b), and Al Salerno (3b).

The $5,000 reward added to the drama.

In the third pitch of the at-bat, Maris deposited the ball 360 feet into the lower right field seats where Durante made the catch. The ball went over outfielder Lu Clinton's head into the outstretched hand of Durante. The crowd of 23,154, roared with approval. Maris described the moment in *Roger Maris at Bat*, written by Jim Ogle: "I couldn't even think as I went around the bases. I couldn't tell you what crossed my mind; I don't think anything did. I was in a daze. I was all fogged out from a very, very hectic season and an extremely difficult month.… I began to come to as I got to the dugout."

That gave the Yankees a 1–0 lead, which proved to be the final score, and they finished 109–53 for the season. The 163-game season was the result of a tie. Bill Stafford pitched six shutout innings. He was relieved by Hal Reniff and Luis Arroyo who also pitched scoreless innings. Arroyo pitched the final two frames.

There are two broadcasts of the call, one by Rizzuto on CBS Radio and the other by Barber on WPIX TV. Mel Allen can also be heard in the Barber call.

The Rizzuto Call

And they're standing up waiting to see if Maris is going to hit number 61.
Here's the wind-up, the pitch to Roger. Way outside, ball one.
And the fans are starting to boo. Maris only has, including this time, three times at bat—and unless the Yankees get a rally that's all he'll have to try and get 61 on the year.
Here's the wind-up—the pitch.

Low, ball two.

That one was in the dirt. And the boos get louder.

Two balls, no strikes on Roger Maris. Here's the wind-up ... fastball, hit deep to right! This could be it! Way back there! Holy Cow, he did it! Sixty-one for Maris. Look at that fight for the ball out there.

Holy cow, what a shot!

The Barber Call

Fast ball is wide—lays off it—ball one.
Low—ball two.
The crowd is reacting negatively. They want to see Maris get something he can swing on.
There it is—number 61—$5,000 somebody.
He got his pitch—$5,000. Here is the fellow with 61, you're seeing a lot today.

Barber then says to Mel Allen, "You haven't seen anything like this have you?"

Allen answered, "Nobody's ever seen anything like this."

Roger Maris trotted out the historic home run. Maris shook hands with Crosetti as he reached third base. At home plate he was greeted by Berra and Yankee bat boy Frankie Perdenti before he got to the dugout where he was welcomed by a fan who jumped onto the field and then by his excited teammates.

Hector Lopez and Blanchard pushed Maris out to the dugout's top step, where he took off his Yankee cap and quickly waved it, acknowledging the fans' cheers. He tried twice to get back into the dugout, but Howard joined Lopez in straight-arming him to keep him from returning to the semi-privacy of the Yankee bench. He came out to take a bow. He reentered the dugout with the crowd still roaring. At that point Lopez, Skowron, and Joe DeMaestri pushed him onto the field and would not let him in the dugout.

Mantle ended with 54 homers. It's the only time in baseball history that two teammates hit at least 50 home runs in the same season.

PA announcer Bob Sheppard was so impressed with Maris' accomplishment that within five minutes of the historic clout, he wrote the following, "Roger Maris Says His Prayers."

> They've been pitching me low and wide and tight.
> I've been tense and nervous, drawn and paillard.
> But my prayers are full of joy tonight.
> Thank you, Lord, for Tracy Stallard.

Sheppard handed the poem over to Mel Allen, who read it to his listeners before the game ended and said, "If you want copies of Bob's poem, write to Yankee Stadium." Sheppard was deluged with mail in the coming days.

It should be noted that Maris hit home runs 59, 60, and 61 without Mantle batting behind him.

Maris received an avalanche of congratulations, but one stood above the rest. Kevin Kernan in *The Yankees Century Series* wrote, "Of all the congratulations Maris received for the feat, one meant the most to him. It read: 'My heartfelt congratulations to you on hitting your 61st home run. The American people will always admire a man who overcomes great pressure to achieve an outstanding goal.' It was signed by President John. F Kennedy."

On October 4, 2022, Maris' AL single-season home run record was shattered by Yankees right fielder Aaron Judge when he hit his 62nd home run of the season. The historic shot came against Texas Rangers right-hander Jesus Tinoco to open the second game of a split doubleheader at Globe Life Field in Arlington, Texas. Statcast projected a 391-foot drive toward the left field seats. The ball marked "C 13" for authentication purposes was secured by Cory Youmans, a fan seated in section 31, row 1, seat 3. For security reasons Youmans and the treasured ball were hustled through the concourse. Youmans is a vice president at Fisher Investments, which manages $197 billion worldwide. At this writing he was not sure what he would do with the souvenir. "If ever sold at an auction, it could go for millions of dollars," Ken Goldin, of Goldin Auctions, told CBS News. Judge's AL home run record, in addition to his .311 batting average, 131 RBI and monster 1.111 OPS, earned him AL MVP honors by the Baseball Writers Association of America. It was the 21st MVP award won by a Yankee player. Judge's monster season led to an unprecedented nine-year, $360 million contract. And on December 21, 2022, he was named the 16th Yankees captain. Honors continued as the Associated Press named him the Male Athlete of the Year. The last Yankee to win the award was Ron Guidry in 1978, with Maris, Mantle, and DiMaggio among the other past Yankee recipients.

Ironically, Ruth, Maris, and Judge all hit more home runs on the road than they did at Yankee Stadium during their record-breaking years. The Babe hit 28 at home and 32 on the road; Maris hit 30 at home and 31 on the road; and Judge went yard 30 times at Yankee Stadium and 32 times on the road.

Judge received many congratulatory messages, including from several Hall of Fame players and President Joe Biden.

What's in a Number?

Numerology is the pseudoscientific belief in an occult, divine or mystical relationship between a number and one or more coinciding events. The number 9 trailed Maris during his career. As a Yankee and Cardinal, Maris wore number 9. He broke into the majors with a nine-game hitting streak. When he played for the Cardinals, he hit his first National League home run on May 9, 1967. The ball was ironically caught by Strasberg. He was sitting in row 9, seat 9 in right field at Forbes Field in Pittsburgh. Strasberg not only developed a huge collection of Maris memorabilia, but he also established a lifelong relationship with Maris and his family. In 1965 Strasberg asked Maris for a bat and a home run ball. "He gave me a bat," said Strasberg, "but Maris stated, 'You'll have to catch the ball.'" As fate would have it, the ball was the one Strasberg grabbed in Pittsburgh.

The Judge-Maris numerological comparison is eerily interesting.

Maris wore number 9 and Judge wore 99; Maris hit 61 HRs in '61 and 61 years later Judge broke the record; both played right field and eclipsed right fielder Babe Ruth's record of 60. Judge tied Maris' record on September 28 at Rogers Centre in Toronto where Roger Maris' son, Roger Maris, Jr., was seated with Judge's mother, Patty, in the front row on top of the Yankees' dugout. Roger Jr. followed the team for nine days but did not make the trip to Texas.

And strange but true, on a night when Judge, wearing number 99, hit number 62, the Yankees 3–2 loss gave the team a record of 99–62.

The Mythical Asterisk

In truth, there has never been an actual asterisk in the record book but rather a parenthetical annotation "162-game season" following Maris' 61 home runs. MLB actually had no direct control over any record books until many years later. It all was merely a suggestion on Frick's part and Young's asterisk idea has been nothing but a long-standing myth.

Roger Angell, the scholarly writer and fiction editor for the *New Yorker*, died in 2022. His life spanned all 27 Yankees world championships. He saw them all from Ruth to Judge. Angell, writer of unparalleled prose, was critical of the asterisk idea. He noted as many had before him that it was curious that numerous other seasonal records that have been established since the beginning of the 162-game season—including stolen bases, at-bats and pitchers' strikeouts—do not bear, as he called it, "the ugly tick." Angell opined that Frick's thinking was partisan because he was once a ghostwriter for the Babe.

In 1991 Angell wrote, "Frick's asterical campaign was not quite a disinterested one, since Frick, a former sportswriter himself, had been a coeval and an adulating biographer of the Babe."

In his eloquent way, Angell continued, "There is no wish here to revive the shoutings and buzzings that accompanied the Maris achievement thirty years back, but I think the present commissioner and some brave committee should meet one of these days and quietly wield an eraser, instead of waiting for some young slugger to come along and do it for them with his bat."

Inspired by Angell's opinion, the discourse thankfully died. Commissioner Fay Vincent convened the Committee for Statistical Accuracy, and the 162-game notation was repealed. "I'm inclined to support the single-record thesis, and that is Maris hit more home runs in a season than anyone else," Vincent said in an article in *Deseret News*. Thus, the "separate records" delineations were forever abolished.

In retrospect, even though Maris played in a 162-game season as compared to Ruth's 154, Maris had only seven more plate appearances than the Bambino (698–691). Because of a tie game, the Yankees actually played 163 games in '61. Maris played in 161 of them.

For the second consecutive year Maris was voted the AL MVP. He hit .269, leading the league in home runs (61), RBI (141), runs (132) and total bases (366). His OPS was a gaudy .993.

In '62 the pressure intensified as many fans believed he should hit 62 homers or at least 60. He batted .256 with 33 home runs and 100 RBI, not Ruthian, but pretty damn good. Yet the press continued its detrimental coverage of Maris. UPI named him the "Flop of the Year."

In the World Series against the Giants, he hit one home run, but it was his defense that garnered headlines. In the ninth inning, he ran down Willie Mays' double and held Matty Alou, the potential tying run, at third base when he made a great throw to second baseman Bobby Richardson, the cut-off man. Richardson fired home to keep Alou from scoring. Although Maris is often credited with the throw, it was Richardson that made the great throw. Richardson went out farther than usual to get the throw from Maris whose arm was barking at the time.

Maris' final two years in pinstripes were not pleasant ones. The Yankee empire collapsed in '65; the team finished in sixth place, their worst finish since 1925. They were getting old all at once and failed to cultivate Black players in their system. The Bombers would not see the postseason again until 1976.

In 1965, Maris, who was hampered by a broken hand, played only 46 games under manager Johnny Keane, the fewest in his career. Although Mantle and Howard also missed large chunks of the season due to injuries, Maris' failure to play at a time when the Yankees clearly needed him only added to the distrust between Maris, the fans and the press. And it also led to Maris distrusting the Yankees. Team doctor Sidney Gaynor and two other doctors claimed they could not find anything wrong with Maris' ailing hand. But the Yankee slugger was convinced the Yankees knew about the injury and they were holding back information because he would increase attendance. The Yankees would deny this.

"He broke his hand sliding home," said Randy Maris. "The Yankees kept it to themselves that his hand was broken. They told him that it was just a sprain. But while in Kansas City, he visited one of his own doctors and found that he had a hairline fracture."

On December 8, 1966, the Yankees traded Maris to the St. Louis Cardinals for third baseman Charley Smith. Maris left the Yankees embittered. The unappreciated Yankee did not return to Yankee Stadium until 12 years after he played his last game for the Bombers in '66. Thanks to the influence of Steinbrenner, Maris returned for Opening Day on April 13, 1978, to help the Yankees raise the 1977 American League pennant. He was joined by Mantle, and for a day, the M&M boys graced the hallowed stadium.

The Cardinals played Maris in right field and moved right fielder Mike Shannon to third base. Maris responded well in his new digs. Although he hit only 14 homers in two seasons in St. Louis, he helped the Cardinals win two National League pennants and a World Series. In the decade of the sixties, Maris played in seven World Series, the most of any player in the major leagues. He appeared in five with the Yankees and two with the Cardinals. In the '67 Fall Classic he helped lead the Cardinals in their seven-game Series win over the Red Sox when he hit .385, including a home run.

Maris retired after the '68 campaign with a lifetime .260 everage that included 275 home runs and 850 RBI. Should he have a place in Cooperstown? He did win back-to-back MVP awards and shattered a long-standing home run record. He was also one of the best outfielders of his era. One thing is unassailable: he was an elite player.

I met Maris at a postgame hotel party following the 1984 Cracker Jack Classic game in Washington, D.C. I was at the bar having a drink when he walked up with one of his sons—I believe it was Roger. I asked Maris what aspect of his career he thought was underrated. "I feel I was a good all-around player," he said. "I had good speed, a good arm and could play the outfield." It was common for Maris to dive into the right field seats at Yankee Stadium and rob hitters of home runs. Colavito, who was a teammate of Maris in Cleveland, sang praise for him and Tony Oliva. "They were the two most underrated players in my era," stated Colavito. In 2021, Oliva was elected to the Hall of Fame by the Golden Days Era Committee.

The Yankees retired Maris' number 9 and Howard's number 32 at the 1984 Old-Timers' Day. "I think the most memorable thing for me and my family was the day they retired his number 9 at Yankee Stadium," said Randy. "Although there is no cute tale, I feel it was one of the happiest days of his life. For me, to be there and see the joyous look on his face, recognizing the admiration of the Yankee fans, it was all I could do to hold back my tears. For someone who for so long endured the label by the press of 'surly' and 'hard to get along with,' it was a sigh of relief to see just how well he was loved and admired by so many people."

In 1984 Maris was diagnosed with lymphoma. With treatment it appeared that the cancer had gone into remission. He made his final trip to Yankee Stadium in April 1985 when he received the team's Lou Gehrig Pride of the Yankees Award the night before the season opener. In all of his returns to Yankee Stadium he was greeted warmly by the fans which helped bury the haunting ghosts of the past.

In 1985 his condition deteriorated. On Saturday, December 14, 1985, Roger Maris died at age 51. The funeral in Fargo and the memorial service at St. Patrick's Cathedral in New York served as impromptu Yankee reunions. The outpouring of emotion and the presence of baseball royalty reflected his accomplishments and respect among the baseball establishment.

Maris' name was prominently in the news in 1998 when Mark McGwire and Sammy Sosa staged a home run race, the modern-day version of the M&M boys. Both sculpted sluggers shattered Maris' single season mark. McGwire ended with 70 and Sosa with 66. Many baseball pundits believed that the two sluggers helped to save the game of baseball from the unpopular 1994–95 players' strike along with Cal Ripken and his record consecutive game playing streak that ended at 2,632 games on September 20. Ironically, McGwire was born on October 1, 1963, two years to the day after Maris hit his record-breaking home run.

The excitement generated by the McGwire-Sosa home run barrage was a far cry from the fairly dismal attention that Maris received when chasing Ruth. The Maris family was very supportive of McGwire, the new single season home run champ— that is, until the performance enhancing drug revelations took center stage several years later, by which time Barry Bonds had surpassed McGwire with 73 home runs in 2001.

Three times Sosa hit more than 60 home runs in a season. The *New York Times* reported that Sosa is one of 104 players who tested positive in baseball's anonymous 2003 survey. "I think there needs to be a distinction," Randy Maris said to ESPN writer Ian Begley. "Obviously, unfortunately I think major league baseball turned an eye to that era." Randy wants to see major league baseball make a note that McGwire, Sosa, and Bonds were all linked to steroids.

Legal Issues

After Maris' retirement, Cardinals owner Gussie Busch set Maris up with a beer distributorship in Gainesville, Florida. The Maris Distributing Company, operated by Maris and his brother Rudy, served as a distributor for Anheuser-Busch in central Florida. There were bright business years, but things turned dark when the distributorship was taken away from the family. In 2001, the Maris family filed a $1 billion defamation lawsuit against Anheuser-Busch. The lawsuit, filed in Alachua County Circuit Court, accused Anheuser-Busch of smearing the Maris reputation by publicly claiming the family's beer distributorship had poor business practices. The allegations included claims the distributorship sold outdated beer, falsified documents, and engaged in fraud, according to the lawsuit. The family reportedly won a $50 million judgment, plus $22.6 million in interest.

In 2005, Anheuser-Busch, the largest U.S. brewer, agreed to pay $120 million to settle continued lawsuits brought by the Maris family. The legal fight between

Anheuser-Busch and the Maris family had consumed eight years, three trials and millions of dollars in legal fees. The Maris family reportedly asked for $5 billion.

In 2001, the Maris family was at Yankee Stadium to commemorate the 50th anniversary of the '61 season. At the ceremony, Yankees captain Derek Jeter, wearing white gloves, carried the bat Maris used to hit the record-breaker onto the field. Durante, also wearing white gloves, brought the ball onto the field. Both the bat and ball were on loan from the Hall of Fame.

For a brief time, it was 1961 again.

18

Don Larsen
The Imperfect Yankee

"The only thing Larsen fears is sleep."
—Jimmy Dykes
(Baltimore Orioles manager)

On the morning of October 8, 1956, Joel Alderman, an attorney and freelance writer friend of mine from New Haven, was driving to Yankee Stadium to attend Game Five of the World Series. In just a couple of hours he would witness perhaps the most historic game in Series history when Don Larsen pitched a perfect game and beat the Dodgers, 2–0, to give the Yankees a 3–2 lead in the Subway Series.

It certainly was one of the biggest stories in the annals of major league baseball history, but within every huge, well-known story, there are scores of lesser ones. Alderman provides this incredible anecdote.

"I was in a car with some friends and the traffic had stopped on the way to the stadium," Alderman recalled. "Another car was on our left, a convertible with the top down. And who was it but Ted Williams."

Alderman figured the "Splendid Splinter," who was arguably the greatest hitter ever, was on his way to the stadium to attend the game. And because the Red Sox weren't involved, there'd be less chance that he'd be bothered by the writers, with whom he had been feuding throughout his career, or the fans, whom he often seemed to resent.

Anyway, having recognized Williams, Alderman shouted over to him, "Hi, Ted! And who do you like today?"

"Teddy Ballgame" knew Larsen was set to start that game for the Yankees. He'd faced Larsen plenty of times. He yelled back at Alderman, "You better watch out. He's gonna be real tough."

"And then, he kept on going," said Alderman. "He was driving to Florida."

Alderman wondered whether friends who weren't in the car that day would ever believe his tale of that brush with the baseball great, so he collected the necessary documentation.

"I wrote a letter to Williams, and I said that I was in that car, and I would appreciate if he would answer in writing that it actually did happen that way," said Alderman. "Well, not only did I get a letter back from Ted saying, 'Yes, it did happen,' he said he was using *my* letter to prove to *his* friends that it happened."

Ted Williams had delivered one of the greatest understatements of all time with the assessment that Larsen would be "real tough" on this Monday afternoon in the Bronx.

The Imperfect Yankee

In October of '56, Doris Day sang "Whatever Will Be, Will Be (Que Sera, Sera)." It was a perfect fit for Larsen's personality. They called him "Gooney Bird" because of his flaky nature and "The Ghoul" for his love for reading morbid comic books. His teammates called him "Night Rider" because of his high-octane nightlife. He was a soft-spoken free spirit who could party with the best. "Don had a startling capacity for liquor," said Mantle. "Larsen was easily the greatest drinker I've known, and I've known some pretty good ones in my time." During spring training in '56 Larsen wrecked his brand-new Oldsmobile by driving it into a St. Petersburg, Florida, telephone pole at 4 or 5 o'clock one morning. He admitted that he had been drinking at several bars earlier in the night and said he had fallen asleep at the wheel. When Yankees manager Casey Stengel heard the news, he remarked, "He was either out pretty late or up pretty early."

Larsen was a mediocre 81–91 pitcher with a 3.78 ERA. The journeyman right-hander was the last surviving pitcher of the old St. Louis Browns, a team that moved to Baltimore for the start of the 1954 season. In '54 he was a paltry 3–21, but two of his wins were against the Yankees. His 21 losses marked the only time he led the league in anything. On November 17, 1954, he was involved in a 17-player blockbuster transaction that brought Larsen and pitching ace Bob Turley to the Yankees. He was only 10–33 with the inept Browns/Orioles before landing on healthy Bronx real estate where he went 45–24 from 1955 to 1959.

Larsen was tough in October. Although he is best remembered for his perfecto in '56, in Game Three of the '57 Series, his first Series outing after his no-hitter, he pitched 7⅓ innings of solid relief to beat the Milwaukee Braves, 12–3. In Game Three of the '58 Fall Classic, with the Yankees behind two games to none, he pitched seven shutout innings to beat the Braves 4–0 in a Series the Yankees would win after being down three games to one.

Larsen was a good-hitting pitcher and batted eighth in the Yankee lineup on occasion. His lifetime batting average of .242 with 14 homers is exceptional for pitchers. In '53, playing for the Browns, he collected a streak of seven consecutive hits. During the '56 season he hit a grand slam off Red Sox pitcher Frank Sullivan. On August 17, 1958, Larsen pinch-hit for pitcher Art Ditmar in the top of the third inning at Boston. Facing Ike Delock, he hit a bases-empty homer deep to center field in the Yankees' 6–5 loss. That season he hit .306 and belted four home runs. His OPS was a remarkable .935.

In '54, Larsen, while pitching for the Orioles, met the future Vivian Larsen, a 27-year-old telephone operator. He was not interested in marriage, but after Vivian told him she was pregnant, the two married the following year. Larsen wanted the marriage kept secret and went through with the ceremony only because of the baby. Charles Faber wrote in a SABR article, "Three months later he left her with no intention of returning because he was not ready to settle down and preferred a life of free and easy existence."

Although Larsen was perfect on the mound one day in his pitching career, he was far from perfect with his child support payments, and Vivian filed another complaint. She was not about to raise their daughter without financial support from her major-league husband. Vivian moved to New York and in a court settlement collected child-support money.

Faber wrote, "On July 16, 1956, Justice Henry Greenberg of the Bronx Superior

Court awarded Vivian $60 a week from Larsen in support of herself and their daughter, Caroline Jean. Don didn't deliver."

He reportedly owed his wife $420, which led her to file another complaint. Faber added, "Vivian's lawyer, Harry Lipsig, said, 'While this baseball hero is enjoying the luxuries of life and the plaudits of the public, he is subjecting his 14-month-old baby girl and his wife to the pleasures of a starvation existence.'"

A Bronx Superior Court Justice upheld the complaint and ordered the Yankees, Larsen, and baseball commissioner Ford Frick to show cause why his share from the '55 World Series should not be appropriated by the Bronx Supreme Court.

When Larsen arrived at Yankee Stadium on the morning of his perfect game, he found the court order in his locker. He made good for the $420. According to Faber, Vivian's lawyer said, "This man is still no hero. In these proceedings, he has brazenly suggested when his daughter was born, she was immediately to be given out for adoption."

In 1957 Larsen married Corrine Bruess, a flight attendant. They had a son, Scott, and had grandchildren.

I had Larsen on my radio show a couple of times and often ran into him at Old Timers games at Yankee Stadium where he was an annual fixture. He came across as quiet and perhaps a bit shy. One of my lasting images of Larsen is him sitting on the floor in the tunnel not far from the Yankee clubhouse having a beer and a cigarette at an Old-Timers' Day.

The Perfect Game

Prior to Game Five of the '56 World Series, a total of 306 World Series games had been played without a no-hitter being pitched. Larsen not only no-hit the Dodgers but he also pitched a perfect game, his ticket to immortality. Subsequent to this, there has been one other Series no-hitter. It occurred in Game Four of the 2022 Fall Classic when four Houston Astros pitchers, Cristian Javier (6), Bryan Abreu (1), Rafael Montero (1), and Ryan Pressly (1), combined to no-hit the Phils 5–0 at Citizens Bank Park in Philadelphia. But Larsen's perfecto remains the only solo no-hitter in Series history.

If there was an unlikely candidate to accomplish such a feat in the Fall Classic or even finish a game, it was Larsen. During his career he completed only 44 of his 171 starts. It would be safe to say that he closed more bars than he did games. The 6'4" right-hander started 20 games in '56 and completed only six. But in Larsen's four September starts, he went 4–0 and allowed only four hits or fewer in each one. During the season Larsen and Turley both went to the no–wind-up delivery which proved to be effective down the stretch for Larsen.

Stengel and his staff went with the hot hand and started Larsen in Game Two. But the fun-loving right-hander laid an egg, failing to last two innings, allowing four runs as the Yankees blew a six-run lead. He had given up only one hit in that game and was leading 6–1 but walked four batters and the Yankees went on to lose, 13–8. In the postgame, Larsen fumed to reporters, "I don't give a damn if I ever pitch another game for the Yankees or Stengel again! I go out there and break my neck? For what? He had no business taking me out of there! That's the last time I'll get to bed early. I'm gonna start enjoying life again."

Larsen was not aware until the day of the game that he would be pitching Game Five. He was not confident that Stengel would give him another chance, but when he got to the clubhouse, he received the surprise of his career and maybe his life. Yankees coach Frank Crosetti was assigned to place a ball in the shoe of the game's starting pitcher in his locker. When Larsen got to the clubhouse, he was astonished to see the ball in his shoe.

His mound opponent that game was 39-year-old Sal "the Barber" Maglie, who 13 days earlier (September 25) had no-hit the Phils at Ebbets Field to become the oldest National League pitcher to toss a no-hitter at the time.

Lady Luck was on Larsen's side in the second inning when Jackie Robinson hit a sizzler to third base that deflected off the glove of Andy Carey into the hands of shortstop Gil McDougald who threw out Robinson. For the remainder of the game Larsen was virtually flawless. Maglie was superb as well. He allowed only two runs on five hits, one a fourth-inning home run to Mantle who made a great catch of a fly ball off the bat of Gil Hodges in the fifth inning.

Knowing Larsen's endurance problems, the Yankees had to be prepared. After the fifth inning Yankees pitching coach Jim Turner, figuring Larsen would eventually need relief help, told Ford to go down to the bullpen and warm up every inning. "I warmed up in the sixth, seventh, eighth and ninth innings," said Whitey. "I never saw the greatest game ever pitched."

Larsen's teammates tried to avoid him in the dugout as tension mounted each inning. "After the seventh inning I bumped Mantle in the dugout," remembered Larsen. "I said, 'Look at the scoreboard. Wouldn't it be something [if I pitched a no-hitter] with two innings to go.' He walked away from me. The dugout was like a morgue."

In the top of the ninth, the throng of 64,519 roared on every pitch. Among the crowd were future Yankees managers Joe Torre (age 16) and Dallas Green (age 22). Carl Furillo flied to Hank Bauer in right before Roy Campanella grounded to Billy Martin at second. Dale Mitchell, a lifetime .312 hitter, then pinch-hit for Maglie. Mitchell took ball one. He then took a strike. With the count 1–1, Mitchell swung and missed for strike two. Tension was growing with every pitch. He then fouled a ball into the left field stands. With the count 1–2, Bob Wolff, broadcasting on the Mutual Broadcasting System and around the world on Armed Forces radio, made the following call that will remain in the annals of baseball history as Larsen was set to deliver his 97th pitch of the game.

"Larsen is ready ... gets the sign ... two strikes and a ball ... here comes the pitch ... strike three ... a no-hitter, a perfect game for Don Larsen." Berra leaped into Larsen's arms. The unmitigated joy reflected in Larsen's embrace with Berra will never be forgotten.

When giving the count, broadcasters always give the balls before the strikes. But Wolff did the opposite. When I asked him why, he replied, "I never thought about that before. But the reason I did was because I covered the Washington Senators for many years and the scoreboard at Griffith Stadium had the strikes before the balls."

Umpire Babe Pinelli (real name Rinaldo Angelo Paolinelli), working his final game ever behind the plate, raised his right arm at approximately 3:15 p.m. indicating strike three. Berra leaped into Larsen's arms while fans roared with excitement. Contrary to reports, this was not Pinelli's final game of his career. He umpired the last two games of the Series on third and second base.

Critics have cried that the pitch was outside, but Larsen said, "It was close enough that he half swung at it. Today, the umpires wouldn't be so hesitant in calling it a strike."

It was difficult to determine if the pitch was a called strike or if the strike was called

At the July 27, 1996, Old-Timers' Day at Yankee Stadium, Don Larsen was honored on the 40th anniversary of his perfect game.

because Mitchell failed to check his swing. But Larry Gerlach, writing in *The SABR Book of Umpires and Umpiring*, solved the mystery in an interview he did with Pinelli.

"There was no doubt in my mind about the pitch," said Pinelli, who had an eight-year big league career as an infielder spent mostly with the Reds in the 1920s. "Larsen hit the corner of the plate with a beautiful fast ball that was just high enough. It was easy to call—and I called it." Pinelli made no mention of a check swing. The strikeout was Larsen's seventh of the game.

The moment Pinelli's arm shot upward for strike three, Vin Scully, then a 28-year-old Dodgers broadcaster, gripped one of baseball's great moments with his silky voice when he said, "Got him. The greatest game ever pitched in baseball history by Don Larsen, a no-hitter and a perfect game in the World Series." However, he incorrectly added, "Only one perfect game has ever been pitched but that was in the course of the regular season. But when you put it in the World Series you set the biggest diamond in the biggest ring." Prior to Larsen's masterpiece five perfect games had been pitched, three since 1900—Cy Young (1904), Addie Joss (1908), and Charlie Robertson (1922).

Yankees announcer Mel Allen did the first half of the game on TV before turning the mic over to Scully. Apparently adhering to superstitious custom, Allen did not say that Larsen was pitching a perfect game. After the third out in the top of the fifth, he said, "And that's the 15th man he's retired." Scully picked up on that and continued, "That's the 16th man, that's the 18th, that's the 20th...."

In retrospect, however, Scully was critical of his work and the broadcast. "Today I would say, 'Call your friends, this fella is pitching a perfect game!'" the iconic broadcaster told Daniel Riley in a 2011 interview for *GQ Sports*. "Anyway, it was just, 'Foul ball, ball two,' because we were intimidated by the idea we were talking too much. So, I can't watch it. I was just so dull professionally, and so different from what I would've done under the same circumstances today. I've never watched it again. Never."

Larsen applauded the game Berra called that day. "I don't recall shaking Yogi off the entire game," he noted. "I never had such good control." But in an article published in the *Beckley Post-Herald*, Larsen said, "I only shook off a couple of Yogi's signals, but he stuck with them, so I went ahead and pitched what he called. I'm glad of it."

Only once the entire contest did Larsen reach a count of three balls to a batter, Pee Wee Reese in the first inning.

When the game ended Larsen was not aware that he had pitched a perfect game. "I didn't know what a perfect game was," he acknowledged. You can't blame him. He was six years old in '22 when Robertson, pitching for the White Sox, was perfect against the Detroit Tigers at Navin Field.

What would become writer Dick Young's most famous sentence as a sportswriter did not appear under his own byline. While covering Larsen's gem, New York *Daily News* writer Joe Trimble struggled to find appropriate words to begin his story. Young reached over and typed seven words into Trimble's typewriter: "The imperfect man pitched a perfect game." Shirley Povich of the *Washington Post* was a bit more elaborate in summing up the improbable turn of events: "The million-to-one shot came in. A month of Sundays hit the calendar. Hell froze over. Don Larsen pitched the first perfect game in World Series history."

Larsen owned the city that night. He and his close friend Arthur Richman partied together. When Richman called the Copacabana for a reservation for seven, he was told they were totally booked. But upon the mention that Larsen was part of the party, the Copa set up a separate table right in front, where the group became part of comedian Joe E. Lewis' show.

Because of his after-dark reputation, untrue stories circulated that Larsen was out late the night before the perfect game and was skunk drunk.

Not true.

Arthur Richman was Larsen's best friend and served as his best man when he got married. "We were together the night before at Bill Taylor's place," recalled Richman, who at the time was a writer with the New York *Daily Mirror*. "Taylor was a backup outfielder with the New York Giants and had a restaurant and bar at 57th Street across from the Henry Hudson Hotel. We took a cab together and went home. I had him home by 11:30 p.m. He stuck a twenty-dollar bill in my hand to give to my mom."

"I don't go to church," said Larsen. "Tell your mother to give it to the synagogue for me." He then went out and had a pizza.

Rickerby's Photo

Arthur Rickerby was a *Life* and UPI photographer who covered the fall of Japan in World War II, the Kennedy White House, and numerous political figures. He was in the press bus a few cars behind President John F. Kennedy when he was assassinated in Dallas on November 22, 1963. But seven years earlier, he was at Yankee Stadium for the perfect game when he worked magic with his camera. The photo I'm referring to shows Larsen, second baseman Billy Martin, and the Yankee Stadium auxiliary scoreboard in right center field that detailed the entire situation including the inning, the score, the batter, the count, the number of hits and the number of outs. It was the iconic photo that underscored the importance of the moment.

When I was writing for *Sports Collectors Digest* in the 1980s, I was told to contact Rickerby's widow, Wanda, who lived in West Hartford, Connecticut. Mrs. Rickerby lived in her late husband's veritable museum of classic photographs. Her large collection of baseball photos was impressive. She explained how her husband, who died in 1972, was able to capture a monumental piece of baseball history with his 35 mm camera.

The 35 mm had been around for many years, but it was not produced in abundance. Rickerby's dedication to a more flexible camera and the pursuit of a more natural photojournalism garnered him a nomination for a Pulitzer Prize and allowed him to take one of the most historic photos in baseball history. "Sensing history was about to be made, Arthur was able to change his position from the photographer's well to behind home plate because he used the 35 mm camera that offered him the mobility to move around because of its smaller size," explained Mrs. Rickerby. "The other photographers had the big, clumsy [heavy plate] cameras."

1956 Corvette

Larsen became *Sport* magazine's second recipient of their World Series MVP award which was a creamy-white '56 Corvette. Dodgers pitcher Johnny Podres won it the year before. "I had the car about two or three years," Larsen said. "I should have locked it up. I sold it to a lady who got into a wreck."

What was strange was that *Sport* made their MVP choice before the Series ended. "I got the car in Brooklyn after the sixth game," revealed Larsen. "I thought it was unusual that they would make their selection before the Series ended." (The Series was tied 3–3.) "They took a picture of actress Rita Moreno with me. I drove the car to the Bronx that day and had it shipped home."

The Yankees won Game Seven, 9–0. Berra lobbied Stengel to start 24-year-old Johnny Kucks because of his sinker. Fly balls in Ebbets Field often never came back. Kucks blanked the Dodgers on three hits. Skowron's grand slam and Berra's two homers led the offensive charge.

That winter, Weiss sent Larsen a contract calling for a $1,500 raise of his $12,000 salary in '56. Larsen, furious, sent it back to Weiss with a note: "If you will forget you ever sent me this, I'll forget I ever got it." Larsen reportedly was asking for $27,500 but signed for $18,000. However, he made an estimated $35,000 in endorsements and appearances immediately after the perfect game (more than his salary in any one major league season), including $6,000 for appearing on Bob Hope's TV show and getting to meet James Cagney, Lucille Ball and Desi Arnaz. Larsen frequently appeared at card shows and other events later in life.

Larsen was sent to the Kansas City A's in the trade that brought Maris to the Yankees on December 11, 1959. Call it fate or whatever, the imperfect Yankee continued to add chapters in an uncanny way to the storied Yankee history. Believe it or not, six years to the day later, on October 8, 1962, Larsen beat the Yankees, pitching a third of an inning in relief for the San Francisco Giants in Game Four of the WS. He recorded the final out of the sixth inning with the score tied 2–2. The Giants then scored four runs in the top of the seventh en route to a 7–3 win. Because Larsen was the pitcher of record when the Giants took the lead, he was credited with the win. Billy O'Dell pitched the last three innings for the Giants and earned the save retroactively as it was not an official stat at the time.

Larsen's perfect game was the last by a Yankee until May 17, 1998, when David Wells was perfect against the Minnesota Twins at Yankee Stadium. Wells, a free spirit like Larsen, wrote in his 2004 memoir, *Perfect I'm Not: Boomer on Beer, Brawls, Backaches, and Baseball*, that he was half drunk when he pitched his perfecto. Baseball's most beloved badass later clarified that statement that he was hungover, not drunk.

On July 18, 1999, Larsen was on hand to throw out the first pitch to Yogi Berra on Yogi Berra Day at Yankee Stadium. In a script made for Hollywood, David Cone then pitched a perfect game against the Montreal Expos in the Yankees' 6–0 win. Cone joined Larsen and David Wells as the trifecta of Yankees to pitch a perfect game. Then on June 28, 2023, Yankees right hander Domingo Germán tossed a perfecto against the Oakland A's at the Oakland Coliseum giving the Bronx Bombers a quartet of pitchers who have hurled perfect games.

In Cone's masterpiece, there was a 33-minute rain delay in the third inning. Cone never went to a three-ball count the entire game and struck out 10. Defensive gems from right fielder Paul O'Neil, second baseman Chuck Knoblauch and left fielder Ricky Ledee helped to preserve the perfect game.

As the game progressed, I grew increasingly nervous. I superstitiously would not leave my seat in the press box even to go to the men's room in fear of breaking Cone's luck. In the top of the eighth, Jose Vidro hit a ground ball to Chuck Knoblauch at second base. It was Knoblauch's only chance of the day. At the time he was suffering from the "yips," a term used when a player is having difficulty throwing to a base. I think the stadium crowd had their hearts in their mouths in fear of one of Knobby's erratic throws. But his throw to Tino Martinez was on the money. When Cone got Orlando Cabrera to pop up to Scott Brosius to end the game, the almost 42,000 fans exploded. They had witnessed history.

David Wells no-hit the Minnesota Twins in 1998. Ironically, Wells graduated from the same Point Loma High School in San Diego as Larsen.

Cone dropped to his knees, his mouth open in amazement. He hugged catcher Joe Girardi, then headed for the clubhouse where he celebrated with Larsen and Berra.

"All the Yankee legends here today—Don Larsen, Yogi Berra," Cone said. "It makes you stop and think of the Yankee magic and the mystique of this ballpark."

I was sitting in the press box with my dear friend, Hall of Fame broadcaster Bob Wolff, who was one of the announcers who called Larsen's perfect game on the Mutual Broadcast System and around the world on the Armed Forces radio.

David Cone in the Yankees dugout on September 26, 1999, two months after he pitched his perfect game against the Montreal Expos.

When the game ended, he signed my scorecard.

> Rich—
> What a thrill—
> Don Larsen's here—
> I'm here watching—
> What vivid memories of my broadcasting his perfect game—and now David Cone.
> Fantastic—
> Bob Wolff

I then had Bill Shannon, the official scorer, sign the card before going to the umpires' room where plate ump Ted Barrett put his signature on it. Later I met Larsen at the bar (where else?) in the stadium press room and he signed it. Later I got Berra, Cone, and Joe Girardi, who caught Cone's perfect game, to sign my scorecard. I had a montage made that included my autographed scorecard, media credential and a photo of the celebration pile-up. The one-of-a-kind piece sits in my man cave.

I also have the Rickerby photo of the final pitch autographed by Larsen that includes three-by-five cards signed by Pinelli and Mitchell, who made the final out. That might be a one-of-a-kind item.

Having a drink with Cone was always on my bucket list. In 2018, I made a rules presentation to the Fox Regional Sports broadcasters, producers, and directors at the Terranea Resort in Rancho Palos Verdes, California. "Coney" was there and was as affable as expected. One more item checked off my list. In retrospect the men who pitched the three perfect games as a Yankee were all late-night party guys—an "imperfect trifecta."

Larsen's perfect game was voted the most memorable moment in World Series/All-Star Game competition in baseball's 1976 voting conducted in honor of the nation's Bicentennial celebration. It certainly affected the value of memorabilia from that game.

Larsen explained that the glove, shoes and hat he wore were all silvered. He kept the last pitched ball of the game and gave his uniform to the San Diego Hall of Champions.

Long-time broadcaster Bob Wolff, who announced Larsen's perfect game in 1956, was in the press box for David Cone's perfecto.

In 2012 Larsen announced that he was retrieving the uniform and put it up for auction with Steiner Sports Marketing to raise money for his grandchildren's college education. The uniform sold for $756,000. The winning bidder was Pete Seigel, CEO of Gotta Have It, a New York City gallery that collected and displayed pop-culture memorabilia. Seigel usually bid for wealthy clients, not himself. In today's market I think the uniform would easily sell for more than $1 million.

There are some interesting sidebars here.

Maglie and Larsen were Yankee teammates the following year and in '58. The Barber had a little sand left in his hourglass. He split the '57 and '58 seasons with the Dodgers and Yankees, appearing in 13 games for the Bombers, six as a starter. He went 3–1 with three saves. The Yankees moved Maglie during the '58 season to the St. Louis Cardinals where he finished his career. He is the last player to have played for all three New York teams prior to 1958 when the Giants and Dodgers moved to the West Coast.

In retrospect, it's likely safe to say that stadium public address announcer Bob Sheppard and Torre were the only two in the ballpark for all three perfect games pitched by Yankee pitchers.

Larsen retired in 1968 after pitching for the Yankees, St. Louis Browns, Baltimore Orioles, Kansas City Athletics, Chicago White Sox, San Francisco Giants, Houston Colt .45s, Houston Astros and Chicago Cubs.

After baseball, Larsen worked as a paper company salesman in San Jose, California, then retired to Hayden Lake near Coeur d'Alene, Idaho, 100 miles from the Canadian border, with his wife, Corinne.

Larsen died on January 1, 2020, at age 90 in Coeur d'Alene. He was the last player from that historic box score of October 8, 1956, to pass.

On August 7, 2021, before the Yankees-Mariners game, Larsen's grandson, Justin, a 29-year-old diesel mechanic who lives in Idaho, spread some of his grandfather's ashes in the area of the pitcher's mound on the site of the old Yankee Stadium, now Macombs Dam Park. Larsen had expressed a desire for some of his ashes to be spread there, and that the date would've been his 92nd birthday made it more meaningful. Justin, having received clearance from the TSA, had carried a portion of his grandfather's ashes on his flight.

Joining Justin was his girlfriend, Shelby Hoagland. Both were visiting New York for the first time.

Ken Davidoff, who covered the story in his August 18, 2021, column in the *New York Post*, wrote, "Don Larsen's longtime agent Andrew Levy, whose Wish You Were Here Productions represents athletes for personal appearances and operates a suite at the Stadium, suggested an activity to enhance the trip."

"Andrew asked me, 'Have you guys done anything with your grandfather's ashes yet?'" Justin said. "What better way [to honor Don Larsen] than to throw some [ashes] out at the old stadium?'"

So Justin Larsen joined Levy and friends Ken Thimmel and Joe Torrisi at Macombs Dam Park, approximating the location of the old stadium mound and left a little of Don behind.

"And if they were looking for a sign that this is what Don would have wanted, they quickly found one," wrote Davidoff. "As they were leaving the park to head for the Stadium, the group encountered a woman wearing a shirt with the 'Perfect Game' brand. No matter that the woman hadn't heard of Don Larsen. A sign is a sign."

"That was crazy!" Justin Larsen said.

19

Mel Allen

The "Voice of the Yankees"

Mel Allen was the soundtrack of Yankee baseball from 1939 to 1964. His voice was a staple of my baseball summers. From his perch in the broadcast booth, he took generations of fans along for the ride. "Anybody else after Mel, they're just renting the title," said current Yankees TV announcer Michael Kay.

There are those for whom labels like "legend" are throwaway platitudes, and then there's Mel Allen, truly one of the great broadcasting legends. He had one of the most recognizable voices in radio. His signature greeting of "Hello there, everybody, this is Mel Allen" was familiar to millions. His popularity even reached Hollywood. He appeared in such flicks as *The Babe Ruth Story* (1948), *Naked Gun* (1988), and *Born on the Fourth of July* (1989). I am proud to say he is the most famous man I have personally known in my life and could call him a friend. To think that one day I would be a colleague of his in various projects was beyond my imagination.

Mel Allen, the voice of the Yankees for parts of four decades, relaxes in his Greenwich, Connecticut, condo on January 6, 1996.

19. Mel Allen

I lived in a melting pot neighborhood. A few houses down the street were the Ploski brothers, Bob and John, and they would often play catch with each other. Bob, who was like a big brother I never had, was a pretty good pitcher in his youth, and he would throw to his older brother while I, at age six or seven, sat on the sidewalk with a popsicle stick that served as a microphone. I was Mel Allen and Bob was Allie Reynolds or Vic Raschi.

I can recall the Yankees broadcasting their first spring training game of the year in early March on WINS radio in NYC in the late '40s and early '50s. It was the first sign summer was on the way and school would soon be out. The game was always against the Cardinals since both teams trained in St. Petersburg, Florida, at Al Lang Field, which I thought was a million miles away. In hand would be my '49 Bowman baseball cards while I listened carefully to the radio.

Tony Russo, the son of an Italian immigrant, owned a mom-and-pop store in my neighborhood, the Hill Street Market. He was a devout Yankee fan which served as a common bond for us. As I approached my teen years, this was where I bought countless baseball cards and hung out and talked Yankee baseball with Russo. It was an era of daytime baseball and Russo, draped in his white apron, never missed a pitch with his radio blaring near the meat counter. Allen's voice was as much a part of the store as Gabby Hayes' Quaker Puffed Rice, the Howdy Doody Wonder Bread stickers and photos of the six gorgeous Rheingold contest finalists that ran annually from 1941 to 1964.

In the late '70s I was a columnist for a small publication in Wisconsin called *The Diamond Report*. I knew that Allen lived in Greenwich, Connecticut, about 50 miles from my hometown of Ansonia. Hoping to get an interview, I decided to call him in the summer of '78.

Aware of Allen's iconic status in baseball broadcasting, I was very apprehensive about calling him. I thought to myself, "Why would he give an interview to a fledgling writer who wrote for an obscure baseball publication?"

I had to ask an operator for his telephone number. Thinking it would be unlisted because of his celebrity, when she gave it to me, I was floored. I almost wished the number was unlisted. How would I ever get the courage to call him?

I finally put on my big boy pants and made the call. When he answered, I was shaking in my shoes. I identified myself and told him how much I admired his broadcasting talents and thanked him for the memories he provided over the years.

During the course of our conversation, I requested the interview and was dismayed by his answer: "Call me in a couple of weeks, because I'm busy at this time."

I thought this he was blowing me off. But I did what he said and was pleasantly surprised when he invited me to his condo where he lived with his sister, Esther.

Allen and I hit it off well and the chemistry was natural. A few weeks following my interview he called me and asked if I would be interested in being a research writer for a syndicated radio spot sponsored by the Hartford Insurance Company. These were 45-second spots covering a variety of famous sports events that included boxing and horse racing, among others.

I was in disbelief that the "Voice of the Yankees" would reach out to me. Of course, I obliged before he finished asking the question and it wasn't long before the Allen-Marazzi relationship was running full throttle. He asked me if I would write the script for a between-games doubleheader show he was doing on the radio.

In the late '70s, I hosted a local cable TV show and had Allen on as a guest. I still have a video that covers a small segment of that episode. Following the taping, Allen, his sister, Esther, and I went down to the Ansonia shopping mall where he would help promote a cancer fundraiser sponsored by the Ansonia-Derby Women's Club of which my wife, Lois, was a member. Mel was joined by New York Giants punter Dave Jennings, whom I also got to know through my show.

Allen came gratis and signed many autographs. He and his sister then joined me for a visit to my parents' home. Amazingly, the famed Yankees broadcaster was sitting in the same living room with my mother, father, and Joe Rostreter, one of Dad's friends. I gazed out the window and reflected on the days I would do my Mel Allen broadcasts watching the Ploski brothers play catch literally across the street, about 60 feet or so from where we sat.

It was a surreal experience.

Mel Allen enjoyed a gilded career transcending baseball and other sports. The Yankees' lead broadcaster for 22 years, the celebrated announcer called almost 4,000 games combining radio and TV. He was behind the mic for 20 World Series, 24 All-Star games, and six no-hitters. He was also in the booth for 14 Rose Bowls, five Orange Bowls and two Sugar Bowls, plus numerous horse races, basketball double-headers and rowing regattas. His voice was heard by millions every week in movie theaters on Fox Movietone newsreels.

Allen's homespun Alabama accent and broadcasting style were infectious, colorful and creative. A wise man, he always found a way to sell his sponsors, Ballantine Beer and Ale and White Owl cigars. A home run was a "Ballantine Blast," a great fielding play might elicit "'Little Phil' [Rizzuto] made a great play, and you'll make a great play for yourself if you open up a can of Ballantine Beer." And I wish I had a dollar for every time I heard him say, "Fans, make the three-ring sign and ask the man for Ballantine." The three rings stood for "Purity," "Body," and "Flavor."

A batted ball hit down the line that was just foul would trigger him to declare, "That ball was foul by the length of a White Owl."

Allen was the master of coining monikers. "Strangely I got nicknames from various fields of transportation," he revealed. "'Ol' Reliable' [Tommy Henrich] was the nickname of a railroad that ran through Alabama. It ran from Cincinnati to New Orleans."

In the '50s, the World Series was covered by the broadcasters of the two competing teams. Being affiliated with the dynastic Yankees gave Allen a job virtually every October.

"Was I really a great broadcaster or was I in the right place at the right time?" he modestly asked. "What if I was with a team other than the Yankees?"

Good point. From 1947 to 1964 the Yankees appeared in 15 of 18 World Series.

Born Melvin Israel in Birmingham, Alabama, on February 14, 1913, Mel was the first of three children born to Russian immigrants Julius and Anna Israel. The family lived in small Alabama towns like Johns and Bessemer in Jefferson County just southwest of Birmingham.

Allen grew up tall, smart, and precocious, completing high school at the age of 15. In his adolescence he worked for a time as a batboy in the Piedmont League in North Carolina and even sold soda at Navin Field, the home of the Detroit Tigers located on the corner of Michigan and Trumbull where he saw his first major league game. The park was later named Briggs Stadium and then Tiger Stadium before the Tigers moved to Comerica Park.

"We lived in North Carolina for a while because of my father's business," explained

Allen. "It was there I got involved as a batboy. My mother's folks lived in Detroit, and we visited there in the summer. I sold soda just one day to get into the park for free. They didn't ask me back because I spent my time watching the game instead of selling soda. One day I saw Babe Ruth play in Detroit. It was the only time I ever saw him play."

In 1932, when he was 19, Allen received a bachelor of arts degree from the University of Alabama. He went on the University of Alabama School of Law, completing his law degree in four years. While in college, he did some public address announcing for Alabama football games. Crimson Tide coach Frank Thomas recommended him to do the play-by-play for Alabama football on WBRC in 1935, Allen's first broadcasting job. He then won a fellowship as a speech instructor at his alma mater in the fall semester of '36. But before long he literally talked himself out of his longtime ambition of being a lawyer when CBS Radio in New York offered him a job for $45 a week while he was on a Christmas vacation.

"I drove five of my former classmates to New York, New Jersey, and Connecticut during the Christmas vacation of 1936," he recalled. "I had never been East. At the time I borrowed Daddy's Ford and drove 36 hours non-stop with my friends. It was standard procedure for students to pay $20 round trip. That's where I got the idea of borrowing my daddy's Ford."

One of the guys on the trip was Irving Berlin Kahn, the nephew of the great songwriter Irving Berlin. Kahn was dropped off in Newark, New Jersey. Allen then unloaded three others in New York City before traveling to New Haven, Connecticut, where he took Bert Levy. "While I was in New Haven, I visited the Yale Bowl, which was snow covered," said Allen. "I remember walking out to the middle of the gridiron surrounded by 70,000 empty seats on a cold New England day."

This would not be the last time that Allen would find himself in the Yale Bowl. In the early '50s he broadcast several Yale football games there. Frank Stolzenberg, a 1953 Yale grad, worked as a spotter in the press box for Allen and other broadcasters while a student at the Ivy League school. "My fee was $5 a game," he said. "The first time I worked with Mel, I thought I was getting stiffed by the great Mel Allen, the longtime voice of the New York Yankees. When it was time to pay me, he said he didn't have his wallet but promised he would have his secretary send me a check. True to his word, I received a check for $20, four times what I usually made."

That was the genial man I got to know and love.

Call it serendipity or luck, Allen's trip north would help shape his life for the next 60 years. While staying at Irving Berlin Kahn's house, on a lark he made contact with CBS Radio. He was invited for two auditions and beat out a field of 60 applicants for the job. Melvin Israel took the job as a CBS staff announcer in 1937. He was immediately asked to change his Jewish-sounding surname and decided to take his father's middle name, Allen. His father was not happy, thinking his son was wasting a good education.

His early days in radio were packed with a variety of assignments, such as playing selections on the mighty Wurlitzer organ, signing on the network and disc jockeying dance bands. He cut his teeth as an understudy to broadcasting titans Ted Husing and Bob Trout for sports and special events. At CBS, Allen announced variety shows starring Perry Como, Jo Stafford, and Harry James. He interrupted Kate Smith's afternoon program with a news bulletin reporting the crash of the airship *Hindenburg*. He worked some college football games as well.

Allen particularly impressed his bosses with a long 52-minute ad-lib description of the Vanderbilt Cup yacht race, broadcasting from an airplane overhead, the first time he was ever in a plane. That led to his first baseball assignment as a color commentator on the 1938 World Series when the Yankees swept the Cubs. He worked as an analyst alongside veteran St. Louis broadcaster France Laux.

In '39, he assisted Arch MacDonald covering the Yankees and Giants on CBS. In Brooklyn, owner Larry MacPhail hired Red Barber to do all Dodger home games live. That opened up baseball broadcasting in New York.

In 1940 MacDonald wound up in Washington and Allen became the principal announcer of the Giants and Yankees for the next several years.

It was during Allen's early years as a Yankee announcer that he had a poignant experience involving Lou Gehrig.

"Gehrig was suffering from ALS but would sometimes visit the team during the season," Allen recollected. "On one occasion he came over to me in the dugout and told me how much he liked what I was doing. Lou said, 'You know, Mel, I never understood the importance of your broadcast because I never got to listen. But now I've got tell you that the one thing that keeps me going is hearing your broadcasts.'"

"I excused myself and walked up the runway and cried," he said.

Allen served in the army for three years during World War II, spending most of his time at Fort Benning, Georgia. During his stint he wanted to go to Officer Candidate School, but the army took advantage of his radio talents and assigned him to do weekly broadcasts to help raise the morale of the infantrymen who were preparing to fight the Rome-Berlin-Tokyo Axis.

"I would talk about the different weapons that were used such as the M-1," said Allen. "Behind me they would use live gunfire for sound effects. For obvious reasons they shot blanks."

When Allen broadcast Yankees and Giants games, he didn't travel with the teams. If a team's scheduled game at home was rained out, the broadcasters would pick up the team that was on the road by way of Western Union and he would do recreations inside a studio. "In doing these recreations, I learned to paint the picture," explained Allen. An Allen broadcast allowed the listener to watch the game on the radio as he detailed the game's action. If Raschi was on the mound, he would say, "Raschi goes into the wind-up, around comes the right arm and the pitch...."

In 1946 Larry MacPhail came over to the Yankees from the Dodgers where he was the team's president. He suggested to Giants owner Horace Stoneham that it would be advantageous for both the Yankees and the Giants to get separate stations to carry all of the games, both home and away. According to Allen, "Stoneham was unaware that MacPhail had already set up a deal with CBS."

Stoneham released Allen of his obligation and Allen became one of the most popular Yankee figures through 1964. His popularity equaled that of many of the ballplayers who wore the pinstripes. His fame grew exponentially in the post–World War II pre-television era when radio was still king.

"I liked working radio more than television," he said. "In radio you painted the full picture as best you could. You were able to put in all the extra strokes. Concerning television, the battle rages on as to how many strokes you should put in and what you should let people watch." The erudite Yankee announcer played on the crowd noise. The excitement in his voice was dictated by the reaction of the crowd.

"Just think of a rowboat in water," he said. "The waves push the boat up and down.

The same thing happens with sound waves. The size of the crowd and the noise will make the announcer react accordingly. One night in Cleveland I was accused of being a turncoat. There were 15,000 fans in Municipal Stadium that held about 78,000. The Yankees won the game 5–1, but every time they got a hit, there was no crowd reaction, not even a negative one. I guess I didn't react the way the Yankee fans back home wanted me to."

"Yankee general manager George Weiss received several letters from irate fans," he went on. "When I returned to New York he called me in, wanting to know what it was all about. Fortunately, Weiss laughed about it."

Critics of Allen charged him with bias and favoritism. To this he responded, "I will readily admit when you are following one team, you are partisan, not prejudiced. To be prejudiced means you can only see one side and dislike the other side. Partisanship means you appreciate both sides but favor one."

"My barometer was the clubhouse," said Allen. "I never had any player with hard feelings toward me. Once I went into the Red Sox clubhouse to talk to Bobby Doerr and while talking to him, Ted Williams called me over to thank me for being nice to him. In most other cities, broadcasters literally rooted for their teams, Pittsburgh and Detroit in particular," he said, referring to Bob Prince and Ernie Harwell. "Phil Rizzuto did it with the Yankees. The only time I ever stood up and cheered was Don Larsen's perfect game in the 1956 World Series. And I didn't cheer into the microphone."

Television went against Allen's grain—it took away his thunder. Red Barber eloquently stated, "On radio, you're an artist. On TV, you're a servant."

Critics claimed Allen's words became extraneous on television. Jack Gould of the *New York Times* often criticized him for talking too much. Others said he rambled or wandered away from the subject at hand. In answer to that Allen replied, "I know people were critical about me talking too much for television. Actually, I was talking about something they couldn't see in the picture, which evidently was a distraction. I guess I could understand that, but I didn't think the fans were getting a full picture by what the camera could pick up."

"When Sandy Amoros made the great catch in the 1955 World Series," he said, "I went ahead and described something the viewers couldn't see on the tube. At the time, Martin was on second and McDougald was on first. I saw the outfield swing around toward right on Berra. Suddenly I looked up and said I never saw a left fielder play as close to center as that. When Amoros made the catch, I was able to describe the whole picture."

Video Replay Pioneer

Allen, who made his celebrated reputation on the radio, surprisingly was a pioneer in baseball television. Most notably he triggered the use of the center field camera and the instant replay.

"In the early '50s with WPIX," he said, "we used to sit around after games and try to come up with ways to improve the telecast. I suggested putting a camera in the center field bleachers to create a different perspective. Up until then, fans viewing the game always saw things from behind the catcher. You always watched the ball going out toward the bleachers."

"We didn't have that many cameras in those days," he went on. "Every once in a while we would use the center field camera. ABC later got credit for it, but we started it at WPIX from Yankee Stadium."

Thus, a new dimension was added to baseball telecasting. In truth, the idea was met with resistance from Weiss, who thought the center field camera would allow opponents to steal the catcher's signals. Reportedly, Weiss allowed three shots a game from center field, then four and eventually five.

CBS-TV director Tony Verna is credited with orchestrating the first use of replay while working the 1963 Army-Navy game when Army quarterback Rollie Stichweh punched in a one-yard touchdown. With Lindsey Nelson at the mic, viewers were able to see a replay of the TD. But Mel Allen would argue that WPIX was the first TV station to use replay. "I used to ask questions such as 'What can you do with tape?' 'How does it work?' 'What if you wanted to show a play over?'" noted Allen. "They explained to me they would call downtown to the WPIX studio from the stadium and would ask them to re-run certain plays."

On July 17, 1959, in a Friday night game at the stadium, Ralph Terry was pitching a no-hitter against the White Sox entering the top of the ninth inning. The crowd of 42,000-plus was roaring with excitement. White Sox outfielder Jim McAnany led off the inning and hit a fly ball to left field that Norm Siebern tippy-toed. The ball dropped at his feet and ruined a no-hitter.

"The tape of the game was in the studio by then," recalled Allen. "Having known what they were able to do at the studio, I said on air to director Jack Murphy, 'Jack, can we view that again?' Murphy ordered it to be re-run. A pitch or two later we were able to show that play over and that was the beginning of replay." It wasn't instant but it was replay.

The White Sox scored two runs that inning and won the game 2–0. Terry ended up pitching a two-hitter but Hall of Famer Early Wynn matched Terry and more, blanking the Yankees on two hits, and was the winning pitcher.

Nobody was better than Allen during rain delays. His talents frequently transformed a dismal afternoon into an amusing one. He was peerless when it came to ad-libbing and generating conversation with an unexpected guest. To be honest, there were times I enjoyed the interviews more than the games. Today when there is a rain delay there's a shift to the studio or a video of a classic game.

"I didn't have material prepared," said Allen. "Broadcasting baseball is a cumulative experience. I would find out if there were any V.I.P.s in the crowd and try to call on them."

His daily search for celebrities once led to a Bing Crosby play-by-play. "One year on Opening Day he wound up doing an inning," chuckled the famed Yankee announcer.

A number of high-profile announcers worked alongside Allen during his tenure with the Yankees. Among the cadre were names like Russ Hodges, Curt Gowdy, Dizzy Dean, Jim Woods, Red Barber, Jerry Coleman, Joe Garagiola, and Phil Rizzuto.

When asked who he most enjoyed working with, Allen answered, "As far as chemistry, Russ Hodges, who went on to become the New York Giants' number one announcer." Allen and Hodges worked together when the Giants and Yankees shared the same radio team. "We could almost read each other's minds," said Allen. "Also, Gowdy was very good." Allen was Gowdy's best man when he married Geraldine Dawkins. The wedding ceremony was held in the Central Presbyterian Church on Park Avenue in NYC. Gowdy left the Yankee broadcasts in '51 to become the anchor announcer for Red Sox broadcasts, a position he enjoyed for 15 summers.

Mel and Red

For many years the two giants in baseball broadcasting in New York City were Allen and Red Barber, who covered the Brooklyn Dodgers from 1939 to 1953. In 1954, Barber moved over to the Yankees broadcast booth joining Allen, the most famous sports announcer in the country. Would there be room for the two?

Barber was hired to handle pregame and postgame shows on televised home games and to work a few innings of play-by-play. He traveled with the team only occasionally. "Mel accepted me as an equal," he wrote in *Rhubarb in the Catbird Seat*. "He could not have been nicer to me either then or all through the years we worked together."

The Yankees had two Southern men with different on-air styles, both behemoths in their craft. Author Curt Smith described them this way: "The Ol' Redhead was white wine, crepes suzette and bluegrass music; Mel was beer, hot dogs, and the United States Marine Band." Jim Woods, who worked with both men, said, "One was a machine gun, the other a violin. Nobody who heard them would have any difficulty discerning which was which."

The play-calling styles of the two were different. Allen would highlight the flight of the ball. He would say, "There's a long drive, that ball is going, going, it is gone." Barber would focus on the outfielder. Perhaps his most famous call is when Dodgers left fielder Al Gionfriddo robbed DiMaggio of a home run or extra base hit in Game Six of the 1947 World Series. He said, "Here's the pitch, swung on, belted … it's a long one … back goes Gionfriddo, back, back, back, back, back, back … heeee makes a one-handed catch against the bullpen! Oh, Doctor!"

Barber brought many country sayings from his Southern upbringing. He would say, "The game is just as tight as a brand-new pair of shoes on a rainy day" or "The bases are FOB—they're full of Brooklyns." His most enduring phrase was "sitting in the catbird seat." In Barber's lexicon, that meant a batter with a three-ball, no-strike count or a team with a comfortable lead.

Barber's best-known innovation for broadcasters was a simple device to remind him to repeat the score frequently for listeners who had just tuned in: He kept a three-minute egg timer hourglass on his desk in the booth. Every time the sand ran down, he repeated the score and flipped it over. Dozens if not hundreds of later announcers adopted this prop.

Fans not only argued who was better—DiMaggio or Williams, and later Mantle, Mays, or Snider—but they also debated the abilities of Allen and Barber. In the tri-state area, it was tribal. If you bled Dodger blue, Barber was your man. If your allegiance was to the Bronx Bombers, Allen was number one.

"Sure, you felt the competition," exclaimed Allen. "Because fans made you feel that. People would write and tell me I stink, that I should take lessons from Red Barber. But I found out that was typical in any city."

Allen and Barber might be revered as the patriarchs of the New York broadcasting scene but the guy with the longest tenure was Rizzuto, who spent 39 years (1957–1995) as a Yankee announcer. Rizzuto cut his teeth under Allen one year after he was released by the Yankees as a player.

"At the time, the Yankees hired the announcers," stated Allen. "Jim Woods had been with us from 1953 to 1956, and Weiss decided to put Rizzuto in the booth. I tried to press George to add Phil but not dismiss Woods, who was brought up from Atlanta. But

Woods was not retained. A lot of things Rizzuto did became popular, such as the birthday routine."

As a member of the media, it was Allen's job to meet and talk with Yankee managers. One of his favorites was Casey Stengel, who piloted the Bronx bombers from 1949 to 1960.

"One year I got down to St. Petersburg, Florida, and they didn't have a room at the hotel," Allen recalled. "Casey was in the bar as usual and would always close it up."

"I walked in the bar about 11:00 p.m. because I heard his voice," he said. "I told Casey that the hotel didn't have my room. He said, 'Don't worry. I've got two beds in my room. You can stay with me.' The problem was he didn't leave the bar until four o'clock in the morning. By the time I got to bed it was about 4:30 a.m. I was tired. I woke up at 8:00 a.m. and Casey was gone. With only three hours sleep he was up and gone for the morning workout."

Firing

It was reported that in the middle of September during the '64 season Mel Allen walked into Yankees co-owner Dan Topping's office to discuss his contract for the next season. This was something Allen had routinely done for more than 20 years with the Yankees. Ralph Houk, the team's general manager, was sitting in the office with Topping when Allen arrived. At the meeting he was told his contract would not be renewed for the '65 season. Since the day he was fired, speculation has persisted regarding Allen's dismissal.

Maury Allen, the longtime scribe of the *New York Post*, had his take on the firing. "It was Houk, the Yankees general manager, who was responsible," said Allen. "Mel talked too much and too loud. Wherever we went Mel would be telling a story about Lou Gehrig or Joe DiMaggio. This was in the '50s and '60s. People got tired of it. I was in the press room one day when Mel was holding court. Houk stormed out and said, 'I can't take it anymore. I've got to get rid of him.' The next day Mel was fired."

There are multiple theories for Allen's demise. During the '63 World Series when the Dodgers swept the Yankees, his voice gave out over the air. Though there were physiological reasons for this, some connected the loss of his voice to the decline of the Yankees. New York *Daily News* writer Dick Young wrote that it was a "psychosomatic failure."

Reportedly, Topping believed that Allen was talking too much on television and pulled him from working the '64 Fall Classic when the Cardinals beat the Yankees in seven games. Others said he was drinking too much.

Another possibility was that Ballantine Beer, the Yankees' longtime sponsor, was cutting back some of its high-level employees including Allen, who made good money. Among the players, only DiMaggio made more money than Allen during the Yankee Clipper's final years. But it remains an enigma how the Yankees could do this to a man who was selected by the television editors of the United States as "America's Best Sportscaster" for 14 consecutive years. To add insult to injury, the Yankees didn't even have the decency to hold a press conference. At the time, Allen was only 51 years old and had a future still in front of him.

"I wasn't surprised, but I was hurt," bemoaned Allen. "There was no reason that I was aware of why I wasn't being retained. I was told the usual thing about the Yankees going in another direction. There was no argument about it. As a matter of fact, I stayed through December to take care of mail that piled up."

Allen confided in me that he had a good idea what happened and would write about it in the future, but he never did.

Following his departure, he did some work with the Milwaukee Braves and Cleveland Indians. It was known in '65 that the Braves would be moving to Atlanta the following season. An Atlanta station hired Allen to broadcast some of the games to the team's future home. But he never did broadcast games in Atlanta. In '68 he was hired to cover the Cleveland Indians.

Mel Allen's journey continued. He was involved in a variety of endeavors. He did public relations work for Canada Dry, called University of Miami football, hosted local and network radio sports shows, and covered the 1966 Little League World Series for a Sacramento radio station. This was a far cry from broadcasting a World Series from Yankee Stadium.

Allen disappeared from the limelight for eight years. "It was as if he had leprosy," *Sports Illustrated*'s William Taafe wrote in a 1985 profile.

The ultimate broadcast celebrity of his day returned to Yankee Stadium on June 8, 1969, where he had the honor of introducing Mickey Mantle on a day the Yankees honored "The Mick."

Thanks to the generosity of Yankees' owner George Steinbrenner, in 1976 Allen was invited to be a part of the ceremony on Opening Day when the Yankees unveiled their refurbished ballpark. Steinbrenner never forgot a 45-minute phone call he had with Allen when he was an assistant football coach at Northwestern University. At the time Steinbrenner was exploring the broadcasting field.

From 1977 to 1985, Allen called a few dozen Yankee games for SportsChannel, a cable network. On July 4, 1983, he had the opportunity to call Dave Righetti's no-hitter. In typical Allen fashion he captured the moment with excitement. "The crowd standing—40,000 plus people in the stands are roaring and Righetti trying to stop Boggs—and he gets him—a no-hitter, a no-hitter, a no-hitter for Dave Righetti. How about that—he got the no-hitter!" he bellowed.

In 1977, Allen was introduced to a new generation of fans across the country as narrator of Major League Baseball's weekly highlight show, *This Week in Baseball*. Fans were again treated to his familiar greeting, "Hello there, everybody. This is Mel Allen."

In 1978, Allen and Red Barber received the first Ford C. Frick Award at the Baseball Hall of Fame. The award honors broadcasters for "major contributions to baseball." (It should be noted, however, that broadcasters are not considered members of the Hall of Fame.) Allen was inducted into the Radio Hall of Fame, the International Jewish Hall of Fame in 1980 and the National Jewish Hall of Fame in 1995.

Thanks to the efforts of former Yankees PR director Marty Appel, who served as VP for public relations for WPIX from 1980 to 1992 and was the executive producer for Yankee telecasts from 1988 to 1992, Allen became the first broadcaster to call a game in seven different decades. Appel brought Allen back one last time on Monday evening, April 30, 1990. The eternal "Voice of the Yankees" joined Phil Rizzuto and George Grande in the A's 6-0 win over the Yanks.

Mel Allen died on June 16, 1996, at age 83 at his home in Greenwich, Connecticut. I attended his funeral service and sat behind Joe DiMaggio, Phil Rizzuto, Yogi Berra, and

George Steinbrenner. We all wore yarmulkes. He was buried in Temple Beth El Cemetery in Stamford, Connecticut. His gravestone reads: "Mel Allen, Beloved son, brother, uncle."

I was privileged to attend his funeral and considered him a friend.

Subsequent to his funeral service, more than a thousand people attended a memorial service in New York's St. Patrick's Cathedral sponsored by the Committee for Christian-Jewish Understanding. On July 25, 1998, a plaque commemorating his career was unveiled in Monument Park at Yankee Stadium.

It was most deserving and long overdue.

How about that!

20

The Pine Tar Game

George Brett is the greatest player in Kansas City Royals history and one of the best to ever play the game. One of four players to collect 3,000 hits, slug 300 homers and steal 200 bases (Willie Mays, Hank Aaron and Dave Winfield are the others), Brett played 21 seasons, winning three batting titles, an MVP award and a World Series ring along the way. But despite all his accomplishments, he may be best remembered for a game at Yankee Stadium on July 24, 1983. Brett had hit a two-out, two-run home run in the top of the ninth off Rich "Goose" Gossage, giving the Royals an apparent 5–4 lead over New York. But then Yankees manager Billy Martin asked the umpires to examine Brett's bat, which they soon determined had excessive pine tar on it. Voiding his home run, they declared the Yankees victors. Brett memorably charged

George Brett's pine tar bat controversy in 1983 continues to resonate among Yankee fans.

from the dugout in a rage, having to be restrained as he screamed at home-plate ump Tim McClelland.

The Royals protested the game and American League president Lee MacPhail, who was the Yankees' general manager from 1966 to 1973, reversed the umpires' decision, a rarity in the game of baseball. He ordered the game to be resumed at a future date with the Royals batting in the top of the ninth with two outs and leading 5–4.

The pine tar controversy was the cause célèbre for baseball in 1983. It exposed a dysfunctional system that primarily involved MacPhail, the Official Playing Rules Committee, and the umpires. MacPhail's ruling proved to be one of the most controversial in the history of the game. Adding intrigue to "the Pine Tar Game" story, an innocent 17-year-old Royals bat boy played a key role.

Before we go to the game, it is important to note how the rule read at the time and review two pine tar bat situations in 1975 with opposite rulings. Rule 1.10 (b) stated, "The bat handle, for not more than 18 inches from the end, may be covered or treated with any material to improve the grip. No such material shall improve the reaction or distance factor of the bat."

Rule 2.00 said, "An illegally batted ball is one hit with a bat that does not conform to rule 1.10 (b)."

If you stop there, it appears that, by rule, Brett used an illegal bat.

Rule 6.06 (a) stated, "A player is out when he hits an illegally batted ball." And Rule 6.06 (d) read, "A player's use of a doctored bat results in the batter being called out, ejected from the game, and the imposition of additional penalties as determined by the League President."

A bat was determined to be doctored if "filled, flat surfaced, nailed, hollowed, grooved or covered with a substance such as paraffin, wax, etc."

What did "etc." mean? Did that include a bat covered with pine tar in excess of 18 inches? Presumably, it did. Looking at the rules just cited, if a batter used a bat that had pine tar in excess of 18 inches from the bat handle, he had hit an illegally batted ball because it did not conform to rule 1.10 (b).

1975 Pine Tar Situations

During the 1975 season there were two incidents involving a pine tar bat ruling. One occurred on the evening of July 19 in Minnesota where the Twins hosted the Yankees and the other took place in Anaheim on September 7 when the Royals played the Angels.

In the top of the seventh of the Yankees-Twins game, Thurman Munson was batting with the bases loaded and two outs when he knocked in Sandy Alomar with a single. Twins manager Frank Quilici complained that the pine tar on Munson's bat exceeded the 18 inches allowed by rules. The bat was checked by plate umpire Art Frantz, who ruled that the bat had exceeded the pine tar limit and called Munson out. Munson lost the RBI, and the Yankees lost the game, 2–1.

"Munson always had a wry sense of humor," recalled Nick Bremigan, who was the first base umpire that night. "When he returned after rounding first base, he kiddingly said to me, 'Better check the ball for blood.' He was referring to the fact that his single was a bleeder, which indeed it was."

"I was aware of what was going on [Frantz checking the bat] and casually said to Munson, 'Checking the ball would probably be irrelevant, because I think you've just been called out,'" Bremigan said.

When Munson realized he was called out, he was furious. He targeted his anger on Quilici and Twins catcher Glenn Borgmann for initiating the bat protest.

Now, let's go to the Royals-Angels game, won by the Royals, 8–7. John Mayberry of the Royals hit two home runs against California. Angels manager Dick Williams argued that the bat Mayberry used for his second home run had pine tar in excess of the 18 inches allowed. But the umpires allowed the home run to stand despite the extra goo. Williams protested the game, but MacPhail ruled that even though Mayberry's bat had excessive pine tar, it was a legal bat.

MacPhail saw pine tar as a misdemeanor, not a felony. The intent of the pine tar rule was to prevent baseballs from being discolored. With the exception of improving the grip, it created no advantage for the batter since pine tar did not affect the distance a ball would travel. The soiled baseballs, on the other hand, led to the need for new baseballs. Rule 1.10 (b), then, was about avoiding unnecessary expenses.

Calvin Griffith, the Twins' frugal owner, led the charge. Griffith was upset about the number of baseballs thrown out of games because they were soiled by pine tar. "For Calvin, everything was dollars and cents and rightfully so," said former umpire Jim Evans, who umpired the Mayberry game.

Yankees manager Bill Virdon never protested Frantz's ruling in the Munson game. If he had protested, MacPhail surely would have reacted as he did in the Mayberry case seven weeks later. But MacPhail's interpretation there did not adhere to the *Official Baseball Rules*, which stated that if a player used a bat that did not conform to the 18-inch pine tar limit, he had hit an illegally batted ball and should be called out.

Here's my question: if MacPhail made a ruling on the pine tar question from the Mayberry protest, why didn't that make its way into clear and specific language in the 1976 *Official Baseball Rules* and future editions?

In 1983, the year of the Brett pine tar game, the four umpires who worked that game in New York obviously interpreted a bat that exceeded the 18-inch pine tar limit as an illegal bat, ignoring the precedent established by MacPhail's 1975 ruling in the Mayberry case.

Bremigan, who assisted me in the first book I wrote, *The Rules and Lore of Baseball*, was considered one of the top baseball rule interpreters of his era. He was an important figure in my life regarding my rules education. Bremigan, who died of a heart attack in 1989, umpired both the Munson and Brett pine tar games. I can only speculate that he carried the weight of making the decision in the Brett game.

Why he ignored MacPhail's ruling in the Mayberry episode is unknown.

The Pine Tar Game

Let's fast forward to that July 24, 1983, Royals-Yankees game, which was played on a sultry Sunday afternoon in the Bronx. At the time, Brett was one of the few players who didn't wear batting gloves. Instead, he relied on pine tar alone to get a good grip on the bat.

The Yankees were in Kansas City July 8–10 when manager Billy Martin and other members of the Yankees team observed excessive pine tar on Brett's bat. But the strategy was to be patient and bring it to the umpires' attention only if Brett did something productive when using the bat. The Yankees certainly were aware of the Munson ruling eight years earlier and thought they had an ace in the hole, if needed. If they were aware of the Mayberry ruling, they ignored it.

The Yankees held a 4–3 lead entering the top of the ninth inning. Yankees reliever Dale Murray retired Don Slaught and Pat Sheridan before U.L. Washington singled to center field. Martin then brought in Gossage to pitch to Brett for the final out. Gossage had pitched a third of an inning in the first game of a doubleheader on Friday, the 22nd, and 2⅓ innings on Wednesday, the 20th, versus the Twins. He should have been rested.

Brett spoiled the day for the Yankees and shocked the 33,944 fans in attendance as he deposited a Goose Gossage pitch into the right field seats to give the Royals an apparent 5–4 lead. As Brett crossed the plate, Martin, ready to protest Brett's bat, approached rookie home plate umpire Tim McClelland.

The Transfer of the Bat

Royals bat boy Merritt Riley's job was to pick up the batter's bat after the ball was put in play and then place it in the bat rack inside the dugout. But for some reason, Riley got caught up in the moment and watched Brett circle the bases.

Just before Washington crossed the plate, Yankees catcher Rick Cerone flipped the bat to Riley who was a bit tardy getting to the plate area. Cerone was then immediately instructed by Martin to recover the bat. "Cerone, being the arrogant guy that he was, grabbed the bat out of my hand," recalled Riley. "He examined the bat thinking Martin wanted it checked for cork. But he saw no evidence of cork and threw the bat down at my feet. I picked it up, but it wasn't long before McClelland took it from me as Martin was making his way out of the dugout."

McClelland then walked toward the pitcher's mound with the bat to huddle with his brother umpires—Bremigan, Joe Brinkman, and Drew Coble. Several Yankees, including Don Mattingly, Graig Nettles, Gossage and Martin, surrounded the umpires and listened intently to their conversation. The umpires then walked to the third base side of the mound where they had a more private meeting.

"Brett paced up and down the dugout," said Riley. "He said to nobody in particular, 'If they call me out, you're going to see four dead umpires.'" McClelland and the rest of the umpiring crew walked back toward home plate where McClelland measured the pine tar on the bat by laying it on the plate, which is 17 inches wide. It was determined that the amount of pine tar on the bat's handle far exceeded the 18-inch limit.

McClelland located Brett in the Royals dugout and, raising his right arm, the umpire called the slugger out. Brett, in a rage, charged McClelland from the dugout. It is an iconic snapshot in baseball time. Brett was restrained by manager Dick Howser and several teammates as well as Brinkman, who had him in a chokehold. This negated the home run and gave the Yankees an apparent 4–3 victory.

The Battle for the Bat

The battle for the bat became the next chapter in this zany episode. While Brett was being restrained, Royals pitcher Gaylord Perry, the noted 44-year-old spitballer, swiped the bat from McClelland. It then fell into the hands of coach Rocky Colavito, who tossed the bat toward the Royals dugout. From there the bat was reportedly picked up by Royals pitcher Steve Renko, who ran up the tunnel adjacent to the Royals' clubhouse where he was stopped by a security guard. McClelland and Brinkman, who were in pursuit of Renko, confiscated the bat. Baseball's version of the *French Connection* had ended.

The umpires sent the bat by courier to MacPhail's office to be examined. Meanwhile, Royals coach Jose Martinez escorted a calmer Brett back to the dugout, followed by Joe Simpson and Howser. The Royals manager returned to the field with Colavito and argued with Bremigan about the ruling to no avail. Frank Sinatra's "New York, New York" blasted over the stadium loudspeakers as Yankee fans euphorically exited the park.

In retrospect, Riley, who became a New York City policeman, possibly could have prevented the pine tar incident if he had picked up the bat in a timely manner and placed it in the bat rack. It might have been impossible for the umpires to determine which bat was used by Brett. "I really believe the pine tar controversy never would have happened if I hadn't done what I did," revealed Riley.

Following the game, Riley was the target of heavy criticism by the Royals for failure to get the bat before Cerone could get his hands on it. "Royals manager Dick Howser was screaming at me," lamented Riley. "I packed things up and went to the clubhouse. When I arrived, the clubhouse guy said, 'I think it's best if you stay out of the locker room. These guys are pretty heated up.' That made me feel worse."

Riley then made his way to the Yankees clubhouse, where he found a more friendly environment. "Coach Jeff Torborg, seeing I was upset, came over to me and said, 'Don't worry about it, the Yankees pay your check. It's not your fault.' I never did hear from the Yankees organization."

Riley hung out there for a while before the visiting clubhouse attendant told him it was safe to return because most of the players had departed. But Brett, who was surrounded by reporters, remained. "After the reporters broke up, Brett made eye contact with me," said Riley. "We always got along well. He used to call me 'Spaulding' in reference to the little brat grandson of Judge Smails in the comedy movie *Caddyshack*. Brett screamed, 'What the hell are you doing?' He then started to smile. He said, 'You owe me.' I answered, 'Whatever you want.'"

The Protest and Decision

Perry was retroactively ejected by MacPhail along with Brett, Howser and Colavito, who were banished for arguing the umpires' decision. Roberts inexplicably received no punishment. Bruce Slutsky, in a SABR article titled "July 24, 1983, Pine Tar Game," wrote, "Dean Taylor, an assistant director of scouting development for the Royals, considered himself a rules buff. It was his opinion that pine tar did not improve the reaction or distance factor of the bat. He told Royals general manager John Schuerholz he thought the umpires had misapplied the rules. Schuerholz found an AL regulation that stated that the use of pine tar should not be considered doctoring the bat. The two wrote a three-page document protesting the game to American League President Lee MacPhail." In reference to the regulation that Schuerholz referred to, Evans stated, "I did not know of any regulation."

On July 28 MacPhail, who had been the Yankees' general manager from 1966 to 1973, made his decision, aided by assistant Bob Fishel, who ironically served as the Yankees' public relations director from 1954 to 1973. Slutsky wrote, "MacPhail upheld the protest, stating, 'It is not in accord with the intent or spirit of the rules and the rules do not provide that a hitter be called out for excessive use of pine tar.' This decision could not be appealed."

To his credit, MacPhail did not throw the umpires under the bus. Instead, he cited the ambiguity of the *Official Baseball Rules.* He laid the responsibility on those in administrative positions, including himself.

Steinbrenner's Pine Tar War

MacPhail ordered the game to be resumed on August 18 with two outs in the top of the ninth inning with the Royals leading 5–4. Needless to say, Yankees owner George Steinbrenner was livid over MacPhail's ruling. "He [MacPhail] is certainly not a scientist and in no position, I feel, to make such a judgment," said Steinbrenner to UPI. "Nor would I be, nor any of my staff or his."

Between the ending of the July 24 game and the resumption of it on August 18, the Yankees fought a series of pine tar wars that even extended into the New York court system. Steinbrenner was fined approximately $300,000 (some say $250,000) by Commissioner Bowie Kuhn after he made the threatening statement, widely reported, that "if the Yankees lose the pennant by one game, I wouldn't want to be Lee MacPhail." He added, "I suggest he go house hunting in Kansas City." The Yankees finished third, seven games out, in '83. There was no need for MacPhail to check real estate listings in Kansas City.

Steinbrenner's clash with MacPhail came to a head over the proposed starting time of the August 18 resumption. After threatening to forfeit the game to the Royals, the Boss stepped back and approved a 2:00 p.m. starting time and a $2.50 charge for a ticket. Steinbrenner's game plan was to make the day a festive occasion, with free gifts and circus acts. He even announced that kids from area day camps would be bused in for the event. But those plans were thwarted because the Royals had a night game in Kansas City on August 17, and MacPhail, citing the basic agreement between the owners and players, stated that the suspended game could not start before 6:00 p.m. on August 18.

Steinbrenner railed against MacPhail. Upset about the starting time of the suspended game, the Yankees' owner accused MacPhail of playing favorites—and depriving kids of a nice day at the ballpark.

The Pine Tar Game adventure continued as two fans filed lawsuits against the Yankees challenging the $2.50 admission charge. The Yankees even hired Roy Cohn, the high-powered trial lawyer.

On the day of the game's scheduled completion, Bronx Supreme Court Judge Orest V. Maresca granted a preliminary injunction blocking the resumption of the game, stating more time was needed to study the lawsuits filed by the two fans. MacPhail appealed Maresca's ruling to the New York Supreme Court Appellate Division in Manhattan. At 3:34 p.m., Justice Joseph Sullivan stayed Maresca's ruling and ordered that the game go on.

At the time the stay was issued, the Royals were sitting in their plane on the tarmac of the Newark Airport. Following Sullivan's decision, they exited the plane and departed to Yankee Stadium, where it was ruled to MacPhail's satisfaction that the game would start at 6:00 p.m.

The Resumption of the Game

A reported 1,245 fans attended the resumed game, which lasted all of 12 minutes. Fans paid $2.50 for a general admission ticket and $1.00 for a bleacher seat. The lawsuit by the two fans went nowhere. The media who covered the game in the press box were each treated to a can of pine tar.

When the game was picked up in the top of the ninth, the Royals led 5–4 because Brett's home run was restored. Pitcher Ron Guidry played center field and the lefty-throwing Mattingly was positioned at second base. Some theorized that Martin made those moves in protest of MacPhail's decision. But most likely Guidry was in center because Jerry Mumphrey had been traded to the Houston Astros, and Mattingly, who pinch-hit for Steve Balboni in the seventh inning, was positioned at second base because Bert Campaneris was injured. Mattingly was the first lefty-throwing second baseman in the major leagues after Cleveland Indians left-handed fireballer "Sudden Sam" McDowell was switched from pitcher to second base for one batter in a July 6, 1970, game against the Washington Senators.

Yankees reliever George Frazier took the mound facing Hal McRae, who followed Brett in the lineup. Brett, Perry, Colavito, and Howser were not on the bench because they had been ejected for their actions on July 24. Colavito never went to the stadium. "Howser gave me permission to spend the day with my family in Reading, Pennsylvania," recalled Colavito. "My son and daughter picked me up at the Newark airport. I met the team the following night in Baltimore."

Brett never joined the team at Yankee Stadium, either. He and Larry Ameche, son of actor Don Ameche, went to lunch at a New Jersey restaurant. At the time, Ameche was a TWA airline rep in charge of Royals charters.

The Yankees stubbornly refused to throw in the towel. Martin had the Yankees appeal that Brett or U.L. Washington had never touched first or second base when Brett hit the July 24 home run. Martin instructed pitcher George Frazier to throw to both bases for the purpose of making the appeal. Each time the umpires denied the appeals. This brought Martin onto the field to meet with umpire Dave Phillips. But Phillips took away Martin's thunder when he provided a notarized affidavit from the original umpiring crew saying that both Brett and U.L. Washington, who was on base at the time of the homer, had touched all the bases.

How did MacPhail's office have such foresight? Steve Wulf wrote in the August 29, 1983, edition of *Sports Illustrated,* "MacPhail and his assistant, Bob Fishel, thought it up after having lunch with some Yankee officials a few weeks ago. Fishel had suggested that the Yankees promote the suspended game in a big way—little pine tar bats and such—but the Yankees reacted in such negative fashion that Fishel and MacPhail realized that the Yankees had not yet begun to fight. So, they anticipated the appeal and subsequently requested that umpire Joe Brinkman's crew notarize a letter."

George Maloney, the plate umpire for the resumed game, announced that the

Yankees were playing the game under protest which created the oddity of two opponents protesting the same game. But the protest was DOA.

More than three weeks after the inning began, Frazier struck out McRae to end the top of the ninth. Royals reliever Dan Quisenberry then retired Mattingly, Roy Smalley and Oscar Gamble to preserve the Royals' 5–4 win. Gamble grounded out to second baseman Frank White, who flipped the ball to first baseman John Wathan for the game-ending out. Martin unsuccessfully argued that Quisenberry should not be eligible to pitch because he was on the DL for the July 24 game. The winning pitcher for the Royals was reliever Mike Armstrong and the loser was Goose Gossage.

Before the 1984 season, the Official Playing Rules Committee clarified the so-called "pine tar rule" to stipulate that a violation of the 18-inch limit shall call for the bat's removal but not for the nullification of any play that results from its use.

In 2010, Major League Baseball added a comment to rule 3.02 (c). It reads in part, "If no objections are raised prior to a bat's use, then a violation of Rule 3.02(c) on that play does not nullify any action or play on the field and no protests of such play shall be allowed." In essence, it indicates that excessive pine tar on a bat is a benign violation.

But why didn't the Official Playing Rules Committee pay any attention to MacPhail's 1975 Mayberry ruling? And why didn't MacPhail direct the committee to include an amended rule 1.10 (b) in the 1976 *Official Baseball Rules*? It took nine years instead.

Another question: Did the umpires have access to the regulation that Schuerholz cited in arguing that the treatment of a bat with excessive pine tar was not an illegal bat? Apparently not.

In short, the pine tar incident revealed that a dysfunctional system existed at the time. There was, to quote a famous line from *Cool Hand Luke*, a failure to communicate.

Aftermath

Martin and the Yankees had had their eye on Brett's bat since the teams' previous series in Kansas City. The game plan was to remain mute until Brett did something positive with the sticky bat. Interestingly, though, the pine tar bat that Brett used in the Yankees-Royals series in early July was broken in the July 23 game, one day before the controversial July 24 game. In other words, the bat used on July 24 exceeded the pine tar rule but was not the same bat the Yankees targeted two weeks earlier. That bat ended up in the hands of Riley, as a gift from Brett. "I still have the bat in my house," said Riley. "Back then, we were permitted to bring broken bats home."

As for Brett, he quipped, "The pine tar game was the greatest thing to ever happen to me. Before that, I was the hemorrhoid guy. After that, I was the pine tar guy. What would you rather be? It's pretty simple to me."

After the MacPhail reversal, Brett eventually got the bat back and used it again for a couple of games before he realized he was using a historic bat that had value.

For a while, Brett displayed the bat at a restaurant he owned called C.J. Brett's in Hermosa Beach, California. But then Brett decided to sell it. "Brett first sold the bat to collector Barry Halper for $25,000," wrote Tyler Kepner in the *New York Times* on July 24, 2008. "Realizing it should go to the Hall instead, Brett got it back from Halper six months later for the same $25,000 price. In thanks, he gave Halper the bat he used to hit three homers in a 1978 playoff game."

Finally, the bat made its way to Cooperstown, where it has rested since 1987.

Wathan, the Royals first baseman who recorded the final out when the game was resumed on August 18, had possession of the ball for a time. "Halper invited teammate Leon Roberts and me to his home the following season when we were in New York and I gave him the baseball free of charge," said Wathan.

The home-run ball was caught by a journalist, Ephraim Schwartz, who reported in an article at InfoWorld.com that he sold it and his game ticket stub to Halper for $500 and 12 Yankees tickets. Halper also acquired the signed business card of Justice Maresca, who had issued the injunction, and the can of Oriole Pine Tar Brett had used on the bat.

Gossage later signed the pine tar ball to Halper, "Barry, I threw the fucking thing!"

21

Joe Torre

"The Godfather"

Joe Torre steered the Yankee ship from 1996 to 2007 during which time the Yankees won four world championships in his first five years falling one short of Casey Stengel's ML record of five consecutive titles from 1949 to 1953. When he was originally hired, the *New York Daily News* headlined him as "Clueless Joe," but his status rose to the title of "The Godfather." He was soft spoken and had the face of calm, but despite his relaxed, composed demeanor, he was unflappable and audacious. The skipper was still water that ran deep. He earned the ultimate respect of his players. Derek Jeter addressed him as "Mr. Torre." And he was able to escape Steinbrenner's firing, an amazing accomplishment in itself.

He was the gatekeeper of the Yankees: the clubhouse was his, and the team was his. You can't get better credibility than taking a ride down the Canyon of Heroes in four of his first five years.

Torre was a master psychologist. He would quietly call out his players, but he was no shrinking violet. When he felt the need to impose his will he would do so privately. There was a game when Paul O'Neil didn't hustle to first base on a ground ball. The next day O'Neil looked at the posted lineup and noticed he wasn't listed.

O'Neil got the memo.

On occasion, Torre might want to admonish a player, but he brought in other players to give the appearance it was a group session rather than a solo beatdown. Although Torre had control of his players, he empowered the players to police themselves.

Torre was media savvy. He held his pre-game press conferences in the Yankee dugout. Unless you got a seat early near where he normally sat in the middle of the dugout, it was difficult to hear his answers.

Torre enjoyed above average success as a player. In his 18-year career (Braves, Cards, Mets) he hit .297 with 252 home runs and 1,185 RBI. His OPS was a healthy .817. Before he was hired to manage the Yankees on the recommendation of senior advisor Arthur Richman, he piloted the three teams he played for with little success, winning 894 games against 1,003 losses. Conversely, in the 12 seasons he shepherded the Yankees, they went to the postseason each year, winning 10 division titles, six AL pennants, and four world championships. His '98 team won a then–AL record 114 games and marauded their way to a World Series title, losing only twice in the playoffs. Overall, he won 1,173 games against 767 losses which catapulted him to the Hall of Fame for his managerial success. After Torre left the Yankees, he managed the Dodgers for three years (2008–2010), going 259–227. He won two division titles and finished fourth his final season.

This all proves that you have to have chicken to make chicken salad. Managers win games with good players, but those around Torre would tell you that when he came to the Yankees, he was the right person for the right job at the right time.

1996 Yankees

The saga of the '96 Yankees was made for Hollywood. It was a team engulfed in adversity. In May, pitcher David Cone underwent surgery to remove an aneurysm in his right shoulder. If he had continued pitching undiagnosed, he could have lost his arm. Torre's brother Rocco, a New York City police officer, died in June of a heart attack. During the World Series, Torre's brother Frank awaited a donor heart in Columbia Presbyterian Hospital. The night before Game Six, Frank underwent a successful heart transplant. The surgery was performed by Dr. Mehmet Oz, who would become a well-known doctor with his own television show.

The Braves were strong favorites to win the Series. It was a daunting task for the Yankees who had to face three future Hall of Fame pitchers in five of the six games. I attended Game One of the Series with my youngest son, Brian. The right arm of John Smoltz and the bat of 19-year-old Andruw Jones proved too much for the Yanks in the Braves' 12–1 blitz. Jones homered in his first two WS at-bats, duplicating the feat of the A's Gene Tenace in the '72 Series. Greg Maddux put away the Yankees in Game two.

Yankees manager Joe Torre (right) and brother Frank enjoy time together in Joe's office on June 7, 1997.

Before the game, Torre told Steinbrenner the Yankees would win it in six. "I was standing in the hallway near Torre's office when Steinbrenner walked in his office," recalled Yankees media relations director Rick Cerrone. "Steinbrenner said, 'Go get 'em, we need this one tonight.'"

"Joe answered, 'I'm not too sure about tonight, but don't worry, Boss, we go to Atlanta. That's my town. We'll take three straight and win it for you on Saturday night [in New York].'"

As if destiny had preordained it, Torre proved to be prophetic.

Down two games to none the Yankees traveled to Atlanta and swept the next three. Cone pitched six innings allowing one run in the Yankees' 5–2 win in Game Three. Jim Leyritz' game-tying (6–6) three-run homer in the eighth inning off Mark Wohlers in Game Four led to an 8–6 win and changed the Yankees' fortunes and history. Leyritz, who was called "The King," hit eight home runs in 61 official postseason at-bats in his career. Pettitte was superb in Game Five pitching 8⅓ shutout innings and O'Neil's spectacular game-ending catch is burned in my memory. The Series resumed in New York for Game Six on October 26.

It was a challenge for the Yanks because they were facing Maddux, who might have been the best pitcher in baseball and had dominated the Yankees in Game Two. In the bottom of the third, the Yanks had O'Neil on third and one out. The Braves had the infield in and Marquis Grissom, the center fielder, was playing shallow and shaded toward right when Joe Girardi hit the ball over his head and ended up on third base with the most celebrated triple in Yankees history that literally shook Yankee Stadium as more than 56,000 fans roared hysterically.

Joe Girardi hit the most famous triple in Yankee history in Game Six of the 1996 World Series. He managed the Yankees from 2008 to 2017.

I was at the game with my son, Rich. It was no doubt the loudest moment I ever experienced at the stadium. It gave the Yankees a 1–0 lead in a game they would win, 3–2. When third baseman Charlie Hayes nestled under a foul fly ball off the bat of Mark Lemke for the final out of the Series, the Stadium was mass hysteria. "They have surmounted every challenge, they have climbed every mountain and the New York Yankees are world champions," boomed an emotionally-charged John Sterling, the Yankees' longtime radio voice. It was a pulse-pounding finish to an amazing World Series.

Yankees third baseman Charlie Hayes made the final putout of the '96 WS when he caught Mark Lemke's foul ball.

And it wasn't long before Wade Boggs was taking a victory lap on the back of a police horse, pointing to the heavens, in celebration of the victory. The moment became perhaps the most iconic image from the Yankees' 1996 world championship season, their first in 18 years. It certainly was upsetting for Red Sox fans to see Boggs, the face of the Sox for more than a decade, in merriment in, of all places, Yankee Stadium. Boggs does not remember how he got on the horse, but it's a touchstone memory among Yankee fans of all generations. What might be forgotten is that Wetteland closed all four games for the Bronx Bombers.

On this October night, "the City That Never Sleeps" celebrated in its inimitable style. The post-game party that flowed into the streets outside the stadium was a sight I will never forget. It extended to a horn-blowing motorcade down Broadway. The fairy tale '96 season had a happy ending. Cone and Frank Torre had successful outcomes, and the Yankees paraded down the Canyon of Heroes after winning their 23rd world championship.

When the Yankees won the '96 Series, it was the climax of a baseball career for Torre that had its ups and downs. No one had ever taken longer to get to the Series—4,272 major-league games as player and manager before his first Series game in '96. As he stated in *Chasing the Dream*, "It had taken getting traded twice and fired three times."

Collectibles

The next season I polled Torre and several players on the following question: What is your most cherished collectible from the '96 season or World Series? Following are some of the responses.

Joe Torre: "The lineup cards."

Joe Girardi: "I have the home plate from Doc Gooden's no-hitter signed by Doc."

Charlie Hayes: "I've got the ball from the final out. The ball is in a safe deposit box. I wrote, 'Last out, 1996 World Series' on the ball. I've been offered money for the ball, but money can't buy love. I also have my gloves, spikes, and my jersey."

Ironically, Wells graduated from the same Point Loma High School in San Diego as Larsen.

Derek Jeter: "I kept my jersey with the World Series patch and two or three signed balls."

Andy Pettitte: "I have a team photo of the pile [after Game Six]. Everybody in the picture signed it."

Bernie Williams: "The uniform I wore in Game Six. I wore it at some of the clinics I did in the off season."

Dwight Gooden: "I have a signed World Series ball by the team, and I also have a ball from the no-hitter I pitched."

Graeme Lloyd: "I have a photo of my father and I in the clubhouse with the World Series trophy after Game Six."

Paul O'Neil: "My uniform with the World Series patch."

Mariano Rivera: "Joe DiMaggio signed a ball for me but I'm not a collector."

Wade Boggs: "My hat. Hats are pretty sentimental to guys."

George Steinbrenner: "The win. It was the most remarkable win I have ever seen. I have never seen a World Series as thrilling as that one. I admit I was getting ready for my concession speech. There will never be a World Series greater than that one."

Bobby Murcer: "After 33 years I sat in the stands for Game Six as a fan. I was one of the biggest fans and I thought the Yankee fans were great. My original seats were located down the right field line. But before Game Six I went in to congratulate George [Steinbrenner]. George saw where I was sitting, and he graciously gave me a better seat behind the Yankee dugout. Because I never went outside with my new tickets, they were never torn. So, I got the guys [the players] to sign my unblemished tickets to Game Six."

The Evil Empire

The Yankees became the team that Yankee detractors loved to hate. In December 2002, Red Sox team president Larry Lucchino unwittingly referred to the Bronx Bombers as the "evil empire." Lucchino was angry at the Yankees for edging out the Red Sox for high-profile free agent pitcher Jose Contreras. New York signed the Cuban defector to a four-year deal worth $32 million just a week after inking Japanese outfielder Hideki Matsui to a contract. Lucchino told the *New York Times*, "The evil empire extends its tentacles even into Latin America."

Despite his Hall of Fame managerial stint with the Yankees, Torre could not escape criticism. Some said he did his best work in the clubhouse, not on the bench. Following the 2004 season when the Yanks blew an unprecedented three games to zero lead against the Red Sox in the ALCS, I had Don Zimmer as a guest on my show. He was not with the Yankees in 2004. The 2003 season was his final year as the Yankees bench coach when he was tied to Torre's hip. We talked about the 2004 collapse after the Bombers had the Sox in the deepest of holes, down three games to none.

"Zim" was surprised that the Yankees didn't run on knuckleball pitcher Tim

Wakefield and didn't bunt on Curt Schilling and his bloody sock. Schilling pitched well in Game One with a torn tendon sheath in his ankle. Before Game Six, Dr. Bill Morgan sutured the tear in a relatively experimental procedure first tried on a cadaver. During the game the blood visible on Schilling's white sock worn under his baseball socks was the result of the stitches pressing against the tendon. The bloody sock had no effect on Schilling's splitter and the Yanks never tested his mobility.

Schilling loaned his bloody sock to the National Baseball Hall of Fame. But it wasn't there long. Schilling started a video game company called 38 Studios which got a $75 million loan from the state of Rhode Island. The company went belly-up, and the state sued Schilling in 2012. 38 Studios would file for bankruptcy and had to pay the state back $61 million.

Perhaps not coincidentally, Schilling auctioned his bloody sock in 2012. Al Tapper, a collector from New York, bought it for $92,613. The garment became part of what Tapper calls a one-of-a-kind collection that includes the original home plate from Yankee Stadium, the boxing gloves Sugar Ray Leonard and Roberto Duran wore during the "No Mas" fight in 1980 and letters written by Babe Ruth to his mistress, Joe DiMaggio to Marylin Monroe and Mickey Mantle to his wife.

The Night of the Midges

If there was one game Torre would like to have back it would be Game Two of the 2007 ALDS when the Indians beat the Yankees 2–1 in 11 innings.

Andy Pettitte had pitched 6⅓ shutout innings before putting runners on first and second. Torre went to the bullpen and brought in Joba Chamberlain. The 21-year-old rookie fireballer had pitched to an 0.38 ERA in 19 regular-season appearances, striking out 34 batters. He had exhibited good control, walking six and throwing one wild pitch over his first 24 big league innings.

Like the Allstate insurance ad, it appeared the ball was in good hands.

Chamberlain escaped the seventh inning by striking out Franklin Gutierrez and retiring Casey Blake on a fly ball to right field. The Yankees held a 1–0 lead. But things went downhill in the bottom of the eighth.

When Chamberlain and the Yankees took the field, the long-legged flies known as midges had arrived from Lake Erie. They were drawn by Northeast Ohio's unseasonable fall warmth (81 degrees at first pitch). In search of mates, a cloud of midges encroached upon the bright lights of what was then called Jacobs Field—and they seemingly centered on the pitcher's mound and Chamberlain. Many were plastered to Chamberlain's neck and arms. The Yankees reliever requested bug spray, as did the Yankees infielders, but it did not seem to have any effect.

Gene Monahan, the Yanks' longtime head athletic trainer, produced a green canister of OFF! bug spray. It not only didn't help, but it also seemed to make matters worse. "I'm trying to throw and then it's getting worse," Chamberlain told Bryan Hoch for MLB.com. "I'm already sweating enough, and I keep hitting the bugs. Geno comes out and [umpire] Laz Diaz was behind the plate; as we all know with foreign substances now, technically what Geno was doing was illegal because it gets sticky. But he's spraying it over everybody, which backfired because they were attracted to the moisture even more."

Diaz, also being attacked, was spraying himself and apparently wasn't concerned about the sticky stuff.

Chamberlain walked leadoff batter Grady Sizemore on four pitches. Sizemore moved to second base on a wild pitch and to third on a sacrifice by Asdrubal Cabrera. Travis Hafner then lined out to first baseman Doug Mientkiewicz. As Victor Martinez stepped in, Chamberlain uncorked his second wild pitch of the inning. The ball was thrown so hard that it bounced right back to Yankees catcher Jorge Posada, about 20 feet from the plate. But Sizemore dashed in from third with the tying run.

In the bottom of the 11th, Torre made another move to his pen, bringing in right-hander Luis Vizcaíno. Kenny Lofton led things off with a walk and went to second base on a single to left field by Franklin Gutierrez. Casey Blake executed a sacrifice bunt, moving the runners up a base. Sizemore was given an intentional free pass. Cabrera popped out to first base for the second out before Hafner laced a single to center field to plate Lofton and give the Indians a 2–1 win and a 2–0 series advantage. They would take the series in four games.

Torre was pilloried for not taking his team off the field because of the insect invasion. Even Roger Clemens said he would have pulled the team off the field. Torre subsequently agreed. It remains one of the greatest regrets of his Hall of Fame managerial career.

The failure of the Yankees to advance beyond the Division Series in 2005, 2006, and 2007 (losing to the Angels, Tigers and Indians) was not acceptable in the eyes of the Yankee brass and their fan base. Whatever air of invincibility had carried the Bronx Bombers along the crest of the title wave had disappeared. After the 2007 season, Torre was offered a one-year contract with a $5 million base pay and $1 million bonuses to be paid for each of three benchmarks the team would reach: winning the American League Division Series; the American League Championship Series; and the World Series. Further, had the Yankees reached the World Series, that would have automatically triggered an option for a new contract the following year. In spite of a pay cut from an average of $6.4 million over the previous three seasons, the new terms would have kept him as the highest-paid manager in the game.

Torre considered the offer an insult and resigned. He managed the Dodgers from 2008 to 2010, winning NL West titles in 2008 and 2009 before losing to the Phils in the NLCS both years. He stepped down after the 2010 season when the Dodgers finished 80–82.

In 2009, two years after he last managed the Yankees, Torre wrote a tell-all book with *Sports Illustrated* writer Tom Verducci titled *The Yankee Years.* On the subject of Steinbrenner, Torre stated, "He would be a tyrant who would second-guess a lot of stuff that you did…. He was resentful of the credit I got…. He wanted to scare you in front of other people. It drove him nuts when it made sense when I talked to him." Torre also threw Cashman under the bus, saying he was not supportive enough. Torre claimed that Cashman never told the front office that he wanted a two-year deal and instead remained silent during Torre's final sit-down with the Yankees brass.

I recall seeing Cashman at a breakfast in Cromwell, Connecticut, shortly after the book was published. "I guess you never know who your friends are," I said to Cashman. Visibly upset, he just shook his head.

ESPN.com's Jerry Crasnick defended Torre and Verducci. "The book is not a first-person tell-all, but rather, a third-person narrative by Verducci, who interviewed dozens of players and team personnel while researching the book."

22

Derek Jeter
The Captain

> "The thing that sets Derek apart from everybody else is that he's not afraid to fail."
> —Charlie Hayes

Winning breeds happiness, and for the most part, the Yankee clubhouse was a pleasant place during the Torre years. And winning was the most important thing to Derek Jeter, who played in more Yankee victories (1,628) than any player in the history of the organization. Because of the way he carried himself with dignity and the respect he had among his teammates, he was named the Yankees' captain on June 3, 2003, a title he held through the 2014 season. No Yankee captain had a longer tenure.

Generally, when a media person goes into the clubhouse there is no pre-planned interview. It's usually a hit-or-miss thing and I was no exception. My objective always was to get a player who was "newsy" and use the tape on my radio show. Jeter was always pleasant to deal with. He was vanilla but accessible to the media. He didn't hide in the players' lounge or the trainer's room.

Many players did promos for my radio show. An example: "This is Derek Jeter, you're listening to *Inside Yankee Baseball* on 600 WICC." That was important to me.

The late writer Roger Angell described Jeter as "imperturbably brilliant." He was baseball's poster boy during his career that lasted from 1995 to 2014. A generational player, there was no greater ambassador to the game. He was an American cultural icon, the son of a black man from Alabama whose biracial identity allowed him to belong to everybody. He went about his craft on and off the field in dignified fashion and was never connected to performance-enhancing drugs. "He's the way you want kids to grow up," said Albert Pujols. "There is nobody perfect on this Earth. Only Jesus was perfect, but Derek was pretty close to being that perfect guy."

"Jete" was all business on the field, but the clubhouse was his playpen. I enjoyed watching the banter between him and Tim Raines when the two lockered near each other between 1996 and 1998.

Jeter played 20 seasons for the Yankees, the most of any player in franchise history. Mariano Rivera is second with 19. It is impressive that during Jeter's 2,747-game career he never fell on the sword of the New York media. As Buck Showalter put it, "He always dealt with the big-league trappings of New York City."

Yankees media relations director Rick Cerrone said, "In the 11 years that I was with the Yankees, I never saw Derek Jeter do the wrong thing or say the wrong thing."

And he was as media polished his rookie year as he was in his later years.

Trust always took center stage in his life, whether it be friends, media, or the front office. He hung out only with his closest friends—those he trusted. In the 2022 ESPN series *The Captain*, he admitted that he probably should have extended himself to other teammates off the field but didn't. Despite being an extremely eligible bachelor his entire career, he managed for the most part to stay away from page six in the New York tabloids, escaping the scrutiny of the gossip columnists. His private life was always sacred and protected. Perhaps he was the contemporary DiMaggio. Even the wedding for the 42-year-old former Yankee star was relatively low-key. Fewer than 100 guests, including friends Posada, Tino Martinez, and Andruw Jones, were in attendance when he married *Sports Illustrated* swimsuit model Hannah Davis, a native of the U.S. Virgin Islands, on July 9, 2016 (the fifth anniversary of his 3,000th hit) in California's Napa Valley. Mariano Rivera, who had already planned a trip to Italy, had to turn down the invitation. The celebrity couple have three daughters, Bella, Story, and River, and a son, Kaius.

Nineteen ninety-seven was the golden age for shortstops. The baseball world was excited about the talents of A-Rod, Jeter, and Nomar Garciaparra. Fans debated who was the best young shortstop of the trio. Jeter and A-Rod, who was then with the Mariners, had been friends for several years and there was no animosity between the two. In future years, their relationship would sour. On August 6, 1999, the Yankees and Mariners engaged in a bench-clearing brawl at Safeco Field in Seattle. As a result of the melee, outfielder Chad Curtis had abrasions on his face; Chuck Knoblauch had a bruised thumb that had to be heavily wrapped; and Girardi had a bruise on his right leg.

It was reported that Jeter and Rodriguez stood off to the side and talked during the brawl, which drew criticism from teammates, notably Curtis. In ESPN's 2022 documentary *The Captain*, Jeter refutes Curtis' account, claiming he wasn't next to A-Rod during the brawl and the two were near each other coming off the field after the fight had ended. Jeter went on to say, "Curtis had issues with everybody."

Following the game, the clubhouse was closed to the media for a significant length of time as it always was. Curtis had his chance to approach Jeter during this time but, according to Jeter, waited until the media arrived to create a big scene. "Chad walked up to me and said, 'I don't like what you did,'" recalled Jeter. "Curtis said, 'I hear you want to hit me, so hit me.' I said, 'Let me get out of here.'"

Curtis, who later apologized, had a tumultuous post-playing career. Known as a religious, Bible-thumping player, he was charged in October 2013 with third-degree criminal sexual conduct. Curtis was a volunteer weight-room instructor and substitute teacher at the time the assaults occurred. Curtis and the Lakewood public schools and its board of education in the Grand Rapids, Michigan, area were the target of the lawsuits by three female students.

He was reportedly giving therapeutic massages to the students when he allegedly molested them. He was sentenced from seven to 15 years in prison and released in 2020 after serving seven. Barry County Circuit Judge Amy McDowell called him a "predator," according to ESPN. Curtis had told McDowell that the three victims lied. He never admitted guilt.

The Greatest Yankee Shortstop

Jeter had the label "star" written all over him early in his career. Rizzuto was asked who the greatest shortstop in Yankee history was.

"The kid is amazing," said Scooter, who was effusive in his praise for the Yankees' young shortstop. "He plays like a guy who's been around for 10 years. I'm trying to think who the best Yankee shortstop I've ever seen is and I keep coming back to this kid." Yet there was talk early in Jeter's career that the Yanks were going to trade him to the Mariners for Felix Fermin.

The Yankee captain was not a get-in-your-face type of leader. He led by example on the field and spoke to teammates privately. The 14-time All-Star garnered five Gold Gloves and five Silver Slugger awards. In the 2000 subway series, the Yankees faced the Mets for the soul of New York City. Before the Series, the Mets' Benny Agbayani predicted the Mets would win in five. Jeter would have none of that. The Yanks were up two games to one when he opened Game Four with a home run. He then tripled and scored in his second at-bat to make it 3–0. The Yankees won the game, 3–2. In the fifth and final game, Jeter tied the contest with his second homer of the Series as the Yankees went on to win 4–2 and clinch the championship. Jeter was voted the MVP of the Series, becoming the first player to be named the All-Star Game and World Series MVP in the same season.

Jeter was impervious to pressure. "Captain Clutch" loved the pomp of the postseason. A lifetime .310 hitter, he hit .308/.374/.465 in 158 playoff games, posting a higher OPS than he did in the regular season. He holds the all-time postseason records for games played (158), runs scored (111), hits (200), total bases (302), singles (143), and doubles (32).

Jete loved the center stage. He appeared on ESPN's *Sunday Night Baseball* 71 times, the most of any player. "I didn't like the time, but I liked the stage," said Jeter, who enjoyed playing in front of large crowds. Jeter, who loved performing in front of audiences, was good theater on and off the field. On December 1, 2001, he hosted *Saturday Night Live*. In the sketch "Yankee Wives," Jeter dressed in drag as Alfonso Soriano's wife. As a prank on Jeter, the *SNL* staff had David Wells and David Cone surprise Jeter when they also showed up in drag in the hilarious scene.

Jeter, born into a multi-racial family, grew up in Michigan but spent his summers in New Jersey with his maternal grandparents. The Jeters overcame the sting of racism. On June 22, 1985, four days shy of his 11th birthday, his family took him to Tiger Stadium when the Yankees, his favorite team, were in town. As a youngster he always said that he would one day be the shortstop for the New York Yankees. His favorite player was Dave Winfield, who went 2-for-4 that day in the Yankees' 4–0 win. Following the game, he was able to get Winfield's autograph.

"That evening he told his parents [Charles and Dorothy], 'One day, you're gonna go to Tiger Stadium and see me play,'" wrote Alan Cohen for SABR. "Two decades later, Jeter recalled, 'I went to sleep that night knowing what I wanted to do with my life. I had great dreams about it. And I'm not sure if I've woken up since.'"

On June 7, 1996, Derek Jeter, in his 68th big-league game, made his first appearance at Tiger Stadium. His parents were there, as they would be for many great moments over his career, culminating in his election to the Baseball Hall of Fame in 2020. For the record, Jeter went 0-for 3 that game but did score a run in the Tigers' 6–5 win.

Jeter, the Yankees' first-round pick out of Central High School in Kalamazoo, Michigan, was the sixth player chosen in the June 1992 MLB amateur draft. The Astros drafted Phil Nevin number 1. Hall of Fame pitcher Hal Newhouser, then a scout with the Astros, wanted Jeter. When they didn't listen to his advice, Newhouser resigned.

Jeter's first two years in the low minors were anything but sensational. He made a total of 98 errors, but his hitting did improve in '93 at Class A Greensboro. He felt overmatched and his confidence was shattered. "I did not want the ball hit to me," he said. Like Mantle many years before him, he was ready to come home.

He debuted on May 29, 1995, in the Yankees' 8–7 loss to the Mariners in the Kingdome after shortstop Tony Fernandez was placed on the disabled list with a strained rib cage muscle. He went 0-for-5. In his first at-bat, he flied to Darren Bragg in short right field. Following the game he and his father Charles went out to dinner at a McDonald's. It was the only place they could find open. The following night he collected his first major league hit, a single to left field off the Mariners' Tim Belcher in the Yanks' 7–3 loss. He made 13 starts and batted .234 before he was optioned back to Columbus. He was recalled in September and appeared in two more games (batted in one), raising his batting average to .250.

Jete was given the shortstop job in '96. He knew that the position was his going into spring training and it was cemented after Fernandez broke his elbow before the start of the season. After homering on Opening Day in Cleveland against Dennis Martinez, like the Energizer Bunny, Jeter kept going, and going, and going. It wasn't long before he stopped being a rookie. He finished the season batting .314 and was voted the American League Rookie of the Year joining Gil McDougald (1951), Bob Grim (1954), Tony Kubek (1957), Tom Tresh (1962), Stan Bahnsen (1968), Thurman Munson (1970), and Dave Righetti (1981) as Yankees who won the Rookie of the Year Award. In 2017, Aaron Judge joined the Yankee ROY winners.

If Jeter made a rookie mistake, it perhaps occurred on October 18, 1996, the day before the scheduled start of the World Series when he left his Mercury Mountaineer parked on the street outside of his apartment on Manhattan's Upper East Side and it was stolen. He was planning to drive to the stadium where the team held their final workout. Jeter was able to bum a ride with catcher Jim Leyritz and made it to practice on time.

Jeter's star was shining his first three years. He was arbitration eligible following the '98 season in which he made $750,000. He asked for $5 million while the team offered $3.2 million. In February of 1999 the arbitrator ruled in Jeter's favor. The Yankees' young shortstop now realized that baseball was a business and his relationship with the front office cooled. In ESPN's 2022 *The Captain*, he said, "One thing with me I'm

This September 23, 1995, photograph is one of the earliest images of Derek Jeter in a Yankees uniform.

very, very, loyal. But loyalty one way is stupidity. I expect the same thing in return. If I feel you're taking advantage or trying to take advantage of me, I'm done."

Jeter again had a contentious experience with the Yankees' front office in 2010 when he was ready for his next contract. He wanted to remain a Yankee and insisted that his negotiations remain private. But it was leaked to the press that he rejected the Yankees' offer of a three-year, $45 million contract. Jeter was coming off an un–Jeter-like season in 2010 when he batted .270 with 10 home runs and 67 RBI. He also struck out 106 times. During negotiations with Cashman, he reportedly asked the Yankees GM what shortstops in baseball were better than him. Cashman answered, "Hanley Ramirez and Troy Tulowitzki." This put a dagger in Jeter's heart.

Cashman challenged Jeter to test the market, another factor that angered the Yankee shortstop. Finally, on December 7, 2010, Jeter signed a three-year, $51 million contract but his relationship with Cashman cooled. The two have subsequently mended their differences. "It has been an incredible honor having a front row seat for one of the great players of all time," said Cashman. "Derek has been a winner every step of the way."

In his 20 seasons, he swung a black Louisville Slugger 72 to the tune of 3,465 hits, 260 home runs, 1,311 RBIs, five world championships, and 14 All-Star games. He ranks sixth on the all-time hit list. On July 9, 2011, Jeter collected his 3,000th hit, a home run off Rays pitcher David Price. Of the 19 players who have recorded their 3,000th career hit since 1961, the expansion era, the only player to reach the milestone in fewer games than Jeter (2,362) was Tony Gwynn, who did it in 2,284 games.

But statistics do not define the total player he was. He was fearless when chasing fly balls whether it was going into the outfield with his back to the infield or diving into the seats with reckless abandon. His plunge into the seats near the third base dugout against the Red Sox on July 1, 2004, is legendary.

Jeter spearheaded many rallies. Unfortunately, there is no stat that shows how many rallies a player starts or what he does to keep a rally going. He was always part of something big. In the decisive Game Six of the '96 WS, Jeter was in the middle of a three-run third-inning uprising that put the Yankees ahead of the Atlanta Braves. His single to left field scored Girardi with the Yankees' second run. Jeter stole second base and scored on a single by Williams. The Yankees won, 3–2.

He had a deep respect for the storied Yankee history. He talked about the ghosts at Yankee Stadium in reference to former Yankee greats when something magical would happen for him and his teammates. He had numerous clutch occasions, too many to mention.

The Yankee shortstop authored several unforgettable moments in the 2001 postseason including his iconic backhand flip toss to nail the A's Jeremy Gimabi at the plate in the seventh inning of Game Three of the ALDS in Oakland. Terrence Long hit a Mike Mussina pitch down the right-field line, where it was fielded by Shane Spencer, who threw wildly over two cutoff men. Like magic, Jeter appeared near the first-base foul line. He snared the ball and shoveled it to Posada. Giambi did not slide and was tagged out to preserve a 1–0 Yankees lead that proved to be the final score. It allowed the Yanks to rebound from a two games to none deficit and win the Series in five before defeating the Seattle Mariners in the ALCS.

He continued his heroics in the World Series against the D'backs.

I was in the press box the night of October 31, 2001, when the Yanks hosted the D'backs in Game Four of the Series. Trailing 3–1, the Yankees were down to their last out when Tino Martinez hit a two-run homer off Byung-Hyun Kim. Martinez came to the Yankees from Seattle along with Jeff Nelson and Jim Macir for Sterling Hitchcock and Russ Davis. Following a slow start (11-for-56) after replacing Mattingly, Martinez became a fan favorite in New York. The rest of the '96 season he hit .302. In his seven seasons in pinstripes, he hit .276 with 192 homers and 739 RBI. His high-water mark came in '97 when he hit .296 with 141 RBI and was the AL MVP runner-up.

In the bottom of the tenth, Jeter walloped a two-out homer off Kim to tie the Series at 2–2. It was past midnight and officially November 1. He was bestowed the moniker "Mr. November."

What's in a number? In his final series in each of the Yankees' 2014 road cities, host teams gave Jeter farewell gifts in recognition of his contributions to the game of baseball throughout his career. In honor of Jeter's number 2, the Mets made a $22,222.22 donation to his Turn 2 Foundation, a non-profit established by Jeter in 1996 to help young people reach their full potential by fostering leadership development, academic achievement, healthy lifestyles and social change.

He had a flair for the dramatic, garnering a walk-off hit in the final game he ever played at Yankee Stadium on September 25, 2014, incredibly the only game he ever played in New York when the Yankees were already eliminated. Thanks to a three-run rally in the top of the ninth that tied the score (5–5), the Bombers were able to bat in the bottom of the frame. With Antoan Richardson on second base and one out, in Jeteresque fashion, he singled to right field off O's right-hander Evan Meek, scoring Richardson to give the Yanks a 6–5 victory. Ironically, standing in the O's dugout was Showalter, Jeter's first skipper when he came up in '95. Yankees TV announcer Michael Kay eloquently captured the drama and moment on the YES network as Jeter walked up to the plate for the last time.

"The script is there, the last page is in Derek's hands," said Kay. "Meek deals, base hit to right field. Here comes Richardson. Here's the throw from [Nick] Markakis. Richardson is safe. Derek Jeter ends his final game with a walk-off single. Derek Jeter—where fantasy becomes reality—did you have any doubt."

Jeter was mobbed by his teammates while the crowd of 48,613 roared hysterically. And to his surprise there was a welcoming crew that included Bernie and Gerald Williams, Joe Torre, Jorge Posada, Andy Pettitte, Mariano Rivera, and Tino Martinez. They all embraced the Yankee captain with hugs and congrats.

Then, in one of the most unforgettable Yankee Stadium moments, Jeter went out to his vacant shortstop position, doffing his cap to the crowd while the Orioles' players stood and acknowledged his magnificent career. Jeter then, in a crouched position, bowed his head to apparently say a prayer of thanks and reflect on his spectacular days in pinstripes.

On January 21, 2020, Jeter was elected to the Hall of Fame in his first year of eligibility by the 397 baseball writers who are the Hall's gatekeepers. He was a sure-thing first-ballot Hall of Famer by any rational measure and should have been a unanimous pick as Rivera was the year before, but one writer failed to vote for him. It is not known which writer opted not to cast a ballot for Jeter, whose percentage edged Ken Griffey, Jr. (99.3 percent) for the highest by a position player. Jeter said that he "couldn't care less" about the snub. Because of the pandemic, the annual induction ceremonies were canceled, but he was honored the following summer in Cooperstown. At the event Jeter asked Cashman to take a walk and the two reconciled their differences stemming from the contract negotiations that were leaked to the media.

Jeter's competitive juices continued to flow after his retirement from the game. In 2017 a group of 16 headed by Florida businessman Bruce Sherman and Jeter completed its purchase of the Miami Marlins from Jeffrey Loria for $1.2 billion. Sherman, the club's chairman and majority owner, became the fourth owner in franchise history, and Jeter, who reportedly invested $25 million, was named the team's chief executive officer, the first black CEO in major league history. Loria made a handsome profit, having bought the team for a reported $185.5 million in 2002. Jeter also helped make history when he named Kim Ng as the Marlins' general manager in November 2020. Ng, a former executive with the Yankees and MLB, became the first woman to be named GM of a big-league team. Ironically, Ng was on the other side of the table when Jeter negotiated his final contract with the Yankees.

Jeter immediately took a sledgehammer to the franchise for fiscal reasons. Stars like Marcell Ozuna, Giancarlo Stanton, and Christian Yelich were all dispatched. In 2020 the Marlins made the playoffs in the 60-game pandemic-truncated season, finishing second in the NL East. They swept the Cubs in the Wild Card Series before being swept by the Braves in the NLDS. But after the fourth year and during the 2022 lockout between the owners and players, Jeter unleashed a bombshell that he was stepping down and also divesting his roughly 4 percent ownership of the club.

"Jeter went into the lockout believing team chairman Bruce Sherman had approved the spending of another $10 million to $15 million on player(s) whenever transactions begin again," wrote the *NY Post*'s Joel Sherman. "And that plan was reversed, in Jeter's understanding. Jeter did not only see that as reneging on a promise, but as a statement against the buildup to try to win—and Jeter was biding the bad times to satisfy his passion to ultimately win."

That's all the Captain ever wanted to do. In 2023 he joined the *MLB on FOX* team.

23

Suzyn Waldman

A Pioneer in Her Field

I have had media credentials at Yankee Stadium for the past 40 years and have encountered many personalities at the big ballyard in the Bronx. If there was ever a profile in courage that I have come across, it is Suzyn Waldman, the longtime WFAN (660) radio color commentator, who has sat alongside veteran announcer John Sterling for the past 19 years covering Yankees baseball. Considered by many a trailblazer and a breakthrough performer, she spent her pre-baseball broadcasting life in the musical theater before invading a world dominated by macho types who held little respect for women in a male-dominated industry. Her 36 years of success is based on her ability to connect with the players and staff on an emotional level. "It's not just stats," she said. "I want to know what a player is feeling."

Broadcaster Suzyn Waldman, a trailblazer in a male-dominated industry, has stood the test of time (courtesy Suzyn Waldman).

Going from the theater to the baseball field was a transition from one stage to another. Because actors are performers and subject to error, it has allowed her to be sensitive to the problems players face. "I see things from a performer's point of view," she said. "When I am interviewing a player, I am going after why he does what he does."

Waldman's acting background prepared her to handle criticism, especially working in a big city. "When you're an actor you have to keep yourself vulnerable," she explained. "I can't let criticism affect what I do."

The fact that she cut her teeth in New York City, the biggest market in the country, and had to overcome issues of credibility primarily because she wore a skirt makes her accomplishments even more enormous. Add to the mix that she conquered breast cancer while she continued working, and we're looking at a remarkable human being. Her life story has been recognized by national TV networks. She has been featured on the *Today Show*, the *CBS Evening News with Dan Rather*, ABC's *20/20*, NBC's *Dateline*, and *The Rosie O'Donnell Show*. On July 25, 2022, Waldman was elected to the Museum of Broadcast Communications Radio Hall of Fame. It was most fitting indeed.

It would be a stretch to say Waldman is to females in the broadcast world what Jackie Robinson was to the advancement of black players in baseball. But it is fair to comment that they both changed the paradigm of their chosen fields and both survived a lonely world riddled by insolent hostility from myopic cynics. Both received death threats and discrimination in different forms. Robinson had to combat racism while Waldman has faced sexism. And both always got back in the batter's box instead of allowing adversity to knock them down and destroy their dreams.

Waldman's unflinching desire to succeed has been her ally. Playing it safe is not her style. She keeps to a motto displayed in her memorabilia room: "Well-behaved women rarely make history." But despite her accomplishments, the multi-talented groundbreaker said, "I'm tolerated but not accepted." She continued, "I was always aware if I messed up someone else wasn't going to get the chance. Women were set up to fail and I wasn't going to fail."

Waldman will be a target of criticism for two reasons: (1) She is a woman acting as an authority in a man's world and (2) she never played the game. To that she scoffs, "There are hundreds of thousands of male obstetricians in this country, what do they know about having a baby? It's ludicrous. This isn't a kidney transplant, it's a game. Mel Allen didn't play major league baseball, nor did Vin Scully or Bob Murphy."

The Clubhouse

Waldman will be the first to tell you that her best work has been clubhouse reporting. She is a superb conduit of information who has stood the test of time. Her longevity covering four decades speaks for itself.

Would she rather do play-by-play?

"I'm not as good on the air as I could have been—I've never been really given a chance," she admitted. But her ability to glean critical information from the private world of the clubhouse creates a unique balancing act with Sterling.

Waldman's assignment to cover the Yankees has been a perfect marriage. For one year she was ignored in the press box because the writers thought she was taking the job of a male reporter. But unlike the narrow-minded knights of the keyboard in press row, she was accepted in the male sanctuary of the clubhouse almost since day one. "The Yankees were great," revealed Waldman. "But in other places it was different. I think the Yankees took a cue from Willie Randolph who was the captain. I was also close with Dave Winfield, Rickey Henderson and Don Mattingly."

Waldman was aware that the print media scribes were ready to pounce on her if she made a mistake. On one occasion Winfield came to the rescue. "Winfield had been in a slump," recalled Waldman. "When I was interviewing him, I had made a mistake on the stats. To protect me, he shut off my tape recorder and said, 'I didn't like the way I answered that question.'"

Although Suzyn had gained acceptance with the Yankee players, that was not the case with Blue Jays outfielder George Bell. At the start of the 1987 season, Bell was snarky, not talking to the New York media, thinking they had cost him the MVP award the year before that went to Mattingly.

One day Bell erupted after a win at Yankee Stadium and the regular beat writers hurriedly gathered around his locker. New on the beat (women had just recently been allowed access to the locker room), Waldman joined the group. "Bell immediately started screaming and yelling at me in Spanish and English," remembered Waldman. "Bell went on, 'I'm not talking to anyone until she leaves.'"

Humiliated but not defeated, she gathered her tape recorder and notebook. She was headed toward the door when she heard Bell's teammate Jesse Barfield ask a fellow writer, "What's her name?" When told, he then called out to her, in a very kind gesture, "Suzyn, I went 3-for-5 today. Don't you want to talk to me?"

The two became friends immediately and their relationship has endured.

At the time, the only other woman covering a team on a full-time basis was Susan Fornoff, a beat reporter for the Oakland A's who worked for the *Sacramento Bee*. "In those days the only time I felt comfortable was when the Yankees played the A's because both teams had a woman reporter covering the team," Waldman said.

During the 1986 season when Fornoff was covering a game between the A's and the Kansas City Royals, she received a pink box with a live rat inside. The rat wore a tag that read, "My name is Sue." The sender of the package was A's veteran Dave Kingman. It was his mindless way of protesting women in the clubhouse. He was fined $3,500 and warned about his future conduct. The 37-year-old Kingman refused to apologize, saying, "I've pulled practical jokes on other people, and I didn't apologize to them," according to Bill Baer of NBC Sports.

Waldman never received a rat in the mail, but she did receive used condoms and feces from irrational sickos.

Background

Raised in Boston, Suzyn grew up a Red Sox fan when names like Frank Malzone, Jackie Jensen and Sammy White were satellites around the iconic Ted Williams. "I used to go to Fenway Park with my grandfather, who had season tickets," recalled Waldman. "Our seats were in the first row directly in back of the Red Sox on-deck circle."

Cute as a button, Suzyn would often stick her head in the Red Sox dugout before games and engage the likes of Johnny Pesky and Williams. She grew very fond of both Boston legends.

When she saw "the Splendid Splinter" kneeling in the on-deck circle, she thought, "If God is a person that's what he looks like." Her affection for and devotion to Williams never waned. He became the real John Wayne in her life. The two reconnected when she sang at a Jimmy Fund function in Boston for the benefit of Sox outfielder Tony Conigliaro who had been hit by a Jack Hamilton pitch on his left cheekbone, sustaining a dislocated jaw and severe damage to his left retina. "My payment was to meet Ted Williams," she acknowledged. "He was the kind of person I thought he'd be. He lived his life the way he wanted."

Since she was four years old, Waldman was trained to be in the theater. She studied at the prestigious New England Conservatory of Music and received a bachelor of science degree in economics and math from Simmons College, now Simmons University, located in the heart of Boston. She started at the conservatory while in high school and continued while matriculating at Simmons. In 2021, Waldman was awarded an honorary doctorate in journalism from Simmons.

Following graduation, she spent 15 years appearing both on Broadway and in touring musical productions. The pinnacle of her show business career was when she starred as Aldonza opposite Richard Kiley in the 1977–1979 revival of *Man of La Mancha*.

"The two years working with Richard were probably the most important years of my life," stated the multi-talented sportscaster. "He was my mentor. I even named one of my dogs after him." Waldman, who also appeared in *Nine* and *No, No Nanette*, was a mainstay on the New York nightclub circuit in the late '70s.

Despite her success on stage and in nightclubs, Waldman never lost her love for sports, especially baseball. The game has been tattooed to her heart since childhood. While still in show business she sang the national anthem numerous times at various big-league venues and arenas before games. As recently as 2020 and 2021 she sang the national anthem on Opening Day at Yankee Stadium.

While performing in Pittsburgh with Kiley in '79, she sang the national anthem during the NLCS between the Reds and Pirates at Three Rivers Stadium. "Richard saw me sing the anthem on television," commented Waldman. "When I returned to the theater, he walked into my dressing room and said, 'This baseball thing—that's where your passion is. Figure it out.'"

She figured it out and took the road to broadcasting.

Everything came together in 1987 for the native of Newton, Massachusetts. Former Red Sox announcer Ken Coleman informed her about the forthcoming debut of WFAN, an all-sports radio station based in New York City. Coleman placed a call to John Channin, the top suit at WFAN, and said he had to meet Suzyn Waldman. That was a giant leap for someone who had never done sports radio, to take her first bite in the Big Apple.

WFAN (660) debuted at 3:00 p.m. on July 1, 1987, billing itself as the world's first 24-hour-per-day sports talk station. The first live voice heard on WFAN was that of Suzyn Waldman, with a sports update, followed by the first show, which was hosted by Jim Lampley. Waldman reported for the station, covering the Yankees and New York Knicks for 14 years, and also served as a talk show host. But the transition into a new career working in the media circus of NYC was fraught with challenges. Her gender was an issue. She was the target of slings and arrows by listeners who questioned her credibility and certain colleagues who saw her as a threat and a job thief.

"I don't think you ever overcome it if you are a female," lamented the veteran radio personality. "Even to this day I think that people are waiting for me to make a mistake. Because of that I am overprepared. I'm terrified of making a mistake. It doesn't happen to men."

Over the years Waldman received many awards for her high-level work, one of which was the International Radio Festival Award for her reporting from the upper deck of Candlestick Park during the Loma Prieta earthquake that rocked the '89 World Series played between the A's and Giants. The 6.9 magnitude event resulted in the death of 63 people while almost 4,000 were injured.

Waldman was covering the Series for WFAN working Game Three. Reliving the day, she said,

> The press boxes were rocking, the football one was swaying, and the stands were shaking. My phone was the only one that didn't go out. I talked over an hour to Gary Cohen, the current Mets announcer, who was back in the station.
>
> I stayed in San Francisco, did Cityside reporting, etc. I hitchhiked out to the where the upper deck of the Nimitz Freeway collapsed and fell on top of the lower deck. I got a ride immediately. Perhaps my World Series credentials which identified me as a member of the press helped.
>
> I think my work during the earthquake led to the writers taking me seriously.
>
> It was quite a time!

Waldman is acutely aware that she is an important channel of Yankee information for her listeners and takes that responsibility seriously. In her early years at WFAN, she was unable to get an interview with Steinbrenner. For obvious reasons it was important to interview one of the most newsy and controversial personalities in the game. But she had not yet proven herself to the irascible owner.

She reasoned that because of her gender, she was never invited to the annual beat writers' luncheon in the late '80s hosted by the Boss at the 21 Club on West 52nd Street. Undaunted, she trailed Steinbrenner and was on him like white on rice. If she was looking for information, a team of wild horses wasn't going to stop her.

Following games, the Yankees' owner would visit the Yankees clubhouse on occasion. When he exited, he would take the elevator upstairs. "If George was in the stadium elevator, nobody else was allowed," revealed Waldman. "I used to run up the ramp and meet the elevator, waiting for George before the door opened."

Waldman assertively promoted herself. She went to the head of sales at WFAN and found out how much they were selling her 5:05 p.m. time slot for. Armed with that information she flew to Tampa and demanded that the Boss would grant an interview. He obliged, but when they met, he told her he didn't like women cops, women fire fighters, and women in sports. "He wanted to see how I would react," she said. "I never perceived that he was being a male chauvinist. He was testing me. He was tough on me for 10 years. He wanted to see if I could take it."

Many would have unfolded like a cheap suit, but not Waldman, who drew on the fundamentals she learned as a stage performer.

With time, the two grew very close. Very few were able to crack Steinbrenner's steel veneer like Waldman. "My relationship with George was everything," she said. "There was a mutual trust." As covered earlier in this book, it was Waldman who brokered the reunion with Steinbrenner and Yogi Berra in January of 1999.

"I brokered the thing with Yogi's son, Dale," explained Waldman. "George kept saying that Yogi would come to the stadium. I said, 'No, George. You're getting on a plane and coming up here to Yogi's museum in Montclair, New Jersey.'" Waldman had pulled off an historic coup on live radio that resonates with time.

When Waldman talked, George listened.

It was bittersweet when she departed WFAN on a full-time basis in 2001 to join the then-new YES Network as a clubhouse reporter and occasional color commentator for Yankees baseball. Waldman, who was the first woman to hold a full-time position as a major league broadcaster, first did play-by-play for nationally televised games on the Baseball Network in 1994–1995 that was established by John Filippelli, the current president of production and programming at YES. She did a few innings each game and in '96 did select Yankee telecasts on WPIX and MSG and in '99 on Fox's WNYW, expanding on her pioneering role to become the first woman to consistently do play-by-play in addition to color for big league baseball. During this period, she continued at WFAN doing talk radio. She also covered WNBA games on the Lifetime Cable Network.

While she was doing TV, Steinbrenner had a unique way of gathering public opinion of her work. "He would go to a restaurant like Runyon's on Second Avenue and kind of disguise himself," laughed Waldman. "He would wear a trench coat, put on sunglasses and go to the bar and say, 'What do you think of that woman?' The reaction was always the same. 'I don't like women in sports, but she is actually okay.'"

Steinbrenner subsequently pushed for Waldman to be in the broadcast booth with Sterling after Charley Steiner left before the start of the 2005 season.

Token Assignments

There have been other women before Waldman who sat behind the mic in the broadcast booth of a major league baseball game, but for the most part it was a gimmick perpetuated by team management. Charlie Finley, the former maverick owner of the Kansas City A's, employed Betty Caywood in the KCMO (710) radio booth for a smattering of games at the end of the 1964 season, joining her with Monte Moore and George Bryson. "The idea is that by putting a woman on the staff we'll appeal to the dolls," Finley said.

"The local chapter of the Baseball Writers Association of America (BBWAA) barred Caywood from the press hospitality room at Fenway Park, so a waiter served her dinner on a tray in the broadcast booth," wrote Warren Corbett for the Society of American Baseball Research. "She made her debut at Yankee Stadium on September 18. Before the game, photographers jammed into the booth to take her picture. Unlike her experience in Boston, however, she was allowed to eat in the press dining area."

In 1977 Charlie Warner, the general manager of Chicago's WMAQ (670), invited Mary Shane to join the White Sox broadcast booth. The idea had White Sox owner and promotion czar Bill Veeck's fingerprints all over it. Her partners included Harry Caray, Lorn Brown, and Jimmy Piersall. "Mary got screwed," stated Waldman. "She was a baseball writer with no broadcasting experience. She was put in the same booth with Caray, a legend, and was only given 20 games to prove herself." Shane and her family moved to Worcester, Massachusetts, where she became a sportswriter for the *Worcester Telegram* in 1981 and along with several women did a yeoman's job covering the Celtics.

And there was Gayle Gardner, the noted ESPN announcer. On August 3, 1993, Gardner became the first woman to do televised play-by-play of a major league baseball game when she called the Colorado Rockies-Cincinnati Reds contest. But like Caywood and Shane, it was a limited gig, not a job.

Just like Jackie Robinson would not be satisfied with the progress the black player has made in baseball, Waldman is not satisfied with the advancement of women in major league baseball broadcasting. "When you consider from the time I broke in at WFAN and did TV work in the mid-'90s, women have not made great on-the-air progress. We've missed two generations," snapped Waldman. "What happened?"

1996

The '96 season represented much more than baseball for Suzyn Waldman and the Yankee family. It was an amalgam of triumphs and tragedies. The Yankees won their first world championship in 18 years but there were several sidebars in one of the most interesting chapters in the club's history.

By '96 Waldman was on a roll when the diagnosis of stage 2 breast cancer hit her like a Mack truck. She faced the debilitating horrors of chemotherapy and the long-range prospects of the insidious disease. But Suzyn had beaten the odds in her professional life and now it was time to attack this medical monster in her personal life. And not for a New York minute did she think about quitting on life or a career she had energetically cultivated. She stared her problem in the eye and didn't blink.

"I didn't have a choice," she declared. "I had to work. I had a house, a mortgage and two dogs. If I stopped, someone else would have had my job. I wasn't going to blow that. I had worked too hard. I fired my oncologist because he wouldn't let me go to spring training."

The treatments that lasted six months left her weak and exhausted, but she worked every day, carrying her microphone and tape recorder with her wherever she went without missing a beat. There wasn't a second when she didn't think she was going to vomit or pass out. "One time while interviewing Willie Randolph I had a wave of nausea," remembered Waldman. "In the middle of the interview, I had to sit down in the dugout. Willie understood and kindly sat next to me while I gathered myself."

A Supportive Boss

The Yankees from the top down were supportive of the woman who had become an integral part of their family. The pillar of the support system was Steinbrenner. "George was always concerned when someone is sick like that," said Waldman. "When the Yankees went on the road, trainers Gene Monahan and Steve Donahue made sure that vials of Neupogen were refrigerated in all the American League clubhouses and in my hotel room." The drug has been used successfully for cancer patients to help stimulate the bone marrow to make white blood cells which helps fight off infection.

Timing and happenstance are critical in life. For Waldman, who was in the middle of her ascent in the broadcast booth, the timing of her illness could not have been worse. "When I got sick, I didn't have a contract for TV. I said to Mr. Steinbrenner, 'I'm not going to lose this job because of cancer, am I? I promise you I won't appear bald in the booth and I won't throw-up on TV.'"

Waldman fought and won her personal battle. And the team she covered won their first World Series in 18 years. Moments after Yankees third baseman Charlie Hayes snared the final put-out in foul territory off the bat of Mark Lemke, cameras showed Waldman hugging Steinbrenner near his suite. When asked about the championship hug, she said, "I think it was for everything. It goes from way back. I was excited for him and some people on that team."

Suzyn Waldman's victory over cancer has served as an inspiration for many including Darryl Strawberry. "When I was diagnosed with cancer, Darryl's mom had just died of breast cancer," she said. "He would try to lift my spirits by giving me a pat on the cheek. Over time Darryl and I became very close."

Two years later it was Waldman's turn to provide strength and hope for Strawberry when the Yankees' slugger faced a battle with colon cancer. "I knew he had cancer before he did from what he was telling me," she said. "We were in Texas in the playoffs. I was with Harold Reynolds from ESPN. Harold called Darryl on his cell phone. When he gasped, 'Oh my God,' I said, 'Give me the phone.' I said to Darryl, 'You're not going to die.'"

She was right.

"When you're told that you have cancer, the only people you want to talk to are those who've had it," stated Waldman. "People in general want to be supportive of cancer patients but their main thing is fear."

On February 18, 1999, the Toronto Blue Jays traded Roger Clemens to the Yankees for pitchers David Wells and Graeme Lloyd and utilityman Homer Bush. Waldman gained much respect from her peers when she broke the blockbuster trade by calling in to the nationally syndicated *Imus in the Morning* show on WFAN. At the time, she was the only radio reporter to travel with the Yankees and her reports had a timeliness that print journalists can only envy. Social media has modified that a bit but her ability to gather Yankee news is unparalleled.

Electronic journalists in New York baseball venues are always under the microscope. From this corner, she was the target of unfair criticism in the following two situations.

Clemens was a Yankee from 1999 to 2003. After a three-year hiatus with the Astros, on May 6, 2007, Clemens announced during the seventh inning stretch that he would be returning to the Yankees for the second half of the 2007 season. Waldman, overcome with emotion, literally screamed with delight. Some viewed this as unprofessional for a major league baseball announcer.

"No one knew he was in the stadium," said Waldman in her own defense. "I didn't either. It was the seventh inning stretch and John was not back in the booth yet. Our engineer said, 'Go.' I started to talk, and the stadium started to shake, and people were screaming. I looked up at the board and there was Roger. I thought it was very dramatic and said, 'Oh my goodness gracious, of all the dramatic things I've ever seen.' And, yes, people made fun of me for that for a year in both New York and Boston—not the fans, just other media."

There's a side note to the story. Waldman added, "When Boston was in shortly after that, I was in the Red Sox clubhouse and Curt Schilling yelled to me, 'Suzyn, outside by third base, five minutes.' I went out there and he came out and said, 'I heard that over and over ... it was not during the action. You did nothing wrong. Don't you ever let people you don't know and who don't care about you dictate how you feel about yourself ... ever!"

"Yup ... Curt Schilling, of all people," she concluded.

Waldman thumbed her nose at the old adage "There's no crying in baseball." During Torre's tenure as Yankees manager, she developed a deep bond with him and broke down on the air following the 2007 ALDS when the Yanks were eliminated three games to one by the Indians. Despite his success it was generally known that Torre would not be returning. It was an end of an era. Tears flowed down her cheeks along with the coaches in the room.

"The breaking up after Game Seven was not because they lost," explained Waldman. "After the game, I made my way right by Joe's office. All the coaches were in there. They were all extremely emotional—Joe, Larry Bowa, all of them. I was describing the scene in there and how they were feeling and got choked up. I thought the fans would like to know that the coaching staff was as devastated as they were, and we all knew that this would be the end of that era. I've always thought I was a conduit between the team and the fans and that's what I was that night. That's who I am, and you can't please everyone."

There's no doubt that Waldman's heart is with the Yankees. But her reporting is not biased. She is not timid about offering criticism of a Yankee player or the organization. Following the 2021 wild card game in which the Red Sox beat the Yankees, she was interviewed by WFAN reporter Sweeny Murti. Waldman was openly critical of the overutilization of the sterile analytics dictated by the metrics geeks. She was irked at the boring style of play the Yankees displayed during the season with excessive strikeouts and a lack of consistency.

"How long do you keep going with the same type of offense?" she complained. "Is Hal [Steinbrenner] listening to the coaching staff and the manager or the analytics department?" she boldly asked in reference to the Yankees' principal owner. "These [players, manager, and coaches] are people, and you can't follow a script. To me it has to be more humanity here. It's not all sitting with an iPad."

What does the future hold for Suzyn Waldman, a self-driven warrior?

"I'm never satisfied," she said. "If there's something else I want to do, I'll figure it out."

Sarah Langs is an MLB.com reporter and researcher who served as an analyst for the first-ever all-female broadcast of a major league game on July 20, 2021, when the Rays hosted the Orioles and has been an instrumental contributor to this book. "Suzyn is a strong, important, pioneering figure in the baseball broadcast field," proclaimed Langs. "We once had a great conversation about representation—how crucial it is for others to see those of minority groups to see themselves reflected in individuals taking on these kinds of roles. I look forward to a day when we've moved past all of the 'firsts,' and these things are more commonplace—when we don't have to qualify something as an 'all-female broadcast' because it is simply a broadcast. But even when we get to that point, it will always be important to remember people like Suzyn, who paved the way."

Epilogue
My Field of Dreams

On April 26, 1972, Lois and I visited her mother, "Mim," during a spring break from our teaching duties. Mim was a huge Yankees fan who lived in Weehawken, New Jersey, where Lois was raised. We decided to go to the stadium and attend the A's-Yankees game. One of the local Hudson County newspapers reported a starting time of two o'clock which was perfect.

When we arrived about 1:30, there were very few people walking in the area of the stadium. I was aware that the early '70s was not a golden era in Yankee baseball and attendance was not good, but I could not believe the minimal activity around the stadium.

We walked down the right field line area to the Yankee players' entrance and asked a security guard why there were so few people. He then informed us that it was a night game and we were about five hours early. I was embarrassed to say the least.

My mother-in-law, who was originally from Ohio, told a little white lie. She said to the guard, "We drove a long distance and we have never been to Yankee Stadium. Is there a chance you would let us in to see the ballpark?"

I had a smirk on my face because I had been there many times over the years, and if I may say, I made a day's pay for a few beer vendors.

To my surprise the security guard said, "Sure. When you go through the door, take a left and keep walking and eventually you will see an entrance to the field." My legs turned to jelly. I could not believe that I would have access to the most historic outdoor arena in the world. I would be taking the same path to the clubhouse area as many Yankees legends had.

It wasn't long before we found ourselves sitting in baseball heaven just to the right of the Yankee dugout. My eyes roamed the 49-year-old baseball cathedral while I reflected on its glorious history.

It was a bright, chilly Wednesday afternoon, and the ground crew was getting ready for the 7:35 night game, hosing down the infield. It really was weird how quiet it was surrounded by 65,000 empty seats. The only noticeable sound was the Number 4 elevated subway train that ran beyond the center field area outside the stadium.

While we were sitting, I noticed the gate to the field was wide open just a few feet away. I said to Lois, "I'm going to go on the field and stand in the first base area." She snapped, "You can't do that, you'll get in trouble." But I figured the worst that could happen would be if we were asked to leave; it was no big deal since there was no game.

So I went out to first base, and nobody bothered to shoo me away. I recall standing there and saying, "This is where Lou Gehrig, Joe Collins, and Bill 'Moose' Skowron stood." I looked up into the third deck behind the catcher and remembered the many games I sat there with my friend Don, who was a diehard Red Sox fan. The upper deck tickets back in the day were $1.75, and if we tipped the usher a few bucks, he gave us box seats closer to the railing.

Now, I was getting a little cocky and Lois was beginning to relax. I went over to where she was sitting with her mother and said, "Let's go out to the monuments that were located in center field." When I was a kid, I thought those were the gravestones of Yankees manager Miller Huggins, Lou Gehrig, and Babe Ruth. Lois was okay with that and we walked out to center field, stepping on the sacred ground where the great DiMaggio and Mantle chased fly balls.

Lois took some photos of the monuments, and we walked back toward the infield. During our return I imagined Bob Sheppard, the noted Yankee Stadium public address announcer, saying, "Your attention, please, ladies and gentlemen, coming in to pitch for the Yankees ... number 25 ... Rich Marazzi ... number 25."

I could not believe that Yankee Stadium had literally become my own playground. I was actually frolicking in my "field of dreams." When we got back to where Mim was sitting, Lois joined her mother while I continued to live out another fantasy. I went into the Yankee dugout, and I had my right leg on the top step and left leg below. My arms rested on my right leg, emulating former managers Ralph Houk and Casey Stengel, who often took that position.

I decided I would do a little role playing and create an imaginary argument with the umpire whose strike zone was terrible. I pointed toward the plate area and carried

I stand at first base in an empty Yankee Stadium in 1972 while my wife Lois and mother-in-law Mim look on.

on for a time. In retrospect, I'm sure the guys on the ground crew had to be wondering who this maniac was walking around the field and talking to himself in anger on the steps of the Yankee dugout.

At that point, I was satisfied and emotionally drained. It was time to go.

Once we got outside the stadium, players from both teams were beginning to file in including Bobby Murcer. One of our students, Danny Blackwell, was a big Murcer fan. I decided to approach Bobby and ask for an autograph for Danny. The affable Yankees center fielder obliged.

We then returned to Weehawken. I'll never forget the euphoria that came over me. It had to be one of the most memorable days of my life. I will always be grateful to that New Jersey newspaper that incorrectly reported the time of the game, to Mim who told a harmless fib, and the security guard who allowed three travelers into the Yankee Stadium for the "first time."

I have had many thrilling moments at the hallowed Bronx ballyard when it was jammed with thousands of roaring fans. But perhaps the most memorable day I ever spent there ironically occurred when the stadium was empty.

As Mel Allen would say, "how about that!"

Bibliography

Allen, Maury. *Where You Have You Gone, Joe DiMaggio? The Story of America's Last Hero.* New York: Dutton, 1975

Appel, Marty. *Pinstripe Empire.* New York: Bloomsbury, 2012.

Bedingfield, Gary. *Baseball in Wartime* newsletter. May 13, 2007.

Berra, Yogi, and David Kaplan. *When You Cone to a Fork in the Road Take It: Inspiration and Wisdom from One of Baseball's Greatest Heroes.* New York: Hachette, 2001.

Bouton, Jim. *Ball Four.* New York: Rosetta Books, 1970.

Brinkman, Joe, and Charlie Euchner. *The Umpire's Handbook.* Lexington, MA: S. Greene Press, 1985, 1987.

Castro, Tony. *DiMag and Mick: Sibling Rivals, Yankee Blood Brothers.* Guilford, CT: Lyons Press, 2016.

Clavin, Tom, and Danny Peary. *Roger Maris: Baseball's Reluctant Hero.* New York: Atria Books, 2010.

Cramer, Richard Ben. *Joe DiMaggio—A Hero's Life.* New York: Simon & Schuster, 2001

Creamer, Robert W. *Babe: The Legend Comes to Life.* New York: Simon & Schuster, 1992.

Dell Magazine. 1956.

Eig, Jonathan. *Luckiest Man: The Life and Death of Lou Gehrig.* New York: Simon & Schuster, 2005.

Gallagher, Mark. *The Yankee Encyclopedia: Volume 3.* Champaign, IL: Sagamore Publishing, 1997.

Gerlach, Larry. *The SABR Book of Umpires and Umpiring.* Phoenix: Society for American Baseball Research, 2017.

Halberstam, David. *The Summer of '49.* New York: William Morrow, 1989.

Joseph, Dan. *The Last Ride of the Iron Horse: How Lou Gehrig Fought ALS to Play One Final Season.* Mechanicsburg, PA: Sunbury Press, 2019.

Leavy, Jane. *The Big Fella: Babe Ruth and the World He Created.* New York: HarperCollins, 2018.

Leavy, Jane. *The Last Boy: Mickey Mantle and the End of America's Childhood.* New York: HarperCollins, 2010.

Lucas, Ed. *Seeing Home: The Ed Lucas Story.* New York: Gallery/Jeter, 2015.

Madden, Bill, and Moss Klein. *Damned Yankees: A No-Holds Barred Account of Life with Boss Steinbrenner.* New York: Grand Central, 1990.

Mandrake, Mark, and Mark Vancil, editors. *New York Yankees: 100 Years—The Official Retrospective.* New York: Ballantine Books, 2003.

Marazzi, Rich, and Len Fiorito. *Aaron to Zuverink: A Nostalgic Look at the Baseball Players of the Fifties.* New York: Stein and Day, 1982.

Marazzi, Rich, and Len Fiorito. *Baseball Players of the 1950s: A Biographical Dictionary of all 1,560 Major Leaguers.* Jefferson, NC: McFarland, 2004.

McMillan, Ken. *Tales from the Yankee Dugout: A Collection of the Greatest Yankee Stories Ever Told.* Champaign, IL: Sports Publishing, 2001.

Miller, Geoff. *Intangibles: Big-League Stories and Strategies for Winning the Mental Game—in Baseball and in Life.* Ashland, OR: Byte Level Books, 2012.

The New York Yankees, 100 Years: The Official Retrospective. New York: The New York Yankees and Ballantine Books, 2003.

Ogle, Jim. *Roger Maris at Bat.* New York: Duell, Sloan, & Pearce, 1962.

O'Neil, Paul, with Burton Rocks. *Me and My Dad.* New York: Harper Paperbacks, 2004.

Pessah, Jon. *Yogi: A Life Behind the Mask.* Boston: Little, Brown, 2020.

Pirone, Dorothy Ruth, and Chris Martens. *My Dad, the Babe: Growing Up with an American Hero.* Boston: Quinlan Press, 1988.

Positano, Dr. Rock. *Dinner with DiMaggio: Memories of an American hero.* New York: Simon & Schuster, 2017.

Ritter, Lawrence S. *The Glory of Their Times.* New York: Macmillan, 1966.

Sabellico, Tom. *I Can See Clearly Now.* Chula Vista, CA: Aventine Press, 2003.

Shah, Diane K. *A Farewell to Arms, Legs, and Jockstraps: A Sportswriter's Memoir.* Bloomington: Red Lighting Books, 2020

Shalin, Mike. *Donnie Baseball: The Definitive Biography of Don Mattingly.* Chicago: Triumph Books, 2011.

Torre, Joe, and Tom Verducci. *Chasing a Dream.* New York: Bantam, 2008

Torre, Joe and, Tom Verducci. *The Yankee Years.* New York: Random House, 2009

Vaccaro, Mike. *1941: The Greatest Year in Sports.* Doubleday. New York. 2007.

Wells, David, with Chris Kreski. *Perfect I'm Not: Boomer on Beer, Brawls, Backaches, and Baseball.* New York: HarperCollins, 2004.

Newspapers

The Albany Evening News
Beckley Post-Herald (West Virginia)
Hartford Courant
New Haven Register
New York Daily News
New York Post
The New York Times
The News and Record of Greensboro
Woman's Wear Daily

Publications

Baseball Digest
Life
New York Jewish Week
New York Post: The Yankees Century
SB Nation
Sports Collectors Digest
Sports Illustrated
The Yankees Century Series

Index

Numbers in ***bold italics*** indicate pages with illustrations

Aaron, Hank 24, 40, 64, 94
Abbott, Bud 84
Abbott, Jim 9, 10, ***10***
Abreu, Bryan 163
Agbayani, Benny 201
Ahearn, Bob 112
Alderman, Joel 122
Allen, Maury 10, 11, 89, 150, 180
Allen, Mel 2, 49, 85, 93, 106, 139, 154, 155, 165, 172, ***172***, 173–182, 207, 217
Alou, Matty 157
Ameche, Don 189
Ameche, Larry 189
Amoros, Sandy 127, 128, 177, 184
Amspacher, Bruce 153
Anderson, Garrett 3
Andrews, Mike 106
Angell, Roger 8, 157, 199
Anson, Cap 64
Appel, Marty 36, 67, 79, 80, 99, ***100***, 103, 111, 181
Appleton, Pete 66
Appling, Luke 95, 138
Armstrong, Louis 147
Armstrong, Mike 190
Arnaz, Desi 167
Arnold, Dorothy 88, 132
Arroyo, Luis 152, 154
Ausanio, Joe 10
Austin, Jimmy 54
Averill, Earl 58

Babich, Johnny 83
Baer, Bill 208
Bahnsen, Stan 202
Balboni, Steve 189
Ball, Lucillle 167
Banks, Ernie 20
Barber, Red 139, 154, 155, 176–179, 181
Barfield, Jesse 208
Barojas, Salomé 31
Barrett, Ted 169
Barrow, Ed 62
Barsocchini, Reno 89
Barth, Bob 114
Bauer, Hank 78, 104, 107, 114, 148, 164
Baylor, Don 116
Bedingfield, Gary 136
Begley, Ian 159

Belcher, Tim 202
Bell, George 208
Bell, Jay 15
Bench, Johnny 124, 143
Bendix, William 50
Bengis, Fred 151
Bennett, Eddie 39, 45, 46
Berg, Moe 58, 59
Berra, Carmen (Short) 111, 128, 131
Berra, Dale 123, 128, 210
Berra, John 118
Berra, Larry 123, 131
Berra, Mike 118
Berra, Paulina 118, 128
Berra, Pietro 118
Berra, Tim 123
Berra, Tony 118
Berra, Yogi 1, 5, 17, 21, 35, 78, 86, 101, 104, 108, 111, 114, 115–117, ***117***, 118–131, 133, 141, 142, 152, 155, 164, 166–169, 177, 181, 210
Bevens, Bill 126
Biden, Pres. Joe 156
Bisher, Furman 25
Bivin, Jim 48
Blackwell, Danny 217
Blake, Casey 198
Blanchard, Johnny 114, 148
Blomberg, Ron 108
Bloomberg, Michael 36
Boggs, Wade 19, 80, 181, 195, 196
Bolling, Frank 130
Bonds, Barry 23, 40
Bonner, Mike 32
Bonney, Bette 82
Bordick, Mike 135
Borgmann, Glenn 185
Boudreau, Lou 35, 86, 138
Bouton, Jim 29, 113, 129
Bowa, Larry 214
Bowsfield, Ted 149
Bradner, Liesl 89
Bragg, Darren 202
Branca, Ralph 126
Brancato, Al 83
Brando, Marlon 32
Breadon, Sam 121
Bremigan, Nick 184–187
Breslin, Jimmy 76
Brett, George 18, 183, ***183***, 184–187, 190, 191

Brewer, Tom 149
Brinkman, Ed 135
Brinkman, Joe 186, 187, 189
Brooke, Holly 110, 111
Brosius, Scott 168
Broussard, Ben 36
Brown, Bobby 118
Brown, Hal "Skinny" 149
Brown, Les 82
Brown, Lorn 211
Brown, Mace 48
Browne, Leo 120
Bryson, George 211
Bumgarner, Madison 126
Busch, Gussie 159
Bush, Pres. George W. 26, 27
Bush, Guy 47, 48
Bush, Homer 213

Cabrera, Asdrubal 198
Cabrera, Orlando 168
Cagney, James 167
Caldwell, Earl 77
Camilli, Dolph 48
Campanella, Roy 124, 125, 128, 142, 164
Campaneris, Bert 189
Cannon, Jimmy 150
Canseco, Jose 14, 98
Capone, Al 76
Caray, Harry 139, 211
Carey, Andy 15, 164
Carrasquel, Chico 31
Carrieri, Joe 93
Carrieri, Ralph 93
Case, George 66
Cashman, Brian 3, 4, 36, 198, 203, 204
Castro, Fidel 149
Castro, Tony 110
Castrovince, Anthony 66
Cavaretta, Phil 95
Caywood, Betty 211, 212
Cecil, Dick 94
Ceres, Jimmy "Peanuts" 83
Cerone, Rick ***2***, 186, 187
Cerrone, Rick 7, 9, 30, 36, 194, 199
Cerv, Bob 152
Chaissin, Charles 131
Chamberlain, Joba 197, 198
Chandler, A.B. "Happy" 49, 137
Channin, John 209

221

Index

Chapman, Ben 47, 77, 80
Chiozza, Lou 49
Christenberry, Maj. Gen Charles W. 90
Christopher, Joe 130
Cimoli, Gino 108
Clair, Michael 50
Clarke, Horace 106
Clavin, Tom 150
Clemens, Roger 23, 24, 198, 213
Cleveland, Pres. Grover 42
Cleveland, Ruth 42
Cline, Patsy 149
Clinton, Lu 154
Cloninger, Tony 130
Cobb, Ty 42, 49, 70, 73, 133, 142
Coble, Drew 186
Cochrane, Mickey 64, 71, 102, 124
Cohen, Alex 201
Cohen, Gary 23, 210
Cohn, Roy 188
Colavito, Rocky 99, 100, 148, 158, 187, 189
Colburn, Charles 89
Cole, Bert 42
Cole, Leonard 41
Cole, Nat King 79
Cole, Natalie 79
Coleman, Jerry 104, 133, 135, 140, 178
Coleman, Ken 209
Collins, Eddie 70, 73
Collins, Joe 86, 125, 141, 216
Colombo, Brother 93
Combs, Earle 66, 82
Como, Perry 175
Cone, David 10, 19, 118, 168, **169**, 193, 195, 201
Conigliaro, Tony 209
Connor, Roger 42
Contreras, Jose 196
Cooper, Gary 67
Corbett, Warren 211
Corcoran, Cliff 48, 50
Cosell, Howard 139
Costabile, Dulio 140
Costanza, George 18
Costas, Bob 114
Costello, Lou 84
Costner, Kevin 8
Courtney, Alan 82
Cousins, Derryl 25
Cox, Bobby 106
Cramer, Richard Ben 77, 78, 90
Crasnick, Jerry 198
Creamer, Robert 47
Cronin, Joe 135
Cronkite, Walter 37
Crosby, Bing 178
Crosby, Bubba 33
Crosetti, Frank 47, 76, 77, 135, 136, 152, 155, 164
Crystal, Billy 8, 30, 98, 113, 150
Curtis, Chad 200
Cutler, Larry 49

Dahlgren, Babe 66
Daley, Bud 152

Daly, Arthur 150
Daly, John Charles 141
Damon, Johnny 36
Daniel, Dan 76, 134, 150
Dark, Alvin 134
Davidoff, Ken 171
Davis, Russ 204
Day, Doris 119, 162
Dean, Dizzy 1, 78
Delock, Ike 162
DeMaestri, Joe 148, 155
DeMuth, Dana 26
Dent, Bucky 13
Diaz, Laz 197, 198
Dickey, Bill 66, 73, 116, 125, 126
DiMaggio, Dom 35, 77, 80, **81**, 126
DiMaggio, Joe 1, 11, 12, 30, 35, 62, 65, 66, 73–81, **81**, 82–94, **94**, 95, 96, 99, 101, 104, 105, 117, 125, 132–134, 136, 142, 144, 156, 179, 179–181, 196, 197, 200, 216
DiMaggio, Joe, Jr. 95
DiMaggio, Vince 77
Dineen, Bill 41
DiRenzo, Tony 55
Ditmar, Art 162
Doerr, Bobby 35, 104, 133, 177
Dolan, Patrick 55
Dolan, the Rev. Thomas S. 54
Donahue, Steve 212
Downing, Al 24
Drebinger, John 85, 127, 132, 134, 135, 150
Dugan, Joe "Jumpin'" 44
Dunphy, Don 82
Duran, Roberto 197
Durante, Rosemarie (Calabrese) 146
Durante, Sal 145, **145**, 146, 147, 154, 160
Duren, Ryne 20, **20**, 21
Duren, Beverly 21
Dye, Jermaine 33

Eckert, William 109
Ehmke, Howard 44
Eig, Jonathan 67
Eisenhower, Pres. Dwight D. 27
Ellis, Ayla 72
Ellis, Bob 69–73
Ellis, Jennifer 72
Ellis, Jill 69
Ellis, Kim 69
Ellis, Scott 69, 70
Embree, Alan 3
Engelberg, Morris 74, 92
Espinoza, Álvaro 31
Esselborn, Emil 132
Evans, Billy 41

Faber, Charles 162, 163
Fain, Ferris 88
Fastook, Eddie 15, 16, **16**, 74, 75
Fein, Nat 50
Feller, Bob 1, 40, 50, 77, 94, 126, 142
Feller, Sherm 30, 106

Felton, Happy 101
Fermin, Felix 201
Fernandez, Tony 202
Ferrick, Tom 86
Filippelli, John 211
Fingers, Rollie 148
Finley, Charlie 91, 211
Fiorito, Len 95
Fischer, Bill 108
Fishel, Bob 79, 80, 188, 189
Fisher, Jack "Fat Jack" 154
Fisk, Carlton 125
Flaherty, Red 154
Ford, Dale 25, 26
Ford, Whitey 1, 40, 91, 94, 114, 119, 127, 129, 131, 152, 164
Fornoff, Susan 208
Fox, Nellie 1
Foxx, Jimmie 58, 77, 109, 135
Foytack, Paul 126
Frazier, George 189, 190
Frick, Ford 137, 149, 153, 157, 163
Fuchs, Emil 48, 49
Furillo, Carl 164

Gagarin, Yuri 149
Gallico, Paul 47
Gamble, Oscar 190
Gandil, Chick 54
Garagiola, Giovanni 120
Garagiola, Joe 120, 178
Garcia, Mike 1
Garciaparra, Nomar 200
Gardella, Danny 136, 137
Gardner, Gayle 211
Gardner, Stephen 91, 92
Garfunkel, Art 95
Gaynor, Dr. Sydney 158
Gehrig, Christina 59, 62, 70
Gehrig, Eleanor (Twitchell) 60, 62, 67–69
Gehrig, Henrich 69
Gehrig, Lou 1, 2, 17, 44–47, 52, 58–65, **65**, 73, **73**, 77, 90, 99, 101, 112, 125, 135, 176, 180, 216
Gerlach, Larry 165
Germán, Domingo 168
Giambi, Jeremy 203
Gibbs, Jake 102
Gibson, Bob 130
Gibson, Josh 11
Gilliam, Jim 128
Gionfriddo, Al 85, 86, 179
Giordano, Anthony 113
Girardi, Joe 169, 194, **194**, 196, 200, 203
Glesson, Jim 121, 122
Goetz, Russ 109
Goldin, Ken 156
Gomez, Lefty 47, 58, 73, 79
Gonzalez, Ray 63
Gooden, Dwight 196
Gorbachev, Mikhail 84
Gordon, Joe 135
Gordon, Sam 146, 147
Gordon, Tom 4
Goren, Herb 142
Goslin, Goose 63

Gossage, Goose 186, 190, 191
Gould, Jack 177
Gowdy, Curt 2, 102, 178
Grande, George 95, 131, 139, 140, 181
Grant, Cary 8, 89, 119
Gray, Pete **8**, 9
Graziano, Rocky 68
Green, Dallas 164
Green, Todd 27
Greenberg, Hank 77, 142
Greenberg, Justice Henry 162
Greene, Amy 90
Greene, Harvey 7
Greenwade, Tom 103
Greinke, Zack 40
Griffey, Ken, Jr. 204
Griffith, Calvin 185
Grim, Bob 202
Grissom, Marquis 194
Grote, Jerry 130
Grove, Lefty 64, 71
Guerrero, Vlad 34
Guidry, Ron 156, 189
Gumpert, Randy 104
Gutierrez, Franklin 198
Gwynn, Tony 203
Gwynne, Fred 19

Hadley, Kent 148
Hafner, Travis 198
Halberstam, David 8, 92, 133
Hall, Jim 36
Haller, Bill 25
Halper, Barry 9, 47, 50, 84, 112, 190, 191
Hamilton, Jack 209
Harder, Mel 75
Harrelson, Bud 9
Harridge, Will 137
Harrington, Marie 57
Harris, Bucky 126
Hartnett, Gabby 47
Harwell, Ernie 177
Hasegawa, Shigetoshi 31
Hatten, Joe 85
Hayes, Charlie 195, ***195***, 196, 199, 213
Hayes, Gabby 173
Haynes, Jimmy 11
Hearn, Jim 134
Heilmann, Harry 42
Henderson, Rickey 14, 40, 116, 208
Henie, Sonja 85
Henrich, Tommy 77, 82, 83, 86, 133, 174
Herbert, Ray 108
Herman, Billy 47
Hermanski, Gene 141
Hernandez, Willie 17
Hildebrand, George 42
Hirschbeck, John 26
Hirschbeck, Mark 26
Hirschbeck, Nikki 26
Hitchcock, Sterling 204
Hoagland, Shelby 171
Hoch, Bryan 197

Hodges, Gil 130
Hodges, Russ 178
Hodgson, Frank 56
Hofman, Bobby 118
Hogsett, Chief 77
Holloway, Ken 63
Honochick, Jim 154
Hope, Bob 167
Hopp, Johnny 86, 87, 104
Hornsby, Rogers 42
Houk, Ralph 106, 129, 149, 180, 216
Houtteman, Art 1
Howard, Elston 152, 155, 158
Howser, Dick 186, 187, 189
Huard, Kevin 110
Hubbard, Cal 134
Hubbell, Carl 135
Huggins, Miller 63, 64, 68, 216
Husing, Ted 175
Huston, Tillinghast L'Hommedieu 41

Idelson, Jeff 7
Israel, Anna 174
Israel, Julius 174

Jackson, Reggie 29, 30, 45
James, Bill 124
James, Harry 175
Jansen, Larry 87
Javier, Cristian 163
Jenkinson, Bill 42, 51–53
Jennings, Dave 174
Jennings, Juanita 54, 57, 58
Jensen, Jackie 87, 104
Jesus (of Nazareth) 34
Jeter, Bella 200
Jeter, Charles 201, 202
Jeter, Derek 5, 19, 26, 36, 125, 160, 192, 196, 199–202, ***202***, 203, 205
Jeter, Dorothy 201
Jeter, Hanna (Davis) 200
Jeter, Kaius 200
Jeter, River 200
Jeter, Story 200
Johnson, Ban 43
Johnson, Billy 103, 104
Johnson, Howard 117
Johnson, Walter 49, 63
Jones, Andruw 193, 200
Jorge, Monica 72
Joseph, Dan 66
Joshua, Von 24
Joss, Addie 165
Joyce, Jim 26
Judge, Aaron 5, 99, 156

Kahn, Irving Berlin 175
Kahn, Roger 8
Kaline, Al 149, 152
Kandle, Kirk 47
Katzman, Harry "Lime" 7
Kay, Michael 80, ***117***, 172, 204
Kaze, Irv 7
Keane, Johnny 158
Keeler, Wee Willie 83
Kekich, Mike 10, 11

Keller, Charlie 77
Kellert, Frank 22
Kelly, Bill 90
Kelly, Edward 39
Kelly, Ray 38, ***38***, 39, 40, 42, 44, 45, ***45***, 46, 47
Keltner, Ken 83, 140
Kennedy, Bobby 96
Kennedy, Pres. John F. 155, 167
Kepner, Tyler 190
Kernan, Kevin 155
Kiley, Richard 209
Kilgannon, Corey 71
Kim, Byung-Hyun 204
Kinder, Edward 56
Kinder, Ellis 133
King, Clyde 116
King, Dr. Martin Luther 96
Kingman, Dave 208
Kinnaman, Bill 154
Kleiber, Paul 83, 84
Klein, Christopher 42
Klein, Moss 116
Klutts, Mickey 31
Knoblauch, Chuck 168, 200
Knott, Jack 77
Kobrin, Bill 90
Koenig, Mark 58
Kohler, David 66
Kosakowski, Don 9, 10, 30, 216
Kosakowski, Don, Jr. 9, 10, ***10***
Kosakowski, Gail 9
Kosco, Andy 106
Koufax, Sandy 68, 94
Krabbenhoft, Herm 63
Kranepool, Ed 130
Krichell, Paul 62, 120, 122, 135
Kubek, Tony 13, ***13***, 14, 102, 109, ***153***, 154, 202
Kucks, Johnny 129, 167
Kuenn, Harvey 126
Kuhn, Bowie 112, 188
Kunath, Cecil 8
Kunath, Dick 8
Kunitz, Al 135

Labine, Clem 128
La Guardia, Fiorello 68
Lampley, Jim 209
Landis, Kenesaw Mountain 42, 59
Langs, Sarah 65, 77, 214
Lariccia, Tony 77
Larsen, Corrine (Bruess) 163
Larsen, Don 5, 29, 117, 118, 128, 129, 148, 161–165, ***165***, 166–171, 177
Larsen, Justin 171
Larsen, Vivian 162, 163
Lary, Lyn 64
Laux, France 176
Lavagetto, Cookie 126
Layton, Eddie 30
Lazzeri, Tony 73
Leavy, Jane 45, 56, 107, 109, 111
Ledee, Ricky 168
Lemke, Mark 195, 213
LeMoine, Bob 48, 49

Index

Lemon, Bob 1, 134
Lemon, Jim 107
Lenz, Jack 35, 44
Leonard, Dutch 63, 136
Leonard, Sugar Ray 197
Levy, Andrew 171
Levy, Bert 175
Levy, George 35
Lewis, Joe E. 166
Leyritz, Jim 194, 202
Liederman, Bill 112
Lincoln, Pres. Abraham 119
Lindell, Johnny 133
Linz, Phil 129, 130
Lipsig, Harry 163
Lloyd, Graeme 196, 213
Lockman, Whitey 134
Lofton, Kenny 198
Lollar, Sherm 126
Lonborg, Jim 106
Long, Terrance 203
Lopat, Ed 141
Lopez, Hector 155
Loria, Jeffrey 205
Luber, Susan 55
Lucas, Allison (Pfeifle) 144
Lucas, Chris 143
Lucas, Eddie 30, 143, *143*, 144
Lucas, Eddie, Jr. 143
Lucas, Red 47, 48
Lucchino, Larry 196
Luciano, Lucky 76
Luciano, Ron 9
Lupica, Mike 139
Lynch, Mike 43

MacDonald, Arch 176
Macir, Jim 204
Mack, Connie 58, 59, 123
MacPhail, Larry 176
MacPhail, Lee 184, 185, 187–190
Madden, Bill 8, 29, 116
Maddux. Greg 193
Madero, Francisco 57
Magerkurth, George 47
Maglie, Sal 128, 136, 164, 170
Malone, Pat 47
Maloney, George 189
Malzone, Frank 208
Mangold, Jeff 24
Mantle, Anna Bea 111
Mantle, Billy 111
Mantle, Danny 111
Mantle, David 111
Mantle, Merlyn (Johnson) 110–112
Mantle, Mickey 1, 5, 14, 17, 21, 29, 31, 35, 51, 80, 97–99, 100, **100**, 101–114, 119, 125, 129, 140, 141, 149–153, *153*, 155, 156, 158, 162, 164, 179, 181, 197, 216
Mantle, Mickey, Jr. 111
Mantle, Mutt 102, 105
Maranville, Rabbit 71
Maras, Corrine (mother of Roger Maris) 147
Maras, Rudy (father of Roger Maris) 147

Marazzi, Brian (son) 94, 193
Marazzi, Lois 13, 14, 32, 79, 94, 142, 146, 174, 215, 216, **216**
Marazzi, Rich 2, 4, 33, 34, 173, 216, **216**
Marazzi, Rich (son) 34, 94, 194
Marberry, Firpo 62, 64
March, David 89
Maresca, Orest V. 188
Maris, Randy 148, 158, 159
Maris, Roger 17, 29, 94, 98, 119, 145–151, **151**, 152, 153, **153**, 154–160
Maris, Roger, Jr. 156, 158, 167
Maris, Rudy 146
Markakis, Nick 204
Marshall, Penny 144
Martens, Chris 57
Martin, Billy 14, 97, 101, 111, 116, 130, 135, 164, 167, 177, 185, 186
Martin, Ruth 69, 70
Martinelli, Giovanni 29
Martinez, Dennis 202
Martínez, José 187
Martinez, Tino 11, 19, 168, 200, 204
Martinez, Victor 198
Marx, Groucho 139
Mathewson, Christy 49
Matsui, Hideki 196
Matthias, Brother 46
Mattingly, Don 17, 18, **18**, 98, 116, 131, 186, 189, 190, 208
Maxwell, Charlie 126
Mayberry, John 185, 190
Mayo, Dr. Charles William 67
Mays, Willie 94, 101, 105, 106, 109, 112, 157, 179
Mazeroski, Bill 101, 129
Mazur, Bill 11
McAnany, Jim 178
McArthur, Gen. Douglas 116
McCarthy, Joe 64, 65, 65, 66, 82, 136
McClleland, Tim 184, 186, 187
McCovey, Willie 24
McDonald, Arch 76
McDougald, Gil 15, 30, 87, 105, 107, 127, 135, 141, 177, 202
McDowell, Amy 200
McDowell, Sam 189
McGowan, Bill 64
McGraw, John 44
McGwire, Mark 14, 159
McKechnie, Bill 48
McKinley, Bill 125
McLain, Denny 108, 109
McLoughlin, Walter 35
McMillan, Roy 130
McMullen, John 116
McNeil, Mim 216, **216**
McRea, Hal 189, 190
Medwick, Joe "Ducky" 120
Meek, Evan 204
Menke, Dennis 130
Merrill, Robert 12
Merrill, Stump 13
Messer, Frank 139
Meusel, Bob 42, 62

Mientkiewicz, Doug 198
Miller, Geoff 41
Miller, Jon 26
Miñoso, Minnie 1, 31, 126
Mitchell, Dale 128, 164, 165, 169
Mitty, Walter 32
Mize, Johnny 35, 86, 95, 104
Molina, Benjie 3
Monahan, Gene 4, 197, 212
Monroe, Marilyn 79, 88–90, 92, 197
Montero, Rafael 163
Montville, Leigh 148
Moore, Johnny 47
Moore, Monte 211
Morante, Tony 33
Morenne, Benoit 46
Moreno, Rita 167
Morgan, Dr. Bill 197
Morgan, Ray 43
Morrow, Edward R. 141
Mossi, Don 152
Mullaney, Dominick 41
Mumphrey, Jerry 134, 189
Munson, Thurman 65, 184–186, 202
Murcer, Bobby 14, 15, 114, 196, 217
Murphy, Audie 122
Murphy, Bob 207
Murphy, Jack 179
Murray, Dale 186
Murray, Jim 62
Murti, Sweeny 214
Musial, Stan 94, 131, 142
Mussina, Mike 203

Nelson, Jeff 19, 204
Nelson, Lindsey 178
Nettles, Graig 147, 186
Nevin, Phil 201
Newcombe, Don 129
Newhouser, Hal 95
Newman, Fred 101
Newsome, Dick 83
Ng, Kim 205

Obama, Pres. Barack 131
O'Dell, Billy 168
O'Donnell, Rosie 207
O'Doul, Jean 89
O'Doul, Lefty 89
Ogle, Jim 150, 154
Ohtani, Shohei 40
Olbermann, Keith 121
Oldin, Paul 36
O'Leary, Charley 55
O'Leary, Helen 55
Oliva, Tony 18, 158
O'Neil, Frank "Buck" 61
O'Neil, Paul 80, 168, 192, 194, 196
Ott, Mel 122
Owen, Mickey 136
Owens, Brick 43
Oz, Dr. Mehmet 193
Ozuna, Marcell 205

Papio, Charles 46
Pappas, Milt 153

Parker, Dave 98
Parnell, Mel 126, 133
Parton, Andy *117*
Pasquel, Bernardo 136
Pasquel, Jorge 136, 137
Patterson, Red 35
Peary, Danny 150
Peckinpaugh, Roger 82
Peek, Jeff 55
Pepitone, Joe 109, 129
Perdenti, Frank 155
Perry, Charles S. 5, 89
Perry, Gaylord 186, 187, 189
Pesci, Joe 19
Pesky, Johnny 126, 133–135, 208
Pessah, John 87, 111, 124, 128, 141
Peterson, Fritz 10, 11
Petrocelli, Rico 106
Pettitte, Andy 19, *19*, 194, 196, 197, 204
Phelps, Anson Green 54
Phillips, Dave 189
Piazza, Mike 23, 24
Pieper, Pat 47
Pierce, Billy 148
Piercy, Bill 63
Piersall, Jimmy 211
Pierzynski, A.J. 33
Pignatano, Joe 130
Pinelli, Babe 164, 165, 169
Pipp, Wally 163
Pirone, Dominick 60
Pirone, Dorothy 54, 56–60
Ploski, Bob 173
Ploski, John 173
Podres, Johnny 127, 167
Posada, Jorge 4, 198, 200, 203, 204
Posey, Buster 126
Positano, Dr. Rock 66
Potter, Brandon 85
Potter, Nels 136
Povich, Shirley 166
Powell, Gen. Colin 84
Power, Vic 148
Presley, Elvis 12
Pressly, Ryan 163
Previte, Pete 113
Price, David 203
Price, Jim 108, 109
Priddy, Jerry 136
Prince, Bob 177
Priore, Nick 75
Pucci, Bill 34
Puckett, Kirby 18
Pujols, Albert 45, 64, 199

Quick, Herbert 69, 70
Quilici, Frank 184, 185
Quisenberry, Dan 190

Radatz, Dick 101
Raines, Tim 199
Ramirez, Hanley 203
Ramos, Pedro 29, 91, 107, 108
Randall, Ed 9, 72
Randolph, Willie 2, 14, 116, 208, 212

Rapuano, Ed 26
Raschi, Vic 35, 104, 129, 133–135, 173, 176
Rather, Dan 207
Rawley, Shane 35
Ray, James Lincoln 68, 103
Reagan, Pres. Ronald 84
Reed, Jack 124
Reese, Pee Wee 124, 126, 142, 166
Reeve, Christopher 8
Reliford, Charlie 23
Reniff, Hal 154
Renko, Steve 187
Reyes, Nap 136
Reynolds, Allie 126, 127, 173
Reynolds, Harold 213
Rice, Grantland 66
Rice, Harry 64
Richards, Paul 124, 125
Richardson, Antoan 204
Richardson, Bobby 102, 114, 157
Richman, Arthur 8, *8*, 9, 10, 17, 133, 166, 192
Rickerby, Arthur 166, 167, 169
Rickerby, Wanda 167
Rickey, Branch 35, 120
Righetti, Dave 98, 181, 202
Riley, Daniel 166
Riley, Merritt 186, 187, 190
Ripken, Cal, Jr. 44, 62, 159
Ripley, Steve 26
Rivera, Jim "Jungle Jim" 1
Rivera, Mariano 4, 5, 33, 34, 36, 196, 199, 204
Rizzuto, Cora (Esselborn) 132, 137, 138, 141
Rizzuto, Phil 35, 76, 89, 95, 99, 104, 119, 132–142, *142*, 143, 144, 154, 174, 177–181, 200, 201
Roarke, Mike 152
Roberts, Leon (?) 191
Roberts, Robin 142
Robertson, Charlie 165, 166
Robinson, Aaron 126
Robinson, Bette 50
Robinson, Earl 154
Robinson, Eddie 50, 107
Robinson, Jackie 22, 35, 126, 127, 142, 164, 207, 212
Rodriguez, Alex 62, 64, 200
Rodriguez, Felix 3, 4, 5
Roettger, Oscar 63
Rogers, Ginger 89
Rogers, Tom *115*
Rolfe, Red 64, 66, 77, 82
Romolt, Jerry 91
Rooney, Mickey 8, 25, 26
Roosevelt, Pres. Franklin D. 68, 85, 120
Root, Charlie 46
Rosen, Bob 9, 70, 71
Rostreter, Joe 174
Rothgeb, Lew 97, 98
Ruffing, Red 57, 73
Ruppert, Jacob 41, *65*
Rushin, Steve 21
Russo, Tony 173
Rust, Art, Jr 11

Ruth, Babe 1, 2, 24, 32, 35, 38–45, *45*, 46–60, 62, 64, 68–70, 73, 86, 89, 101, 109, 112, 125, 135–137, 148, 149, 156, 157, 175, 197, 216
Ruth, Claire (Hodgson) 50, 54, 56–60, 68
Ruth, Helen (Woodford) 54, 56, 57
Ruth, Julia (Stevens) 56, 58, 59

Salerno, Al 154
Sandomir, Richard 139
Sandoval, Pablo 45
Savitt, Alan 110
Schang, Wally 44
Schilling, Curt 197, 213, 214
Schnering, Otto Young 42
Schubert, George C. 88
Schuerholz, John 187, 188, 190
Schultz, Barney 108
Schwartz, Ephrain 191
Schwarzkopf, Gen. Norman *16*
Score, Herb 100, 148
Scott, Dale 26
Scott, Everett "Deacon"
Scully, Vince 165, 207
Seaver, Tom 138, 140
Seigel, Pete 170
Shah, Diane 111
Shane, Mary 211, 212
Shannon, Bill 9, 169
Sharp, Fred 35
Shea, Frank "Spec" 78, 126, 140
Sheehy, Pete 93, 94, 99
Sheppard, Bob 5, 26–28, *28*, 29–37, 99, 155, 216
Sheridan, Pat 186
Sherman, Bruce 205
Sherman, Joel 205
Shor, Toots 85
Shore, Ernie 43
Shotton, Bert 86
Showalter, Buck 199, 204
Shuba, George "Shotgun" 128
Shulock, John 25
Shulte, John 120
Siebern, Norm 148, 178
Siedeman, David 72
Silvera, Charlie 104, 128
Simmons, Al 71, 135
Simon, Paul 95, 98
Simpson, Joe 187
Sinatra, Frank 12, 187
Sisler, George 83
Sizemore, Grady 198
Skowron, Bill "Moose" 103, 114, 152, 155, 167, 216
Slaught, Don 186
Slaughter, Enos 138
Slutsky, Bruce 187
Smalley, Roy, Jr. 190
Smith, Gov. Al 44
Smith, Charley 158
Smith, Curt 179
Smith, Kate 175
Smith, Red 99
Smoltz, John 193
Snider, Duke 106, 179

Soriano, Alfonso 201
Sorrell, Vic 64
Sosa, Sammy 159
Sousa, John Philip 44
Speaker, Tris 70, 73
Spellman, Card. Francis 49
Spencer, Shane 203
Spotola, Bina 84
Spotola, Jerry 83
Staats, Dewayne 13
Stafford, Bill 154
Stafford, Jo 175
Staley, Gerry 152
Stallard, Tracy 145, 147, 154, 155
Stanky, Eddie 126, 134
Stanton, Giancarlo 205
Steigler, Laurel 69
Stein, Herb 33
Steinberg, Mark 150
Steinbrenner, George 8, 9, 15, 16, 16, 36, 65, 74, 75, 116, 117, 131, 134, 181, 182, 188, 194, 196, 210, 212, 213
Steinbrenner, Hal 214
Steiner, Charley 211
Stengel, Casey 21, 44, 58, 86, 87, 99, 119, 126, 130, 132, 135, 142, 162, 163, 180, 192, 216
Sterling, John 195, 206, 207, 211
Stevens, John Paul 47
Stevens, Tom 60
Stichweh, Rollie 178
Stirnweiss, Snuffy 86, 135, 138
Stobbs, Chuck 108
Stokes, Earl Dodge 54
Stolzenberg, Frank 175
Stoneham, Horace 122, 176
Stottlemyre, Mel 106, 130
Strasberg, Andy 150, *151*, 156
Strawberry, Darryl 213
Sturdivant, Tom 129
Sturm, Johnny 82
Sturtze, Tanyon 7
Sullivan, Daniel 60
Sullivan, Ed 141
Sullivan, Frank 162
Sullivan, Joseph 188, 189
Summerall, Pat 113
Summers, Bill 127, 134
Susce, George 137
Szen, David 30

Taafe, William 181
Tapper, Al 197
Taylor, Bill 166
Taylor, Dean 187
Tegenborg, Lars 91, 92
Tenace, Gene 193
Terry, Bill 135
Terry, Ralph 101, 178

Thimmel, Ken 171
Thomas, Frank (football coach) 175
Thomson, Bobby 143
Throneberry, Marv 148
Tiant, Luis 106
Tinoco, Jesus 156
Tobin, Jack 63
Tomanek, Dick 148
Tomei, Marisa 18, *19*
Topping, Dan 35, 85, 86, 105, 180
Torborg, Jeff 187
Torgeson, Earl 11
Torgeson, Ina 11
Torre, Frank 193, *193*, 195
Torre, Joe 3, 4, 22, 33, 164, 192, *193*, 194–199, 204, 214
Torre, Rocco 193
Torrisi, Joe 171
Tortorella, John 146
Tosetti, Linda Ruth 54, *56*, 57–59
Trafford, Abigail 114
Travis, Cecil 136
Tresh, Tom 106, 202
Triandos, Gus 21
Trimble, Joe 166
Trout, Bob 175
Trucks, Virgil "Fireball" 135
True, Roy 112
Trump, Pres. Donald 98
Turley, Bob 128, 129, 162, 163
Turner, Jim 164
Tyman, Debbie 36

Ueberroth, Peter 112
Ulbrich, Weston 55

Vaccaro, Mike 83
Valdivielso, José 31
Vale, Jerry 11, 12, *12*
Valle, Rudy 47
Vangilder, Elam 63
Vázquez, Javier 5
Vecsey, George 150
Veeck, Bill 211
Verducci, Tom 121, 198
Verna, Tony 178
Vincent, Fay 157
Violin, Hank 78
Virdon, Bill 185
Vizcaino, Luis 198

Wagner, Honus 49
Wakefield, Tim 197
Waldman, Suzyn 117, 206, *206*, 207–214
Walker, Rube 130
Wanninger, Pee-Wee 63
Ward, Aaron 62, 63
Ward, Preston 148

Warhol, Andy 33
Warhop, Jack 41
Warner, Brian 91
Warner, Charlie 211
Warp, Harold 47
Washington, U.L. 186, 189
Wathan, John 190, 191
Wayne, John 209
Weaver, Earl 25
Webb, Del 105
Weiss, George 100, 120, 124, 130, 167, 177–179
Welke, Bill 26
Welke, Tim 26
Wells, David 168, *168*, 201, 213
Wetteland, John 20, *20*, 195
White, Bill 139
White, Frank 190, 191
Whitney, Pinky 49
Wight, Bill 35, 104
Wilder, Billy 90
Wilkinson, Bud 148
Will, George 98
Williams, Bernie 14, *143*, 146, 196, 203, 204
Williams, Dick 185
Williams, Gerald 204
Williams, Ted 35, 40, 62, 66, 75, 77, 80, 82, 84, 85, 93, 104, 126, 127, 133, 142, 177, 179, 208, 209
Winchell, Walter 90
Winfield, Dave 17, 73, 116, 201, 208
Witt, Whitey 44
Wohlers, Mark 194
Wolff, Bob 164, 169, *170*
Wolff, Warner 101
Woodling, Gene 126, 141
Woods, Jim 139, 179
Workman, Hank 77, 78
Wright, Kyle 40
Wright, Toby 30
Wulf, Steve 189
Wynegar, Butch 17
Wynn, Early 1, 178

Yastrzemski, Carl 28, 154
Yawkey, Tom 85
Yelich, Christian 205
Yost, Eddie 130
Youmans, Cory 156
Young, Cy 165
Young, Dick 124, 149, 166, 180
Youngman, Harold 105

Zabala, Adrian 136
Zachary, Tom 52
Zernial, Gus 88, 89
Zimmer, Don 22, *22*, 127, 196

www.ingramcontent.com/pod-product-compliance
Ingram Content Group UK Ltd.
Pitfield, Milton Keynes, MK11 3LW, UK
UKHW050531150426
5217IPUK00026B/1887